Shojo Beat

# Fairy Cube

Vol. 1

Story & Art by
**Kaori Yuki**

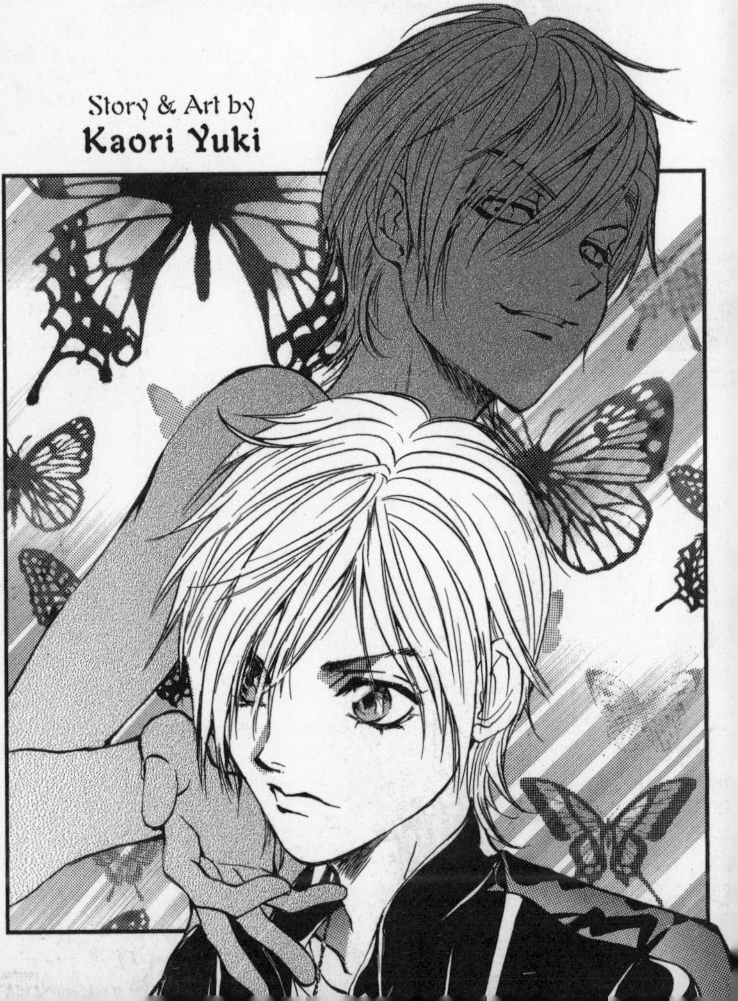

# CONTENTS

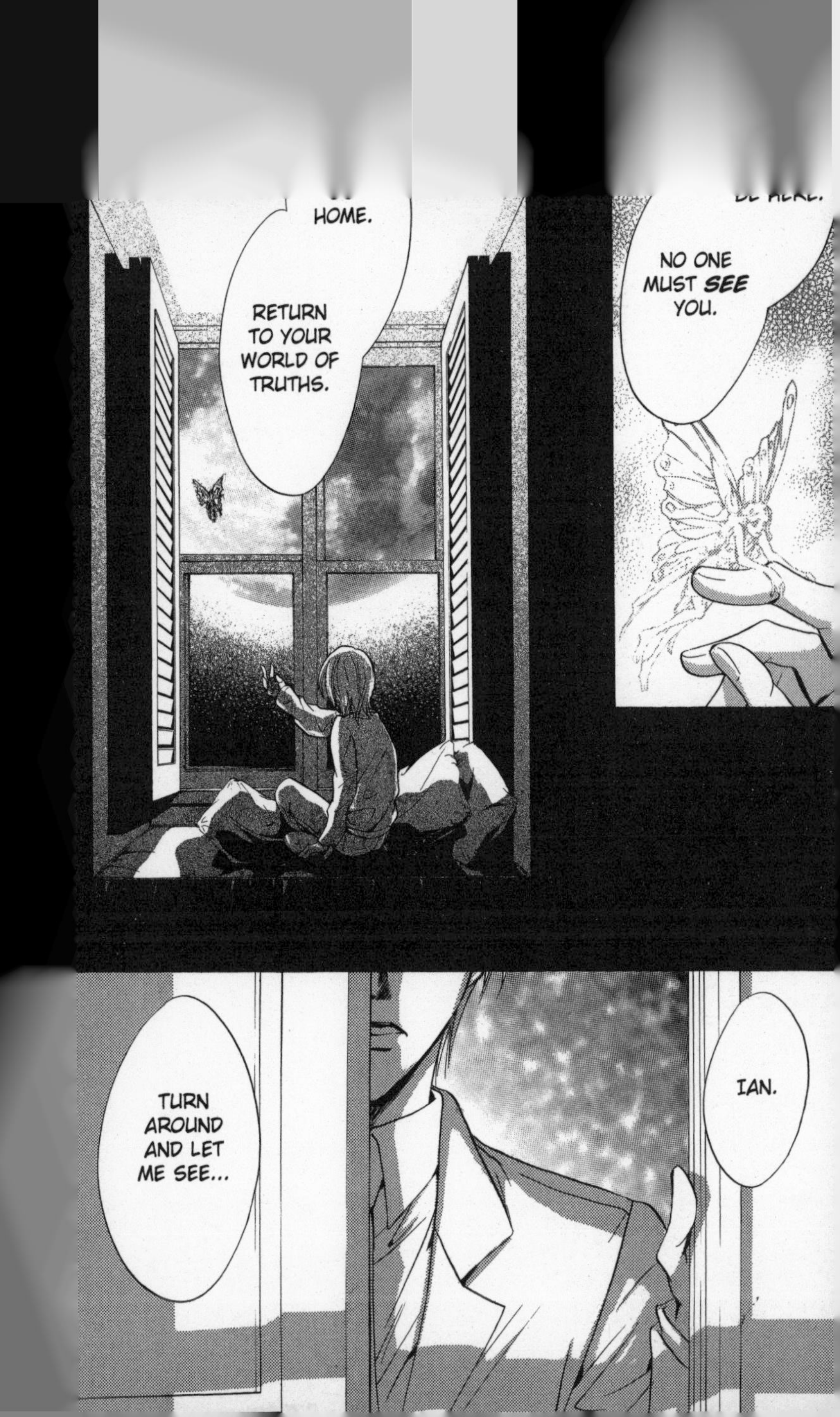
NO ONE MUST SEE YOU.
HOME.
RETURN TO YOUR WORLD OF TRUTHS.
IAN.
TURN AROUND AND LET ME SEE...

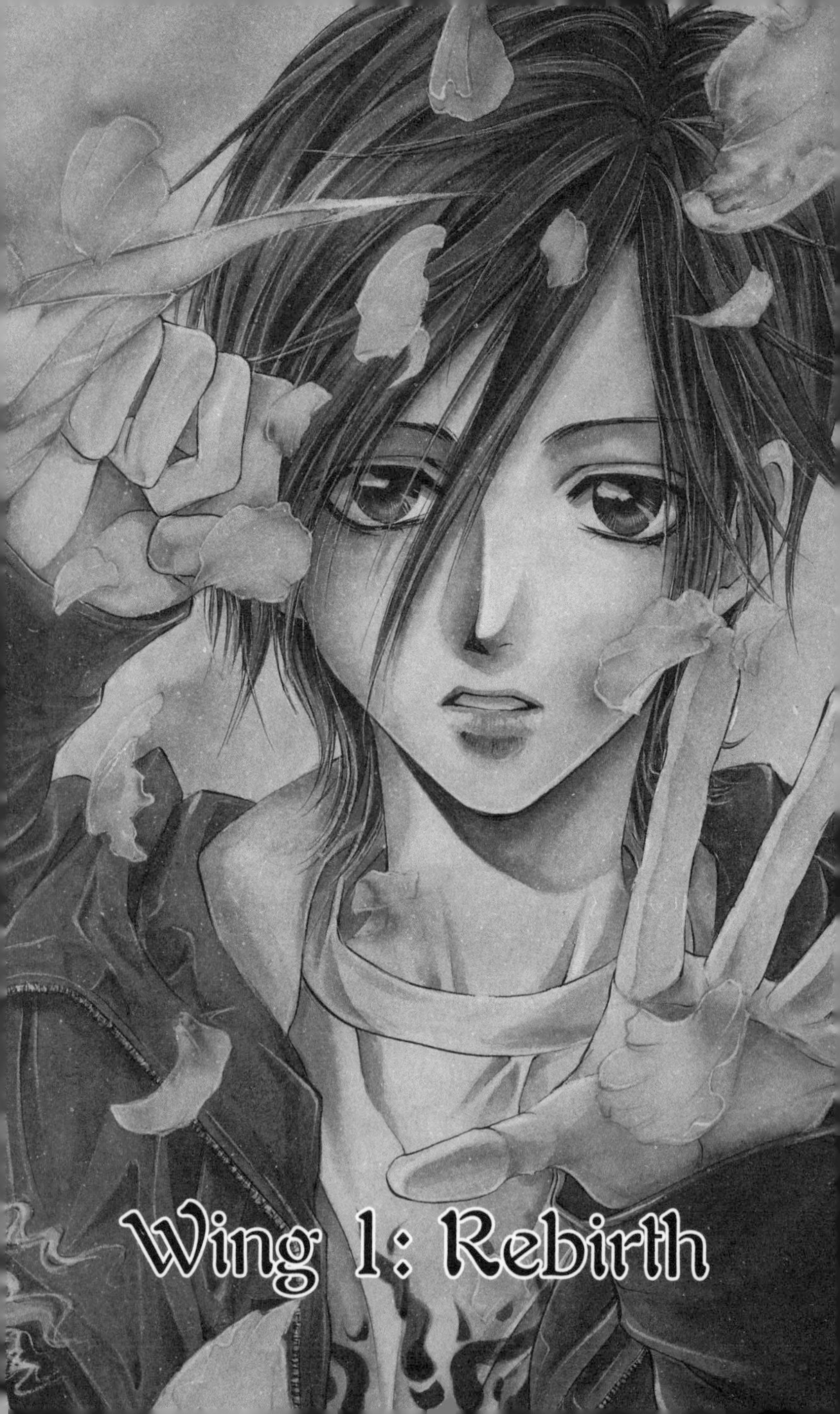

# Wing 1: Rebirth

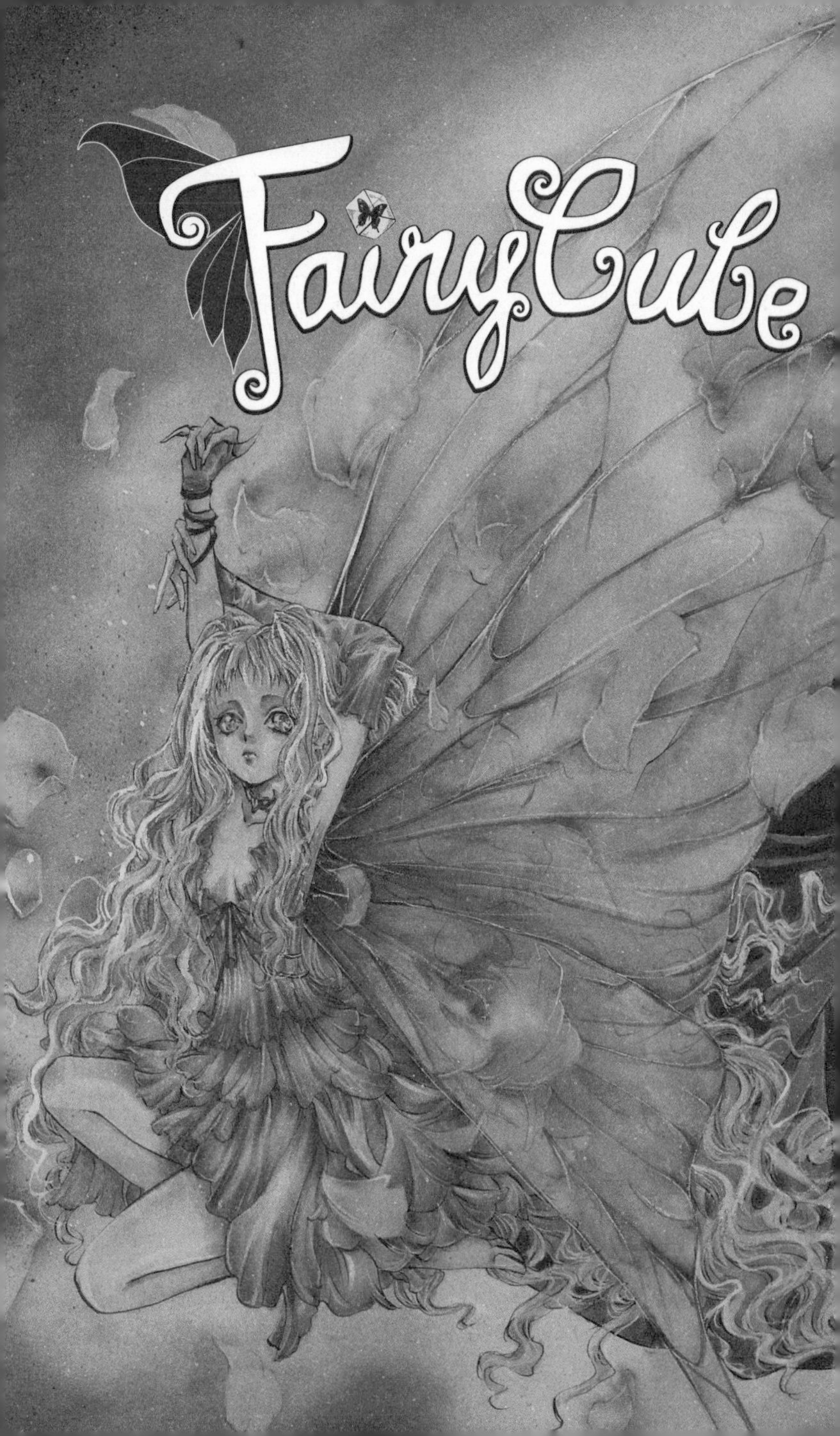
Fairy Cube

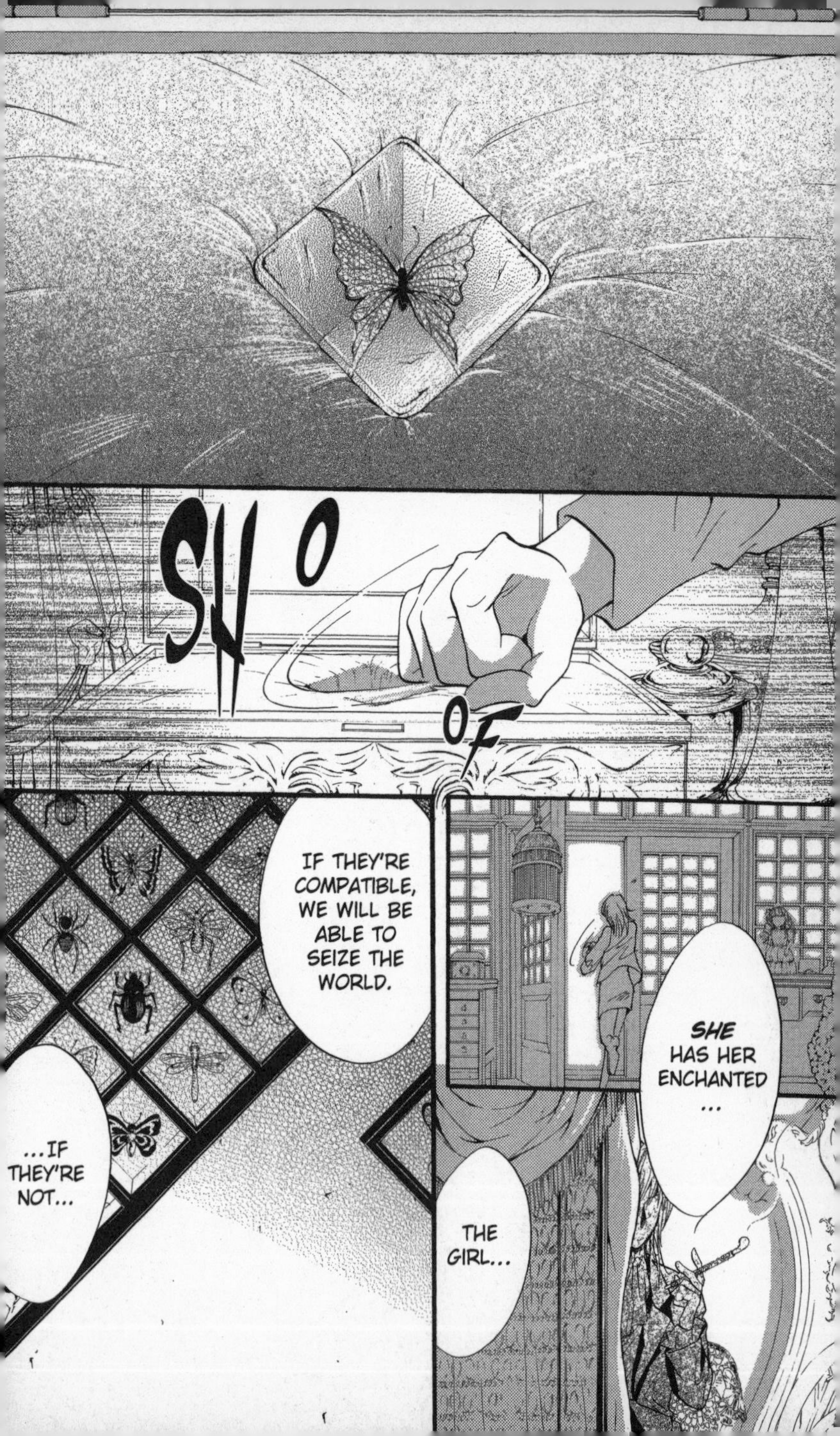
SHOOF
SHE HAS HER ENCHANTED ...
THE GIRL...
IF THEY'RE COMPATIBLE, WE WILL BE ABLE TO SEIZE THE WORLD.
...IF THEY'RE NOT...

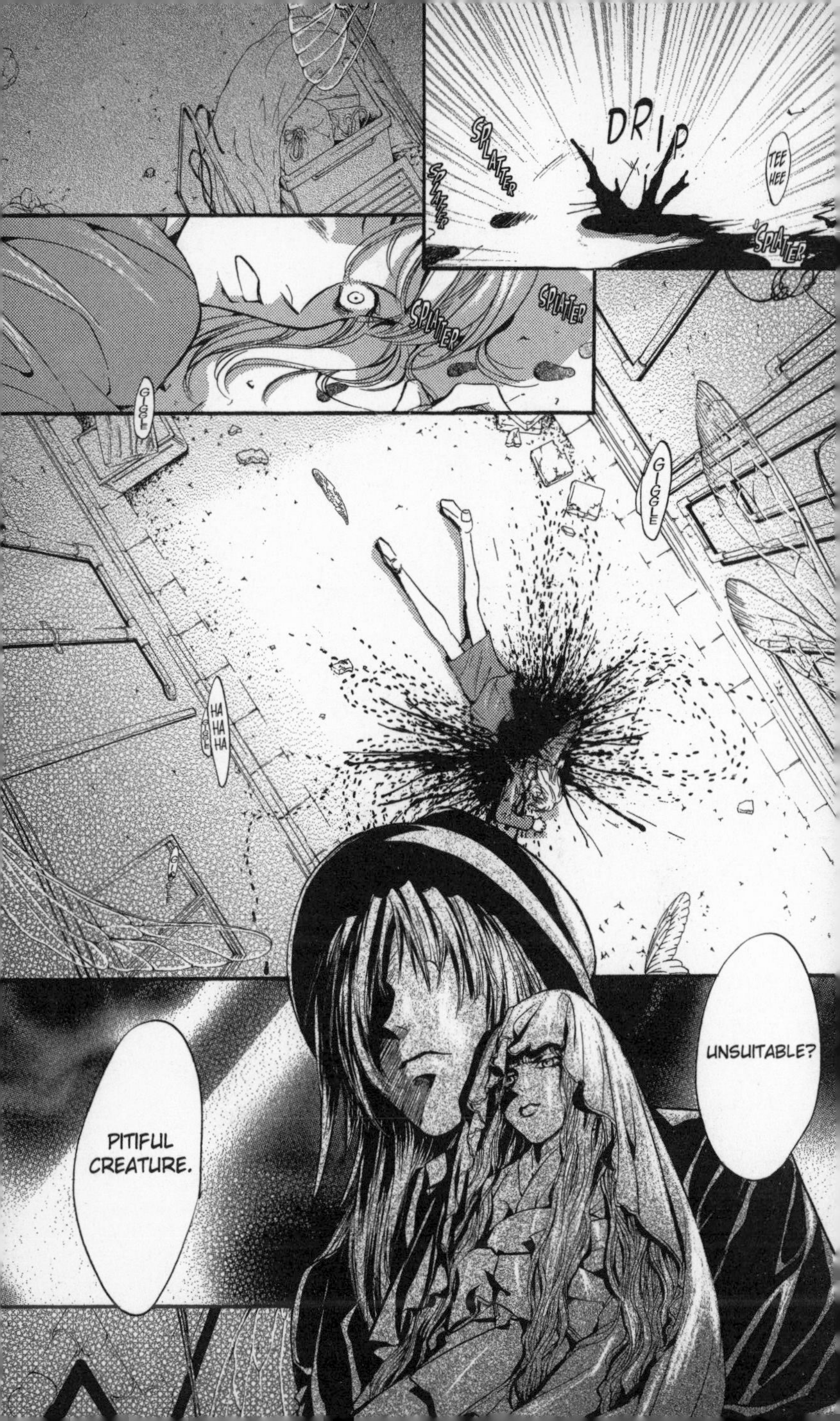
TEE HEE
DRIP
SPLATTER
SPLATTER
SPLATTER
SPLATTER
SPLATTER
SPLATTER
GIGGLE
GIGGLE
HA HA HA
GIGGLE
UNSUITABLE?
PITIFUL CREATURE.

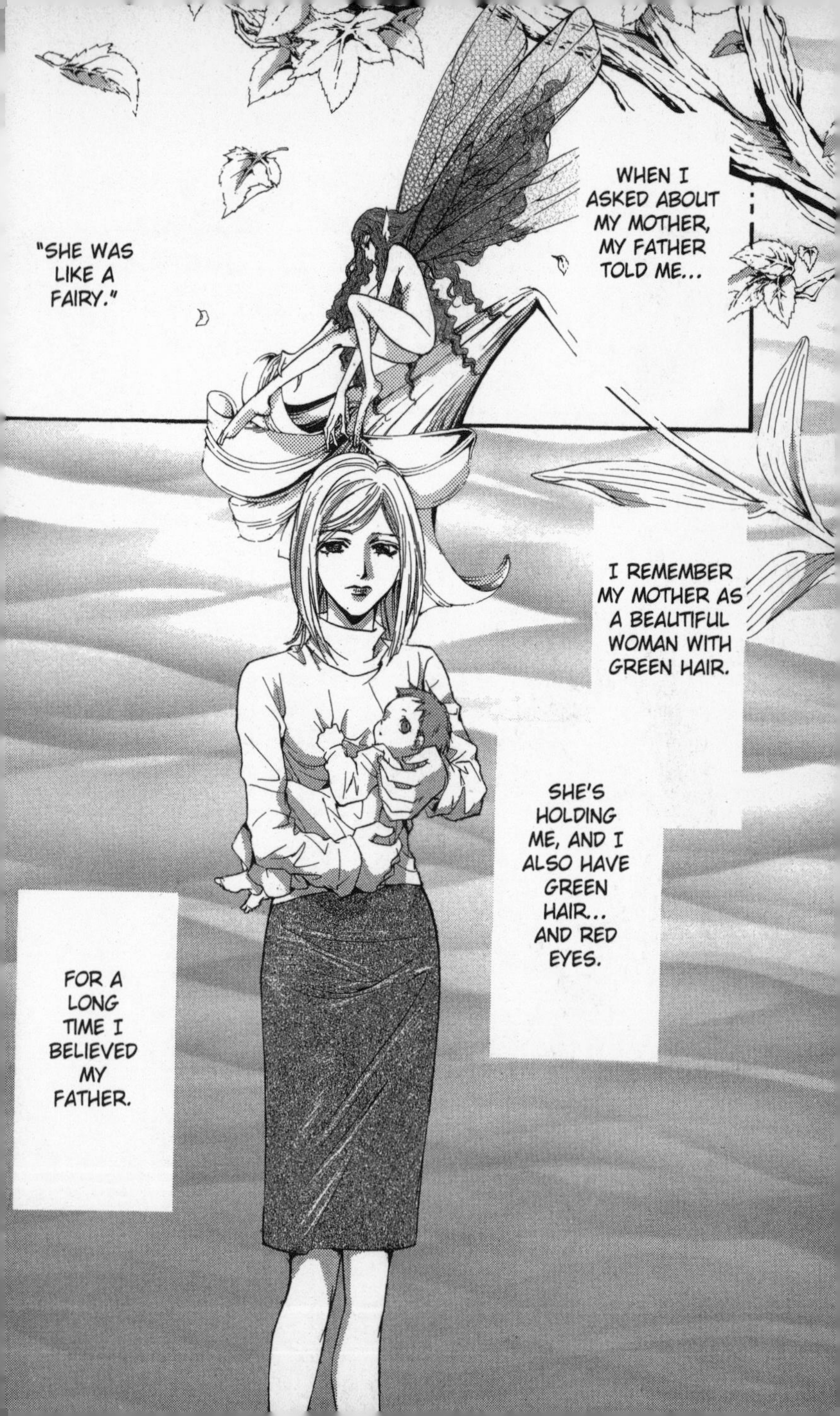
WHEN I ASKED ABOUT MY MOTHER, MY FATHER TOLD ME...
"SHE WAS LIKE A FAIRY."
I REMEMBER MY MOTHER AS A BEAUTIFUL WOMAN WITH GREEN HAIR.
SHE'S HOLDING ME, AND I ALSO HAVE GREEN HAIR... AND RED EYES.
FOR A LONG TIME I BELIEVED MY FATHER.

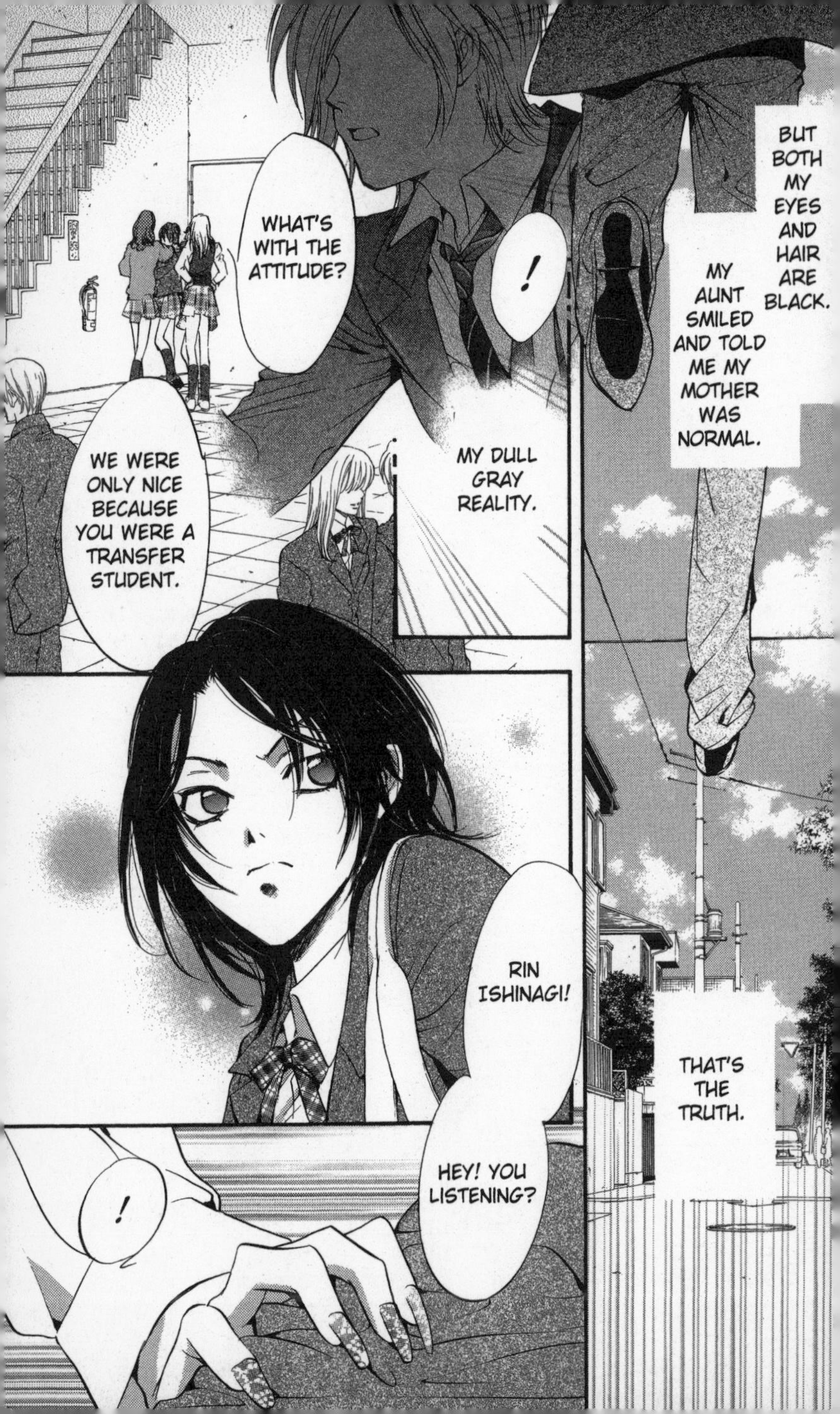
BUT BOTH MY EYES AND HAIR ARE BLACK.
MY AUNT SMILED AND TOLD ME MY MOTHER WAS NORMAL.
THAT'S THE TRUTH.
!
WHAT'S WITH THE ATTITUDE?
MY DULL GRAY REALITY.
WE WERE ONLY NICE BECAUSE YOU WERE A TRANSFER STUDENT.
RIN ISHINAGI!
HEY! YOU LISTENING?
!

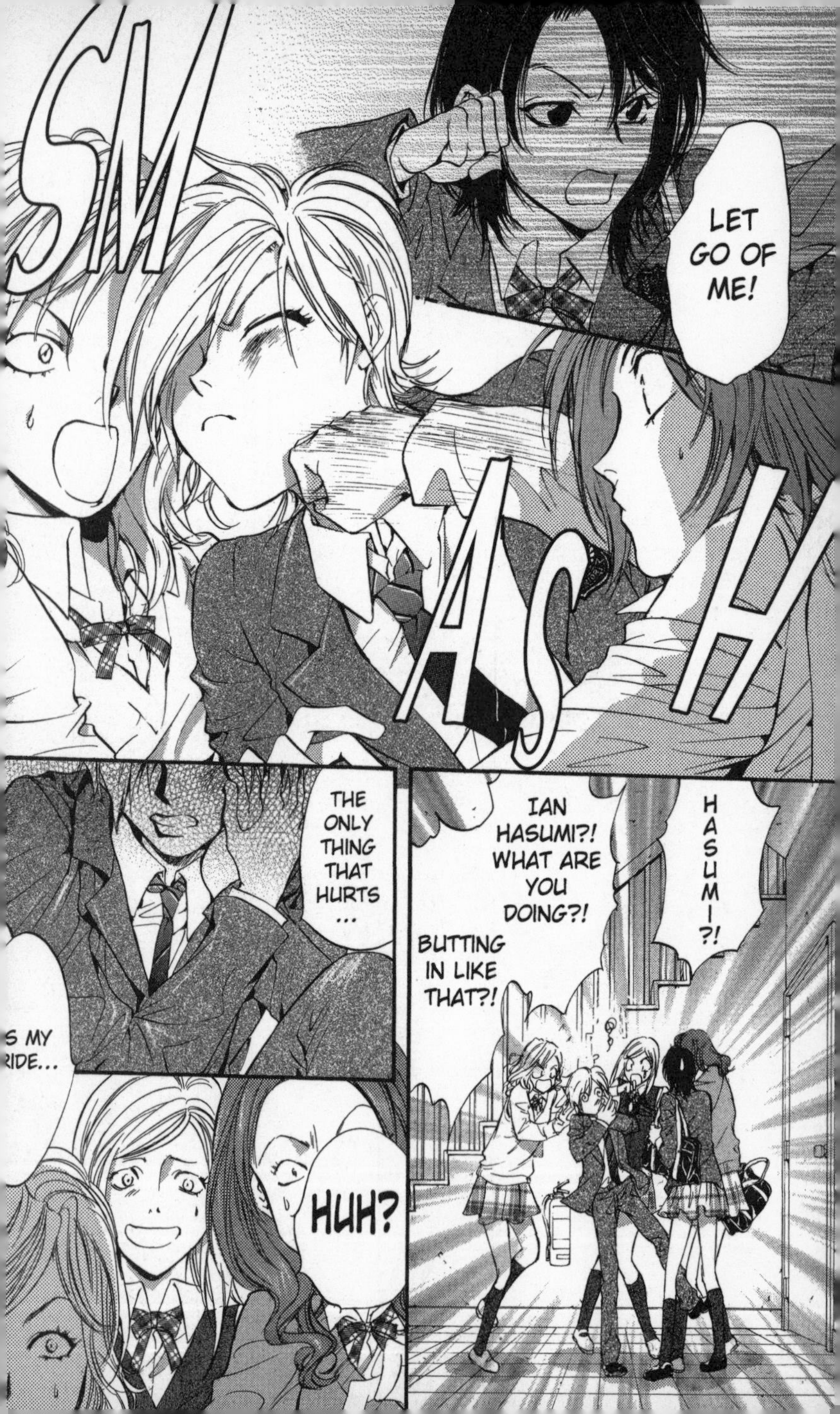
LET GO OF ME!
SMASH
HASUMI?!
IAN HASUMI?! WHAT ARE YOU DOING?!
BUTTING IN LIKE THAT?!
THE ONLY THING THAT HURTS...
S MY RIDE...
HUH?

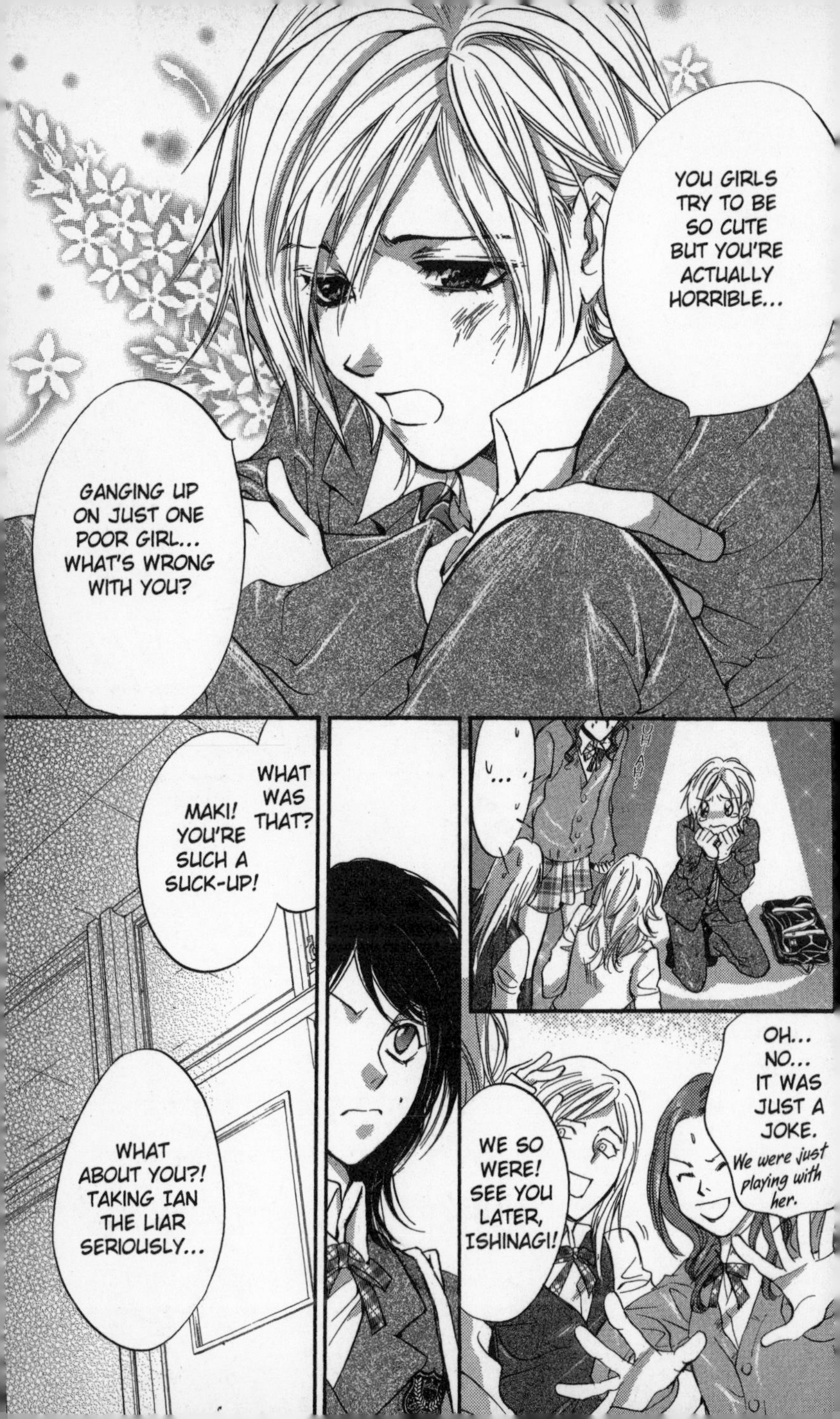
YOU GIRLS TRY TO BE SO CUTE BUT YOU'RE ACTUALLY HORRIBLE...
GANGING UP ON JUST ONE POOR GIRL... WHAT'S WRONG WITH YOU?
...
OH... NO... IT WAS JUST A JOKE.
We were just playing with her.
WE SO WERE! SEE YOU LATER, ISHINAGI!
WHAT WAS THAT?
MAKI! YOU'RE SUCH A SUCK-UP!
WHAT ABOUT YOU?! TAKING IAN THE LIAR SERIOUSLY...

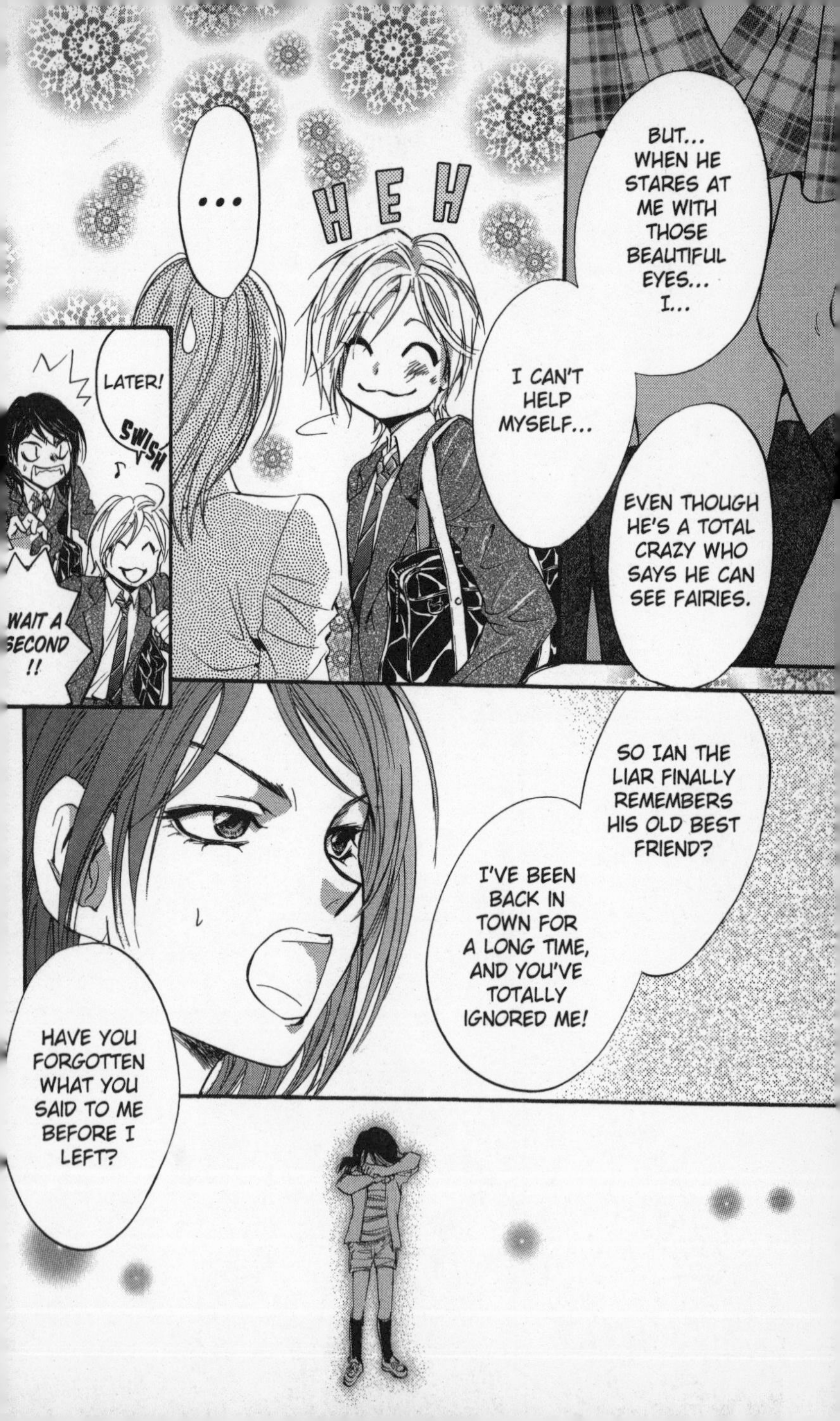
BUT... WHEN HE STARES AT ME WITH THOSE BEAUTIFUL EYES... I...
I CAN'T HELP MYSELF...
EVEN THOUGH HE'S A TOTAL CRAZY WHO SAYS HE CAN SEE FAIRIES.
HEH
...
LATER!
SWISH
WAIT A SECOND !!
SO IAN THE LIAR FINALLY REMEMBERS HIS OLD BEST FRIEND?
I'VE BEEN BACK IN TOWN FOR A LONG TIME, AND YOU'VE TOTALLY IGNORED ME!
HAVE YOU FORGOTTEN WHAT YOU SAID TO ME BEFORE I LEFT?

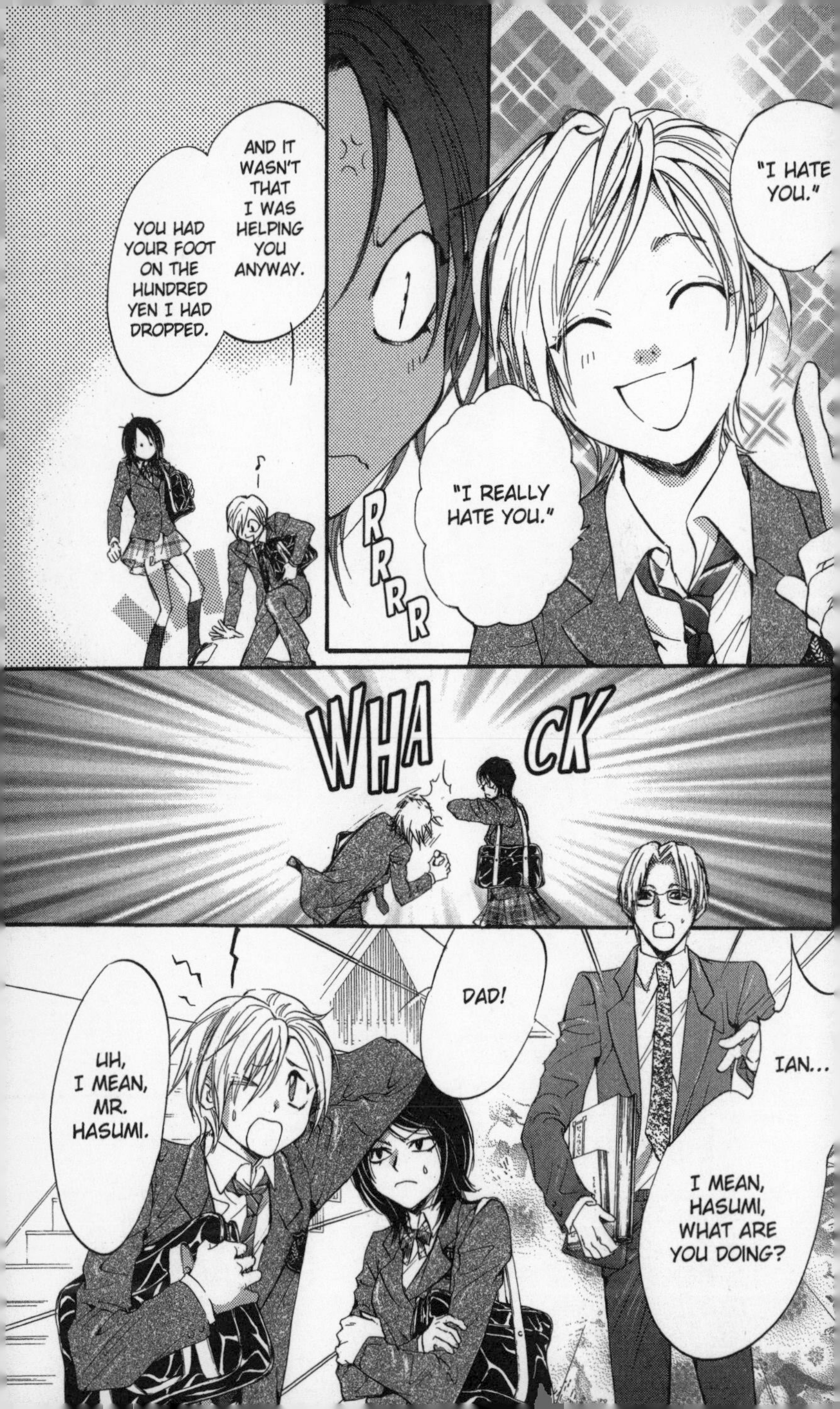
"I HATE YOU."
"I REALLY HATE YOU."
RRRR
AND IT WASN'T THAT I WAS HELPING YOU ANYWAY.
YOU HAD YOUR FOOT ON THE HUNDRED YEN I HAD DROPPED.
WHACK
IAN...
I MEAN, HASUMI, WHAT ARE YOU DOING?
DAD!
UH, I MEAN, MR. HASUMI.

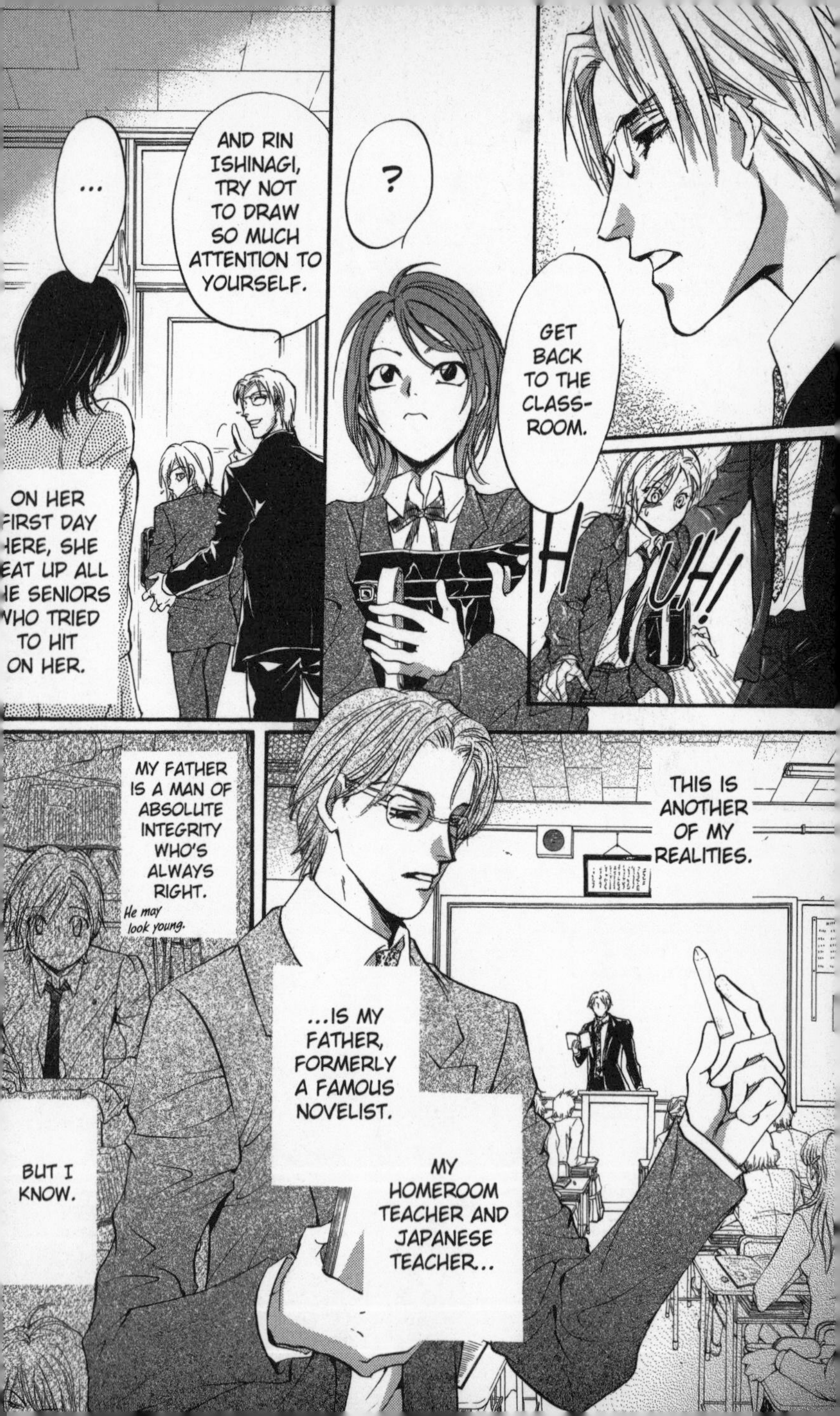
GET BACK TO THE CLASS-ROOM.
HUH!
?
AND RIN ISHINAGI, TRY NOT TO DRAW SO MUCH ATTENTION TO YOURSELF.
...
ON HER FIRST DAY HERE, SHE EAT UP ALL HE SENIORS WHO TRIED TO HIT ON HER.
THIS IS ANOTHER OF MY REALITIES.
MY HOMEROOM TEACHER AND JAPANESE TEACHER...
...IS MY FATHER, FORMERLY A FAMOUS NOVELIST.
MY FATHER IS A MAN OF ABSOLUTE INTEGRITY WHO'S ALWAYS RIGHT.
He may look young.
BUT I KNOW.

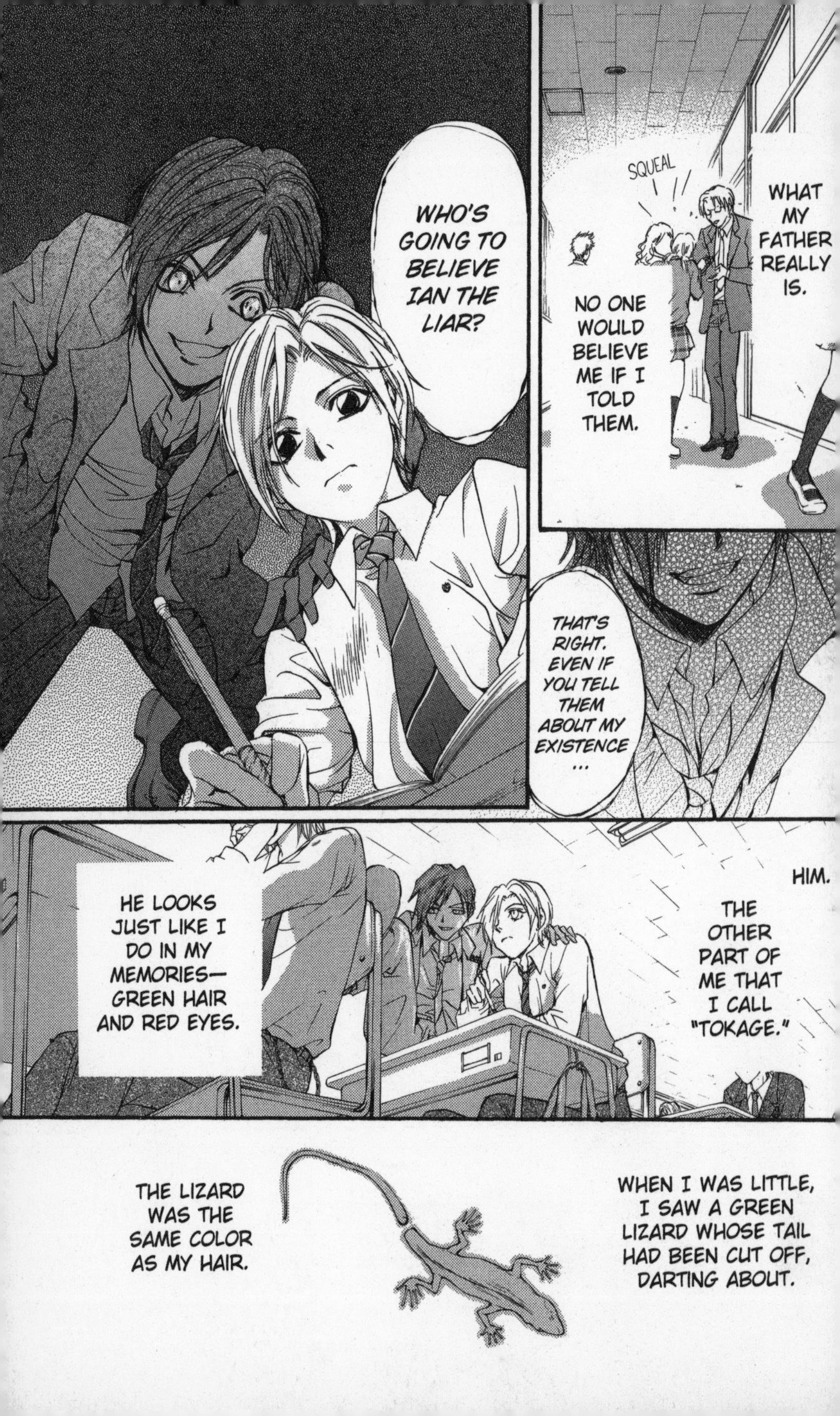
WHAT MY FATHER REALLY IS.
SQUEAL
NO ONE WOULD BELIEVE ME IF I TOLD THEM.
THAT'S RIGHT. EVEN IF YOU TELL THEM ABOUT MY EXISTENCE...
WHO'S GOING TO BELIEVE IAN THE LIAR?
HIM.
THE OTHER PART OF ME THAT I CALL "TOKAGE."
HE LOOKS JUST LIKE I DO IN MY MEMORIES—GREEN HAIR AND RED EYES.
WHEN I WAS LITTLE, I SAW A GREEN LIZARD WHOSE TAIL HAD BEEN CUT OFF, DARTING ABOUT.
THE LIZARD WAS THE SAME COLOR AS MY HAIR.

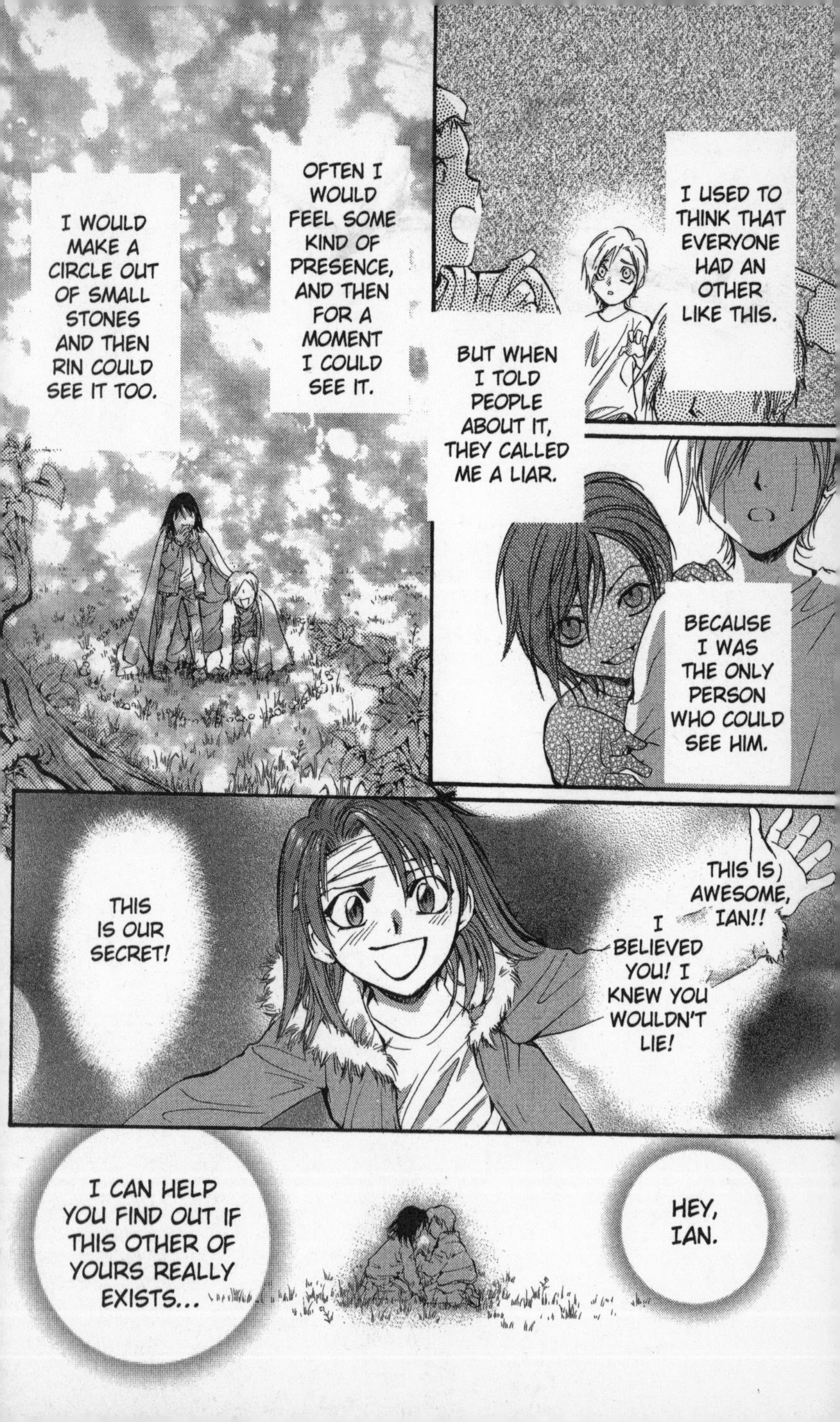
I USED TO THINK THAT EVERYONE HAD AN OTHER LIKE THIS.
BUT WHEN I TOLD PEOPLE ABOUT IT, THEY CALLED ME A LIAR.
BECAUSE I WAS THE ONLY PERSON WHO COULD SEE HIM.
OFTEN I WOULD FEEL SOME KIND OF PRESENCE, AND THEN FOR A MOMENT I COULD SEE IT.
I WOULD MAKE A CIRCLE OUT OF SMALL STONES AND THEN RIN COULD SEE IT TOO.
THIS IS AWESOME, IAN!!
I BELIEVED YOU! I KNEW YOU WOULDN'T LIE!
THIS IS OUR SECRET!
HEY, IAN.
I CAN HELP YOU FIND OUT IF THIS OTHER OF YOURS REALLY EXISTS...

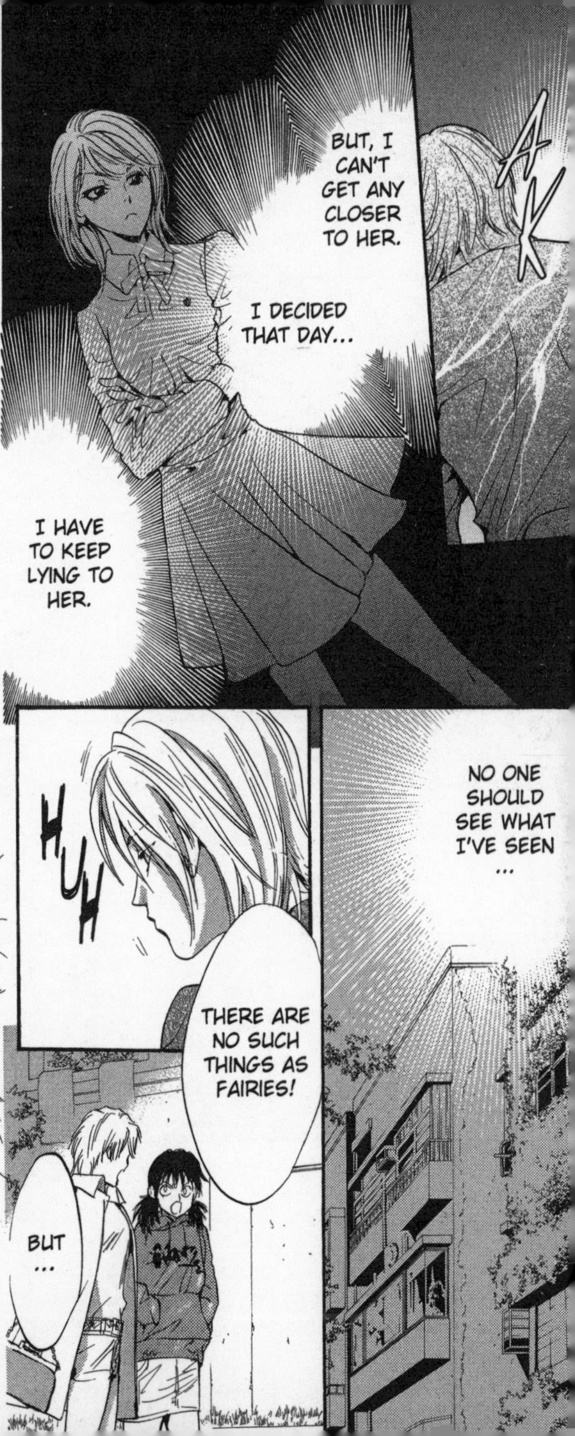
AK
BUT, I CAN'T GET ANY CLOSER TO HER.
I DECIDED THAT DAY...
I HAVE TO KEEP LYING TO HER.
NO ONE SHOULD SEE WHAT I'VE SEEN ...
HUH
THERE ARE NO SUCH THINGS AS FAIRIES!
BUT ...

A new series, a long time in coming... It begins with a dead body...

I wanted to try a short series, so bear with me for a little while.♡

Once I saw photos of the Cottingley Fairies and I remember the shock. But they are real, huh? Fairies...

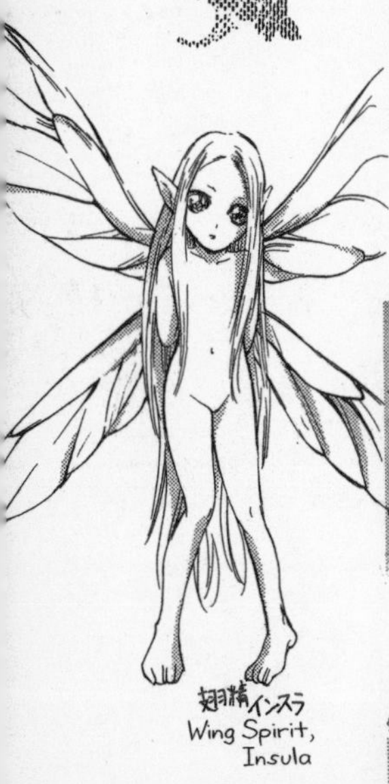

翅精インスラ
Wing Spirit, Insula

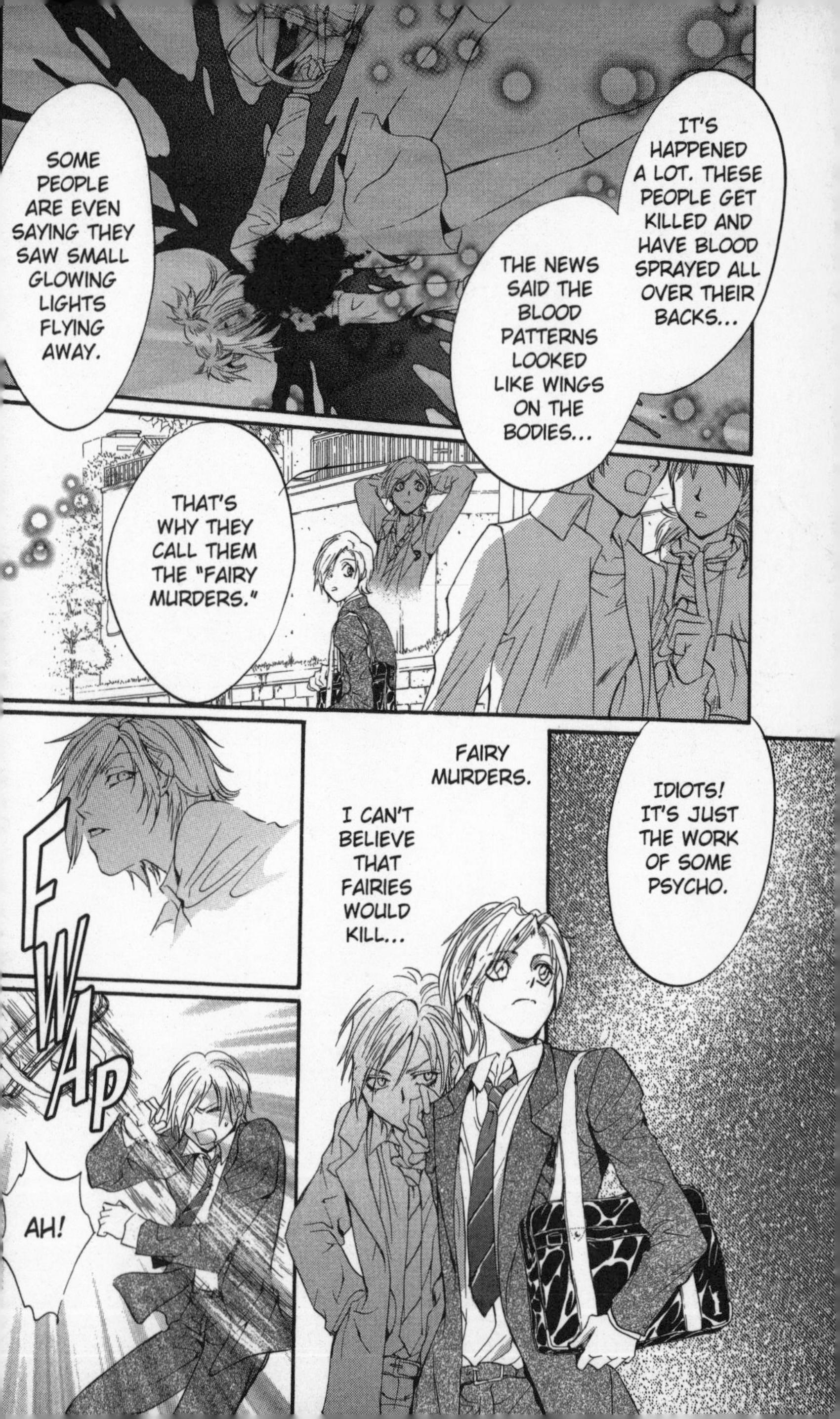
IT'S HAPPENED A LOT. THESE PEOPLE GET KILLED AND HAVE BLOOD SPRAYED ALL OVER THEIR BACKS...
THE NEWS SAID THE BLOOD PATTERNS LOOKED LIKE WINGS ON THE BODIES...
SOME PEOPLE ARE EVEN SAYING THEY SAW SMALL GLOWING LIGHTS FLYING AWAY.
THAT'S WHY THEY CALL THEM THE "FAIRY MURDERS."
IDIOTS! IT'S JUST THE WORK OF SOME PSYCHO.
FAIRY MURDERS.
I CAN'T BELIEVE THAT FAIRIES WOULD KILL...
FWAP
AH!

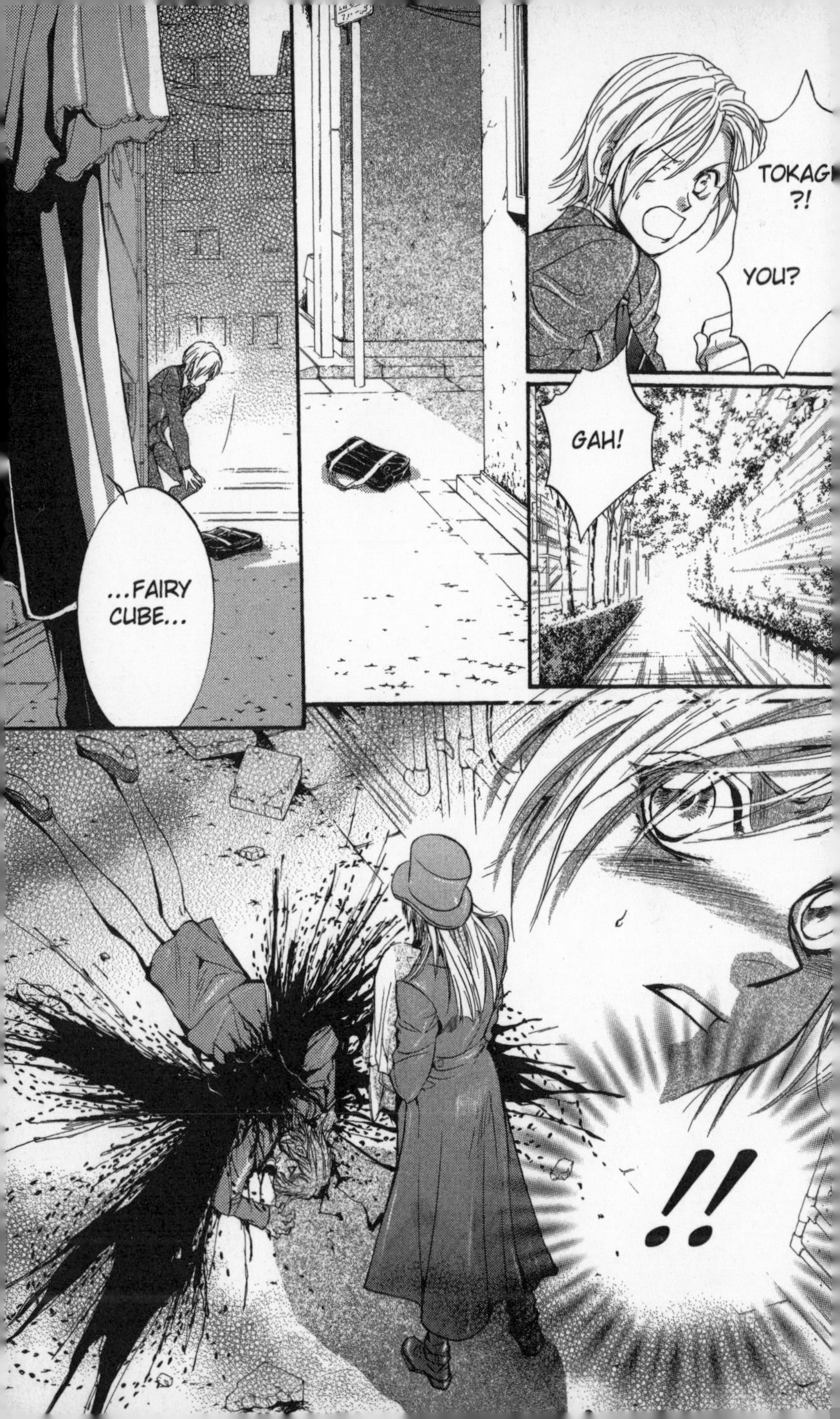
TOKAG
?!
YOU?
GAH!
...FAIRY CUBE...
!!

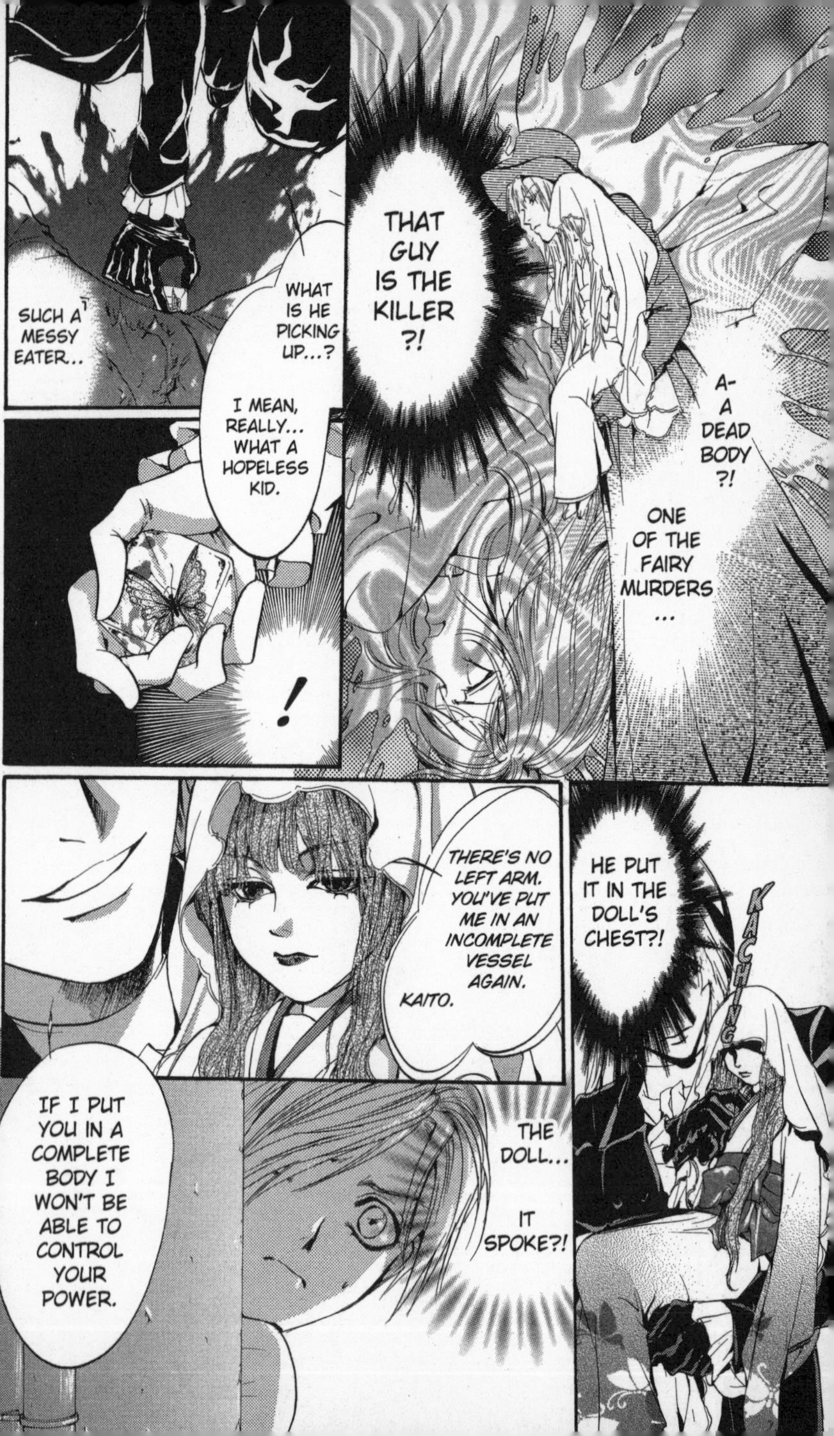
A- A DEAD BODY ?!
ONE OF THE FAIRY MURDERS ...
THAT GUY IS THE KILLER ?!
WHAT IS HE PICKING UP...?
SUCH A MESSY EATER...
I MEAN, REALLY... WHAT A HOPELESS KID.
!
HE PUT IT IN THE DOLL'S CHEST?!
KACHING
THERE'S NO LEFT ARM. YOU'VE PUT ME IN AN INCOMPLETE VESSEL AGAIN.
KAITO.
THE DOLL...
IT SPOKE?!
IF I PUT YOU IN A COMPLETE BODY I WON'T BE ABLE TO CONTROL YOUR POWER.

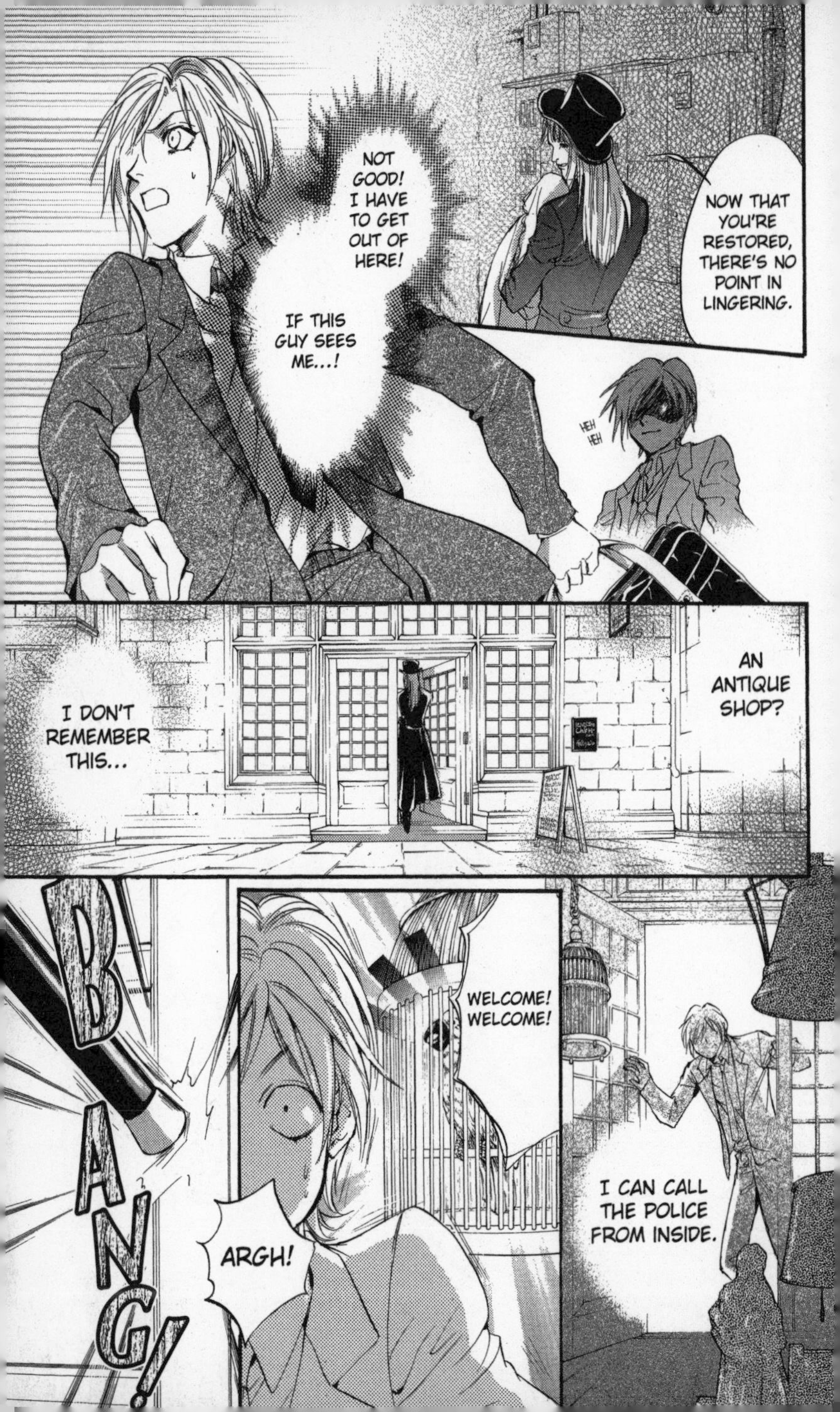
NOW THAT YOU'RE RESTORED, THERE'S NO POINT IN LINGERING.
HEH HEH
NOT GOOD! I HAVE TO GET OUT OF HERE!
IF THIS GUY SEES ME...!
AN ANTIQUE SHOP?
I DON'T REMEMBER THIS...
I CAN CALL THE POLICE FROM INSIDE.
WELCOME! WELCOME!
BANG!
ARGH!

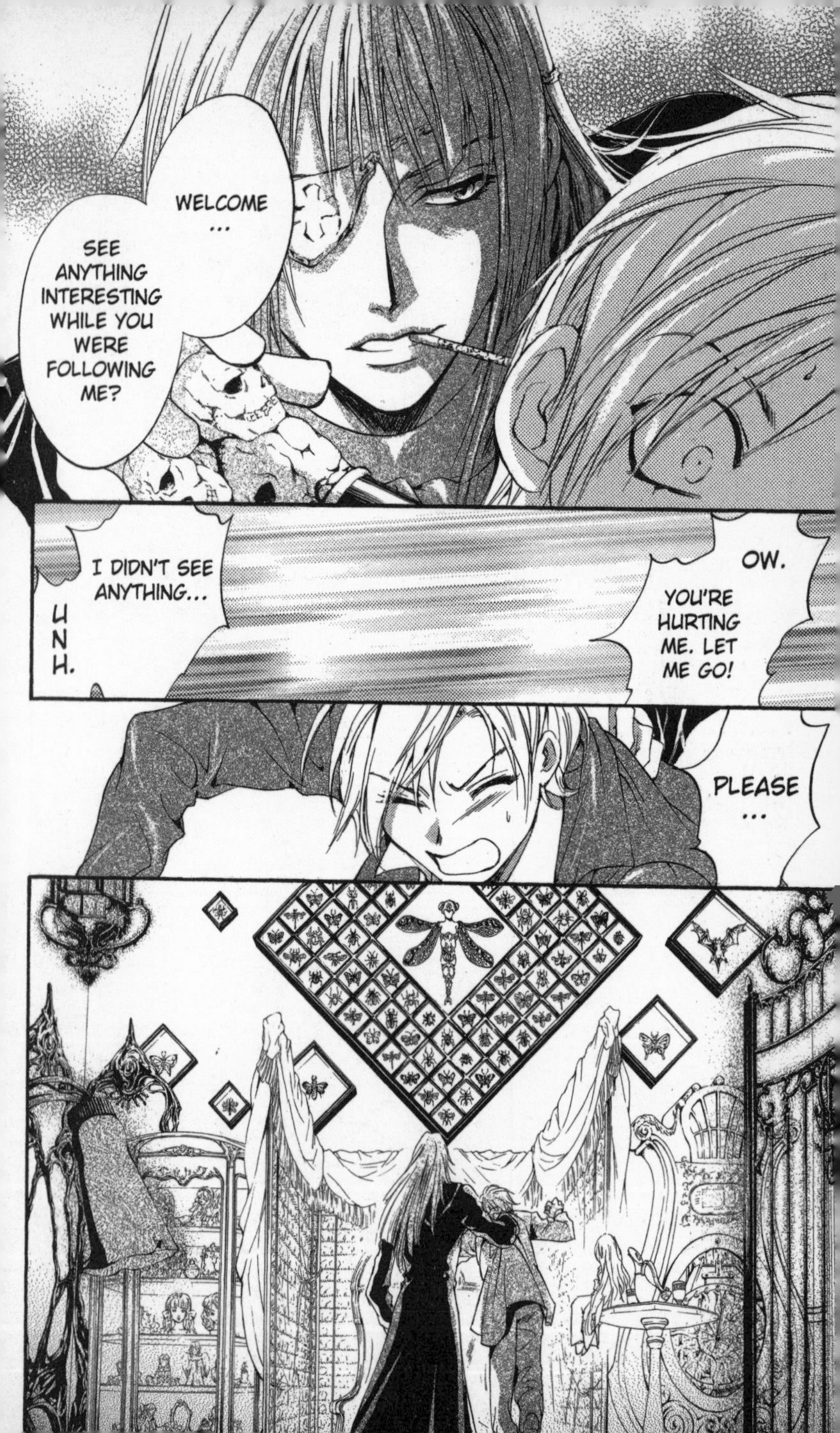
WELCOME ...
SEE ANYTHING INTERESTING WHILE YOU WERE FOLLOWING ME?
OW.
YOU'RE HURTING ME. LET ME GO!
I DIDN'T SEE ANYTHING...
UNH.
PLEASE ...

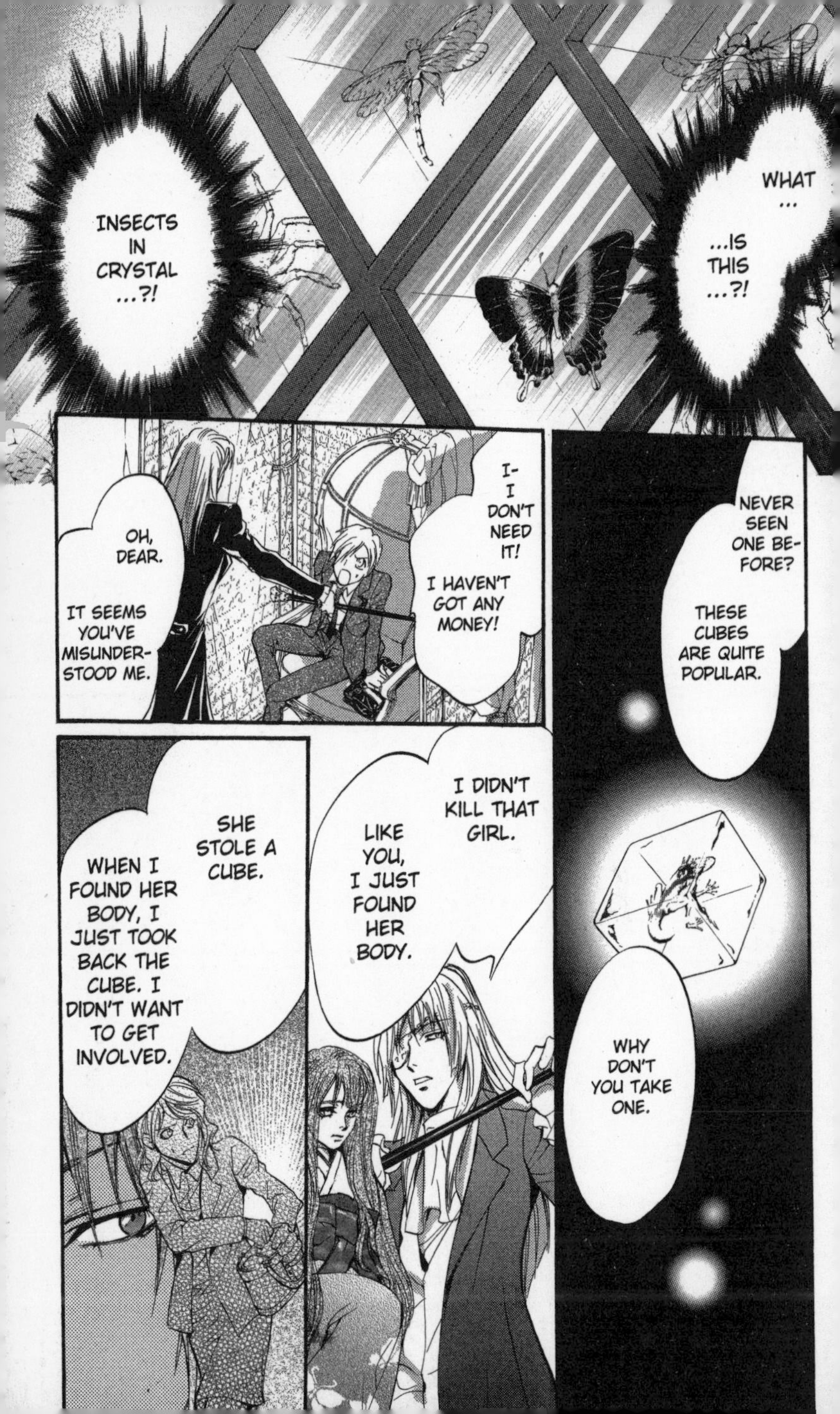
WHAT... ...IS THIS...?!
INSECTS IN CRYSTAL...?!
NEVER SEEN ONE BEFORE?
THESE CUBES ARE QUITE POPULAR.
WHY DON'T YOU TAKE ONE.
I- I DON'T NEED IT!
I HAVEN'T GOT ANY MONEY!
OH, DEAR.
IT SEEMS YOU'VE MISUNDERSTOOD ME.
I DIDN'T KILL THAT GIRL.
LIKE YOU, I JUST FOUND HER BODY.
SHE STOLE A CUBE.
WHEN I FOUND HER BODY, I JUST TOOK BACK THE CUBE. I DIDN'T WANT TO GET INVOLVED.

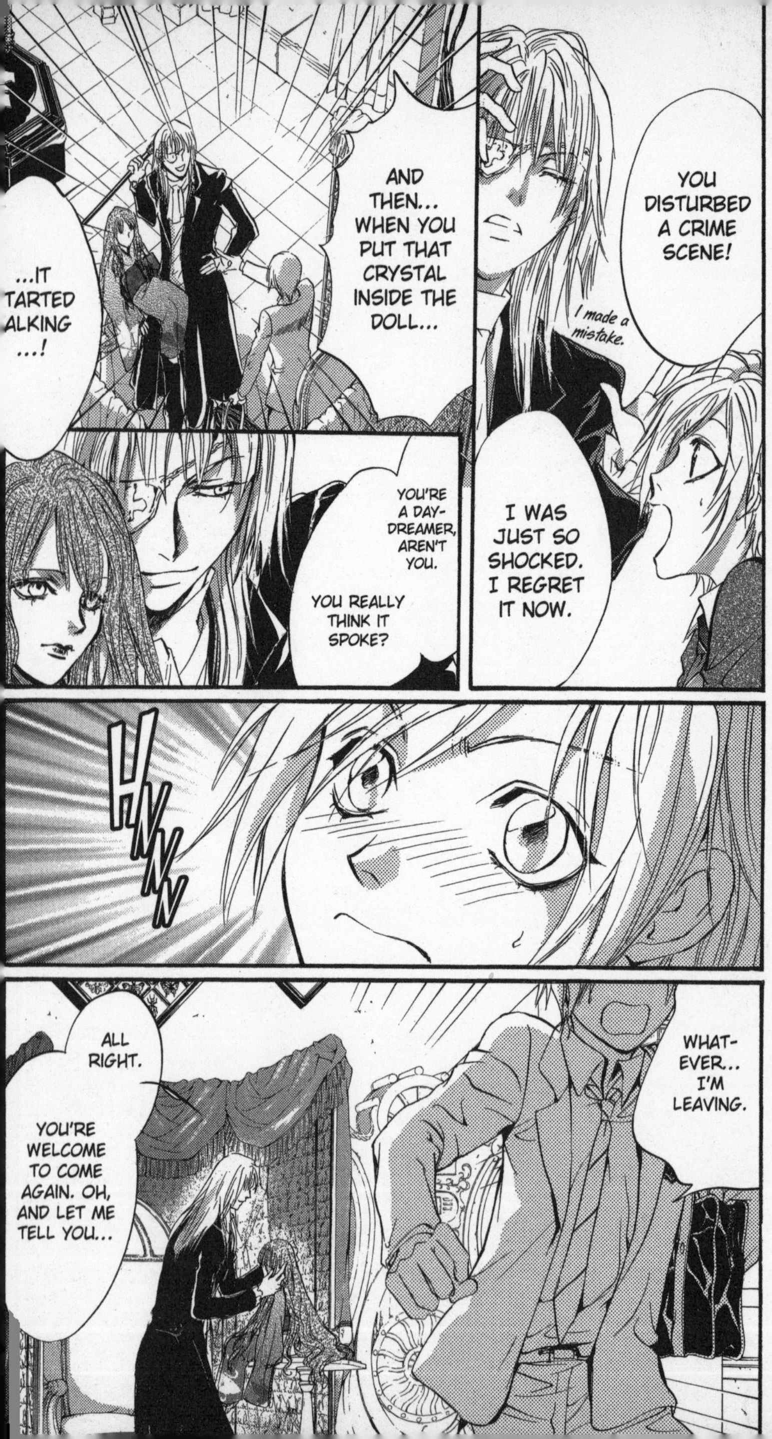
YOU DISTURBED A CRIME SCENE!
I made a mistake.
I WAS JUST SO SHOCKED. I REGRET IT NOW.
AND THEN... WHEN YOU PUT THAT CRYSTAL INSIDE THE DOLL...
...IT TARTED ALKING ...!
YOU'RE A DAY-DREAMER, AREN'T YOU.
YOU REALLY THINK IT SPOKE?
HNNN
WHAT-EVER... I'M LEAVING.
ALL RIGHT.
YOU'RE WELCOME TO COME AGAIN. OH, AND LET ME TELL YOU...

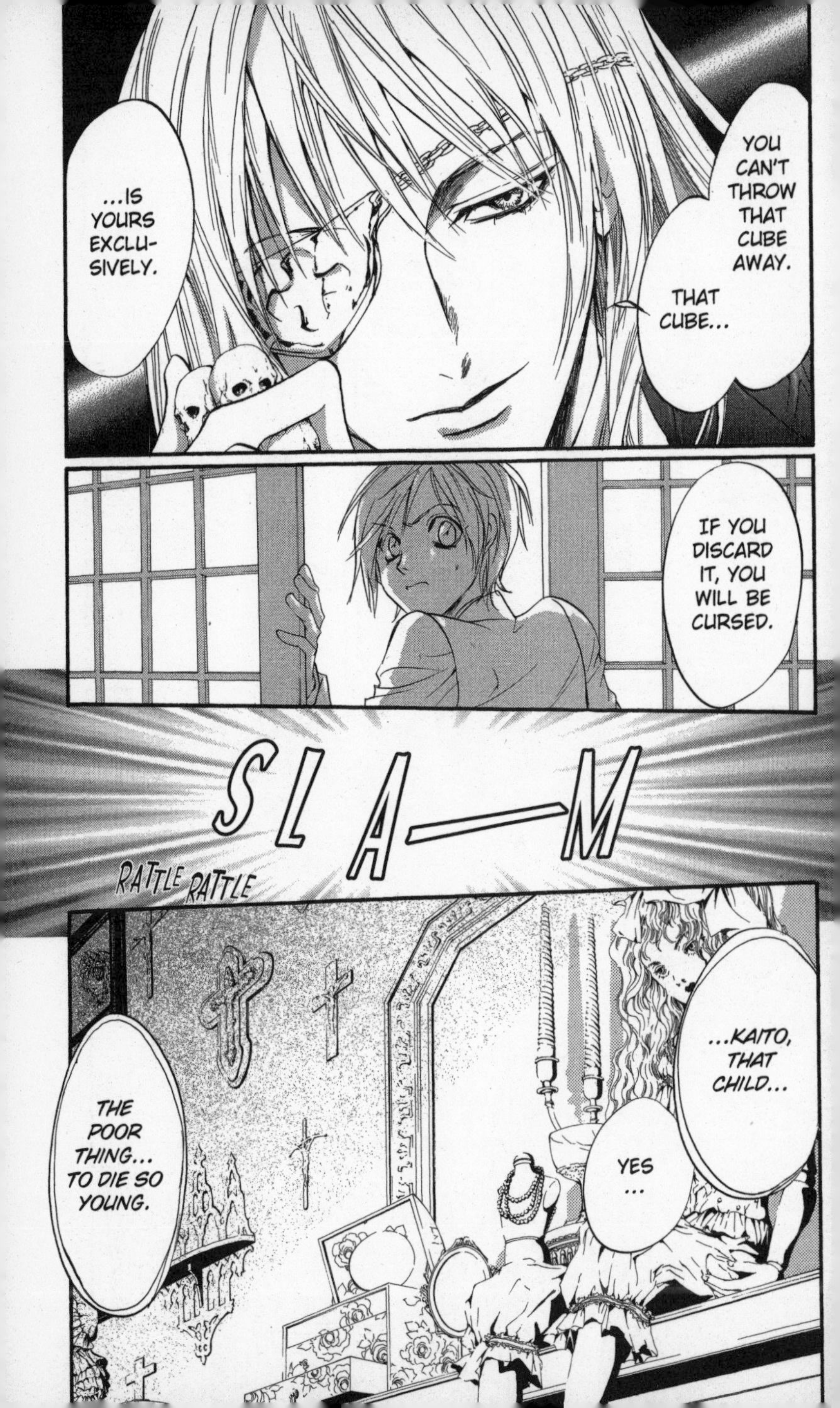
YOU CAN'T THROW THAT CUBE AWAY.
THAT CUBE...
...IS YOURS EXCLU-SIVELY.
IF YOU DISCARD IT, YOU WILL BE CURSED.
SLA—M
RATTLE RATTLE
...KAITO, THAT CHILD...
YES...
THE POOR THING... TO DIE SO YOUNG.

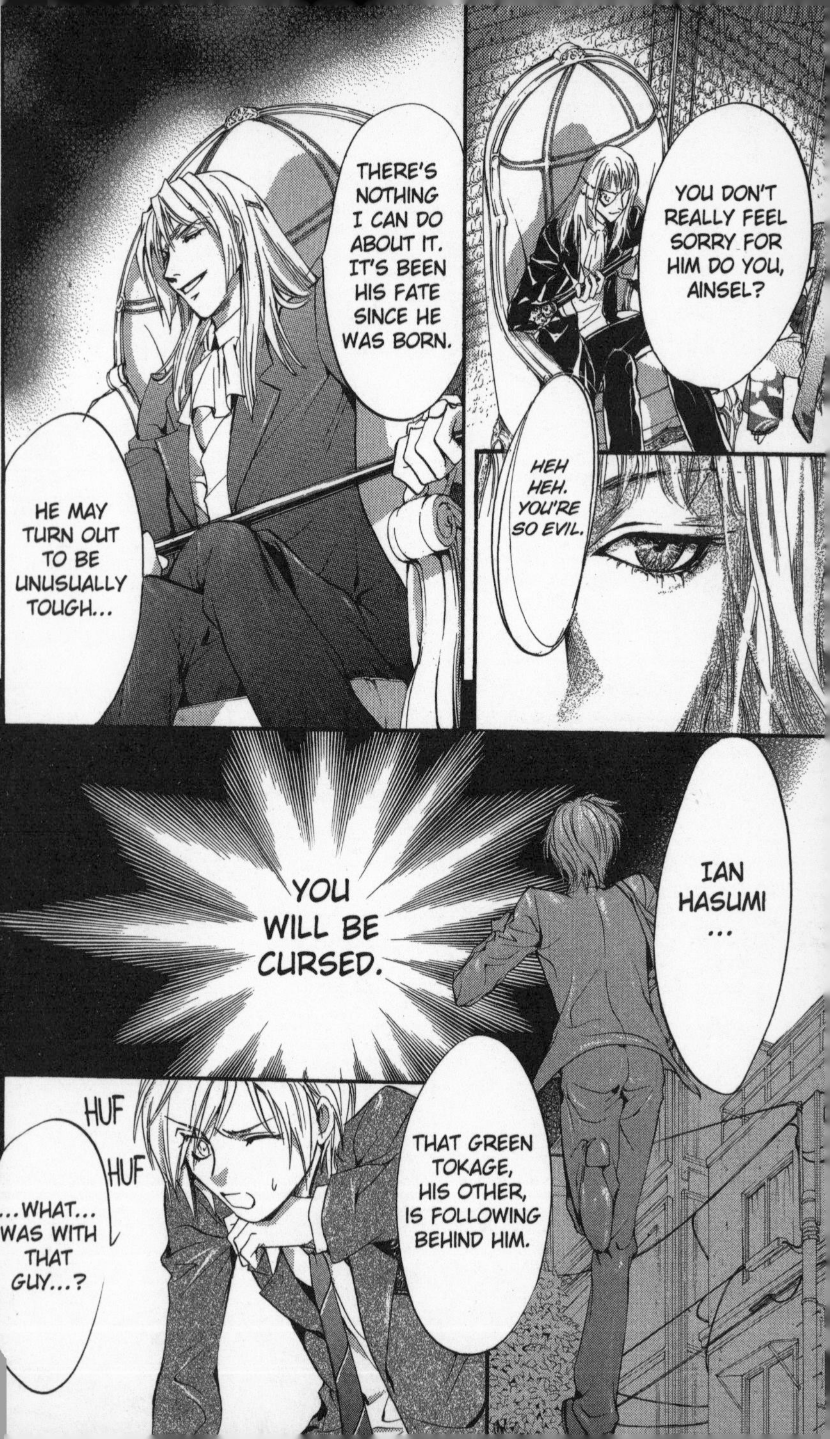
YOU DON'T REALLY FEEL SORRY FOR HIM DO YOU, AINSEL?
HEH HEH. YOU'RE SO EVIL.
THERE'S NOTHING I CAN DO ABOUT IT. IT'S BEEN HIS FATE SINCE HE WAS BORN.
HE MAY TURN OUT TO BE UNUSUALLY TOUGH...
IAN HASUMI ...
YOU WILL BE CURSED.
THAT GREEN TOKAGE, HIS OTHER, IS FOLLOWING BEHIND HIM.
HUF
HUF
...WHAT... WAS WITH THAT GUY...?

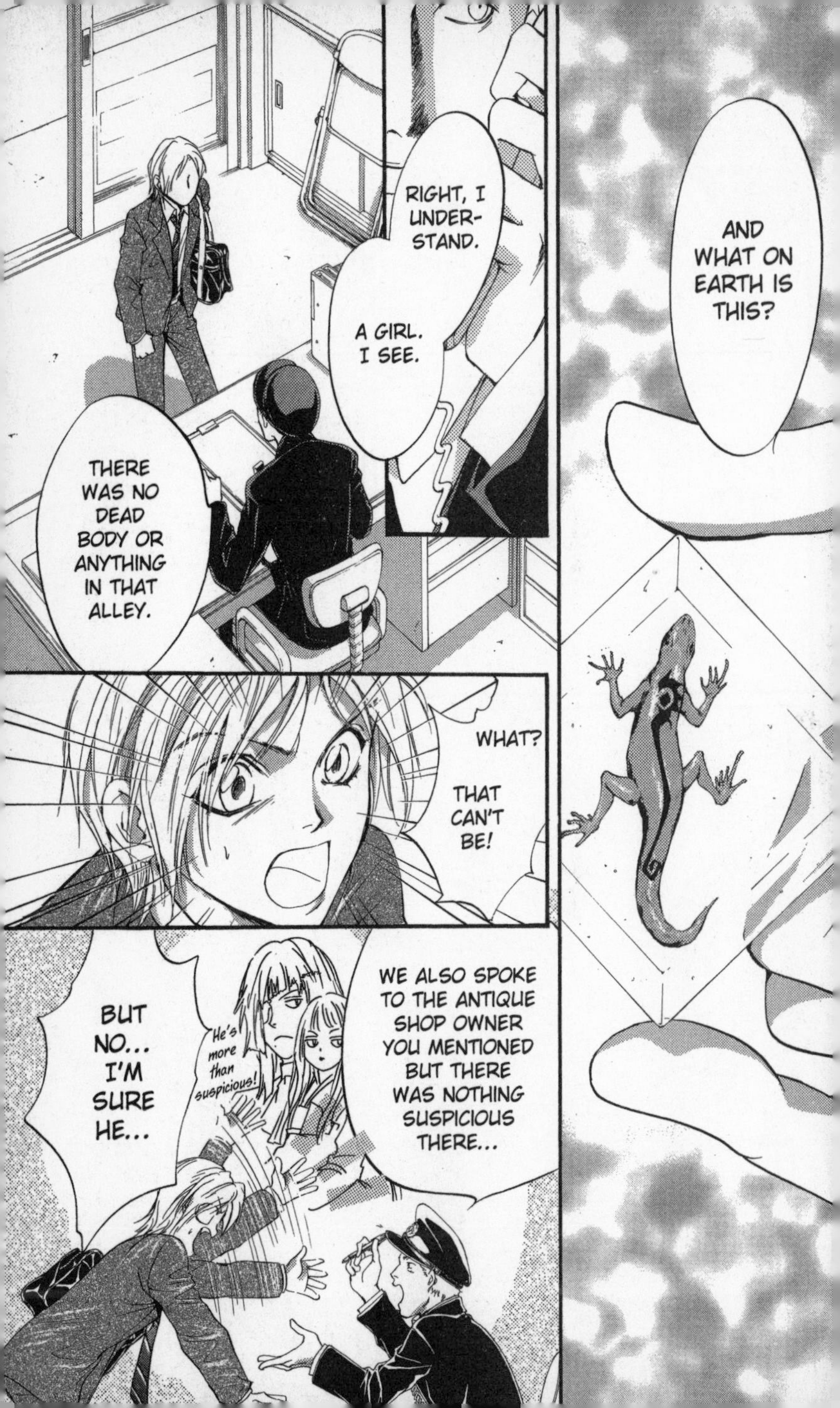
AND WHAT ON EARTH IS THIS?
RIGHT, I UNDER-STAND.
A GIRL. I SEE.
THERE WAS NO DEAD BODY OR ANYTHING IN THAT ALLEY.
WHAT?
THAT CAN'T BE!
WE ALSO SPOKE TO THE ANTIQUE SHOP OWNER YOU MENTIONED BUT THERE WAS NOTHING SUSPICIOUS THERE...
He's more than suspicious!
BUT NO... I'M SURE HE...

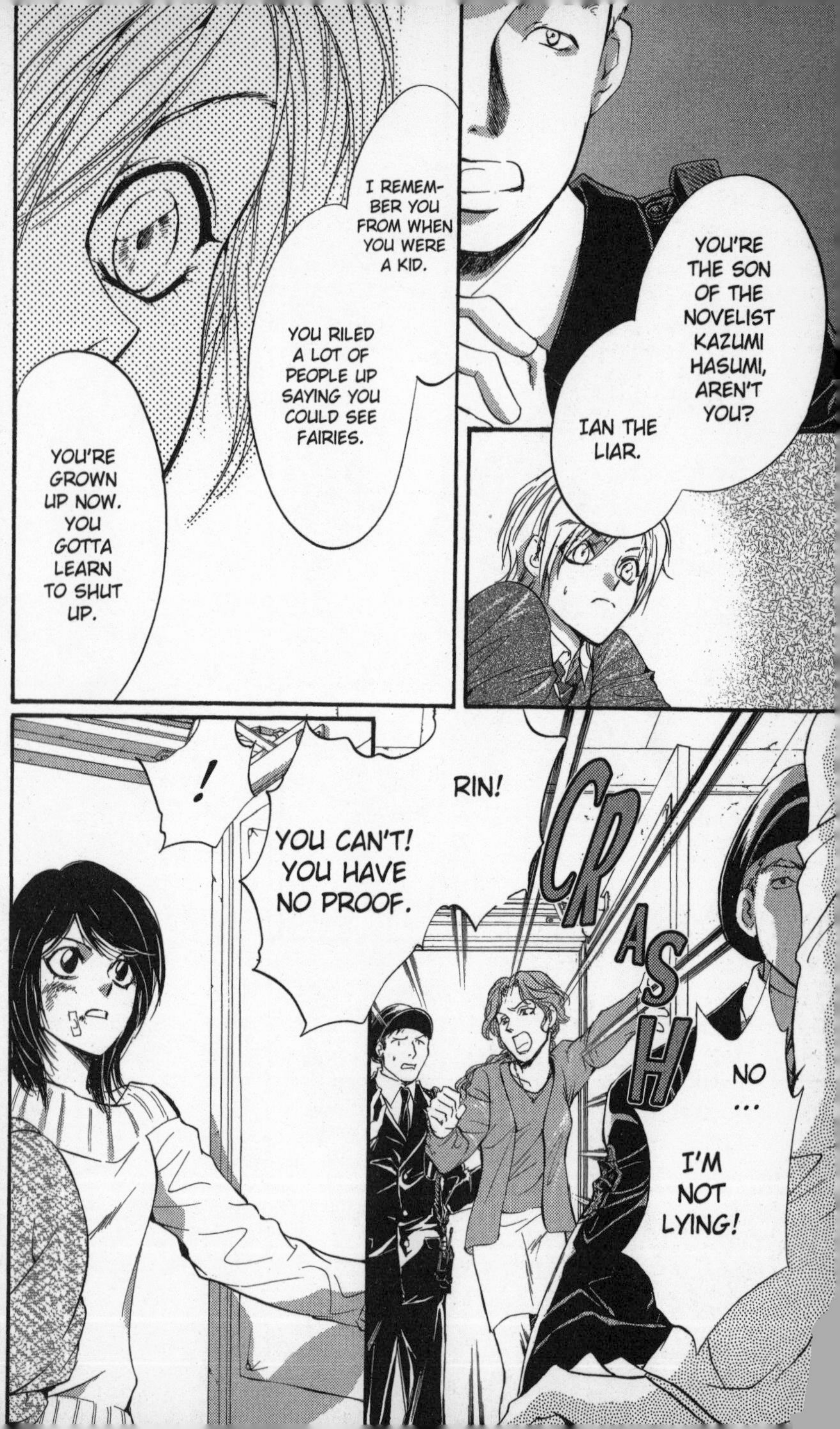
YOU'RE THE SON OF THE NOVELIST KAZUMI HASUMI, AREN'T YOU?
IAN THE LIAR.
I REMEMBER YOU FROM WHEN YOU WERE A KID.
YOU RILED A LOT OF PEOPLE UP SAYING YOU COULD SEE FAIRIES.
YOU'RE GROWN UP NOW. YOU GOTTA LEARN TO SHUT UP.
NO ...
I'M NOT LYING!
CRASH
RIN!
!
YOU CAN'T! YOU HAVE NO PROOF.

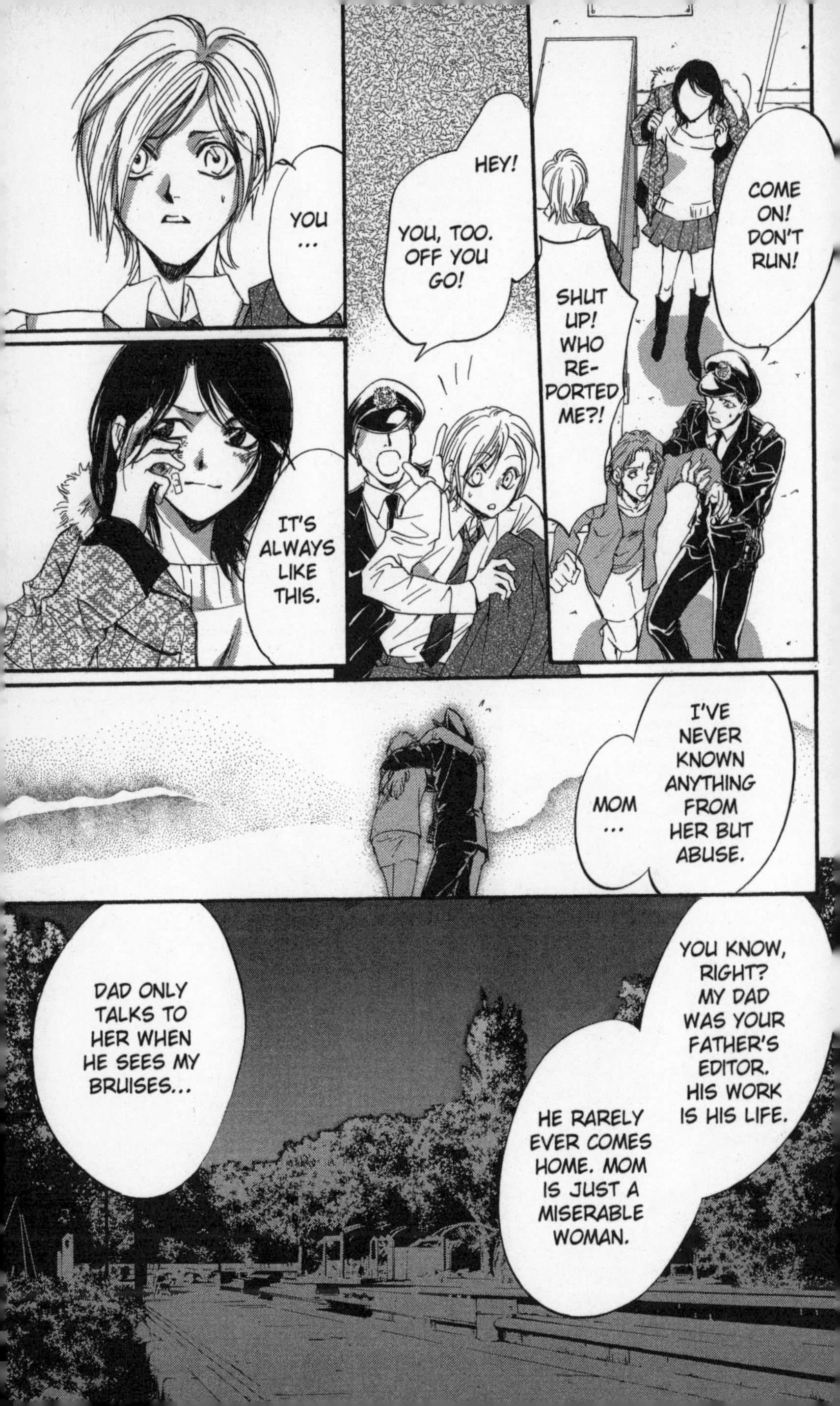
COME ON! DON'T RUN!
SHUT UP! WHO RE-PORTED ME?!
HEY!
YOU, TOO. OFF YOU GO!
YOU ...
IT'S ALWAYS LIKE THIS.
I'VE NEVER KNOWN ANYTHING FROM HER BUT ABUSE.
MOM ...
YOU KNOW, RIGHT? MY DAD WAS YOUR FATHER'S EDITOR. HIS WORK IS HIS LIFE.
HE RARELY EVER COMES HOME. MOM IS JUST A MISERABLE WOMAN.
DAD ONLY TALKS TO HER WHEN HE SEES MY BRUISES...

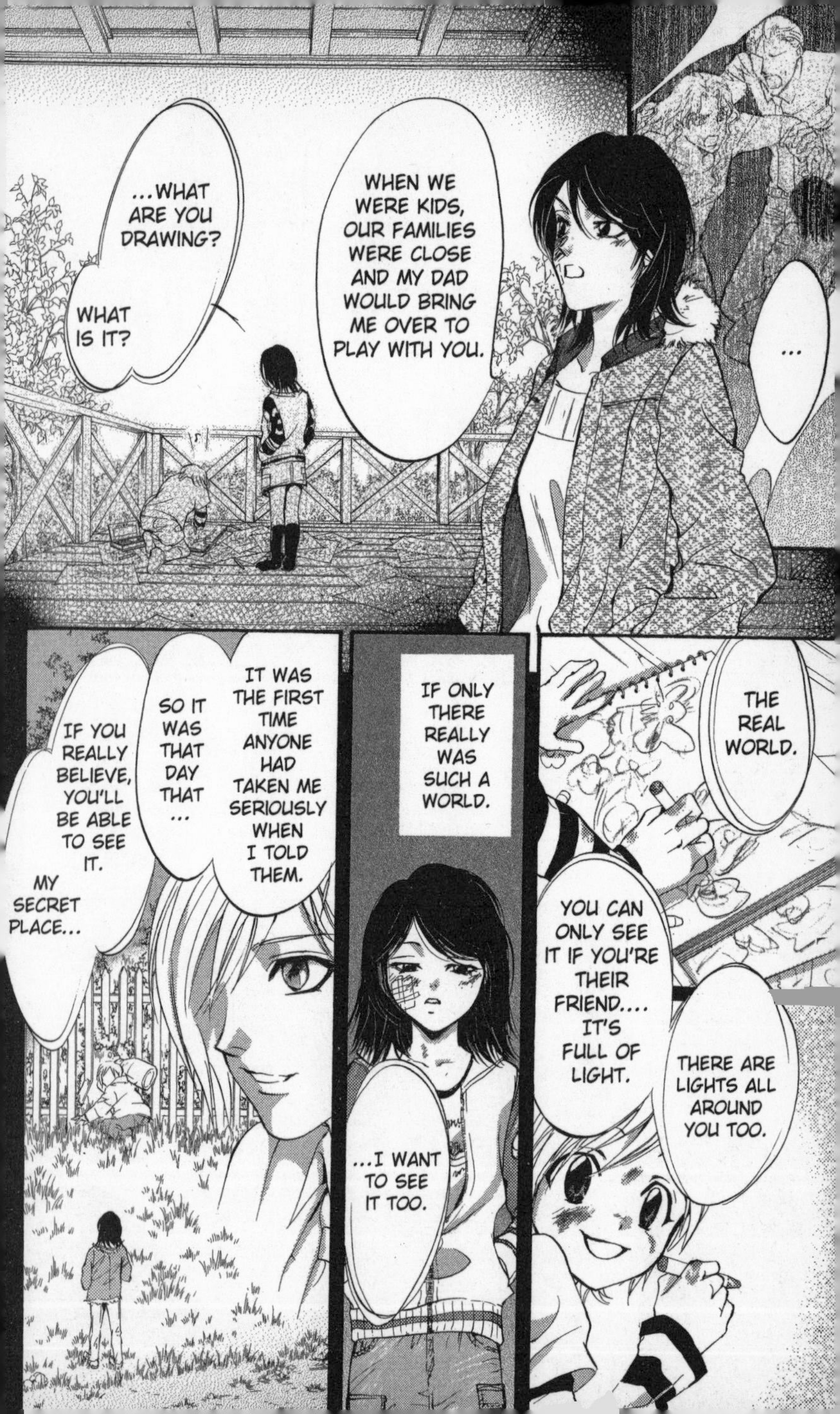
...
WHEN WE WERE KIDS, OUR FAMILIES WERE CLOSE AND MY DAD WOULD BRING ME OVER TO PLAY WITH YOU.
...WHAT ARE YOU DRAWING?
WHAT IS IT?
THE REAL WORLD.
YOU CAN ONLY SEE IT IF YOU'RE THEIR FRIEND.... IT'S FULL OF LIGHT.
THERE ARE LIGHTS ALL AROUND YOU TOO.
IF ONLY THERE REALLY WAS SUCH A WORLD.
...I WANT TO SEE IT TOO.
IT WAS THE FIRST TIME ANYONE HAD TAKEN ME SERIOUSLY WHEN I TOLD THEM.
SO IT WAS THAT DAY THAT ...
IF YOU REALLY BELIEVE, YOU'LL BE ABLE TO SEE IT.
MY SECRET PLACE...

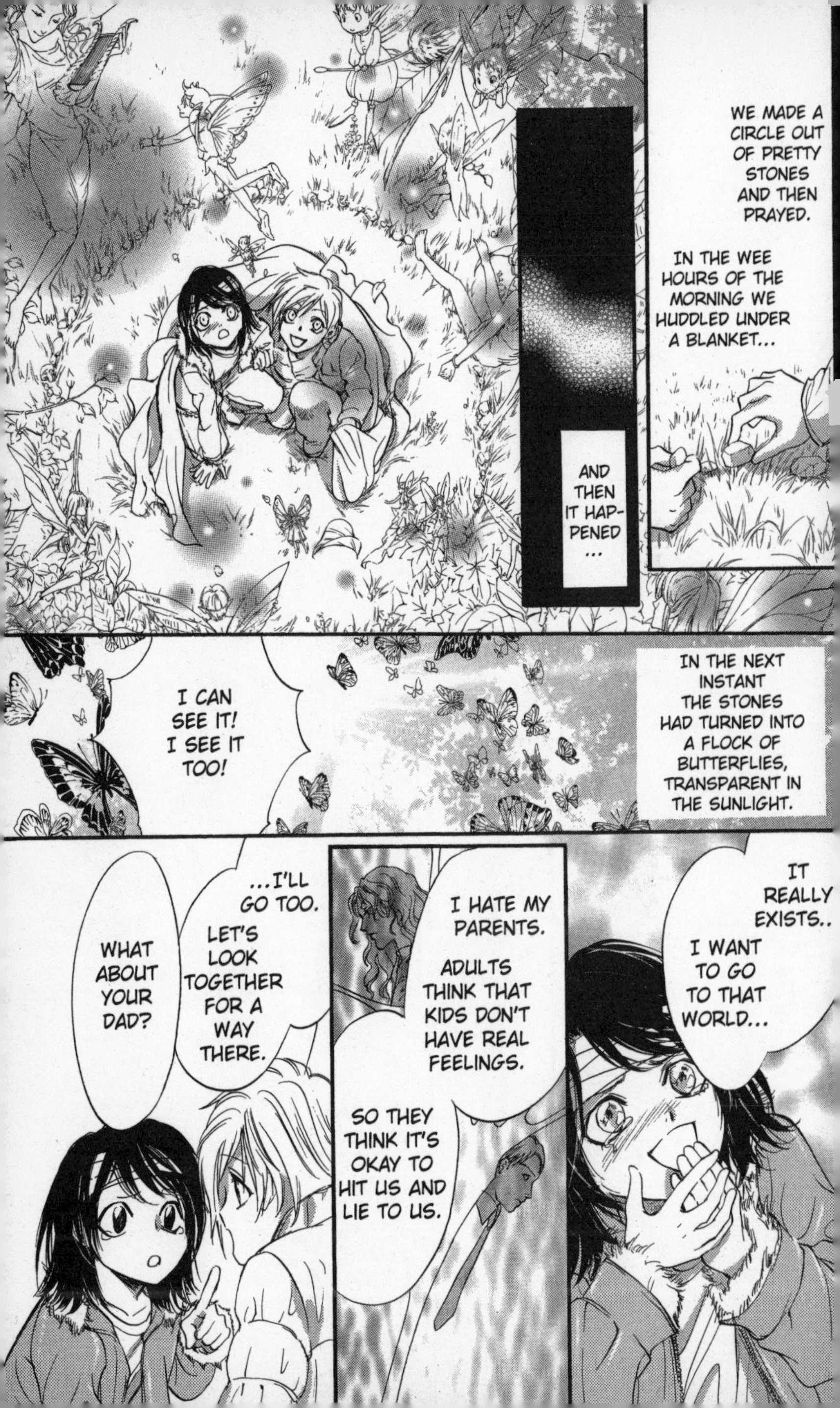
WE MADE A CIRCLE OUT OF PRETTY STONES AND THEN PRAYED.
IN THE WEE HOURS OF THE MORNING WE HUDDLED UNDER A BLANKET...
AND THEN IT HAP-PENED ...
IN THE NEXT INSTANT THE STONES HAD TURNED INTO A FLOCK OF BUTTERFLIES, TRANSPARENT IN THE SUNLIGHT.
I CAN SEE IT! I SEE IT TOO!
IT REALLY EXISTS..
I WANT TO GO TO THAT WORLD...
I HATE MY PARENTS.
ADULTS THINK THAT KIDS DON'T HAVE REAL FEELINGS.
SO THEY THINK IT'S OKAY TO HIT US AND LIE TO US.
...I'LL GO TOO.
LET'S LOOK TOGETHER FOR A WAY THERE.
WHAT ABOUT YOUR DAD?

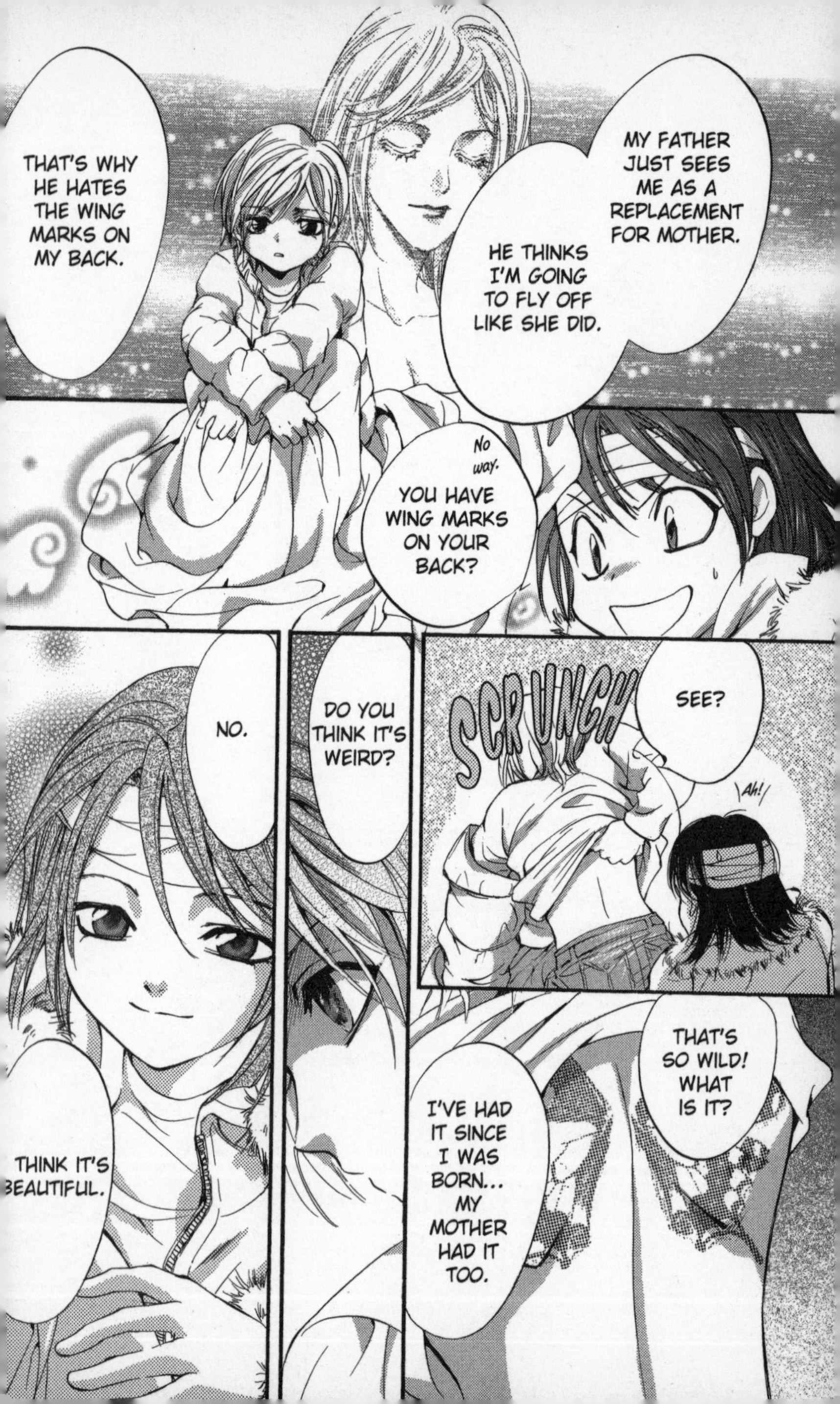
MY FATHER JUST SEES ME AS A REPLACEMENT FOR MOTHER.
HE THINKS I'M GOING TO FLY OFF LIKE SHE DID.
THAT'S WHY HE HATES THE WING MARKS ON MY BACK.
No way.
YOU HAVE WING MARKS ON YOUR BACK?
SEE?
SCRUNCH
Ah!
THAT'S SO WILD! WHAT IS IT?
I'VE HAD IT SINCE I WAS BORN... MY MOTHER HAD IT TOO.
DO YOU THINK IT'S WEIRD?
NO.
THINK IT'S BEAUTIFUL.

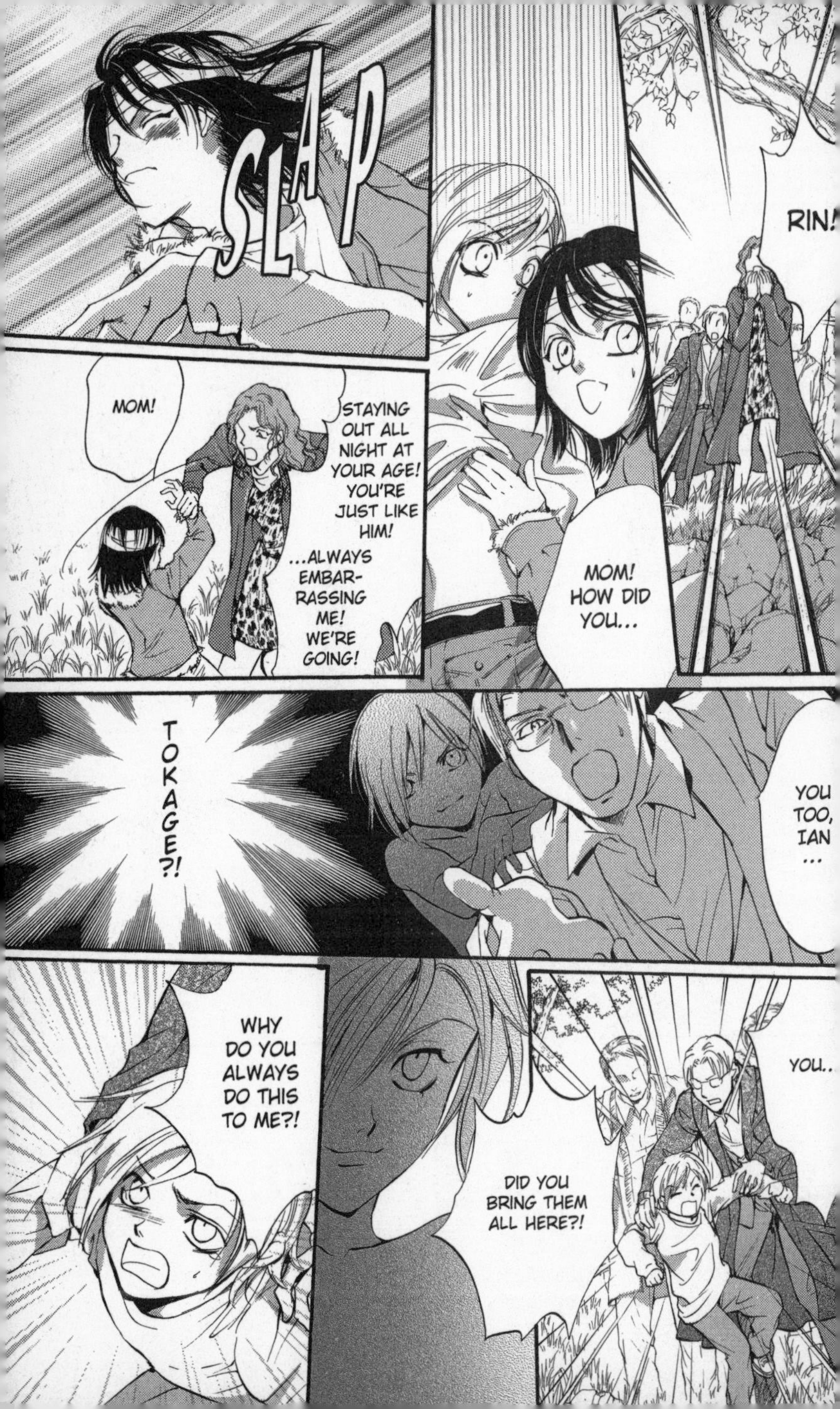

RIN!
MOM! HOW DID YOU...
SLAP
STAYING OUT ALL NIGHT AT YOUR AGE! YOU'RE JUST LIKE HIM!
...ALWAYS EMBARRASSING ME! WE'RE GOING!
MOM!
YOU TOO, IAN...
TOKAGE?!
YOU...
DID YOU BRING THEM ALL HERE?!
WHY DO YOU ALWAYS DO THIS TO ME?!

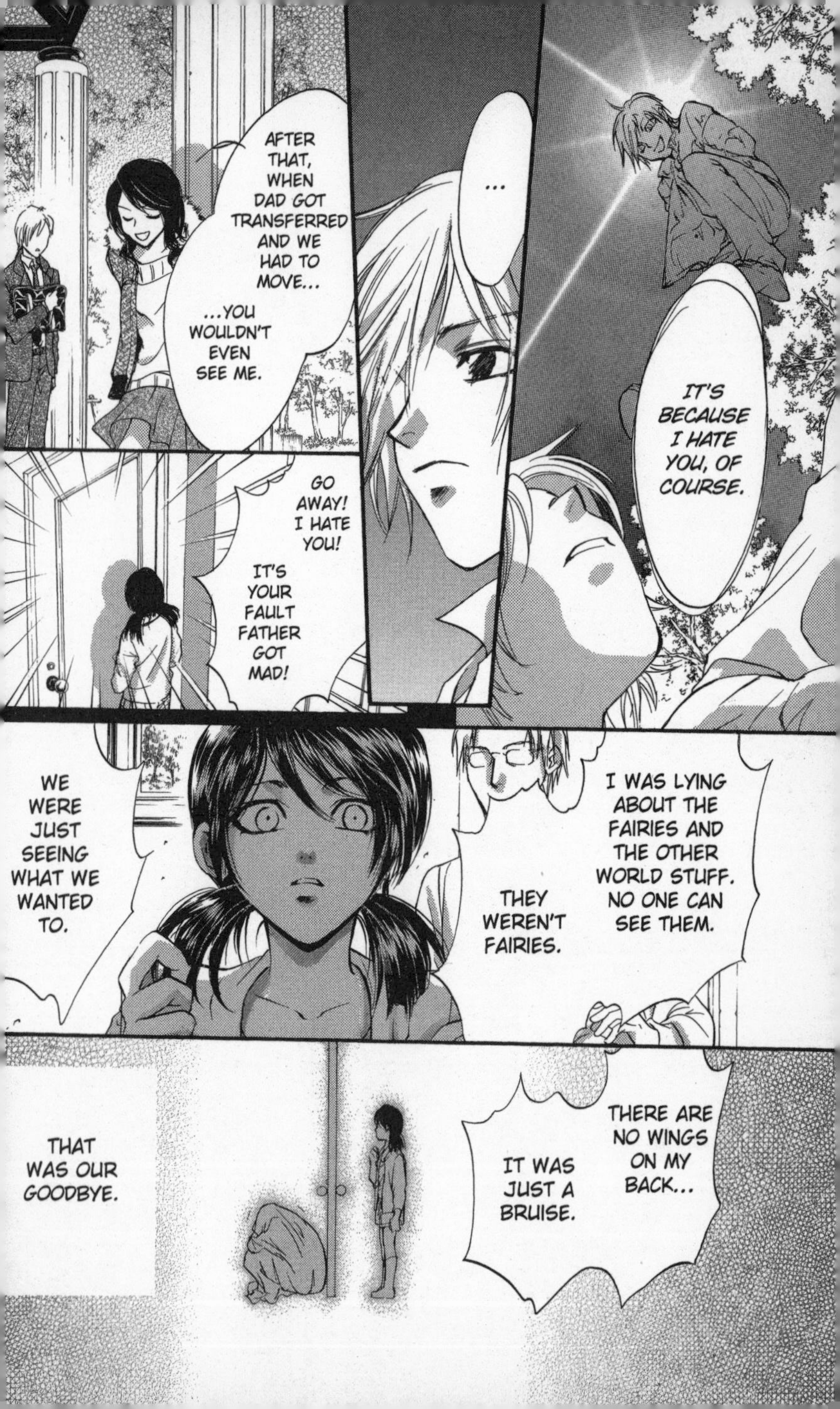
IT'S BECAUSE I HATE YOU, OF COURSE.
...
AFTER THAT, WHEN DAD GOT TRANSFERRED AND WE HAD TO MOVE...
...YOU WOULDN'T EVEN SEE ME.
GO AWAY! I HATE YOU!
IT'S YOUR FAULT FATHER GOT MAD!
I WAS LYING ABOUT THE FAIRIES AND THE OTHER WORLD STUFF. NO ONE CAN SEE THEM.
THEY WEREN'T FAIRIES.
WE WERE JUST SEEING WHAT WE WANTED TO.
THERE ARE NO WINGS ON MY BACK...
IT WAS JUST A BRUISE.
THAT WAS OUR GOODBYE.

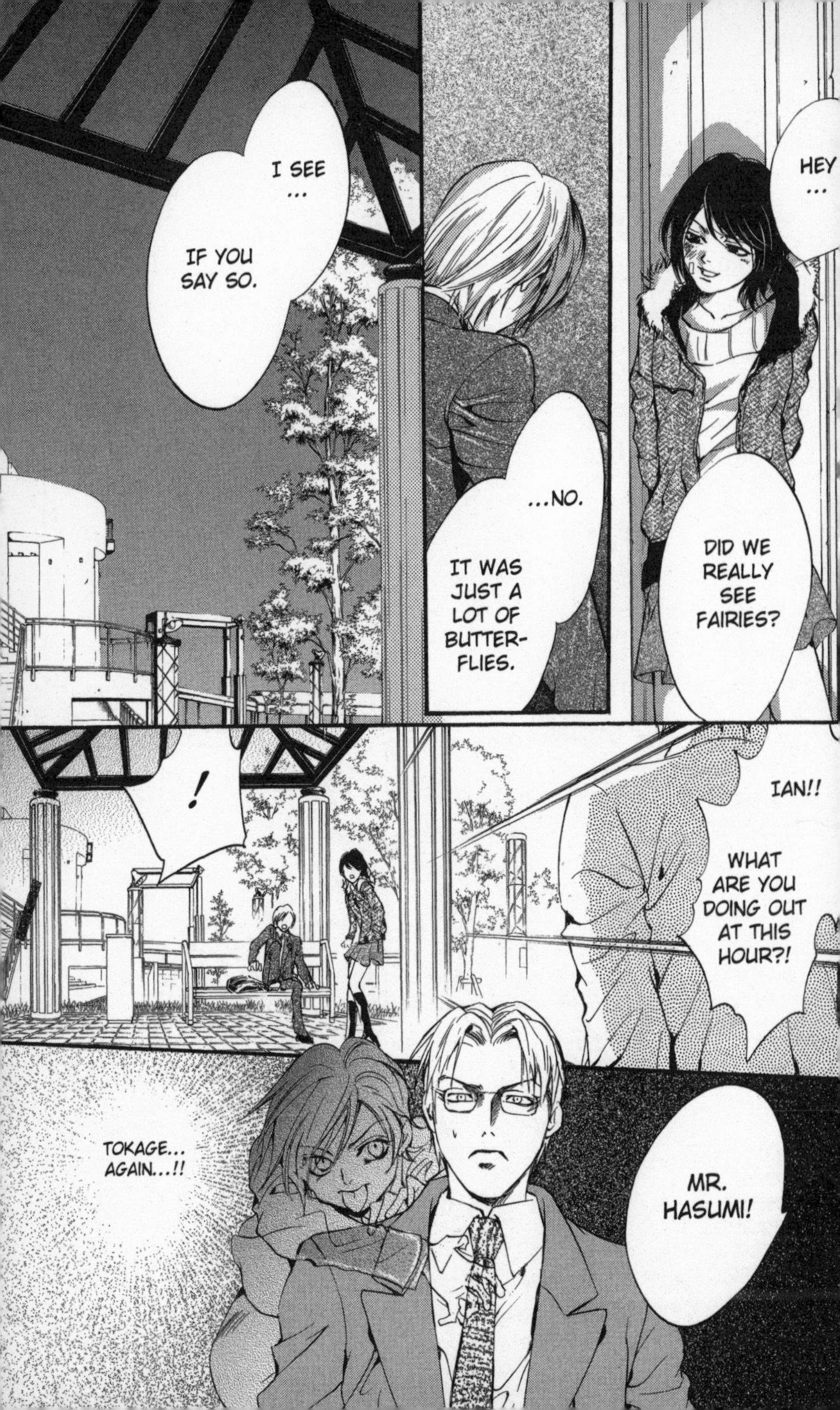
HEY ...
DID WE REALLY SEE FAIRIES?
...NO.
IT WAS JUST A LOT OF BUTTER-FLIES.
I SEE ...
IF YOU SAY SO.
IAN!!
WHAT ARE YOU DOING OUT AT THIS HOUR?!
!
MR. HASUMI!
TOKAGE... AGAIN...!!

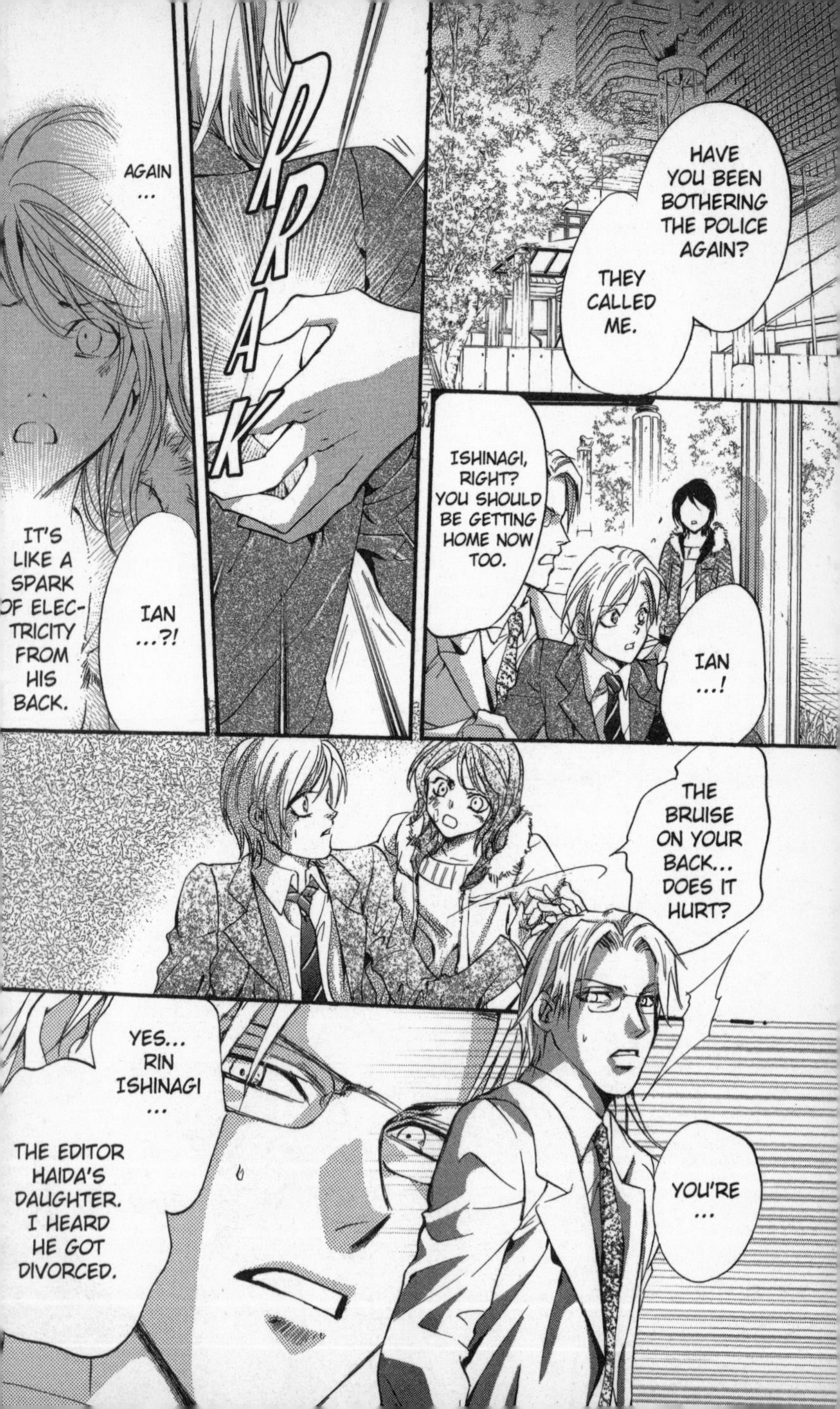
HAVE YOU BEEN BOTHERING THE POLICE AGAIN?
THEY CALLED ME.
IAN ...!
ISHINAGI, RIGHT? YOU SHOULD BE GETTING HOME NOW TOO.
DRRAKK
IAN ...?!
AGAIN ...
IT'S LIKE A SPARK OF ELEC-TRICITY FROM HIS BACK.
THE BRUISE ON YOUR BACK... DOES IT HURT?
YOU'RE ...
YES... RIN ISHINAGI ...
THE EDITOR HAIDA'S DAUGHTER. I HEARD HE GOT DIVORCED.

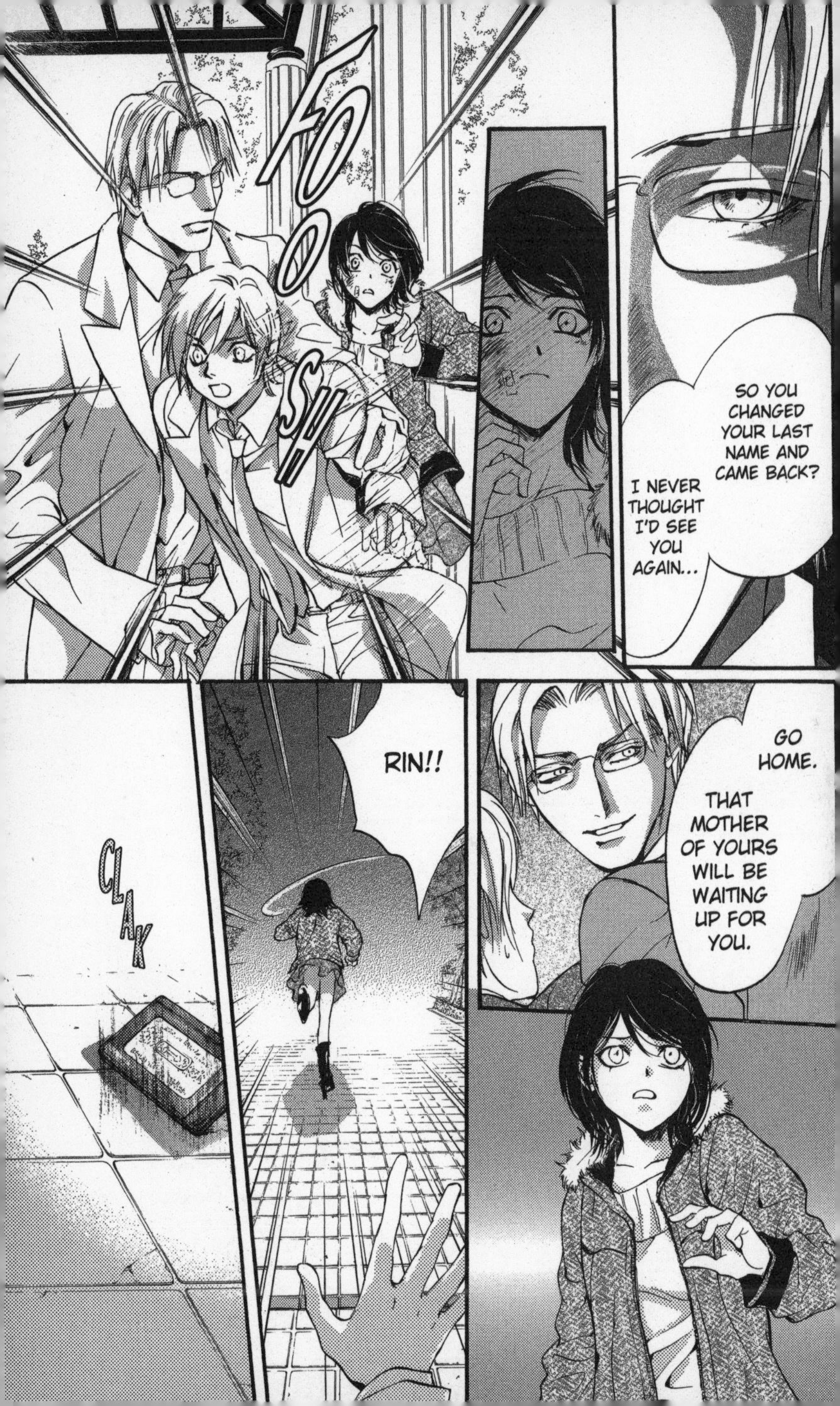
SO YOU CHANGED YOUR LAST NAME AND CAME BACK?
I NEVER THOUGHT I'D SEE YOU AGAIN...
FOOO
SH
GO HOME.
THAT MOTHER OF YOURS WILL BE WAITING UP FOR YOU.
RIN!!
CLAK

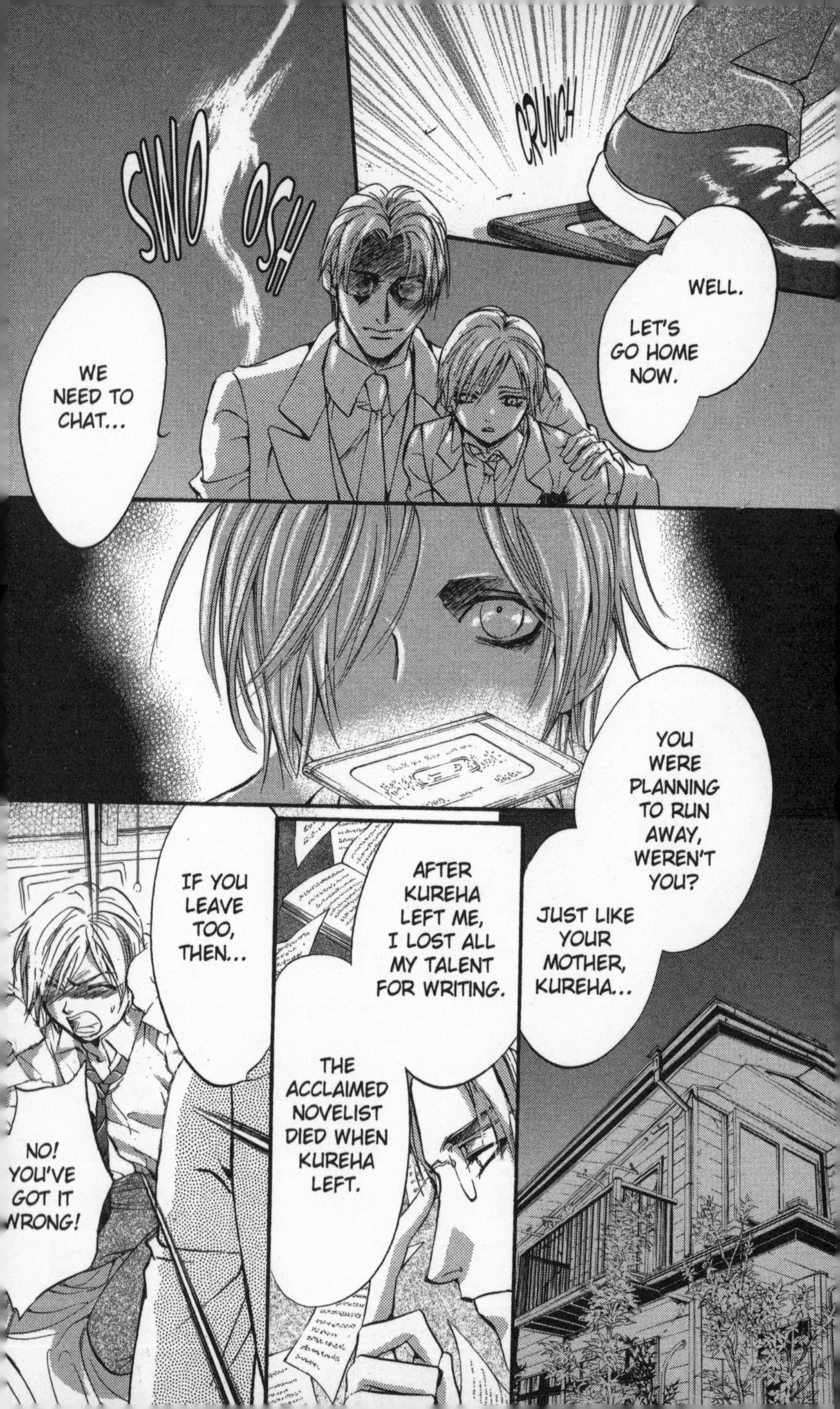
CRUNCH
SWOOSH
WELL.
LET'S GO HOME NOW.
WE NEED TO CHAT...
YOU WERE PLANNING TO RUN AWAY, WEREN'T YOU?
JUST LIKE YOUR MOTHER, KUREHA...
AFTER KUREHA LEFT ME, I LOST ALL MY TALENT FOR WRITING.
THE ACCLAIMED NOVELIST DIED WHEN KUREHA LEFT.
IF YOU LEAVE TOO, THEN...
NO! YOU'VE GOT IT WRONG!

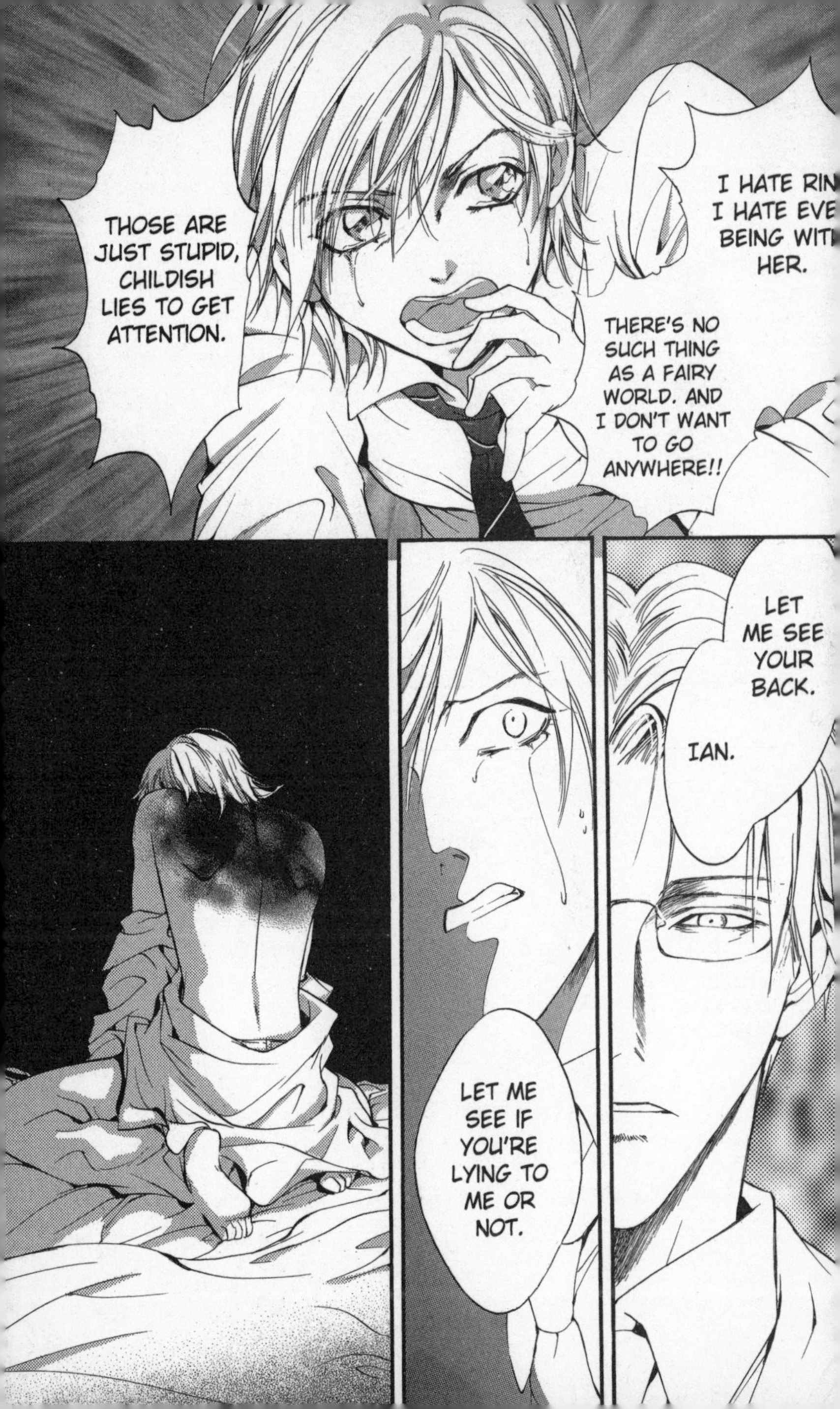
I HATE RIN
I HATE EVE
BEING WIT
HER.
THERE'S NO SUCH THING AS A FAIRY WORLD. AND I DON'T WANT TO GO ANYWHERE!!
THOSE ARE JUST STUPID, CHILDISH LIES TO GET ATTENTION.
LET ME SEE YOUR BACK.
IAN.
LET ME SEE IF YOU'RE LYING TO ME OR NOT.

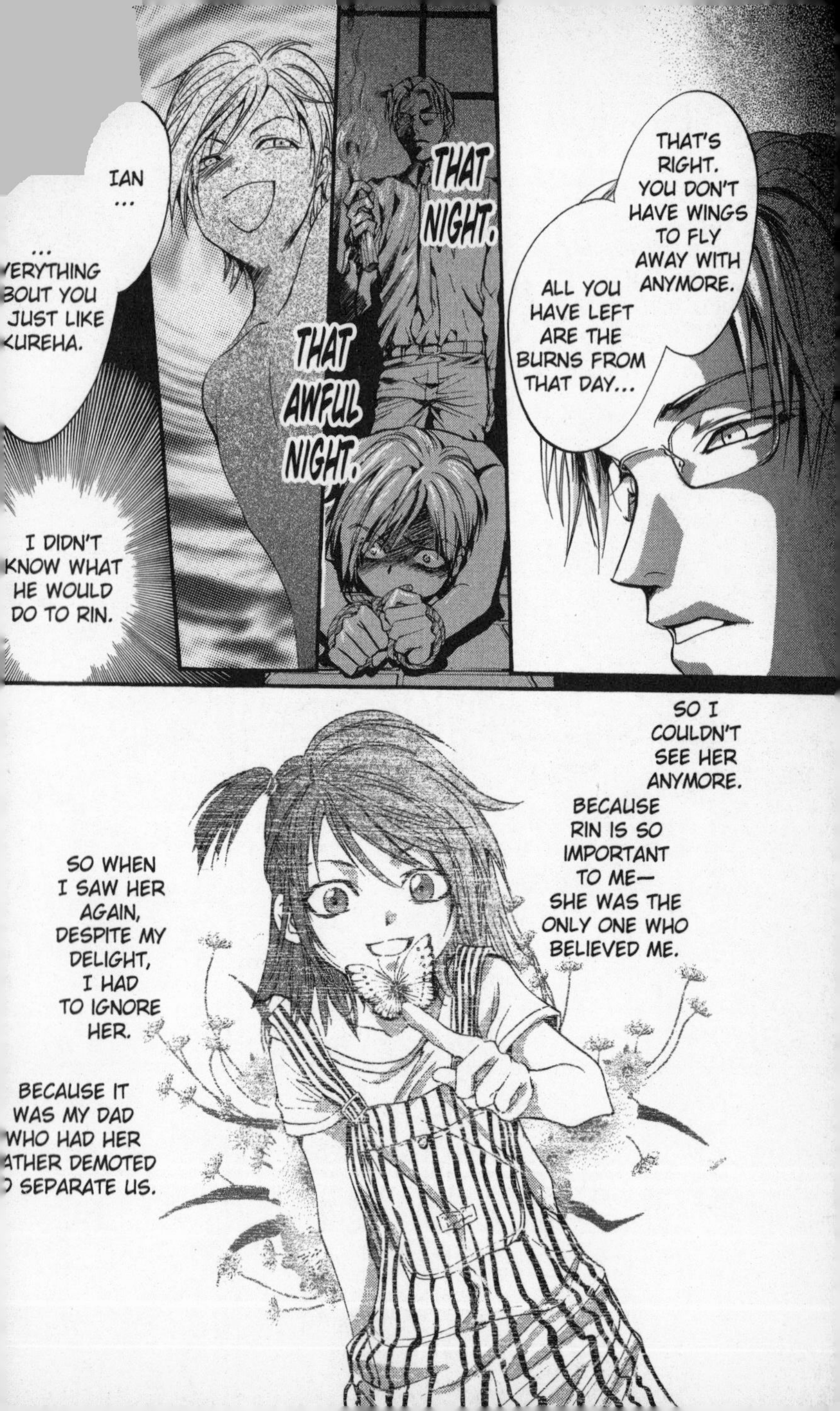
THAT'S RIGHT. YOU DON'T HAVE WINGS TO FLY AWAY WITH ANYMORE.
ALL YOU HAVE LEFT ARE THE BURNS FROM THAT DAY...
THAT NIGHT.
THAT AWFUL NIGHT.
IAN ...
... ERYTHING BOUT YOU JUST LIKE UREHA.
I DIDN'T KNOW WHAT HE WOULD DO TO RIN.
SO I COULDN'T SEE HER ANYMORE.
BECAUSE RIN IS SO IMPORTANT TO ME— SHE WAS THE ONLY ONE WHO BELIEVED ME.
SO WHEN I SAW HER AGAIN, DESPITE MY DELIGHT, I HAD TO IGNORE HER.
BECAUSE IT WAS MY DAD WHO HAD HER ATHER DEMOTED SEPARATE US.

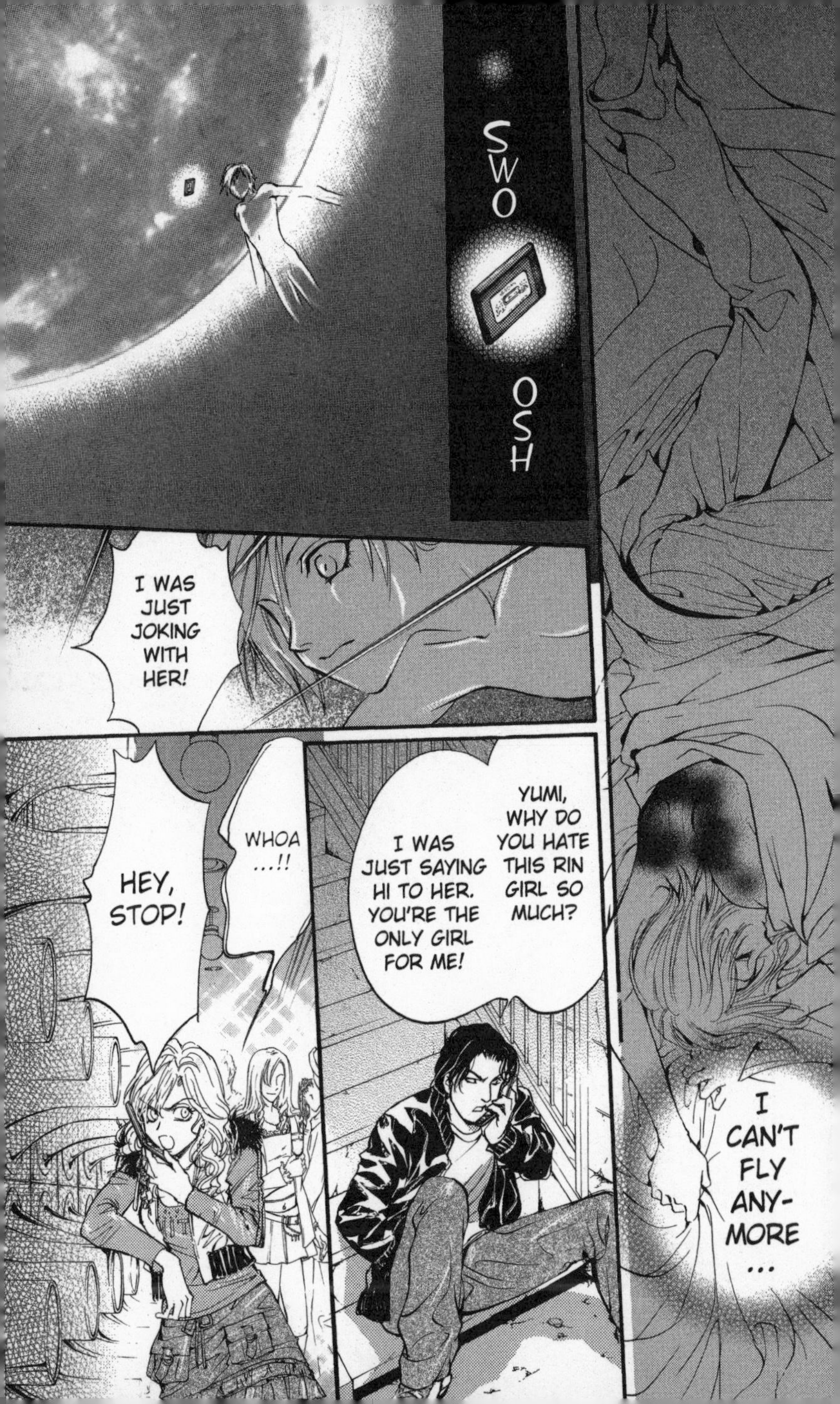
I CAN'T FLY ANY-MORE...
SWO OSH
I WAS JUST JOKING WITH HER!
YUMI, WHY DO YOU HATE THIS RIN GIRL SO MUCH?
I WAS JUST SAYING HI TO HER. YOU'RE THE ONLY GIRL FOR ME!
WHOA ...!!
HEY, STOP!

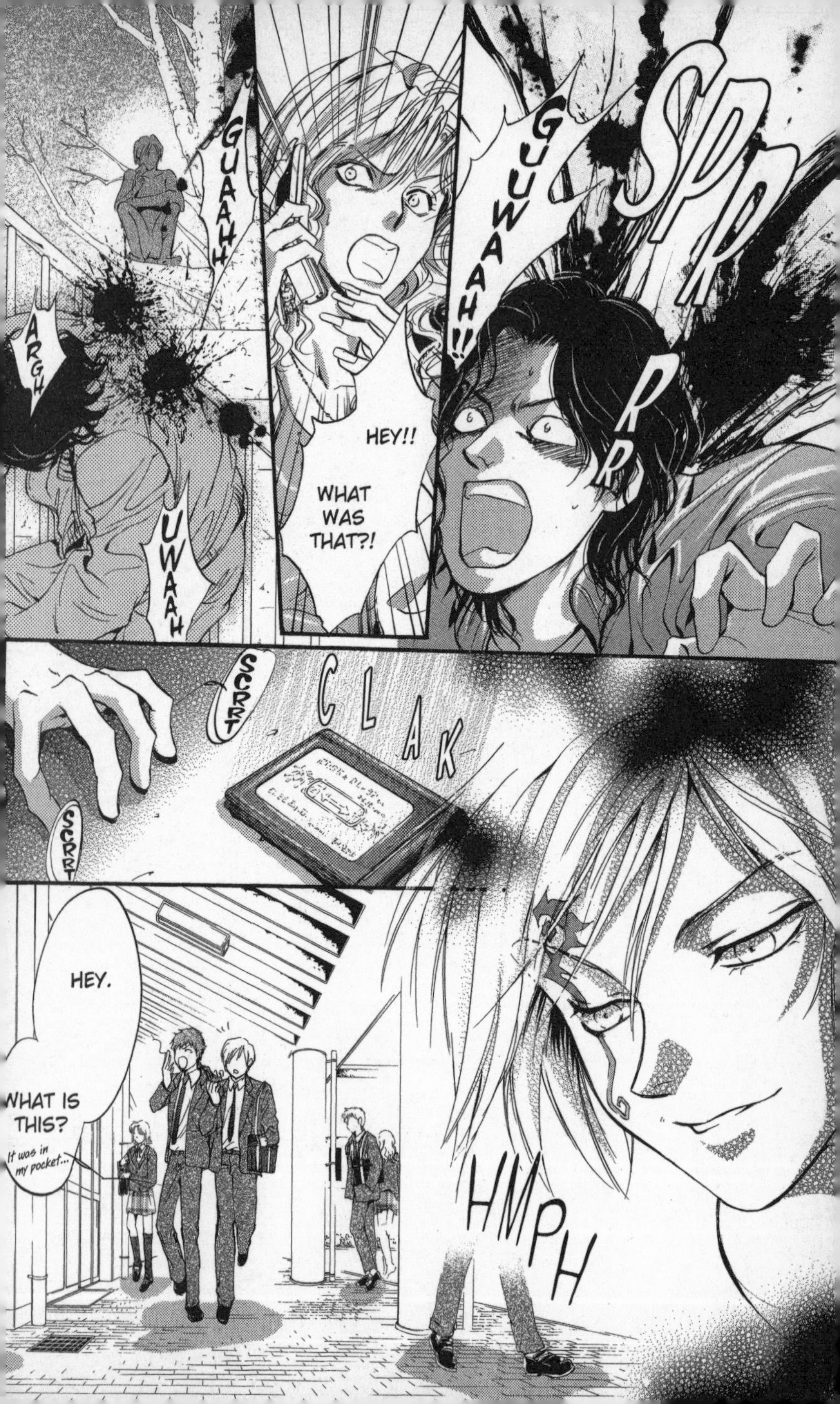
SPRRR
GUUWAAAH!!
HEY!!
WHAT WAS THAT?!
GUAAHH
ARGH
UWAAH
CLAK
SCRRT
SCRRT
HMPH
HEY.
WHAT IS THIS?
It was in my pocket...

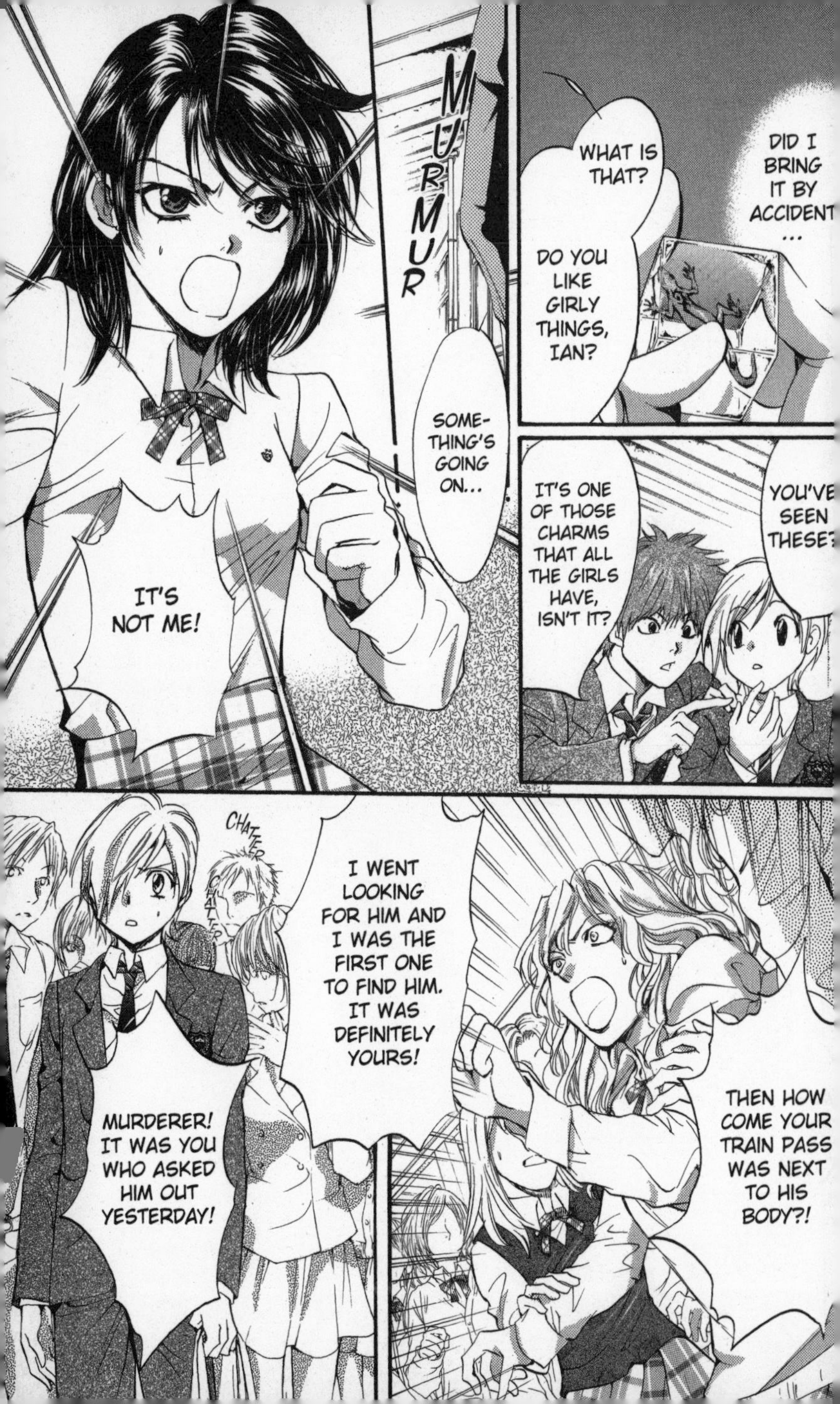
WHAT IS THAT?
DID I BRING IT BY ACCIDENT...
DO YOU LIKE GIRLY THINGS, IAN?
YOU'VE SEEN THESE?
IT'S ONE OF THOSE CHARMS THAT ALL THE GIRLS HAVE, ISN'T IT?
MURMUR
MURMUR
SOME-THING'S GOING ON...
IT'S NOT ME!
THEN HOW COME YOUR TRAIN PASS WAS NEXT TO HIS BODY?!
I WENT LOOKING FOR HIM AND I WAS THE FIRST ONE TO FIND HIM. IT WAS DEFINITELY YOURS!
CHATTER
CHATTER
MURDERER! IT WAS YOU WHO ASKED HIM OUT YESTERDAY!

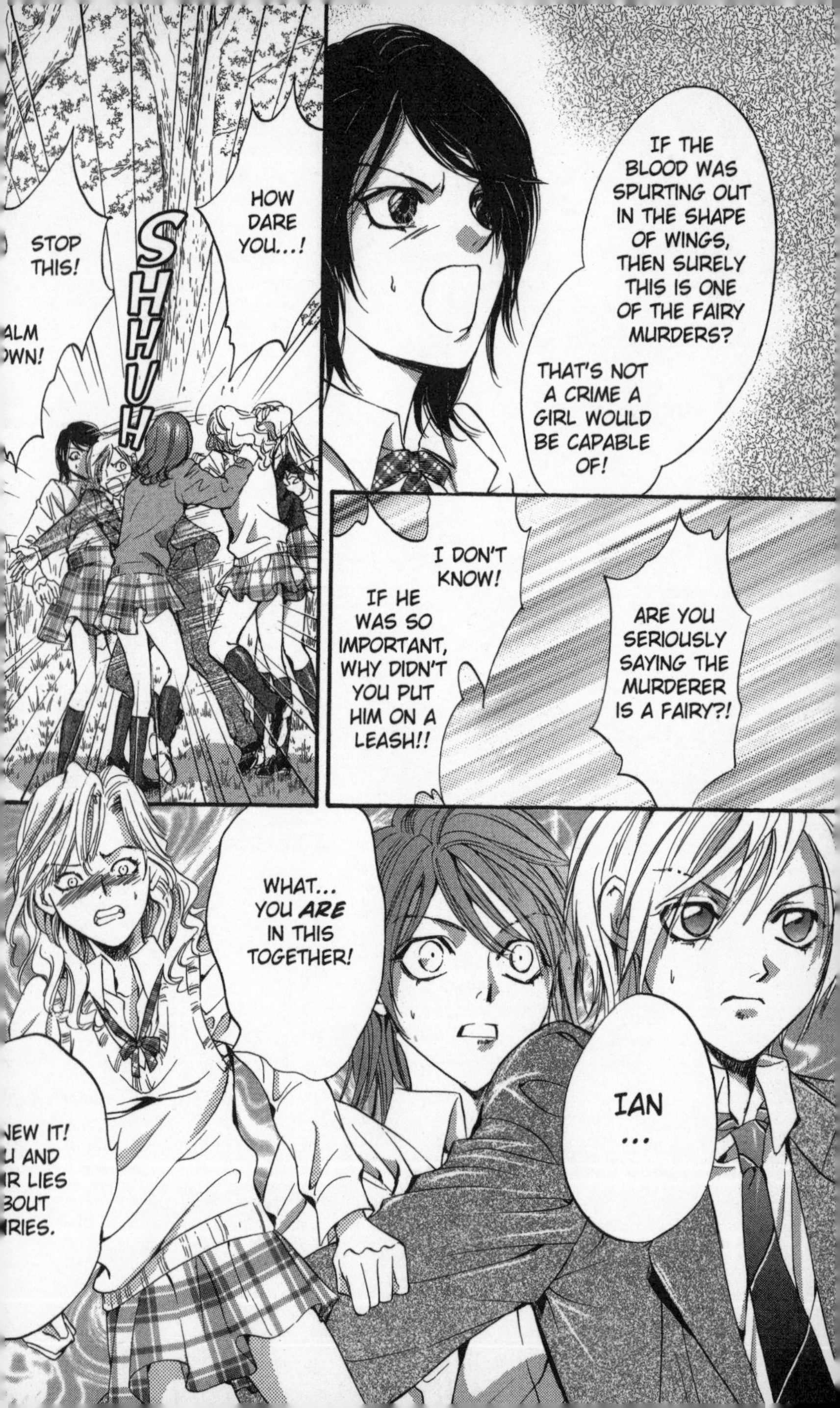
IF THE BLOOD WAS SPURTING OUT IN THE SHAPE OF WINGS, THEN SURELY THIS IS ONE OF THE FAIRY MURDERS?
THAT'S NOT A CRIME A GIRL WOULD BE CAPABLE OF!
ARE YOU SERIOUSLY SAYING THE MURDERER IS A FAIRY?!
I DON'T KNOW!
IF HE WAS SO IMPORTANT, WHY DIDN'T YOU PUT HIM ON A LEASH!!
HOW DARE YOU...!
SHHUH
STOP THIS!
ALM
WN!
IAN ...
WHAT... YOU *ARE* IN THIS TOGETHER!
NEW IT!
U AND
R LIES
BOUT
RIES.

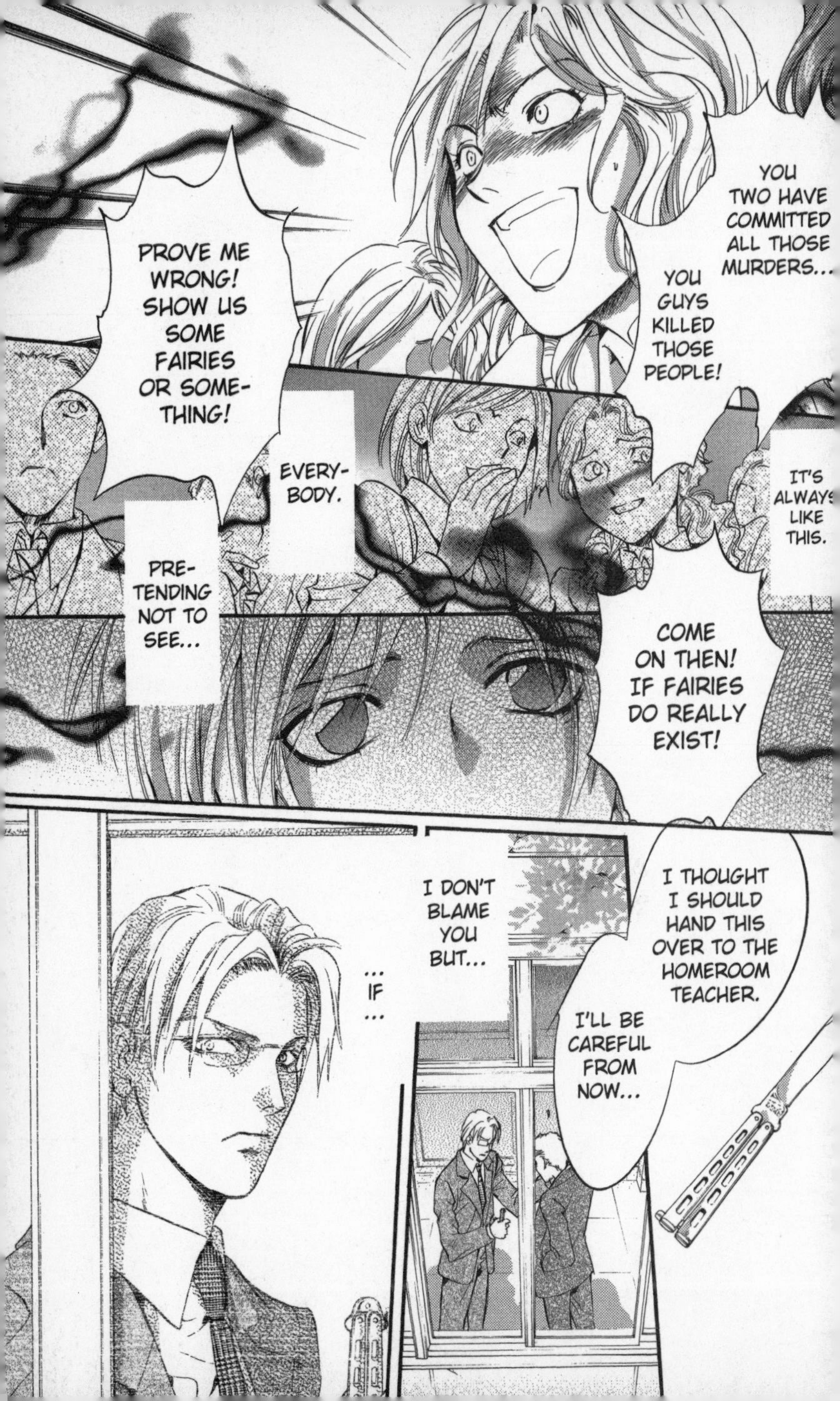
YOU TWO HAVE COMMITTED ALL THOSE MURDERS...
YOU GUYS KILLED THOSE PEOPLE!
PROVE ME WRONG! SHOW US SOME FAIRIES OR SOME-THING!
IT'S ALWAYS LIKE THIS.
EVERY-BODY.
PRE-TENDING NOT TO SEE...
COME ON THEN! IF FAIRIES DO REALLY EXIST!
I THOUGHT I SHOULD HAND THIS OVER TO THE HOMEROOM TEACHER.
I'LL BE CAREFUL FROM NOW...
I DON'T BLAME YOU BUT...
...IF...

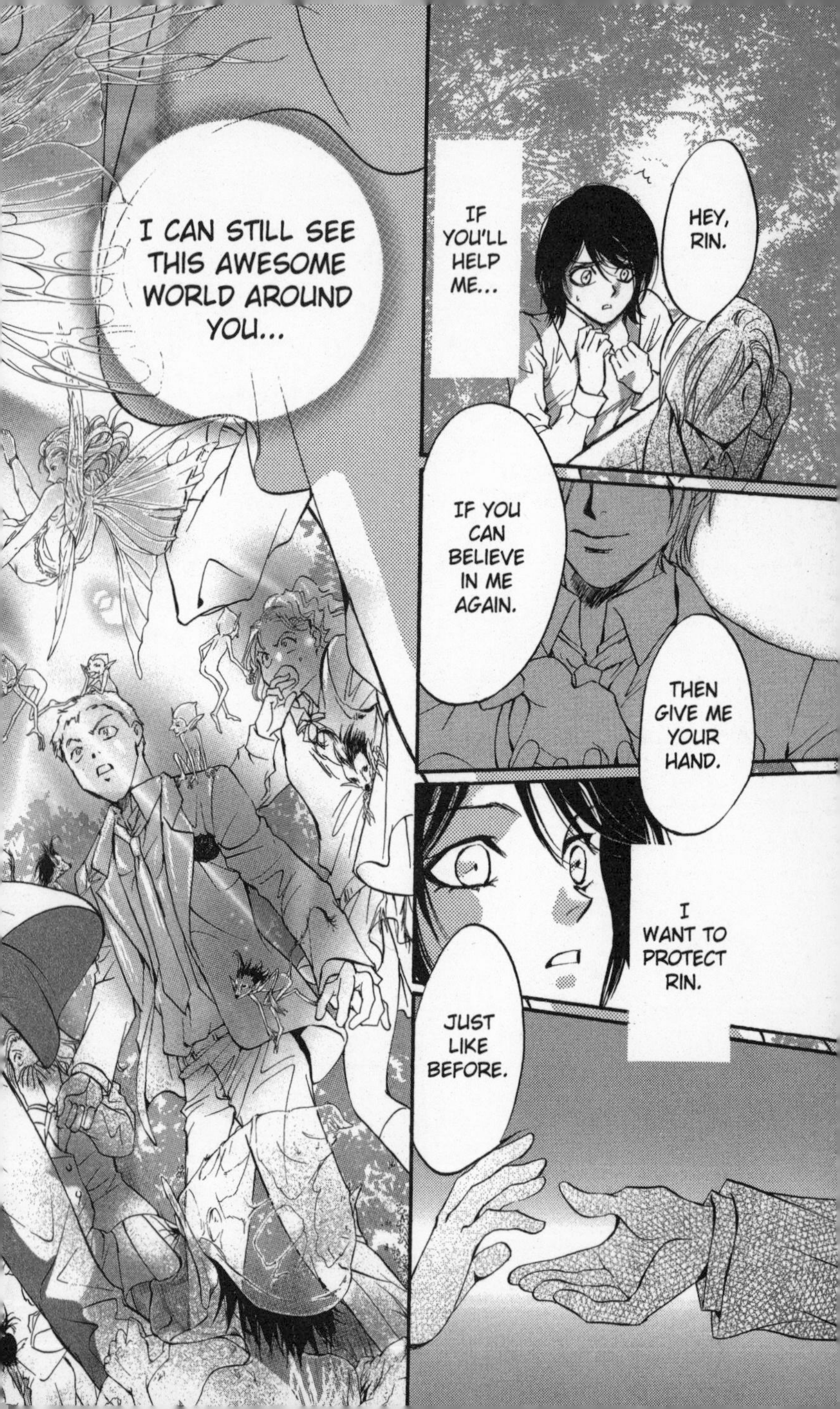
HEY, RIN.
IF YOU'LL HELP ME...
IF YOU CAN BELIEVE IN ME AGAIN.
THEN GIVE ME YOUR HAND.
I WANT TO PROTECT RIN.
JUST LIKE BEFORE.
I CAN STILL SEE THIS AWESOME WORLD AROUND YOU...

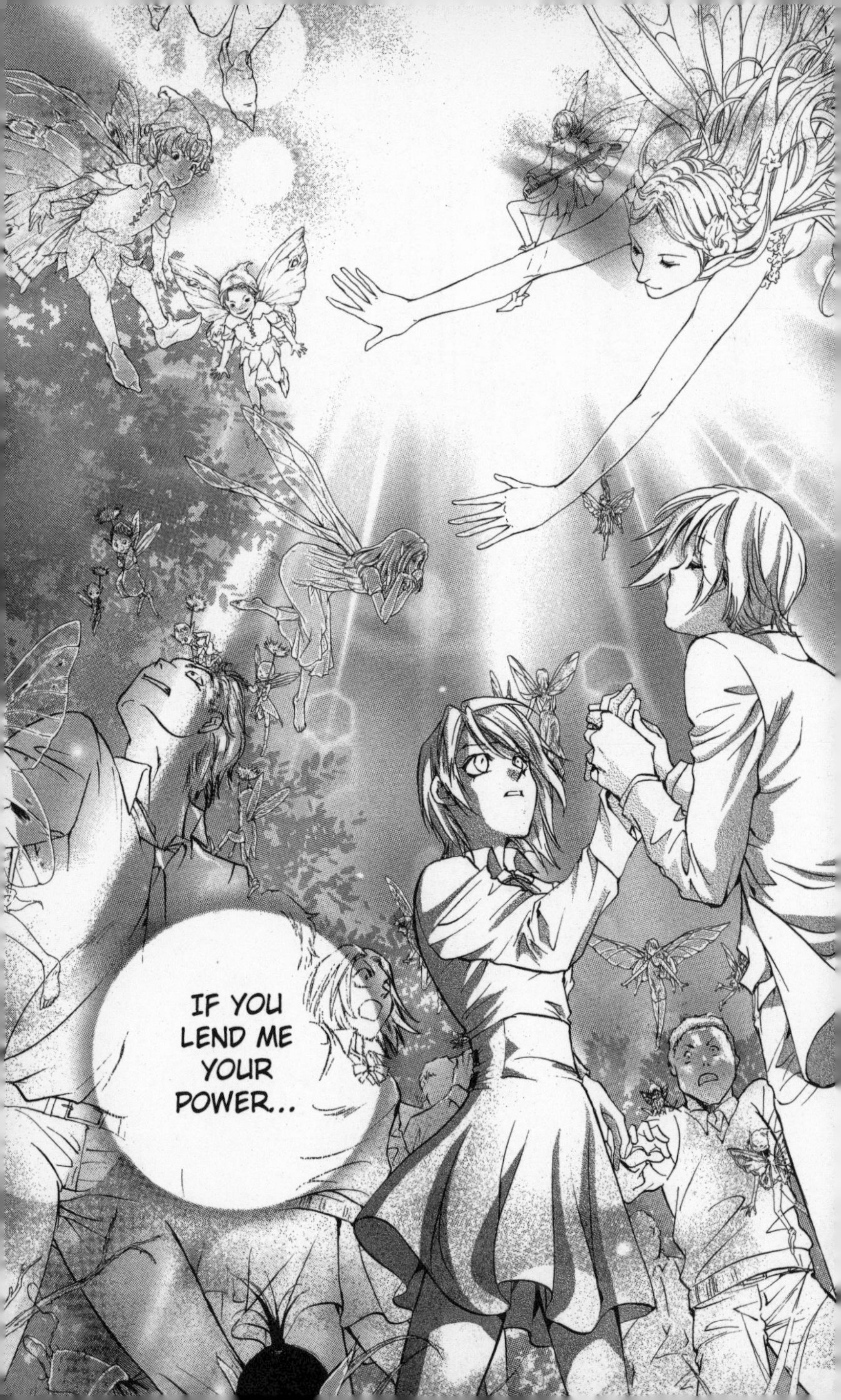
IF YOU LEND ME YOUR POWER...

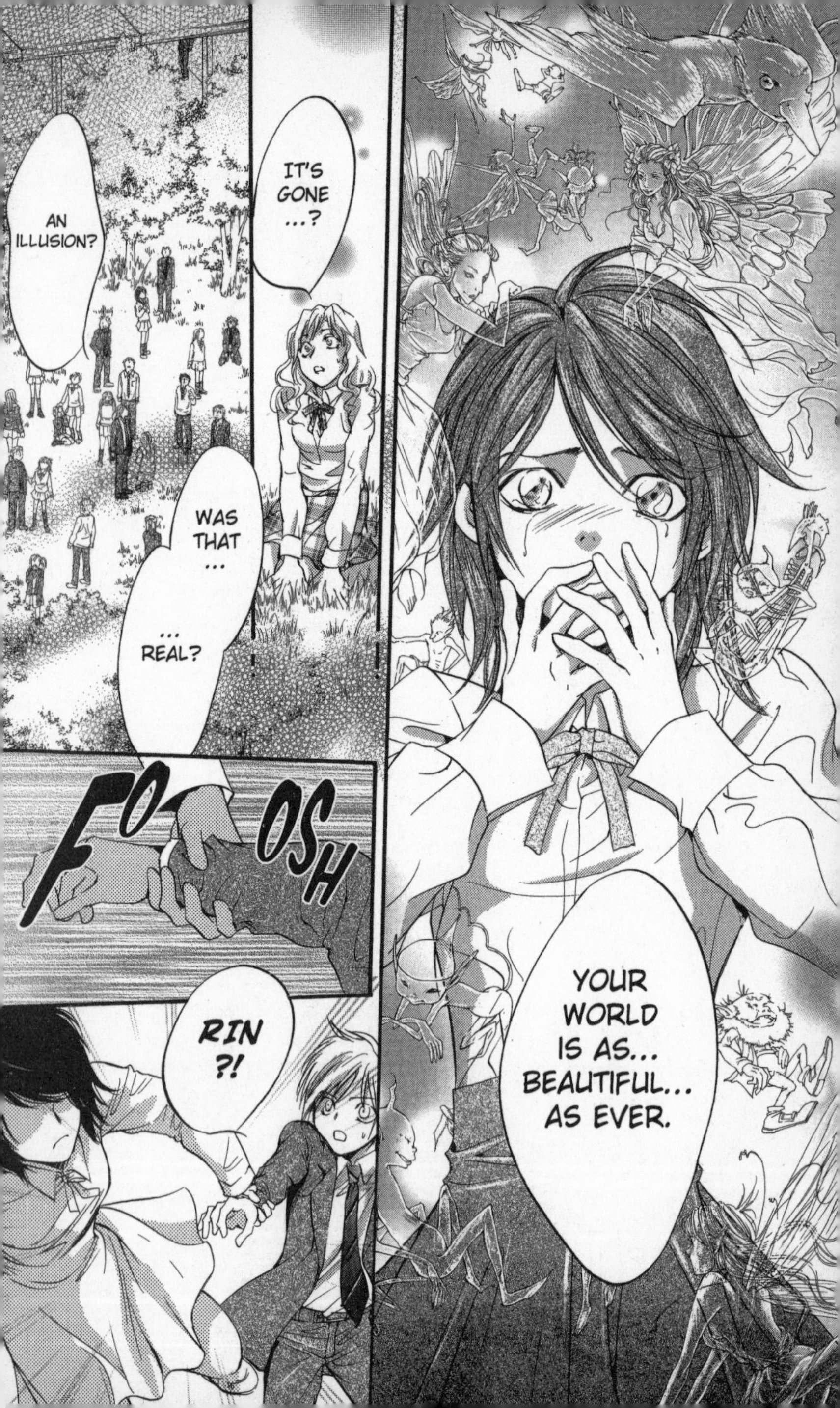
YOUR WORLD IS AS... BEAUTIFUL... AS EVER.
IT'S GONE ...?
AN ILLUSION?
WAS THAT ...
... REAL?
FOOSH
RIN ?!

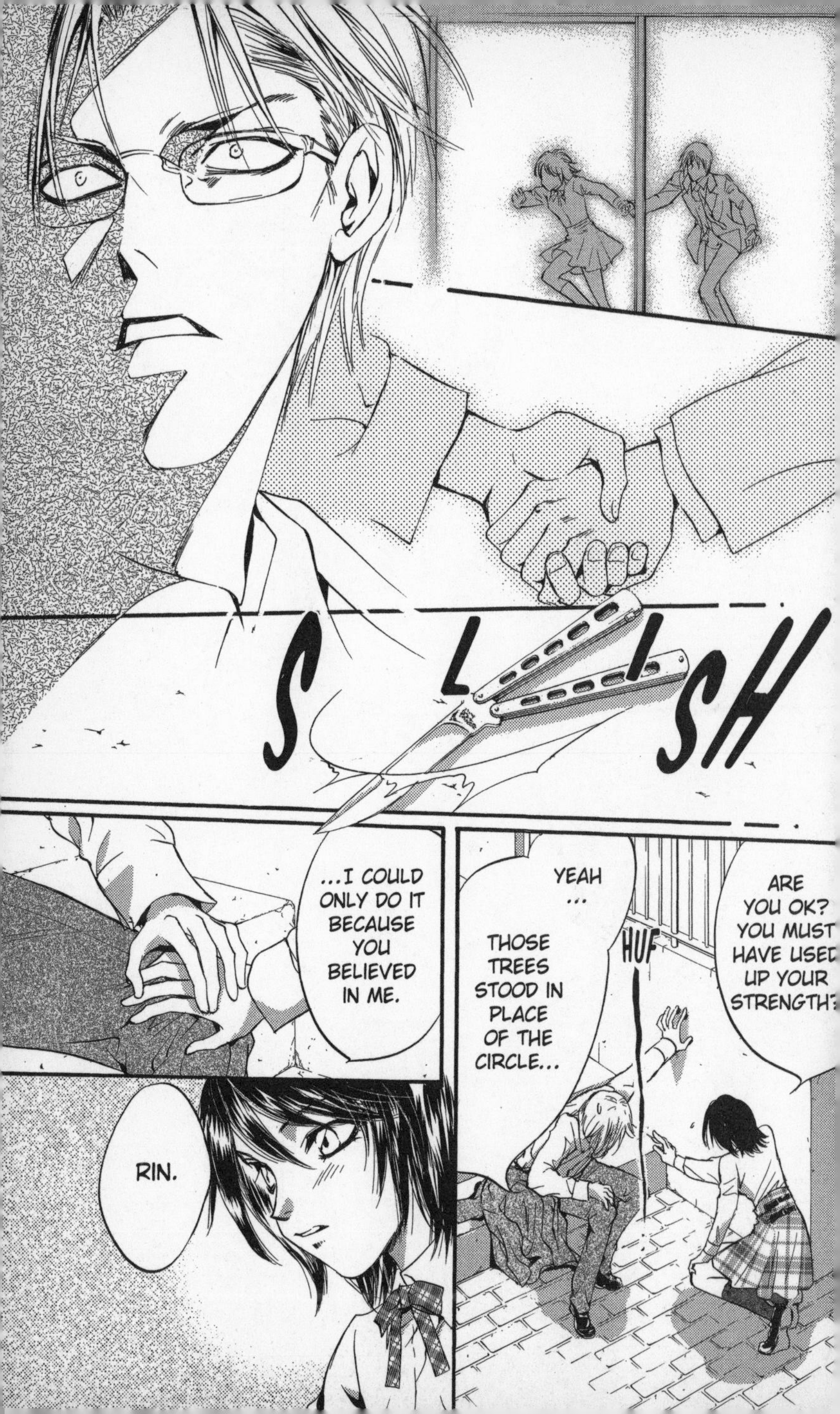
SLISH
ARE YOU OK? YOU MUST HAVE USED UP YOUR STRENGTH?
HUF
YEAH ...
THOSE TREES STOOD IN PLACE OF THE CIRCLE...
...I COULD ONLY DO IT BECAUSE YOU BELIEVED IN ME.
RIN.

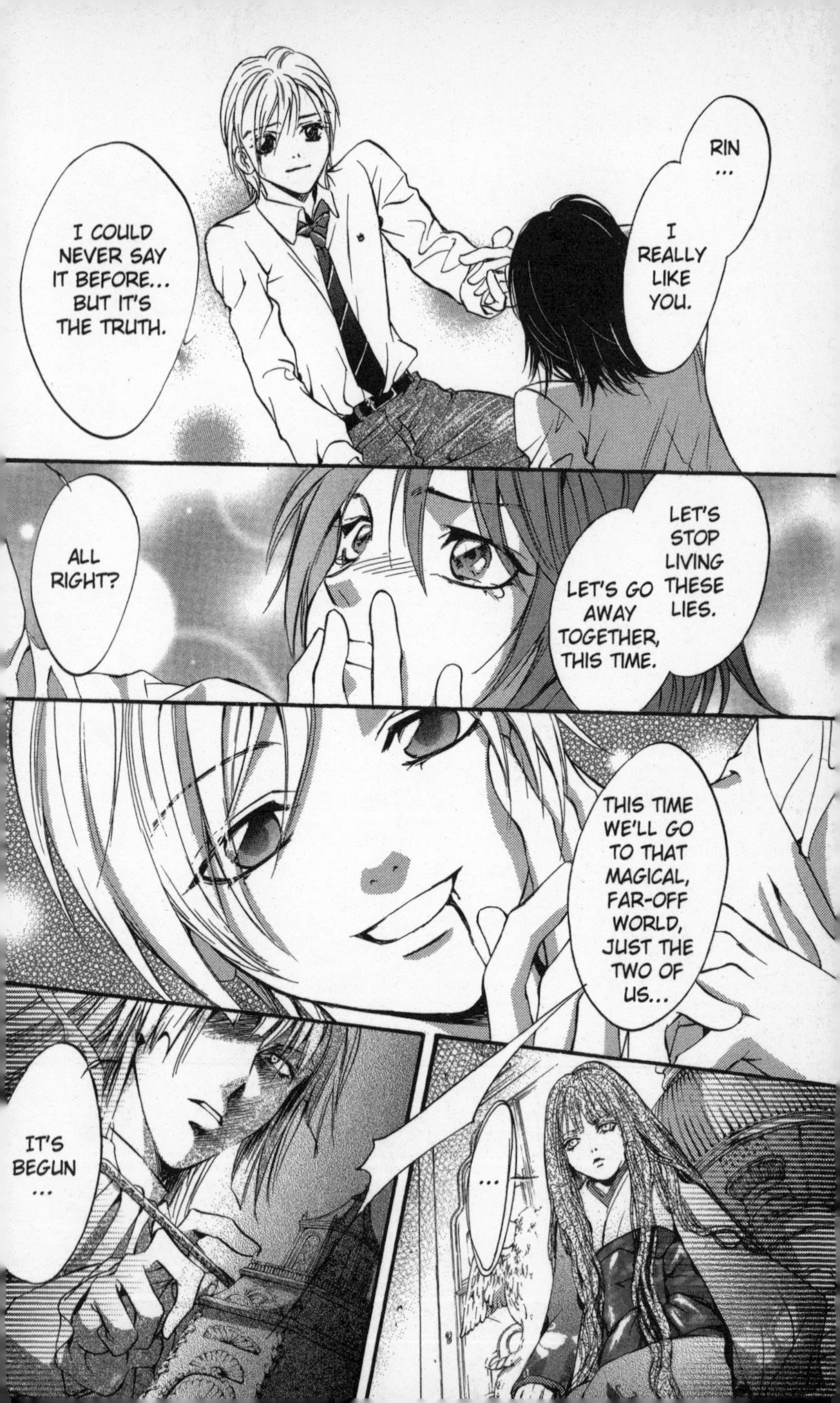
RIN ...
I REALLY LIKE YOU.
I COULD NEVER SAY IT BEFORE... BUT IT'S THE TRUTH.
LET'S STOP LIVING THESE LIES.
LET'S GO AWAY TOGETHER, THIS TIME.
ALL RIGHT?
THIS TIME WE'LL GO TO THAT MAGICAL, FAR-OFF WORLD, JUST THE TWO OF US...
...
IT'S BEGUN ...

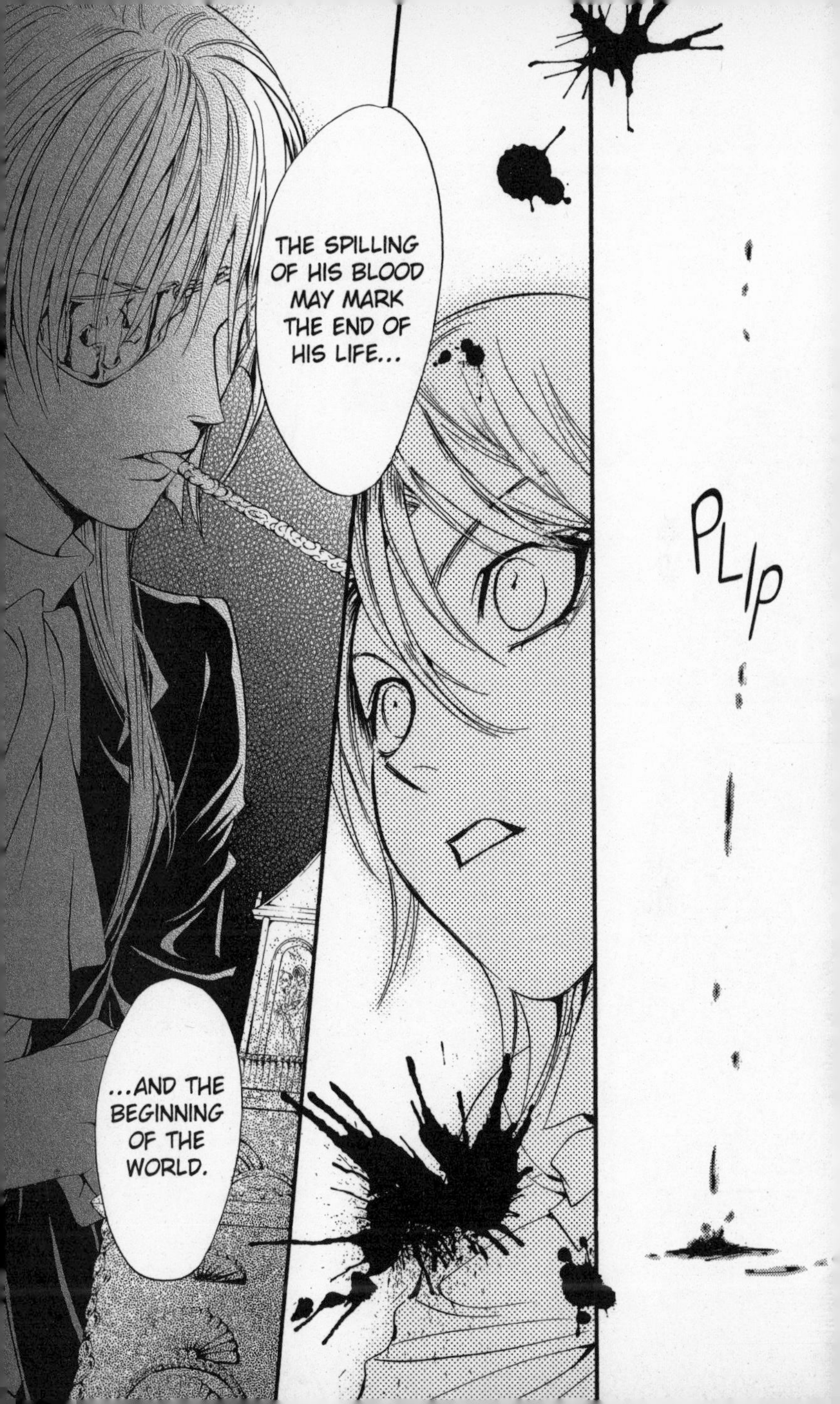
PLIP
THE SPILLING OF HIS BLOOD MAY MARK THE END OF HIS LIFE...
...AND THE BEGINNING OF THE WORLD.

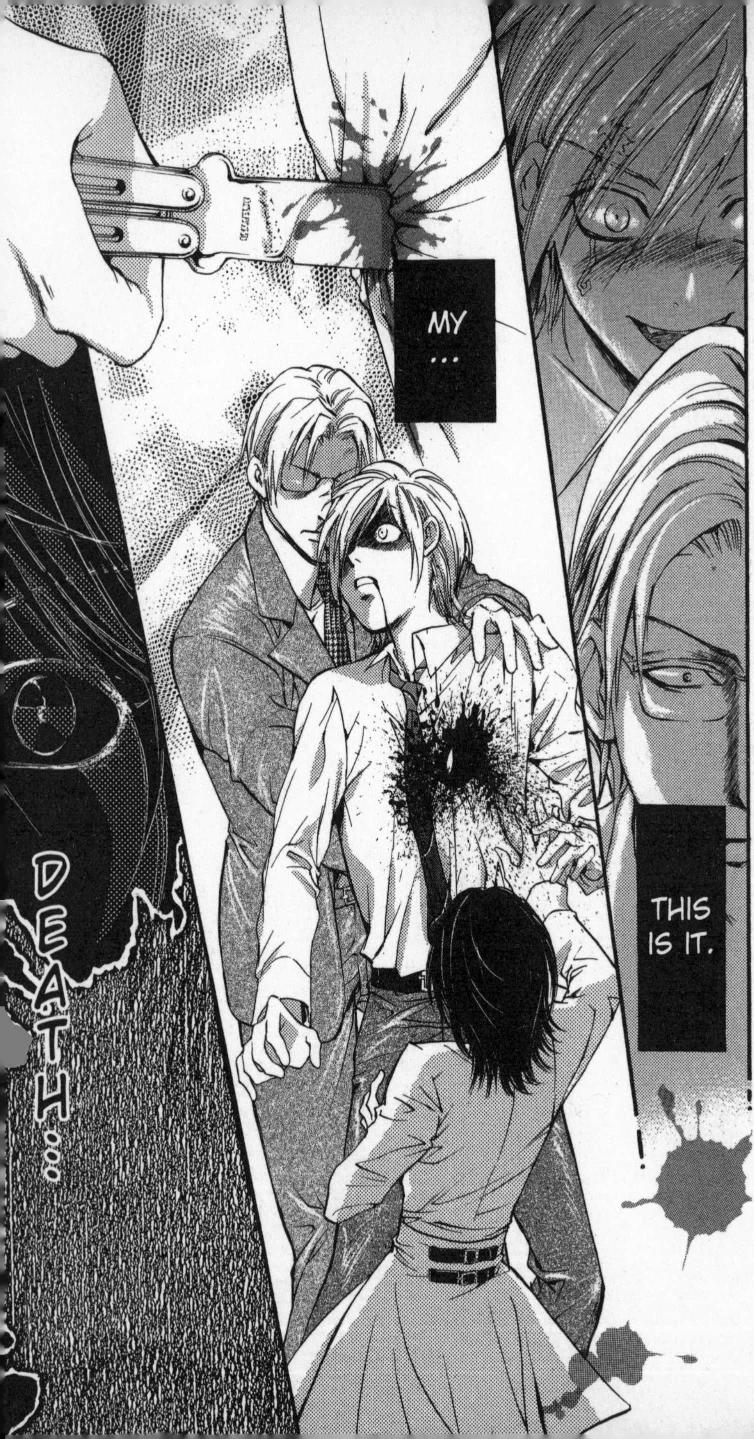
THIS IS IT.
MY ...
DEATH...

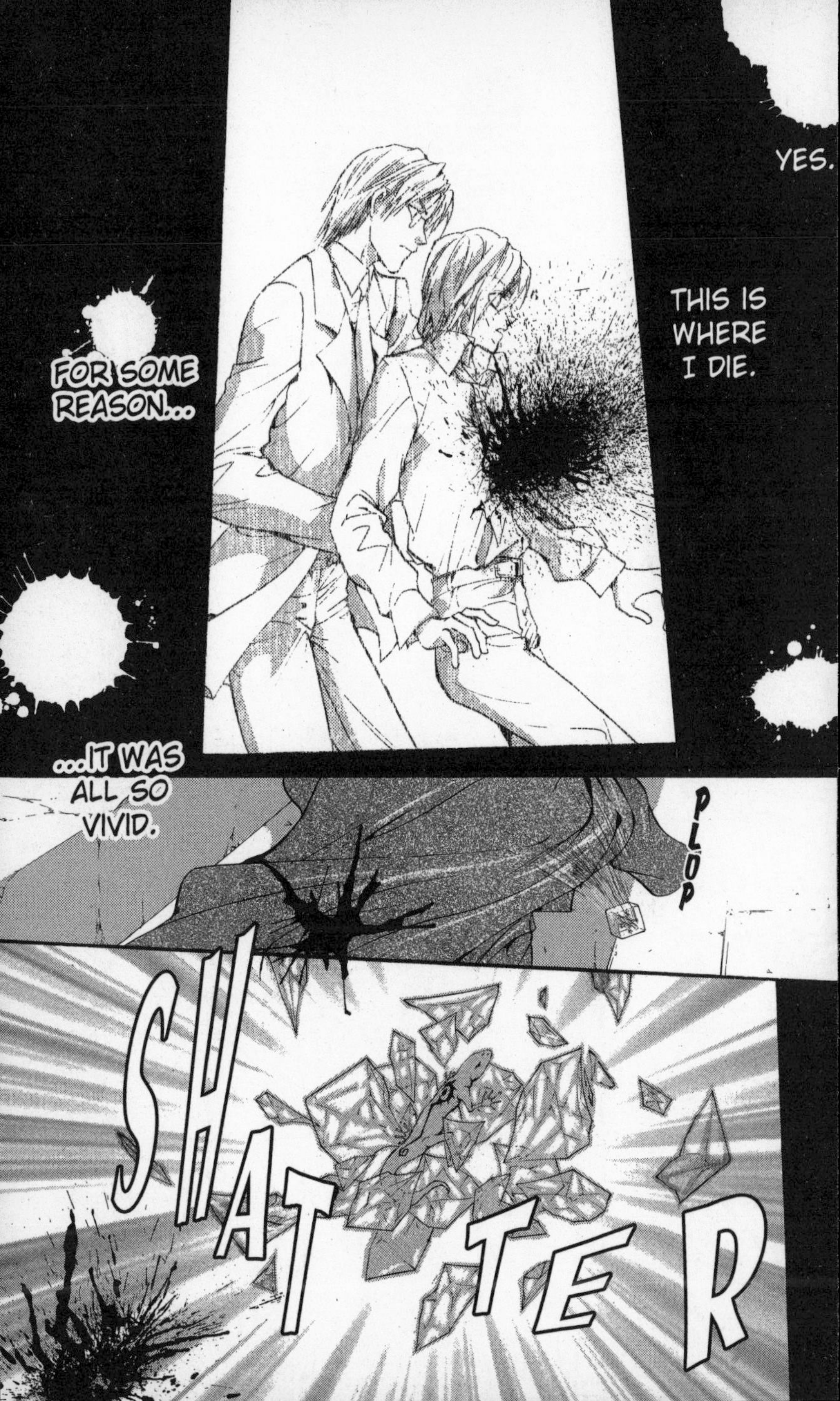
YES.
THIS IS WHERE I DIE.
FOR SOME REASON...
...IT WAS ALL SO VIVID.
PLOP
SHATTER

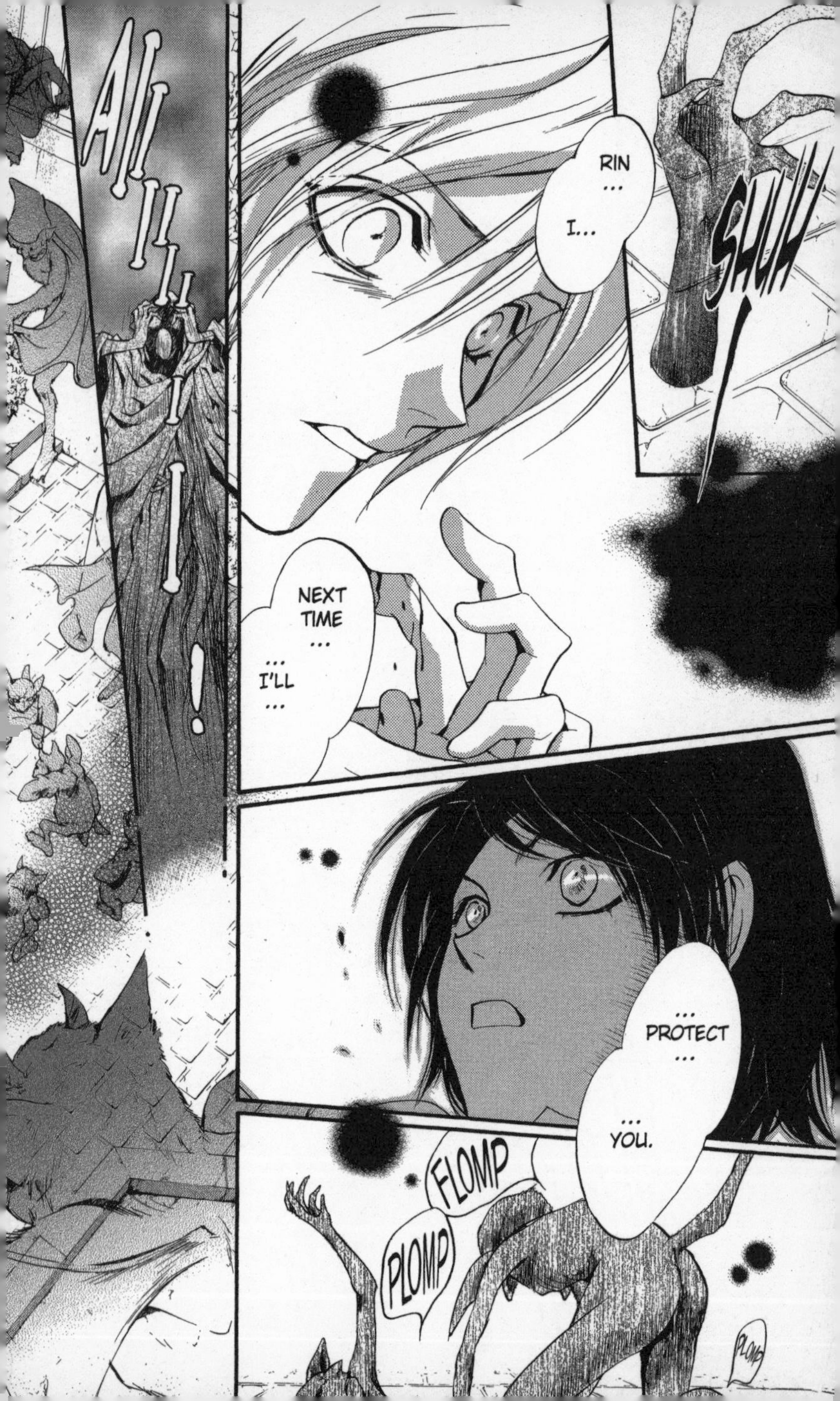
SHUH
RIN ... I...
NEXT TIME ... ... I'LL ...
... PROTECT ...
... YOU.
FLOMP
PLOMP
PLOMP
AIIIIIII
!

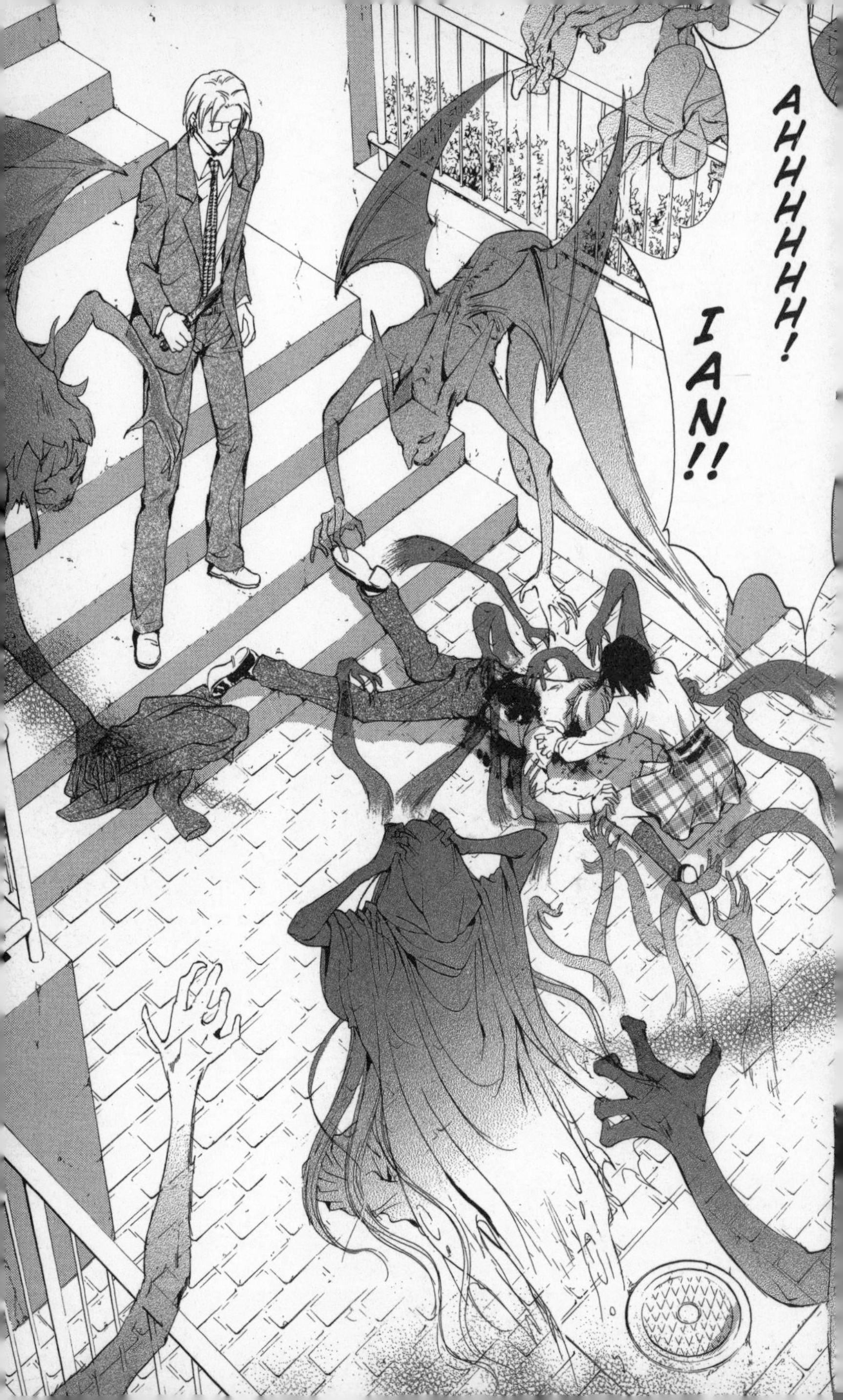
AHHHHHHH!
IAN!!

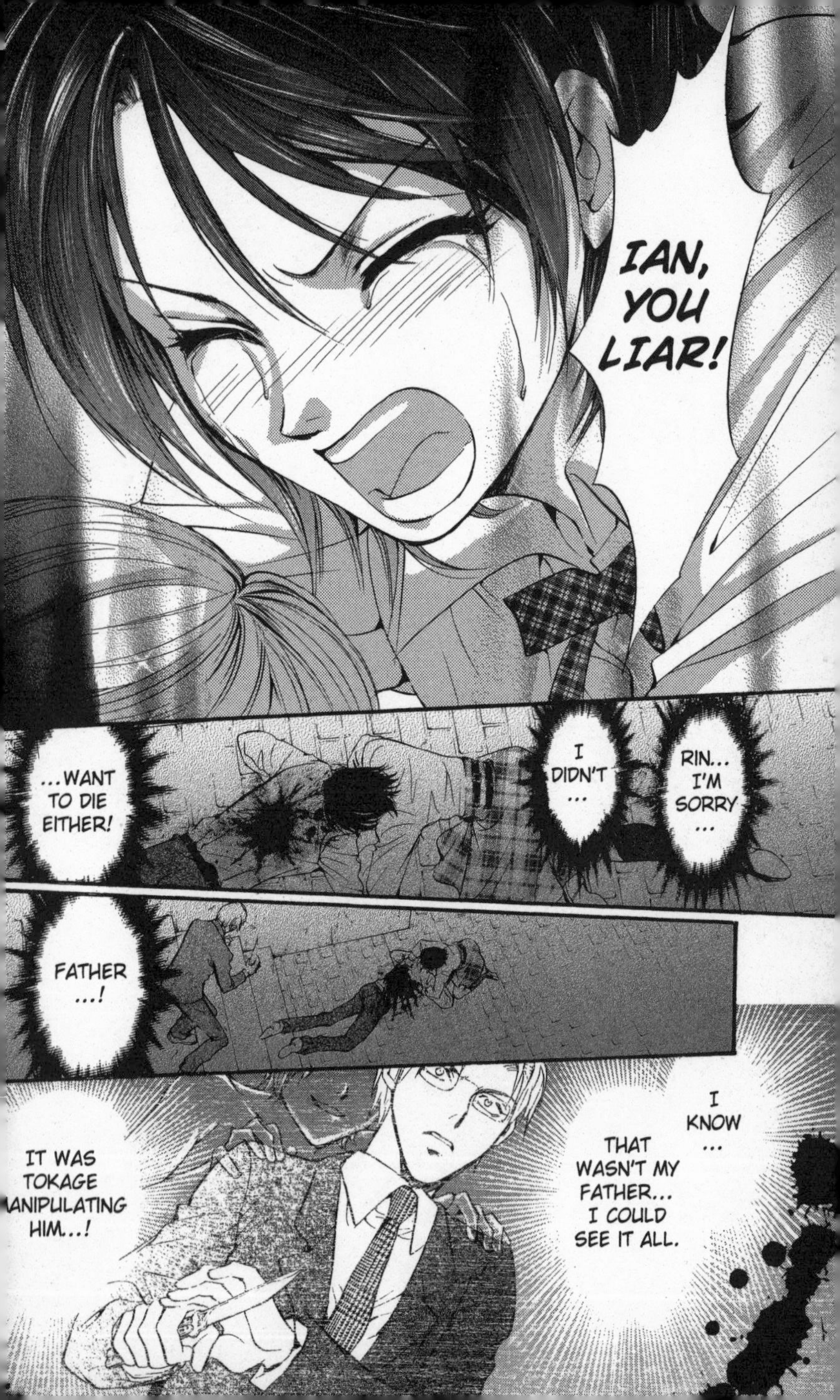
IAN, YOU LIAR!
RIN... I'M SORRY...
I DIDN'T...
...WANT TO DIE EITHER!
FATHER...!
I KNOW...
THAT WASN'T MY FATHER... I COULD SEE IT ALL.
IT WAS TOKAGE ANIPULATING HIM...!

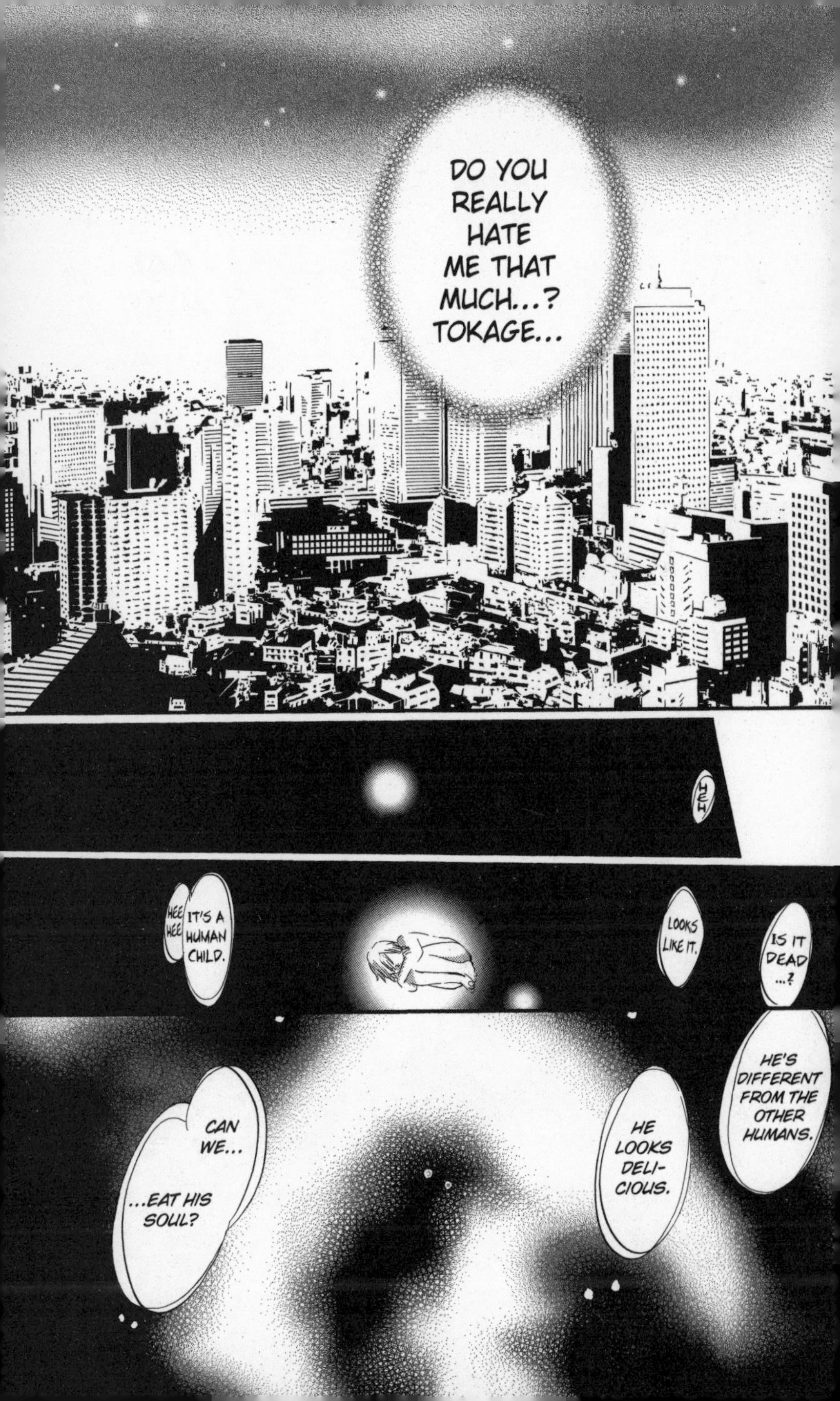
DO YOU REALLY HATE ME THAT MUCH...? TOKAGE...
HEH
IS IT DEAD ...?
LOOKS LIKE IT.
IT'S A HUMAN CHILD.
HEE HEE
HE'S DIFFERENT FROM THE OTHER HUMANS.
HE LOOKS DELICIOUS.
CAN WE...
...EAT HIS SOUL?

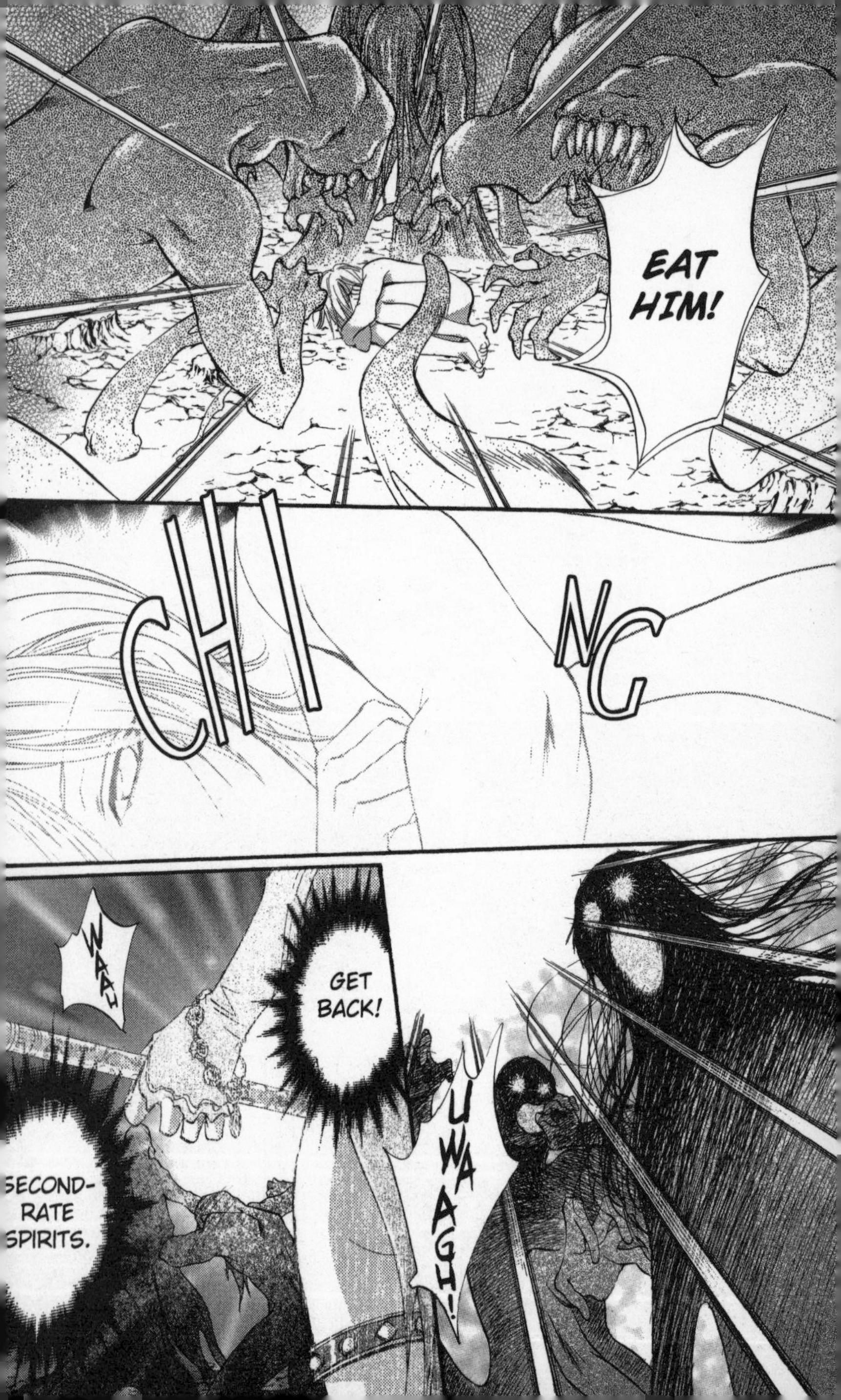
EAT HIM!
CHINC
UWAAGH!
GET BACK!
WAAH
SECOND-RATE SPIRITS.

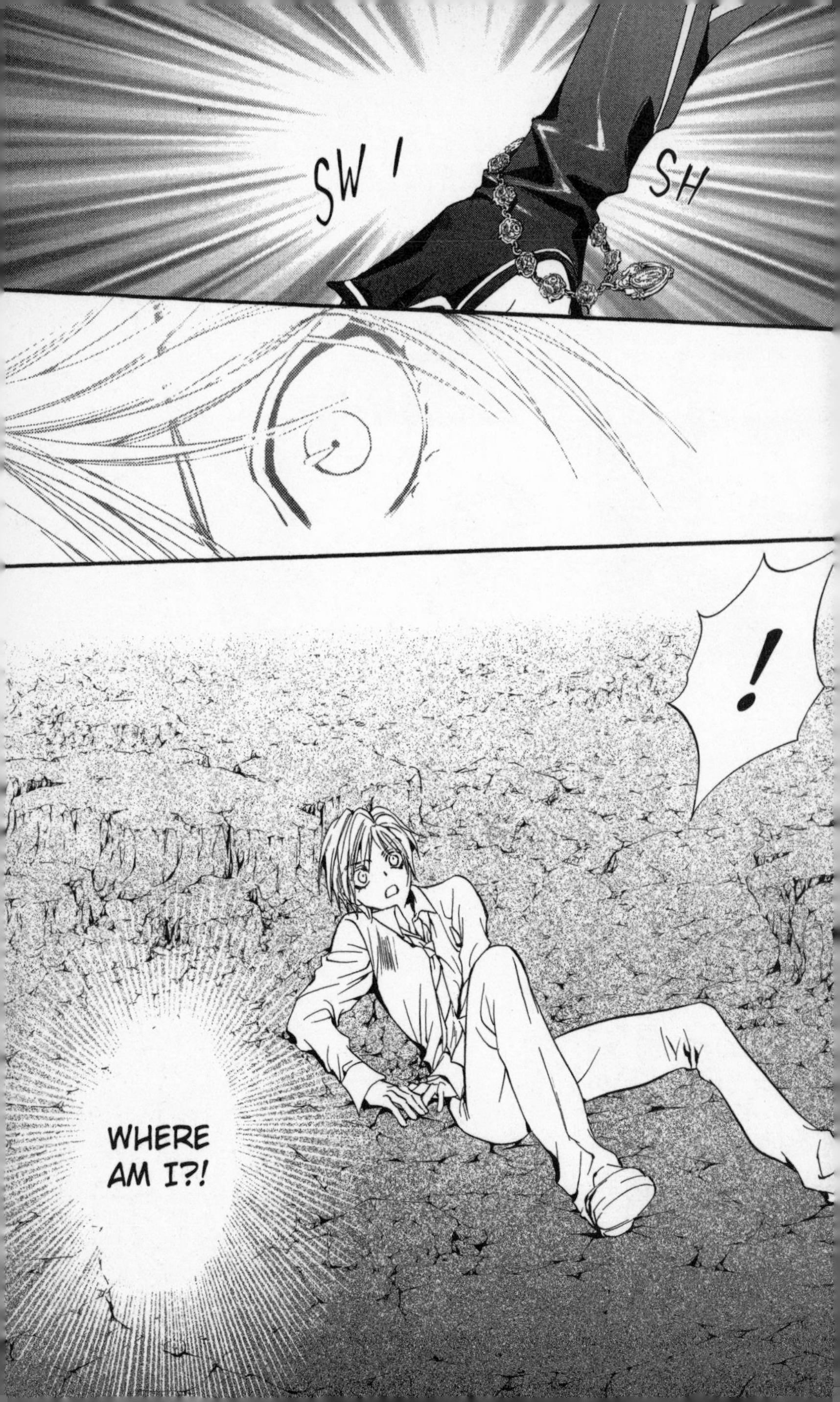
SW I SH
!
WHERE AM I?!

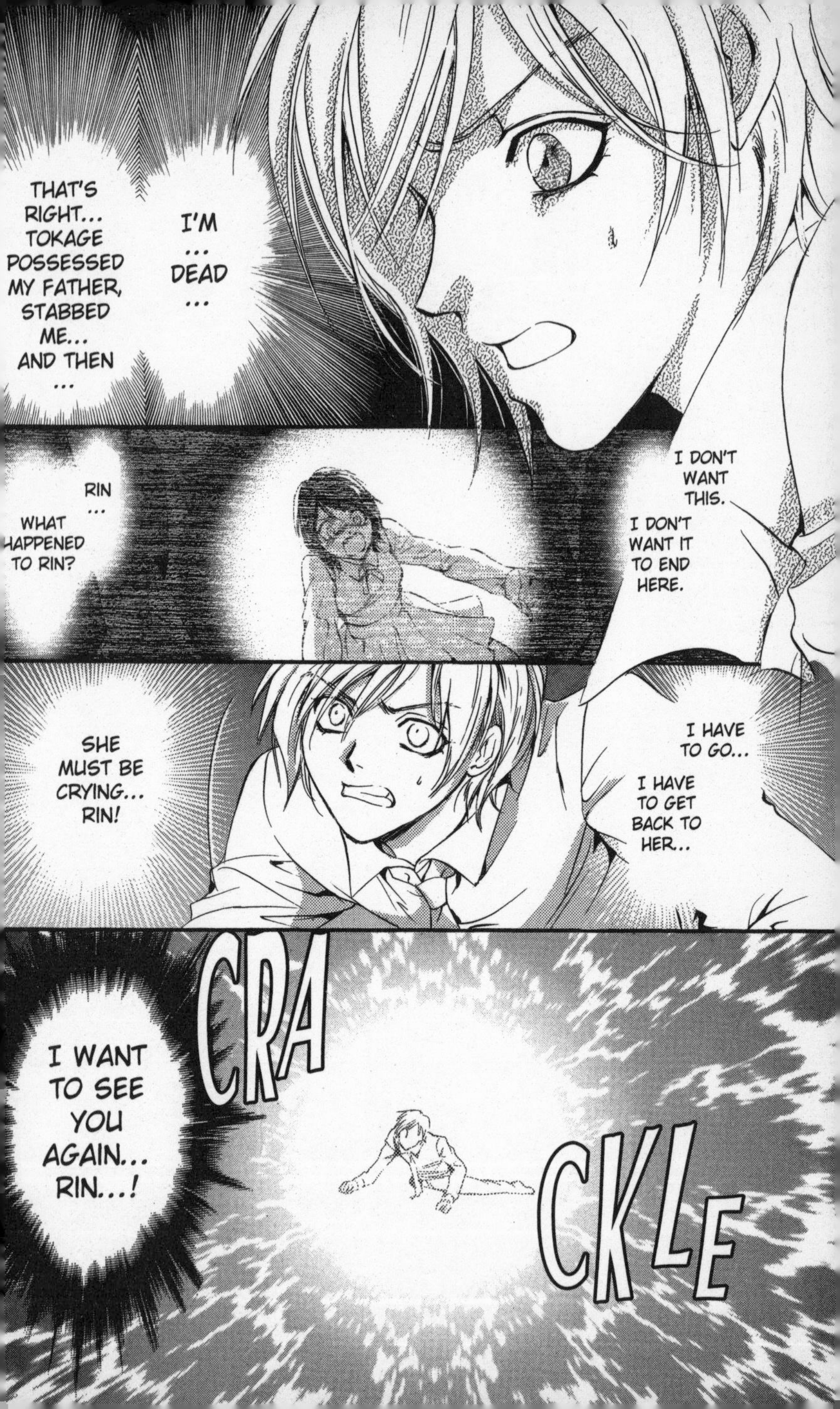
I'M ... DEAD ...
THAT'S RIGHT... TOKAGE POSSESSED MY FATHER, STABBED ME... AND THEN ...
I DON'T WANT THIS.
I DON'T WANT IT TO END HERE.
RIN ...
WHAT HAPPENED TO RIN?
I HAVE TO GO...
I HAVE TO GET BACK TO HER...
SHE MUST BE CRYING... RIN!
CRACKLE
I WANT TO SEE YOU AGAIN... RIN...!

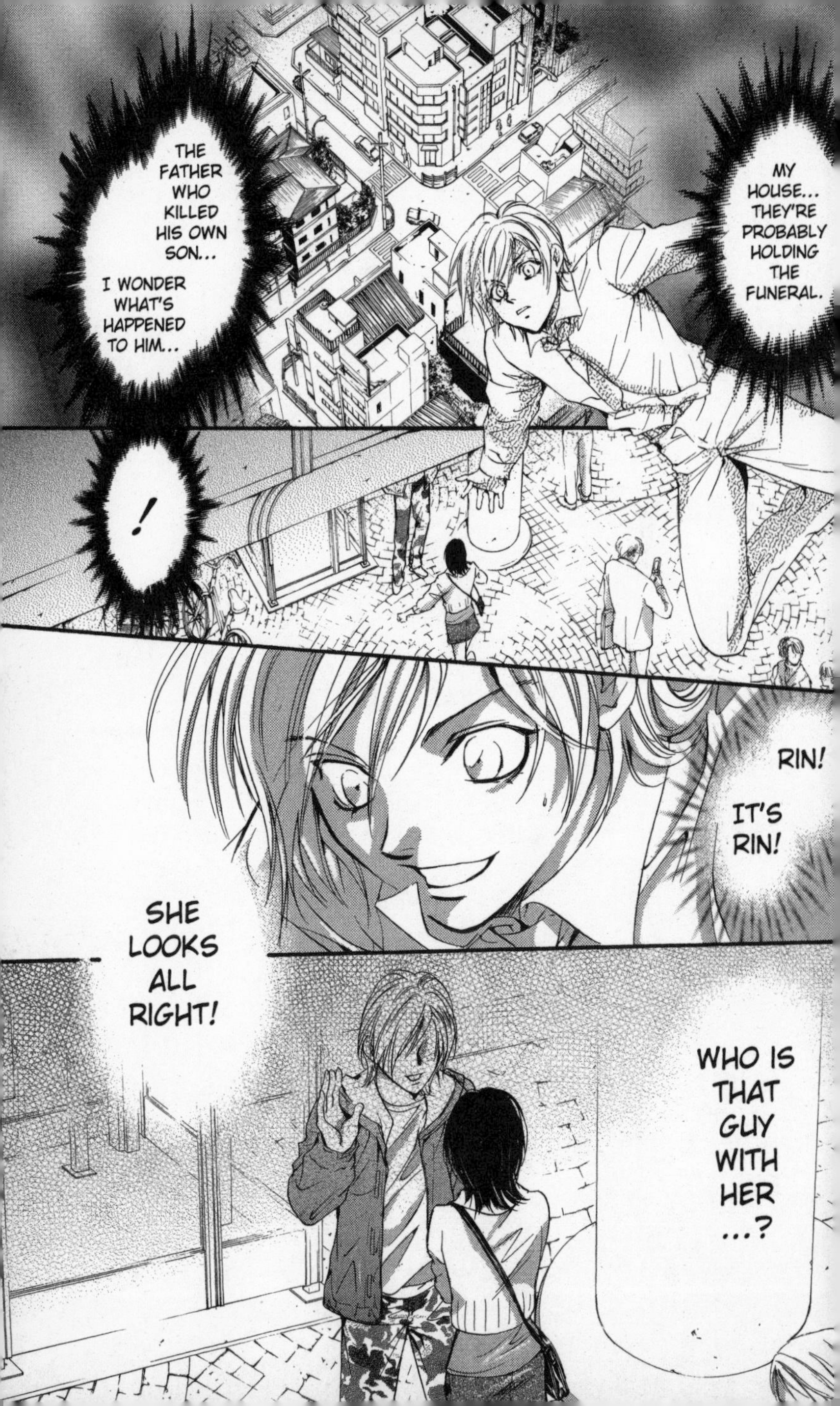
MY HOUSE... THEY'RE PROBABLY HOLDING THE FUNERAL.
THE FATHER WHO KILLED HIS OWN SON...
I WONDER WHAT'S HAPPENED TO HIM...
!
RIN!
IT'S RIN!
SHE LOOKS ALL RIGHT!
WHO IS THAT GUY WITH HER ...?

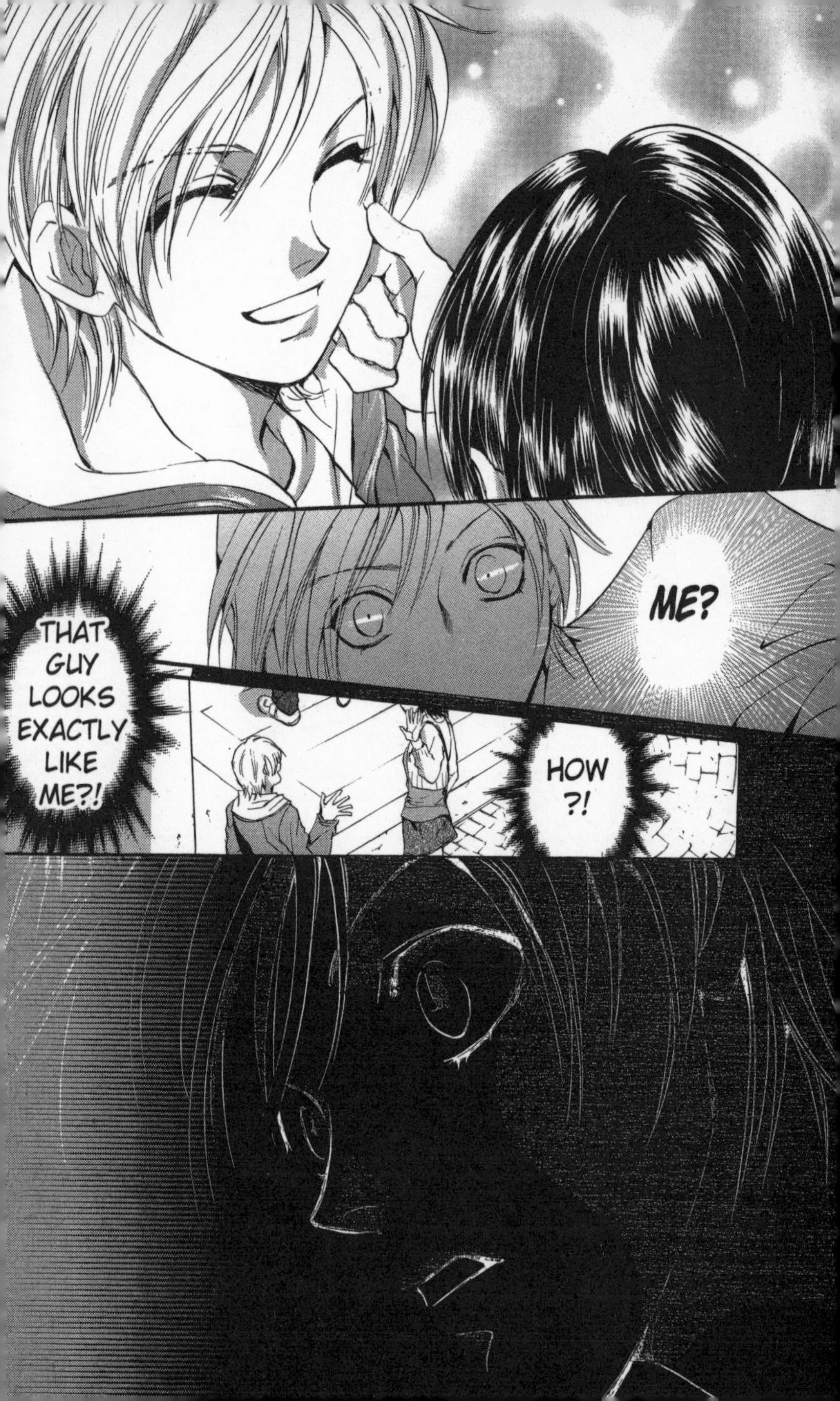
ME?
THAT GUY LOOKS EXACTLY LIKE ME?!
HOW ?!

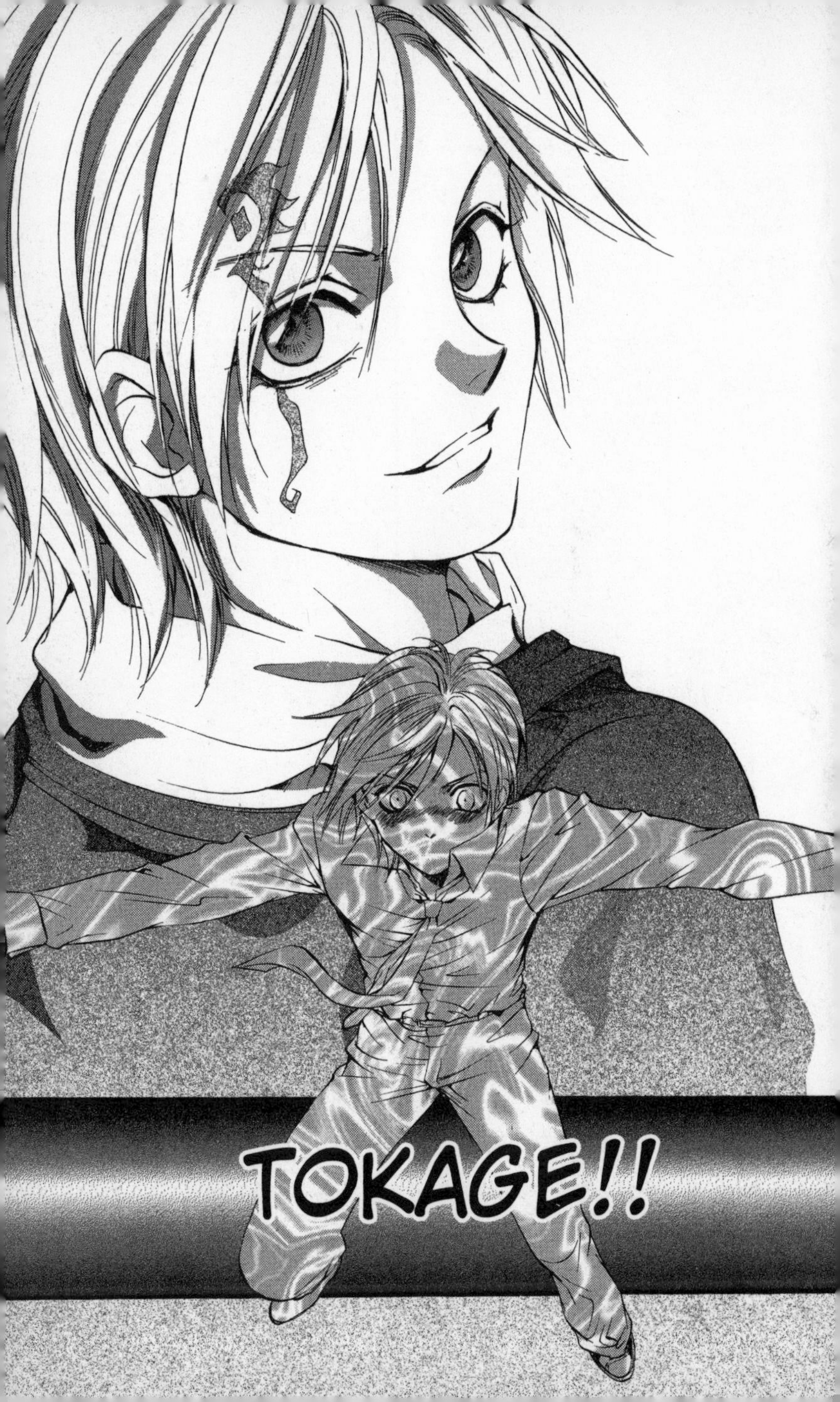
TOKAGE!!

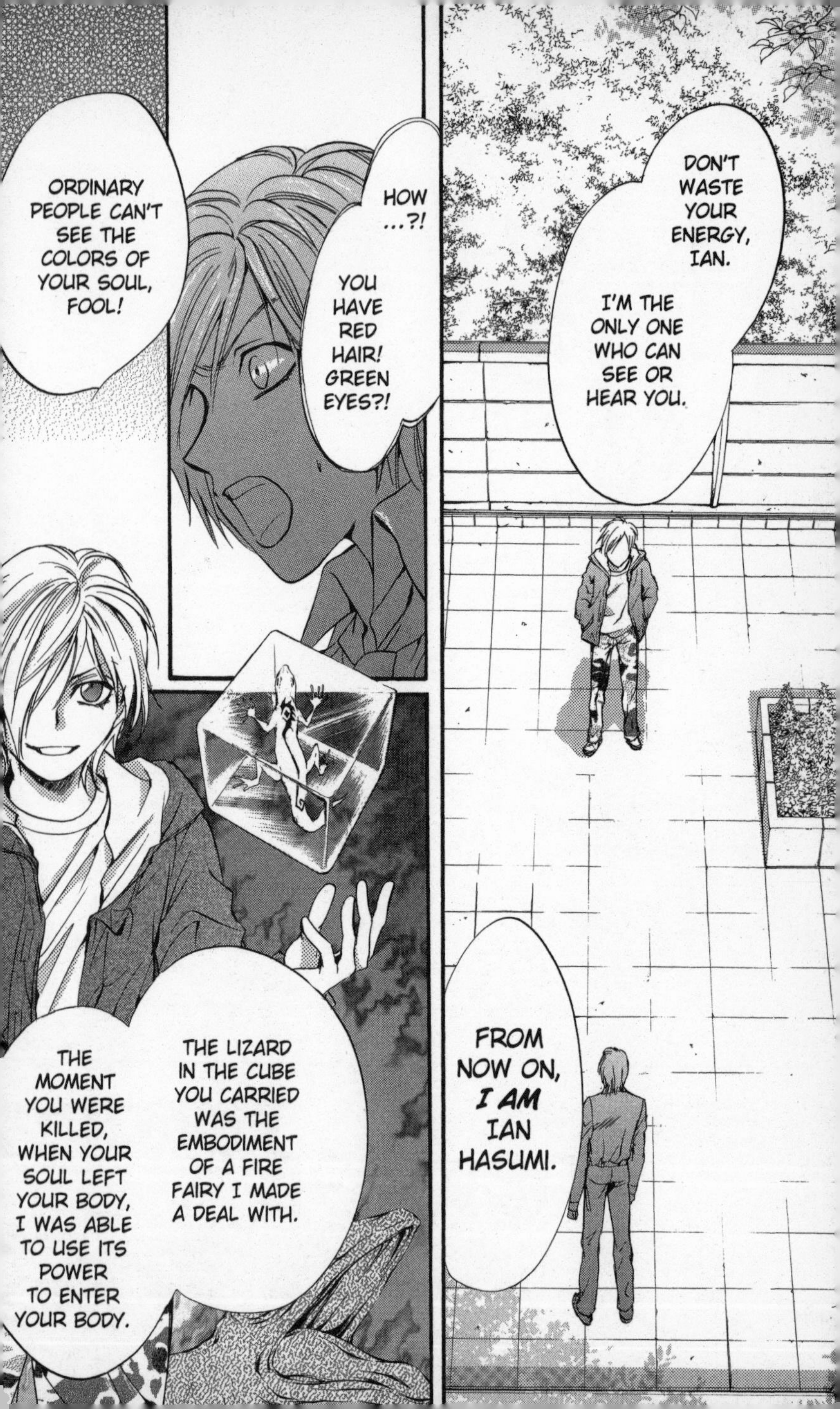
DON'T WASTE YOUR ENERGY, IAN.
I'M THE ONLY ONE WHO CAN SEE OR HEAR YOU.
FROM NOW ON, *I AM* IAN HASUMI.
HOW ...?!
YOU HAVE RED HAIR! GREEN EYES?!
ORDINARY PEOPLE CAN'T SEE THE COLORS OF YOUR SOUL, FOOL!
THE LIZARD IN THE CUBE YOU CARRIED WAS THE EMBODIMENT OF A FIRE FAIRY I MADE A DEAL WITH.
THE MOMENT YOU WERE KILLED, WHEN YOUR SOUL LEFT YOUR BODY, I WAS ABLE TO USE ITS POWER TO ENTER YOUR BODY.

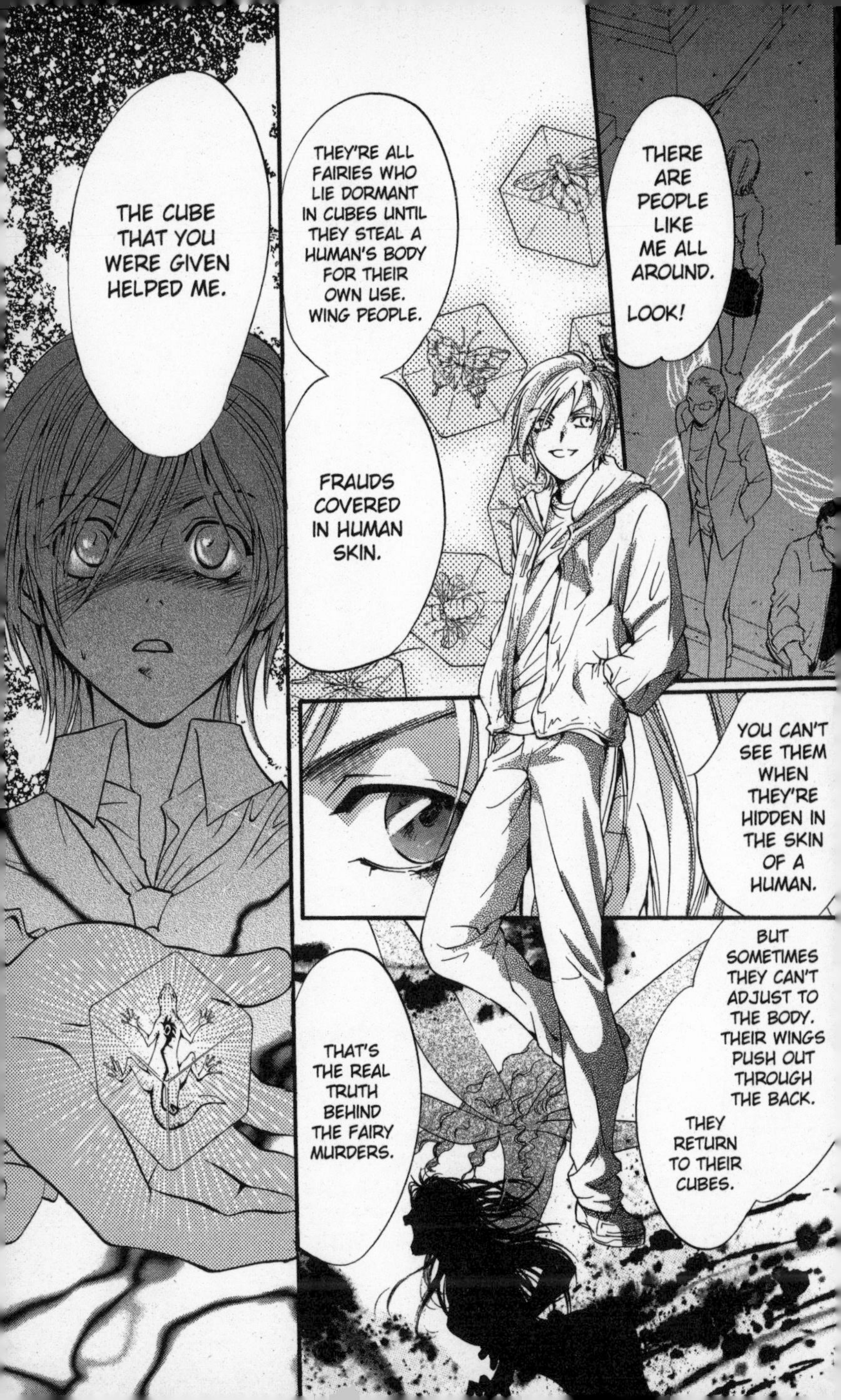
THERE ARE PEOPLE LIKE ME ALL AROUND.
LOOK!
THEY'RE ALL FAIRIES WHO LIE DORMANT IN CUBES UNTIL THEY STEAL A HUMAN'S BODY FOR THEIR OWN USE. WING PEOPLE.
FRAUDS COVERED IN HUMAN SKIN.
YOU CAN'T SEE THEM WHEN THEY'RE HIDDEN IN THE SKIN OF A HUMAN.
BUT SOMETIMES THEY CAN'T ADJUST TO THE BODY. THEIR WINGS PUSH OUT THROUGH THE BACK.
THEY RETURN TO THEIR CUBES.
THAT'S THE REAL TRUTH BEHIND THE FAIRY MURDERS.
THE CUBE THAT YOU WERE GIVEN HELPED ME.

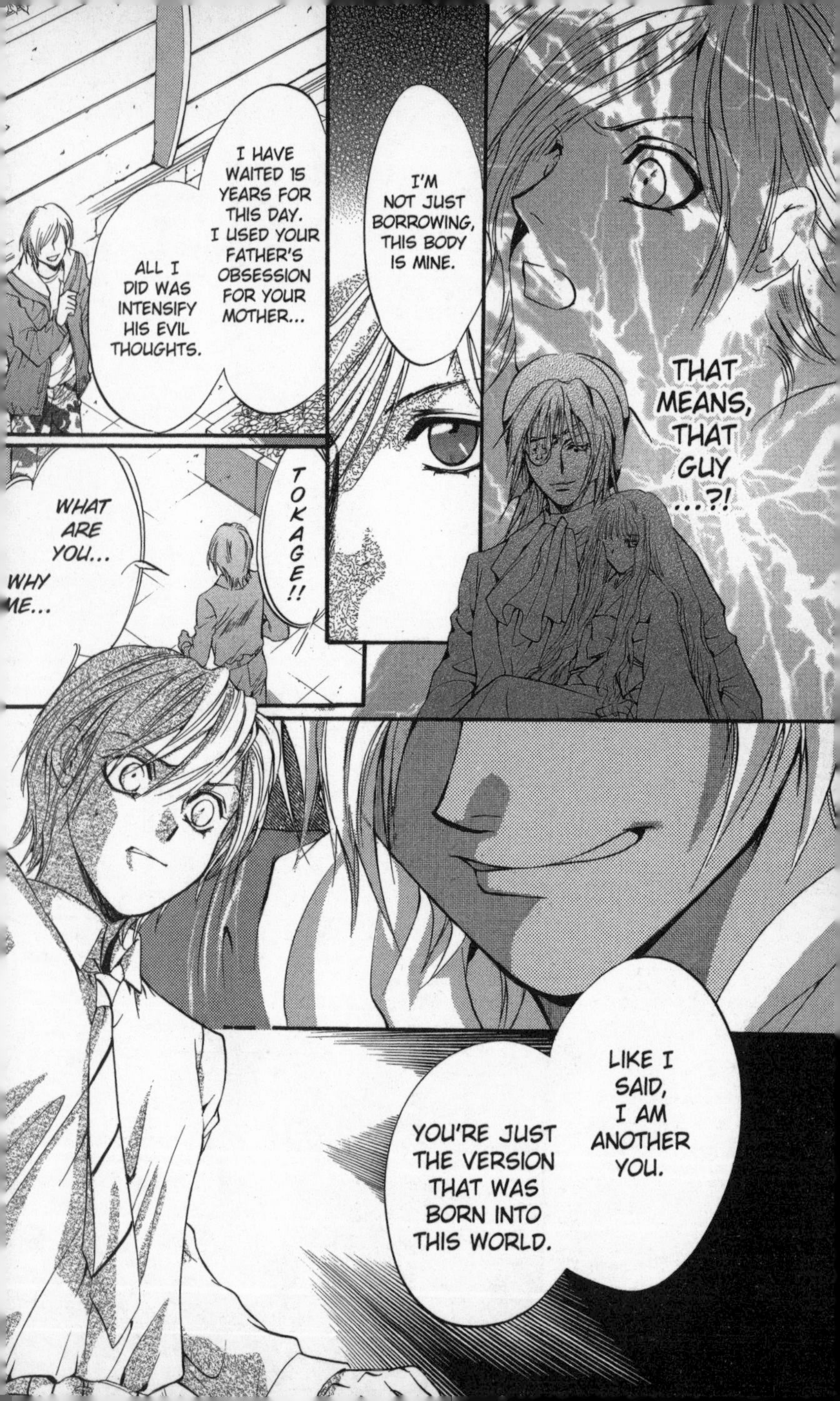
I'M NOT JUST BORROWING, THIS BODY IS MINE.
THAT MEANS, THAT GUY ...?!
I HAVE WAITED 15 YEARS FOR THIS DAY. I USED YOUR FATHER'S OBSESSION FOR YOUR MOTHER...
ALL I DID WAS INTENSIFY HIS EVIL THOUGHTS.
TOKAGE!!
WHAT ARE YOU... WHY ME...
LIKE I SAID, I AM ANOTHER YOU.
YOU'RE JUST THE VERSION THAT WAS BORN INTO THIS WORLD.

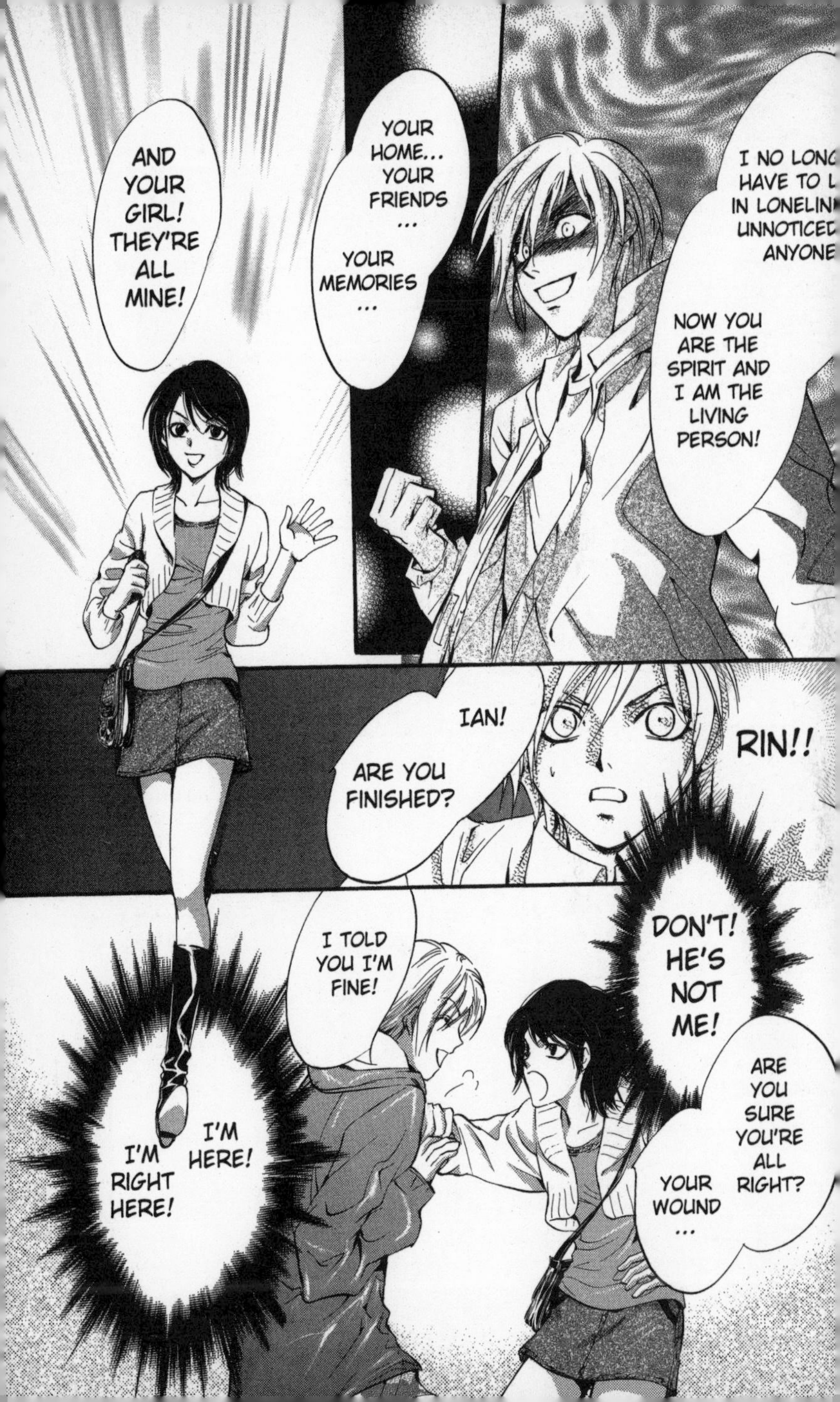
I NO LONG HAVE TO L IN LONELIN UNNOTICED ANYONE
NOW YOU ARE THE SPIRIT AND I AM THE LIVING PERSON!
YOUR HOME... YOUR FRIENDS ...
YOUR MEMORIES ...
AND YOUR GIRL! THEY'RE ALL MINE!
RIN!!
IAN!
ARE YOU FINISHED?
DON'T! HE'S NOT ME!
ARE YOU SURE YOU'RE ALL RIGHT?
YOUR WOUND ...
I TOLD YOU I'M FINE!
I'M HERE!
I'M RIGHT HERE!

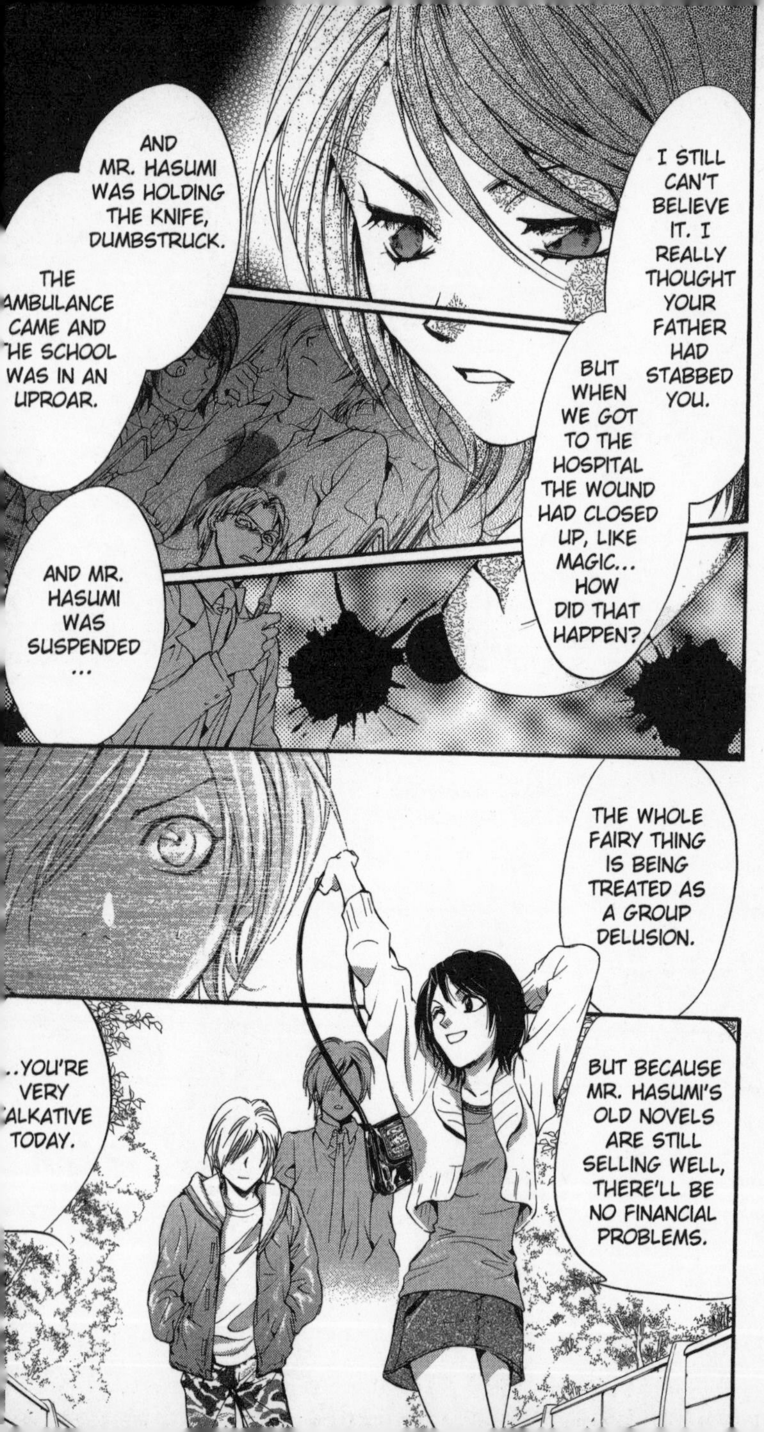
I STILL CAN'T BELIEVE IT. I REALLY THOUGHT YOUR FATHER HAD STABBED YOU.
BUT WHEN WE GOT TO THE HOSPITAL THE WOUND HAD CLOSED UP, LIKE MAGIC... HOW DID THAT HAPPEN?
AND MR. HASUMI WAS HOLDING THE KNIFE, DUMBSTRUCK.
THE AMBULANCE CAME AND THE SCHOOL WAS IN AN UPROAR.
AND MR. HASUMI WAS SUSPENDED...
THE WHOLE FAIRY THING IS BEING TREATED AS A GROUP DELUSION.
BUT BECAUSE MR. HASUMI'S OLD NOVELS ARE STILL SELLING WELL, THERE'LL BE NO FINANCIAL PROBLEMS.
...YOU'RE VERY TALKATIVE TODAY.

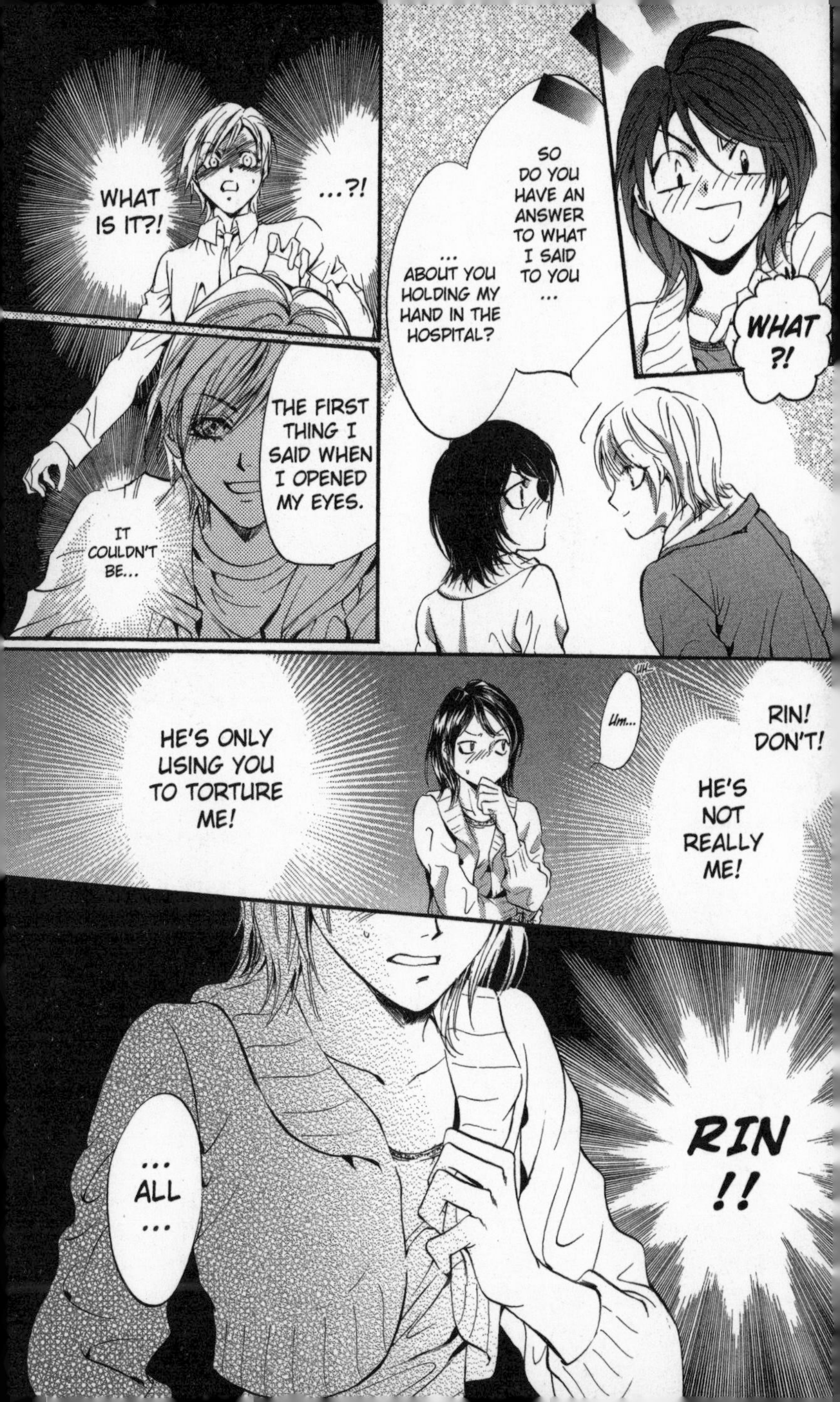
SO DO YOU HAVE AN ANSWER TO WHAT I SAID TO YOU ...
... ABOUT YOU HOLDING MY HAND IN THE HOSPITAL?
WHAT ?!
...?!
WHAT IS IT?!
THE FIRST THING I SAID WHEN I OPENED MY EYES.
IT COULDN'T BE...
RIN! DON'T!
HE'S NOT REALLY ME!
UH...
Um...
HE'S ONLY USING YOU TO TORTURE ME!
RIN !!
... ALL ...

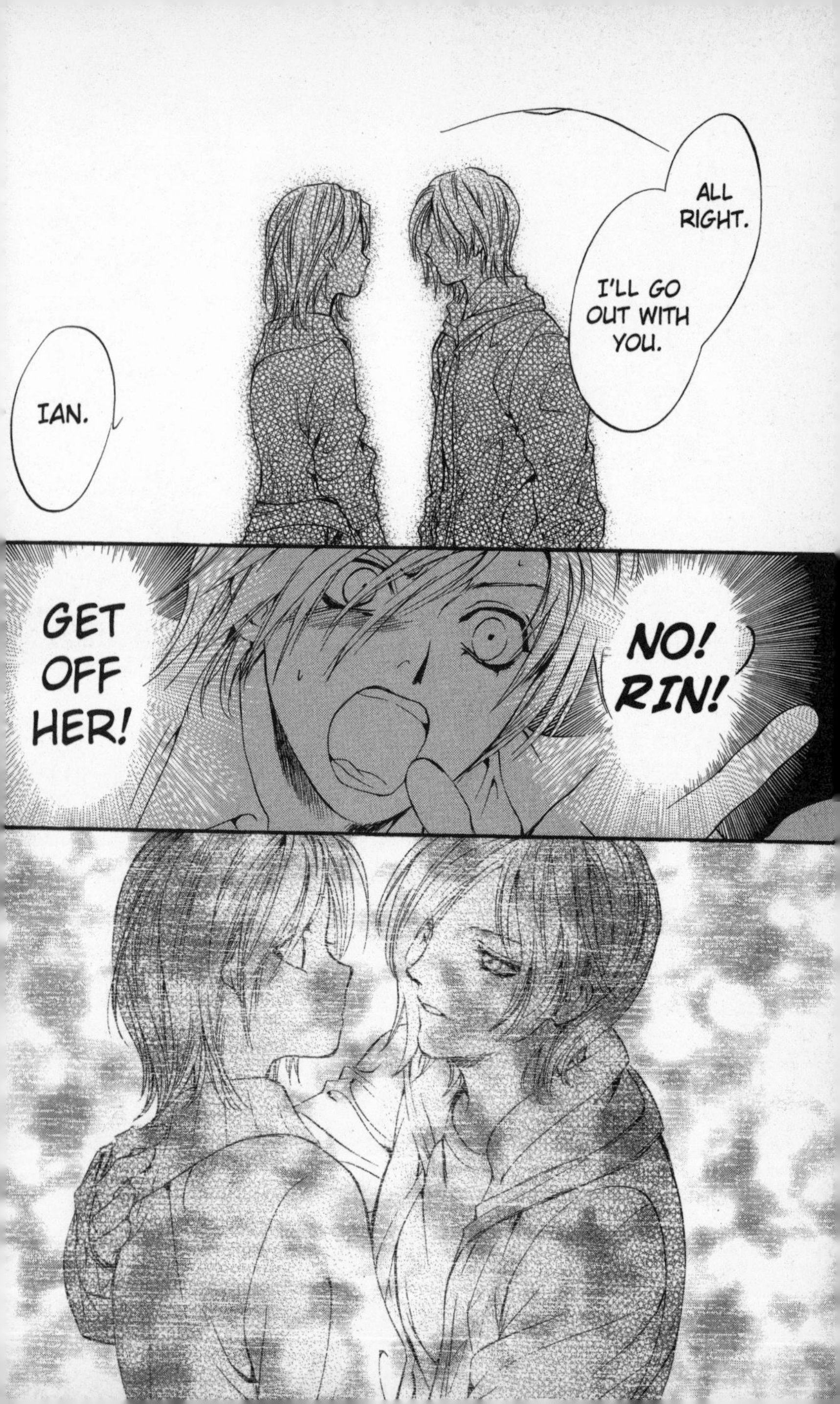
ALL RIGHT.
I'LL GO OUT WITH YOU.
IAN.
NO! RIN!
GET OFF HER!

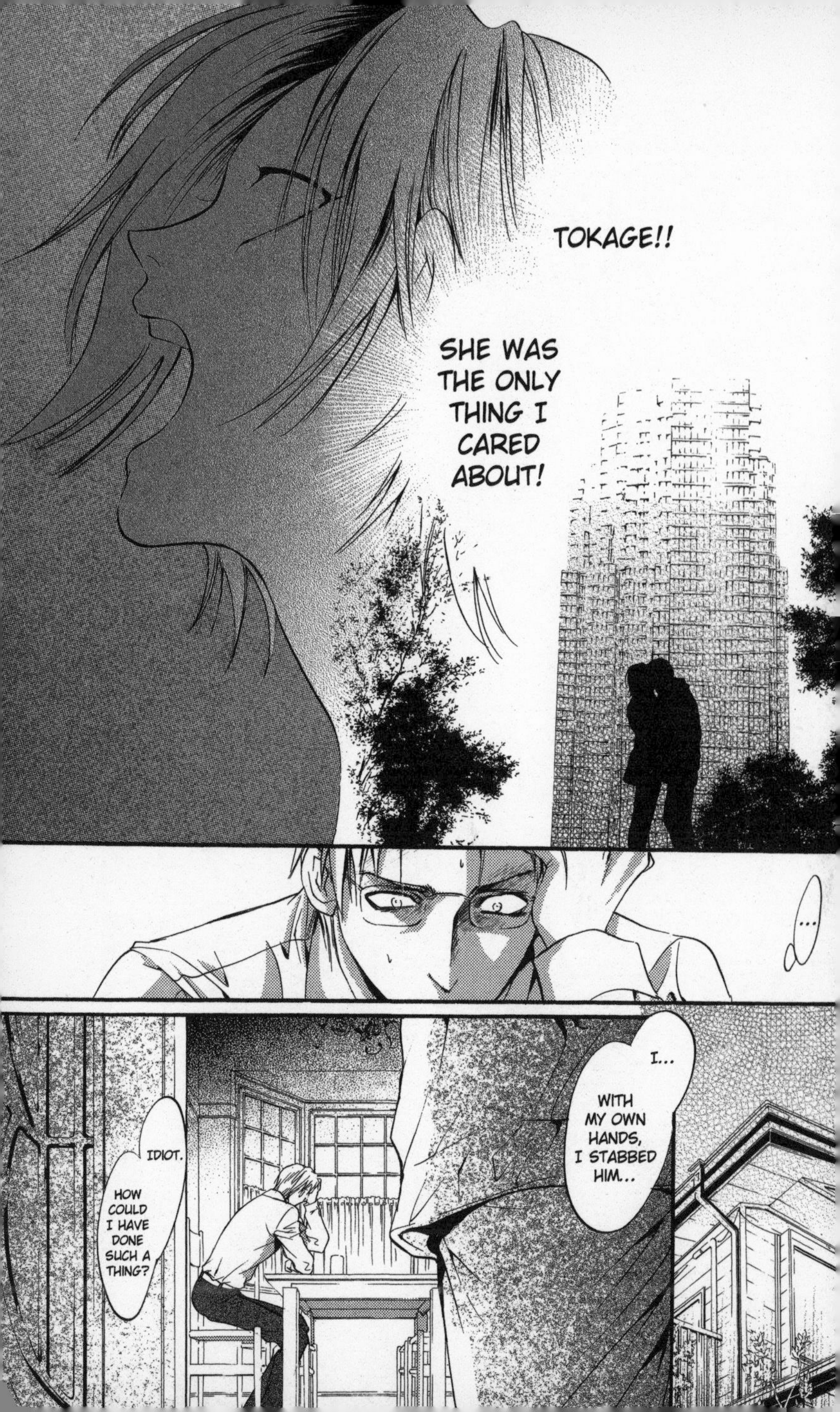
TOKAGE!!
SHE WAS THE ONLY THING I CARED ABOUT!
...
I...
WITH MY OWN HANDS, I STABBED HIM...
IDIOT.
HOW COULD I HAVE DONE SUCH A THING?

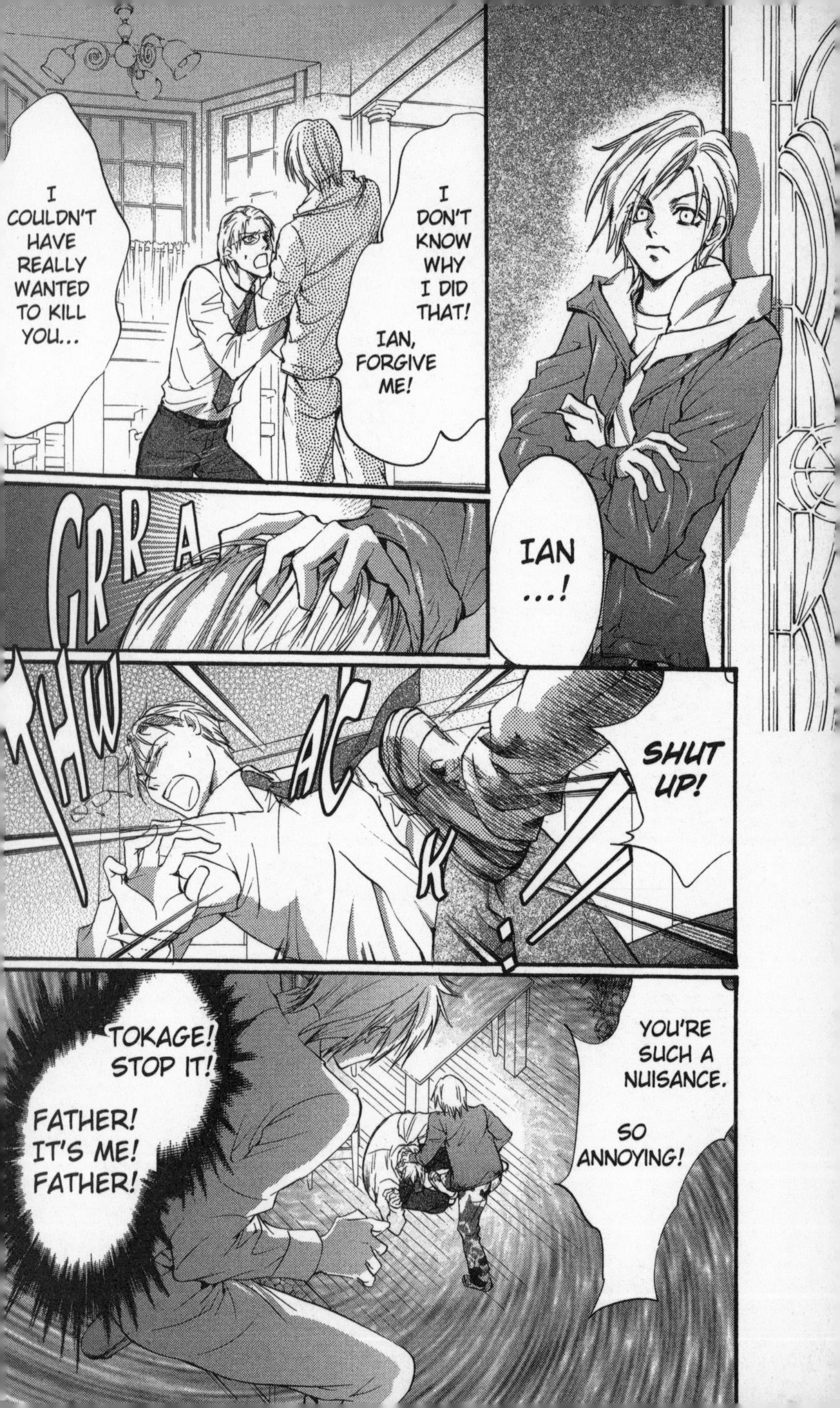
IAN ...!
I DON'T KNOW WHY I DID THAT!
IAN, FORGIVE ME!
I COULDN'T HAVE REALLY WANTED TO KILL YOU...
CRRA
SHUT UP!
THWACK
YOU'RE SUCH A NUISANCE.
SO ANNOYING!
TOKAGE! STOP IT!
FATHER! IT'S ME! FATHER!

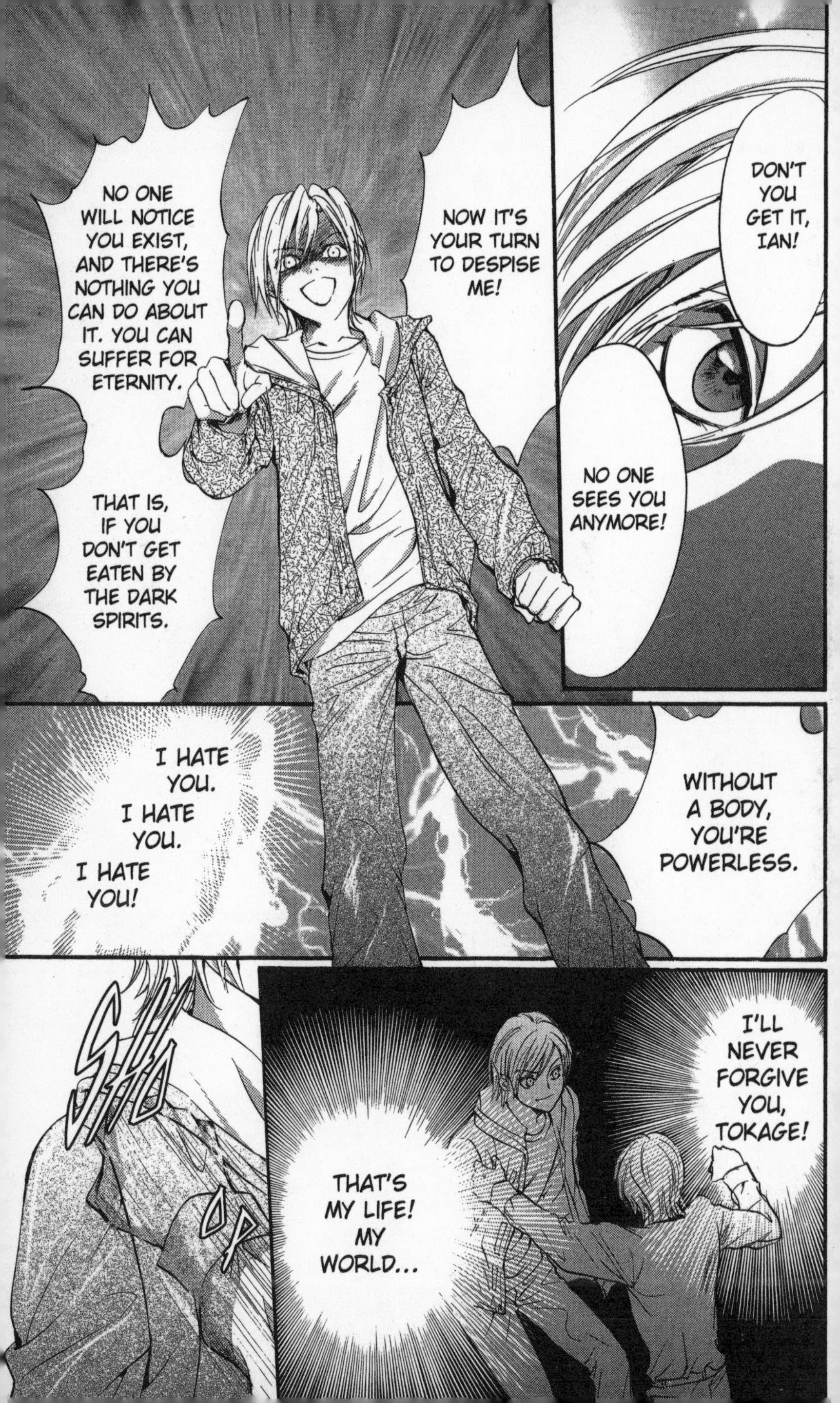
DON'T YOU GET IT, IAN!
NO ONE SEES YOU ANYMORE!
NOW IT'S YOUR TURN TO DESPISE ME!
NO ONE WILL NOTICE YOU EXIST, AND THERE'S NOTHING YOU CAN DO ABOUT IT. YOU CAN SUFFER FOR ETERNITY.
THAT IS, IF YOU DON'T GET EATEN BY THE DARK SPIRITS.
WITHOUT A BODY, YOU'RE POWERLESS.
I HATE YOU.
I HATE YOU.
I HATE YOU!
I'LL NEVER FORGIVE YOU, TOKAGE!
THAT'S MY LIFE! MY WORLD...

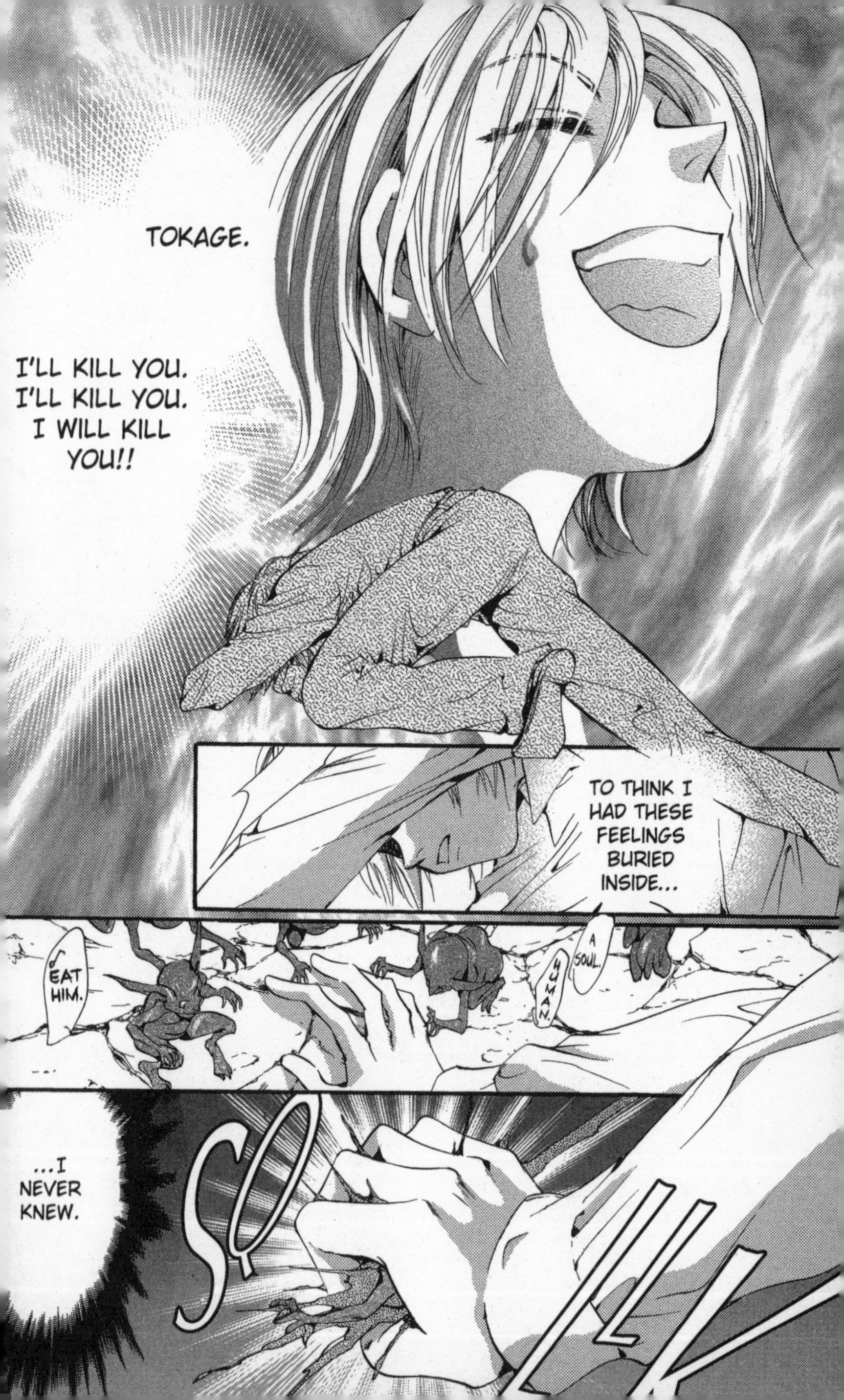
TOKAGE.
I'LL KILL YOU. I'LL KILL YOU. I WILL KILL YOU!!
TO THINK I HAD THESE FEELINGS BURIED INSIDE...
A SOUL.
HUMAN.
EAT HIM.
...I NEVER KNEW.
SQ

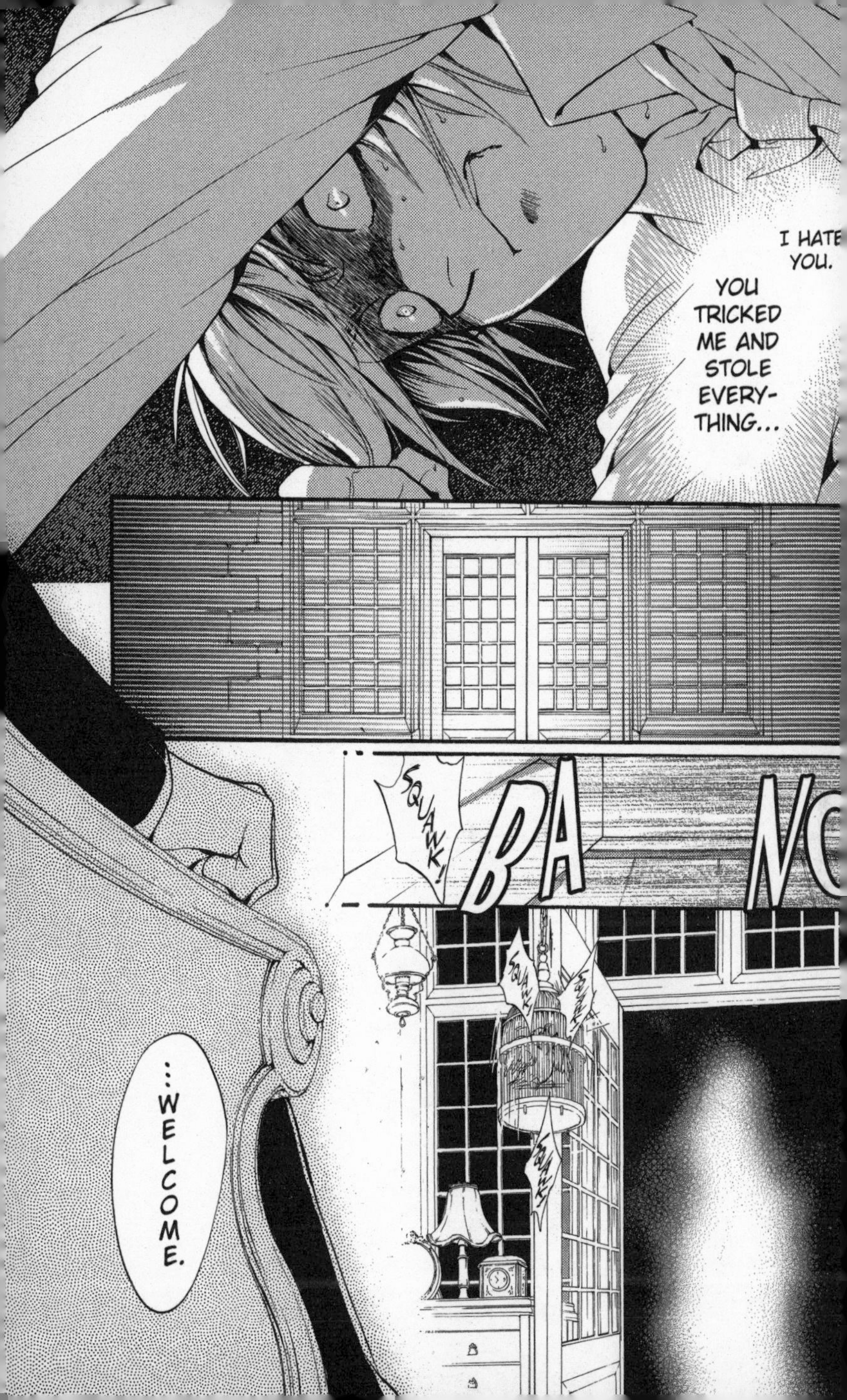

I HATE YOU.
YOU TRICKED ME AND STOLE EVERY-THING...
BA NG
SQUANK!
SQUANK!
SQUANK!
SQUANK!
...WELCOME.

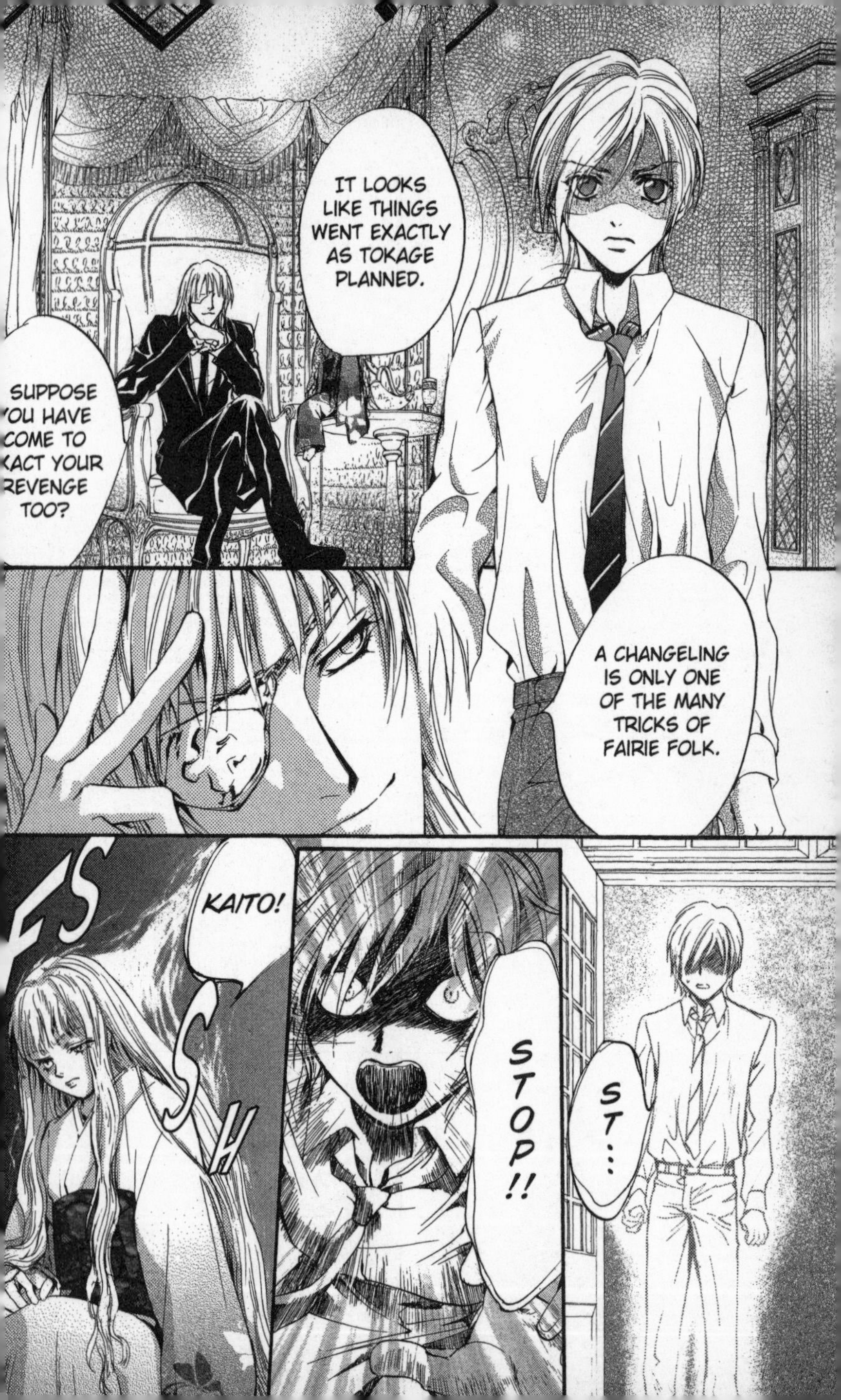
IT LOOKS LIKE THINGS WENT EXACTLY AS TOKAGE PLANNED.
SUPPOSE OU HAVE COME TO XACT YOUR REVENGE TOO?
A CHANGELING IS ONLY ONE OF THE MANY TRICKS OF FAIRIE FOLK.
ST...
STOP!!
KAITO!
SSH

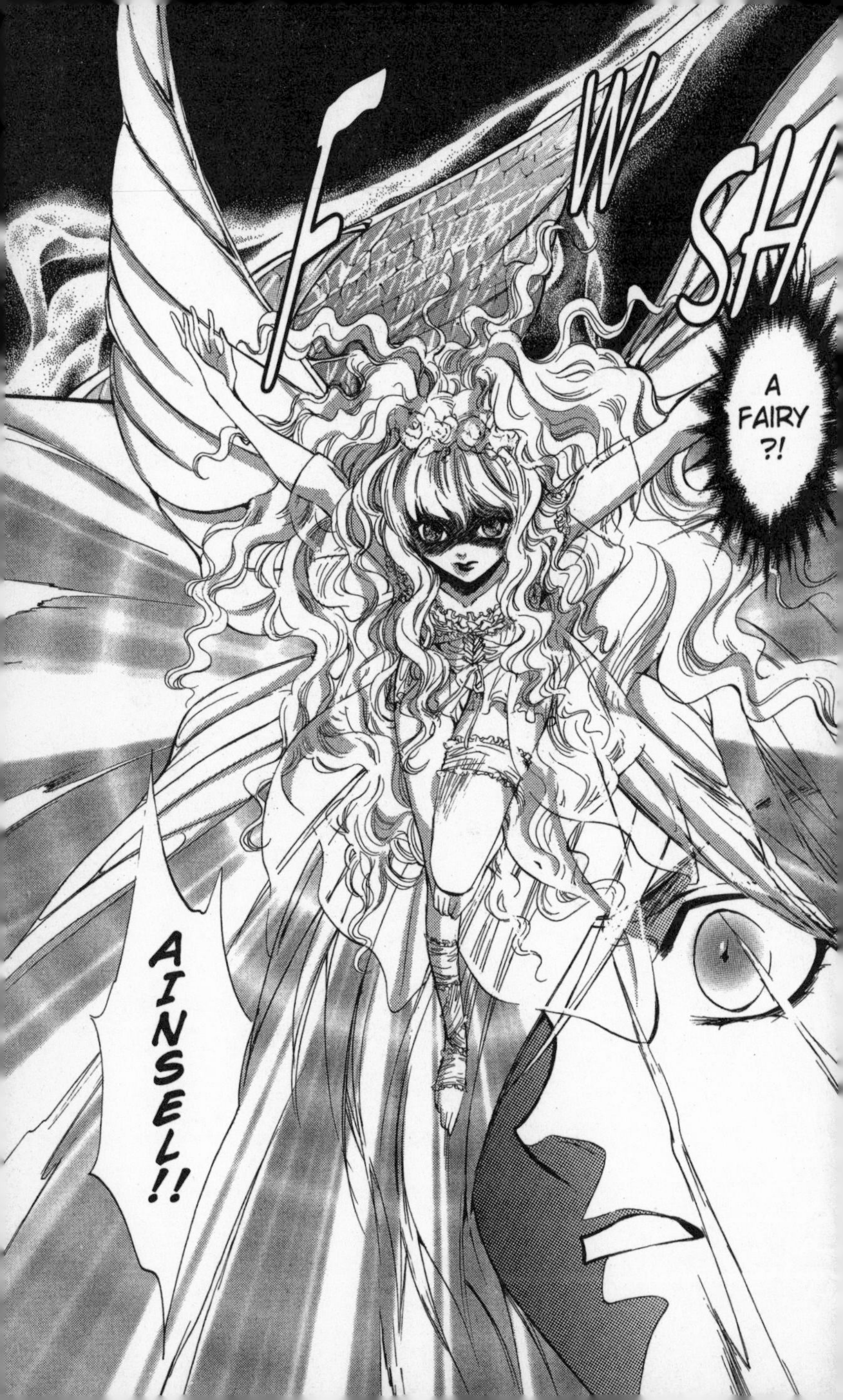
FWSH
A FAIRY ?!
AINSEL!!

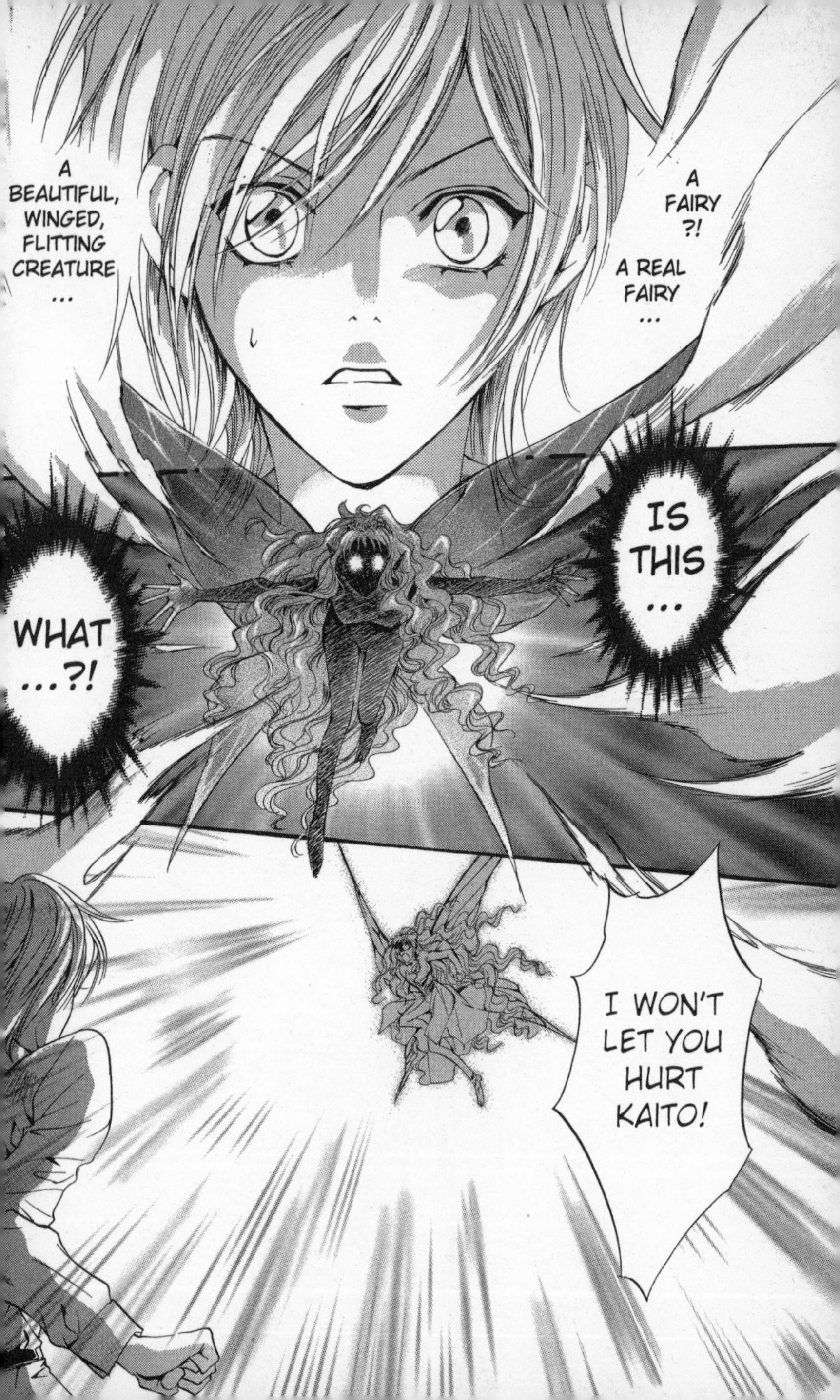

A FAIRY ?!
A REAL FAIRY ...
A BEAUTIFUL, WINGED, FLITTING CREATURE ...
IS THIS ...
WHAT ...?!
I WON'T LET YOU HURT KAITO!

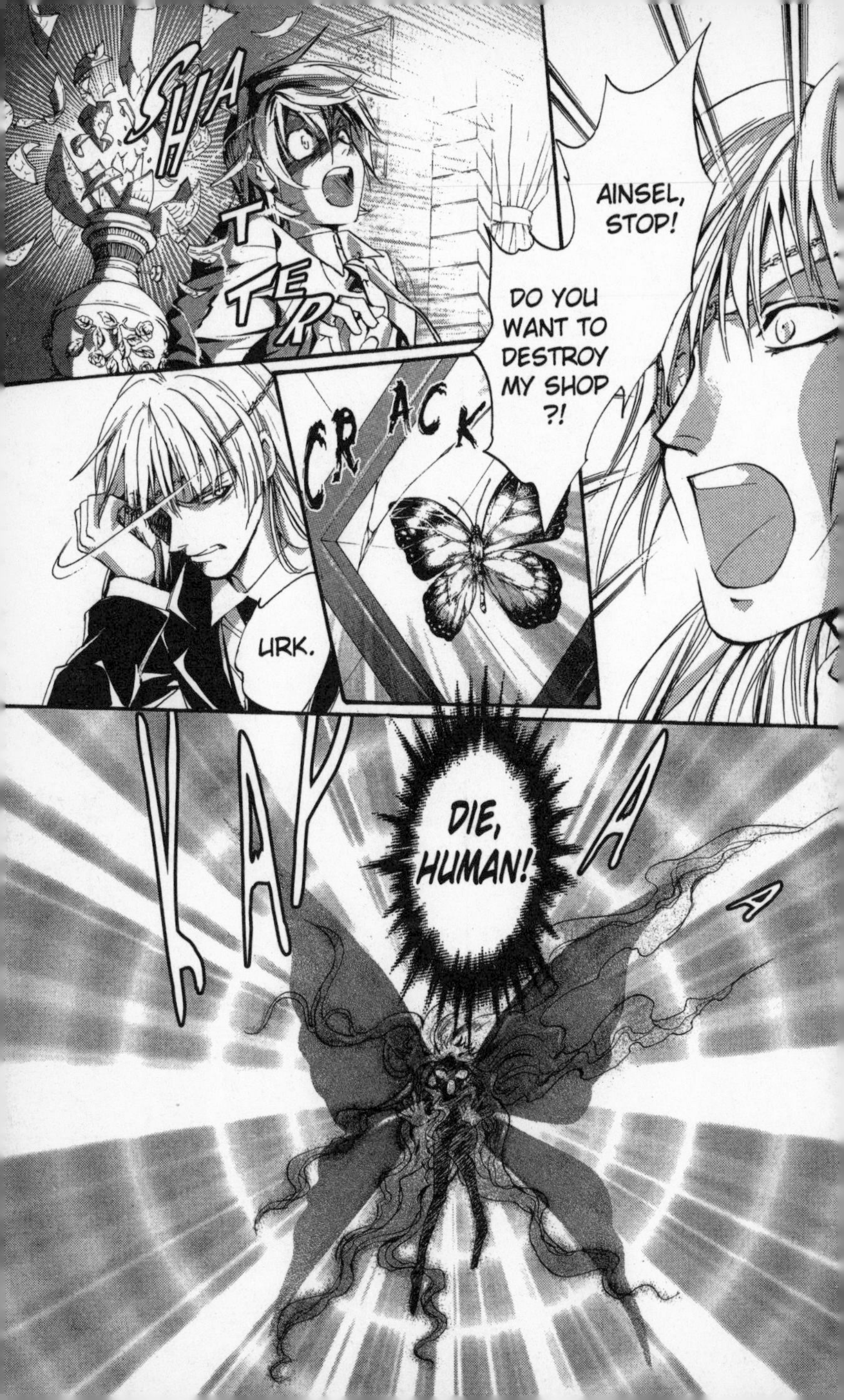
AINSEL, STOP!
DO YOU WANT TO DESTROY MY SHOP ?!
SHATTER
CRACK
URK.
DIE, HUMAN!

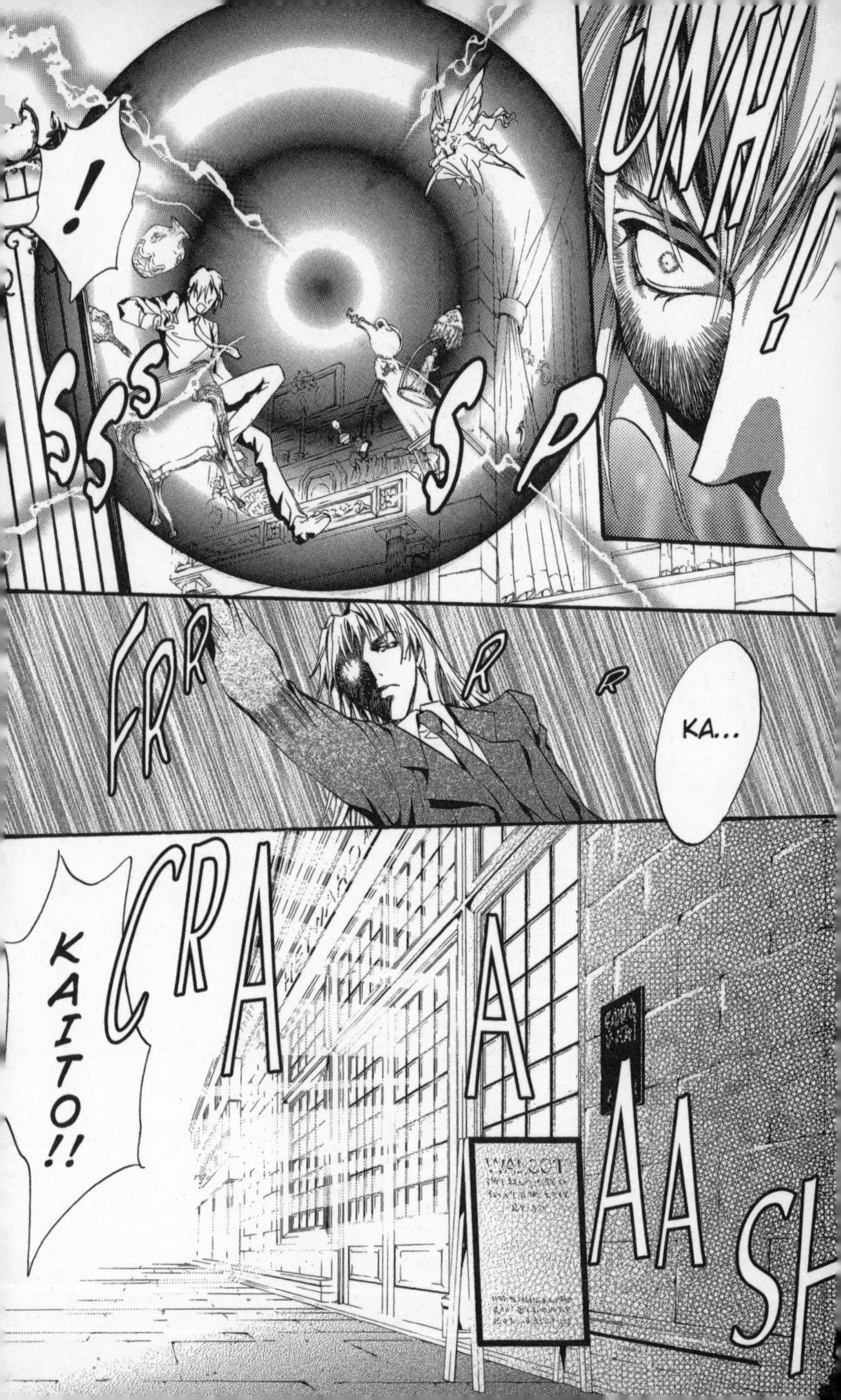

UNH!
!
SSSSP
KA...
FRRRR
CRAAAAASH
WALCOT
KAITO!!

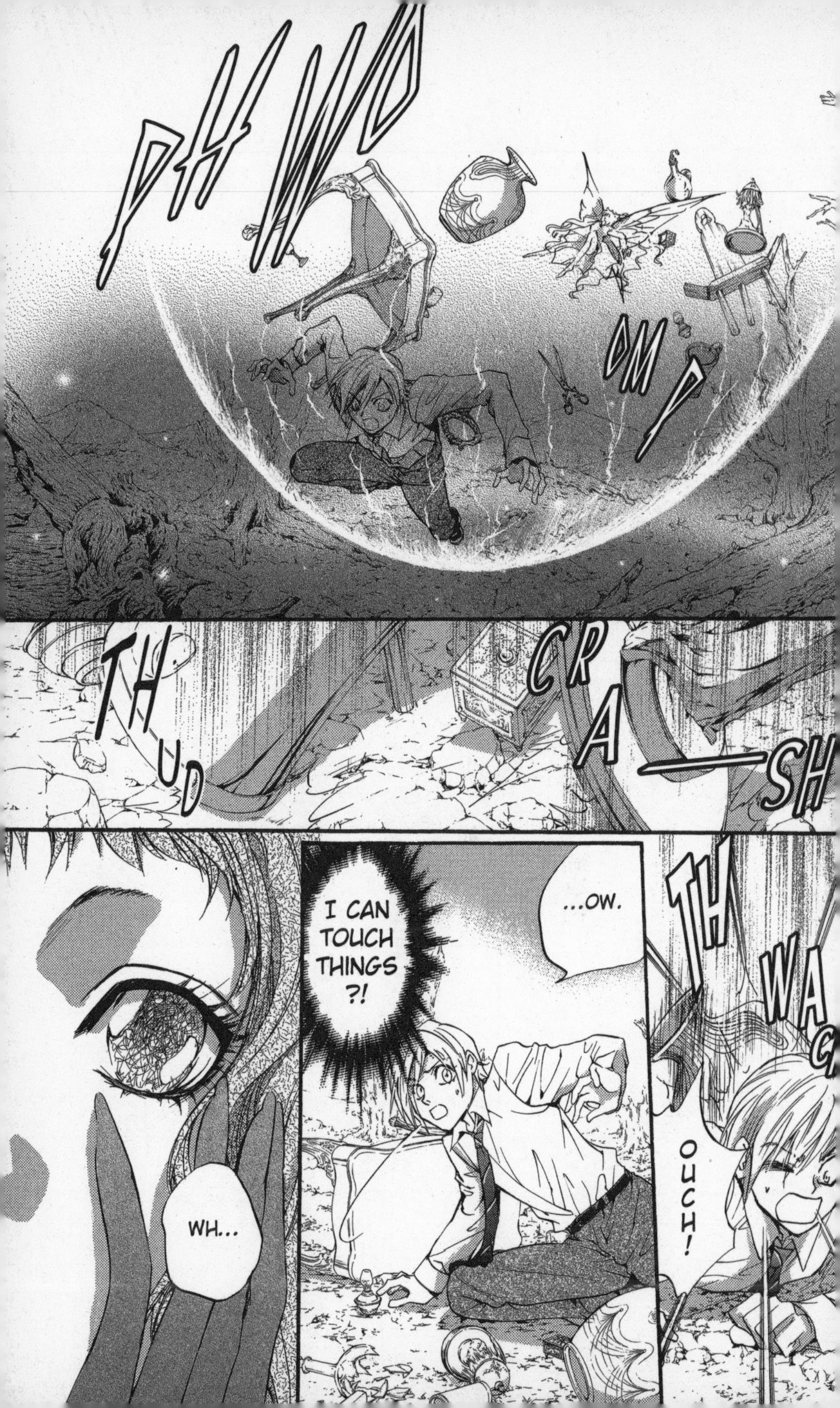
PHWO
OMP
CRA—SH
THUD
THWAG
OUCH!
...OW.
I CAN TOUCH THINGS?!
WH...

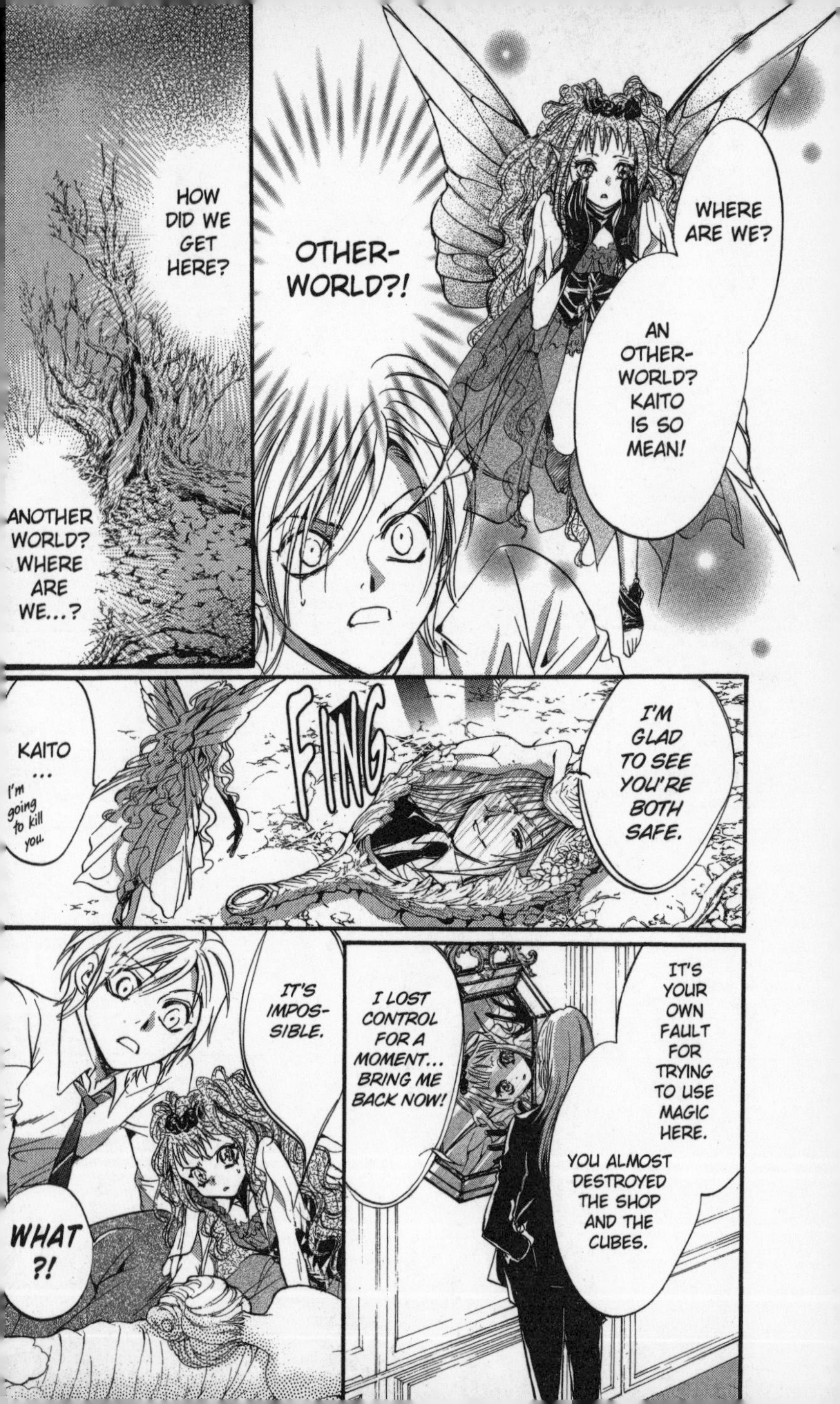
WHERE ARE WE?
AN OTHER-WORLD? KAITO IS SO MEAN!
OTHER-WORLD?!
HOW DID WE GET HERE?
ANOTHER WORLD? WHERE ARE WE...?
I'M GLAD TO SEE YOU'RE BOTH SAFE.
FING
KAITO ... I'm going to kill you.
IT'S YOUR OWN FAULT FOR TRYING TO USE MAGIC HERE.
YOU ALMOST DESTROYED THE SHOP AND THE CUBES.
I LOST CONTROL FOR A MOMENT... BRING ME BACK NOW!
IT'S IMPOSSIBLE.
WHAT?!

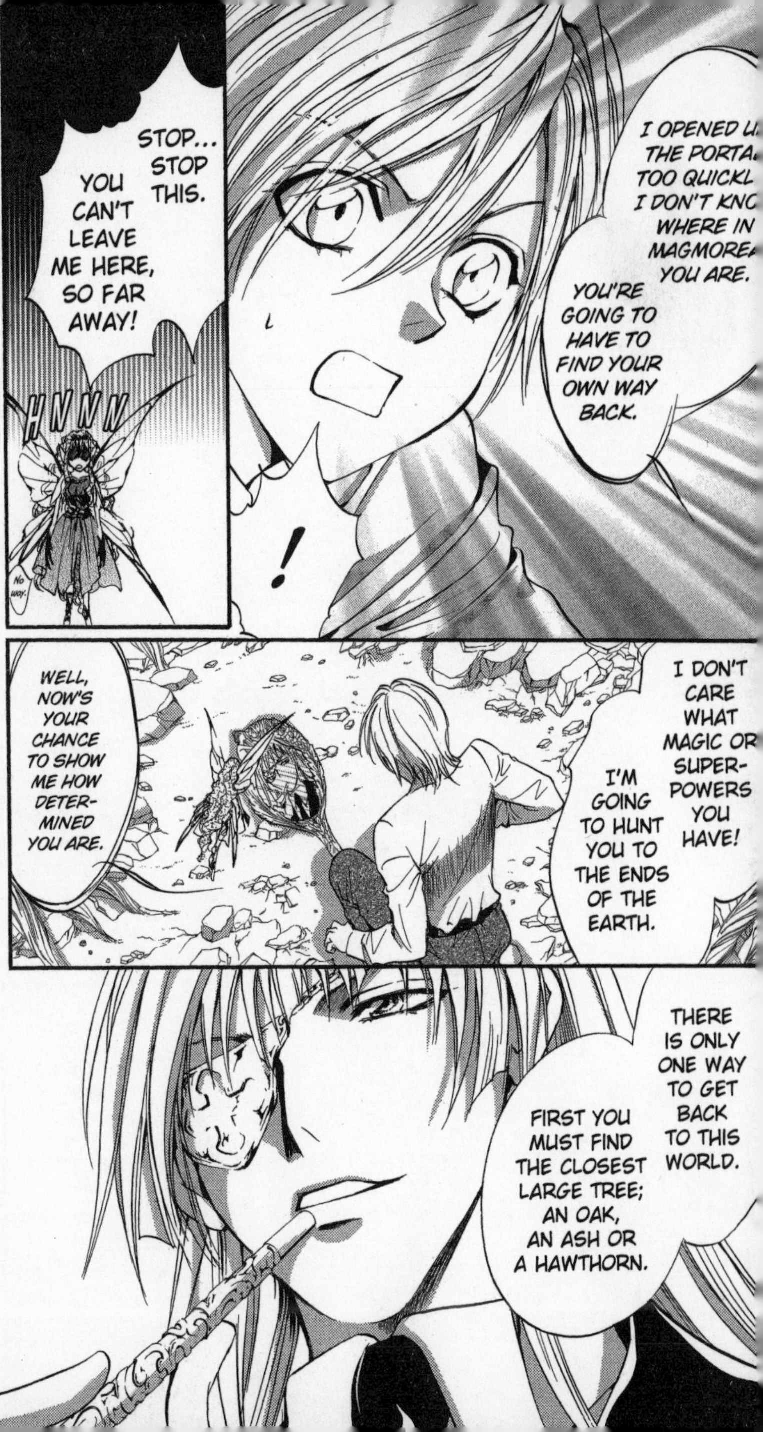
I OPENED U THE PORTA TOO QUICKL I DON'T KNO WHERE IN MAGMORE YOU ARE.
YOU'RE GOING TO HAVE TO FIND YOUR OWN WAY BACK.
!
STOP... STOP THIS.
YOU CAN'T LEAVE ME HERE, SO FAR AWAY!
HNNN
No way.
I DON'T CARE WHAT MAGIC OR SUPER-POWERS YOU HAVE!
I'M GOING TO HUNT YOU TO THE ENDS OF THE EARTH.
WELL, NOW'S YOUR CHANCE TO SHOW ME HOW DETER-MINED YOU ARE.
THERE IS ONLY ONE WAY TO GET BACK TO THIS WORLD.
FIRST YOU MUST FIND THE CLOSEST LARGE TREE; AN OAK, AN ASH OR A HAWTHORN.

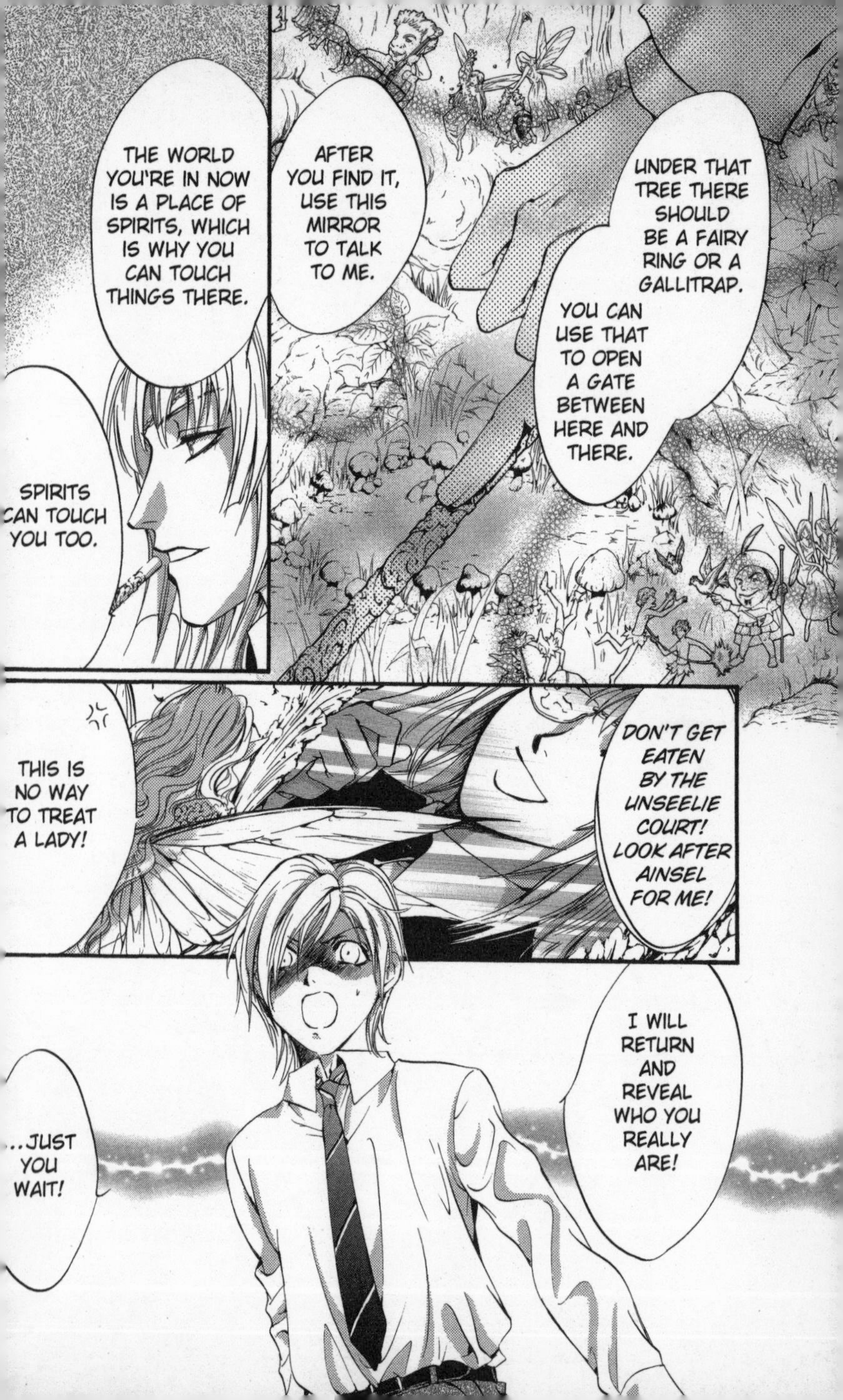
UNDER THAT TREE THERE SHOULD BE A FAIRY RING OR A GALLITRAP.
YOU CAN USE THAT TO OPEN A GATE BETWEEN HERE AND THERE.
AFTER YOU FIND IT, USE THIS MIRROR TO TALK TO ME.
THE WORLD YOU'RE IN NOW IS A PLACE OF SPIRITS, WHICH IS WHY YOU CAN TOUCH THINGS THERE.
SPIRITS CAN TOUCH YOU TOO.
DON'T GET EATEN BY THE UNSEELIE COURT! LOOK AFTER AINSEL FOR ME!
THIS IS NO WAY TO TREAT A LADY!
I WILL RETURN AND REVEAL WHO YOU REALLY ARE!
...JUST YOU WAIT!

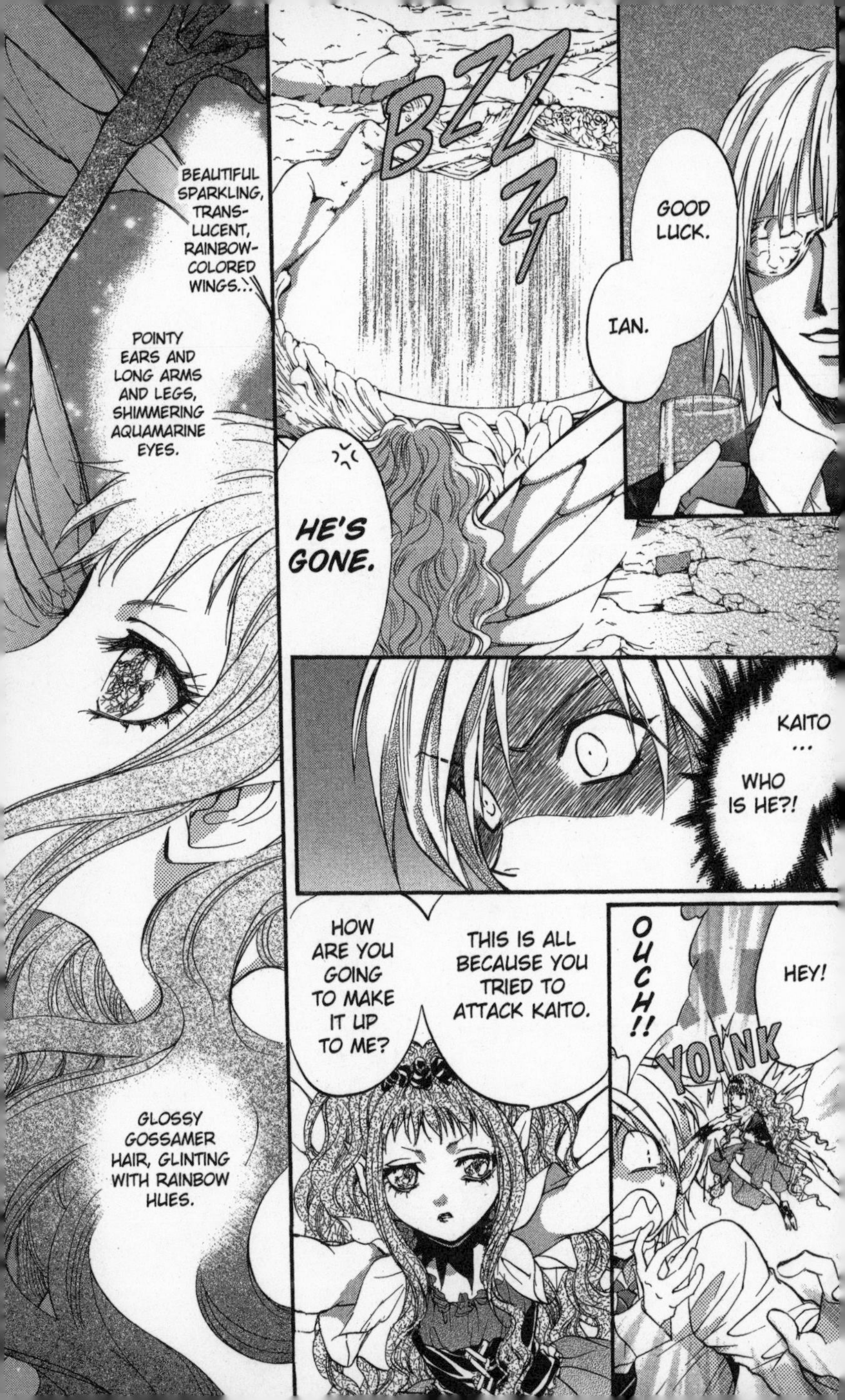
GOOD LUCK.
IAN.
BZZZT
HE'S GONE.
KAITO ...
WHO IS HE?!
HEY!
OUCH!!
YOINK
THIS IS ALL BECAUSE YOU TRIED TO ATTACK KAITO.
HOW ARE YOU GOING TO MAKE IT UP TO ME?
BEAUTIFUL SPARKLING, TRANS-LUCENT, RAINBOW-COLORED WINGS...
POINTY EARS AND LONG ARMS AND LEGS, SHIMMERING AQUAMARINE EYES.
GLOSSY GOSSAMER HAIR, GLINTING WITH RAINBOW HUES.

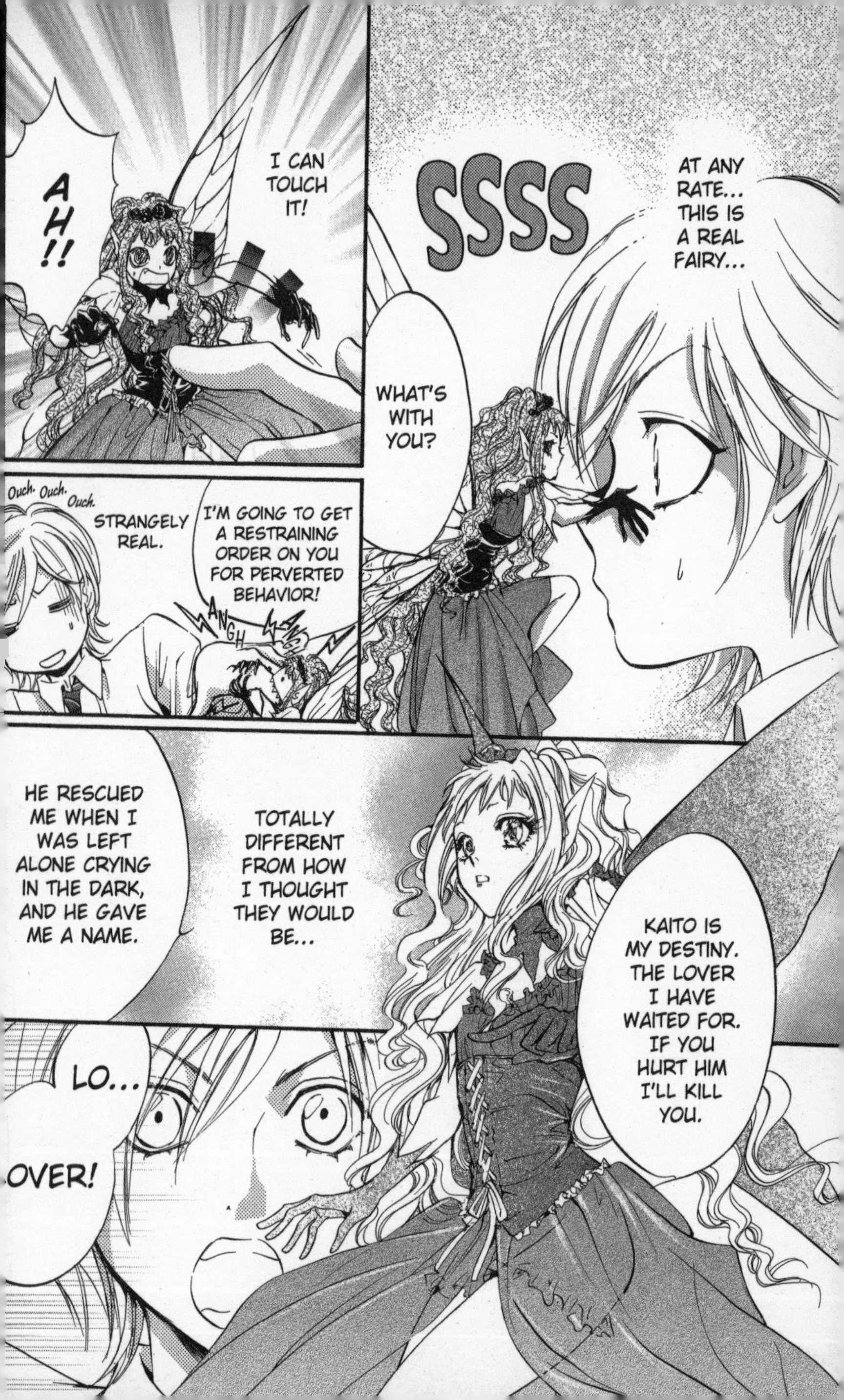
SSSS
AT ANY RATE... THIS IS A REAL FAIRY...
WHAT'S WITH YOU?
I CAN TOUCH IT!
AH!!
I'M GOING TO GET A RESTRAINING ORDER ON YOU FOR PERVERTED BEHAVIOR!
STRANGELY REAL.
Ouch. Ouch. Ouch.
ANGH
ANGH
KAITO IS MY DESTINY. THE LOVER I HAVE WAITED FOR. IF YOU HURT HIM I'LL KILL YOU.
TOTALLY DIFFERENT FROM HOW I THOUGHT THEY WOULD BE...
HE RESCUED ME WHEN I WAS LEFT ALONE CRYING IN THE DARK, AND HE GAVE ME A NAME.
LO...
OVER!

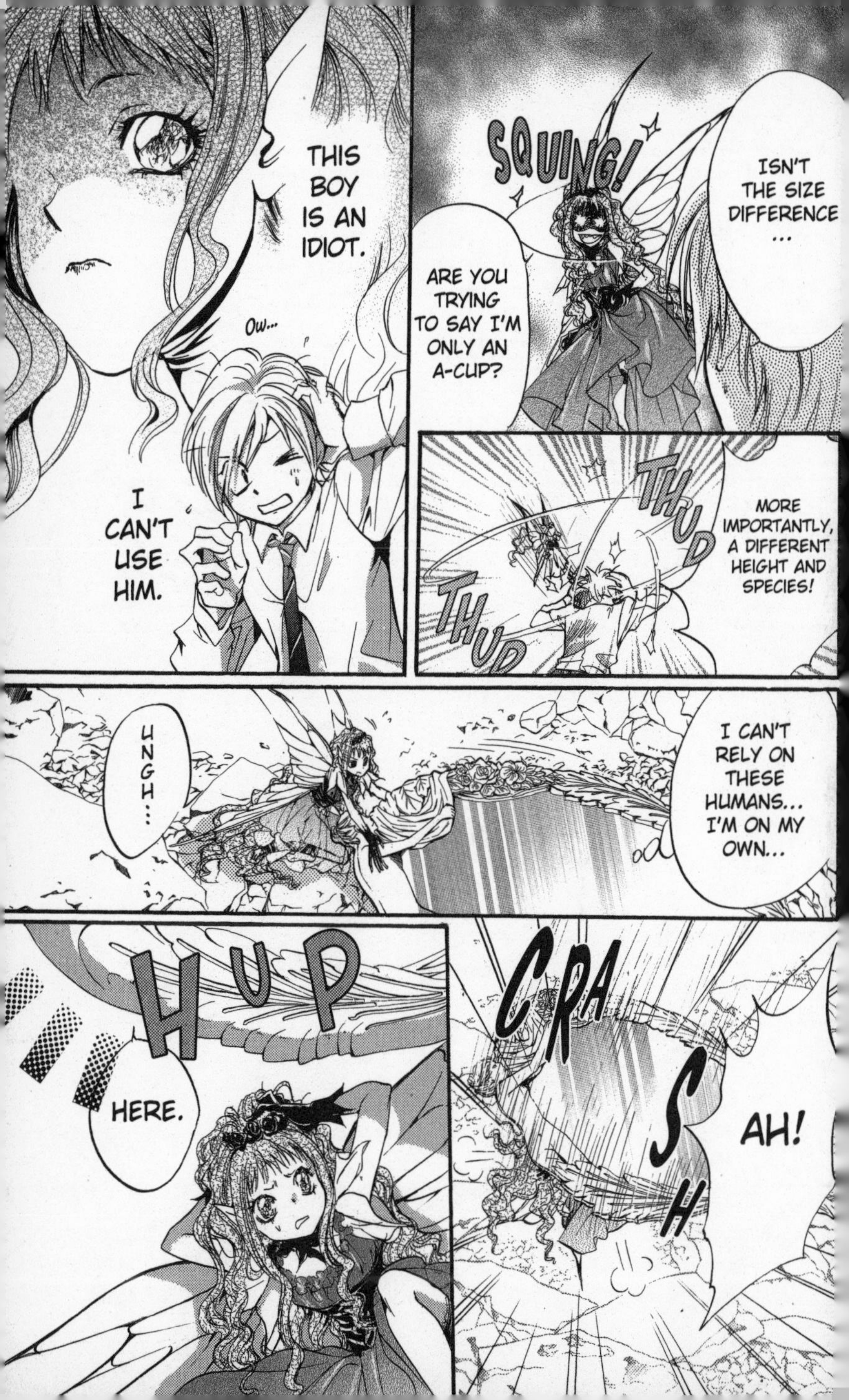
ISN'T THE SIZE DIFFERENCE ...
SQUING!
ARE YOU TRYING TO SAY I'M ONLY AN A-CUP?
MORE IMPORTANTLY, A DIFFERENT HEIGHT AND SPECIES!
THUD
THUD
THIS BOY IS AN IDIOT.
OW...
I CAN'T USE HIM.
I CAN'T RELY ON THESE HUMANS... I'M ON MY OWN...
UNGH...
CRASH
AH!
HUP
HERE.

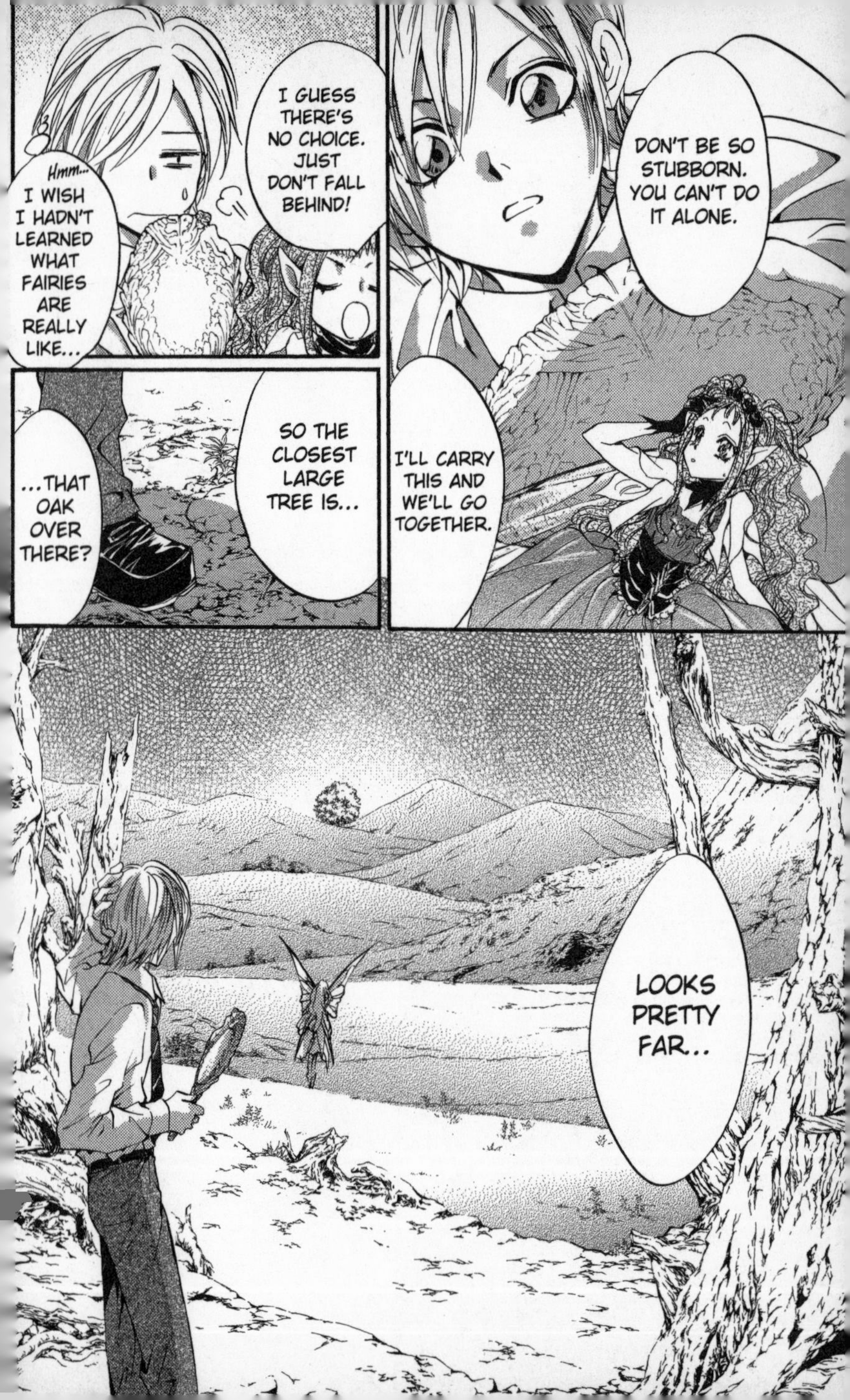
DON'T BE SO STUBBORN. YOU CAN'T DO IT ALONE.
I'LL CARRY THIS AND WE'LL GO TOGETHER.
I GUESS THERE'S NO CHOICE. JUST DON'T FALL BEHIND!
Hmm... I WISH I HADN'T LEARNED WHAT FAIRIES ARE REALLY LIKE...
SO THE CLOSEST LARGE TREE IS...
...THAT OAK OVER THERE?
LOOKS PRETTY FAR...

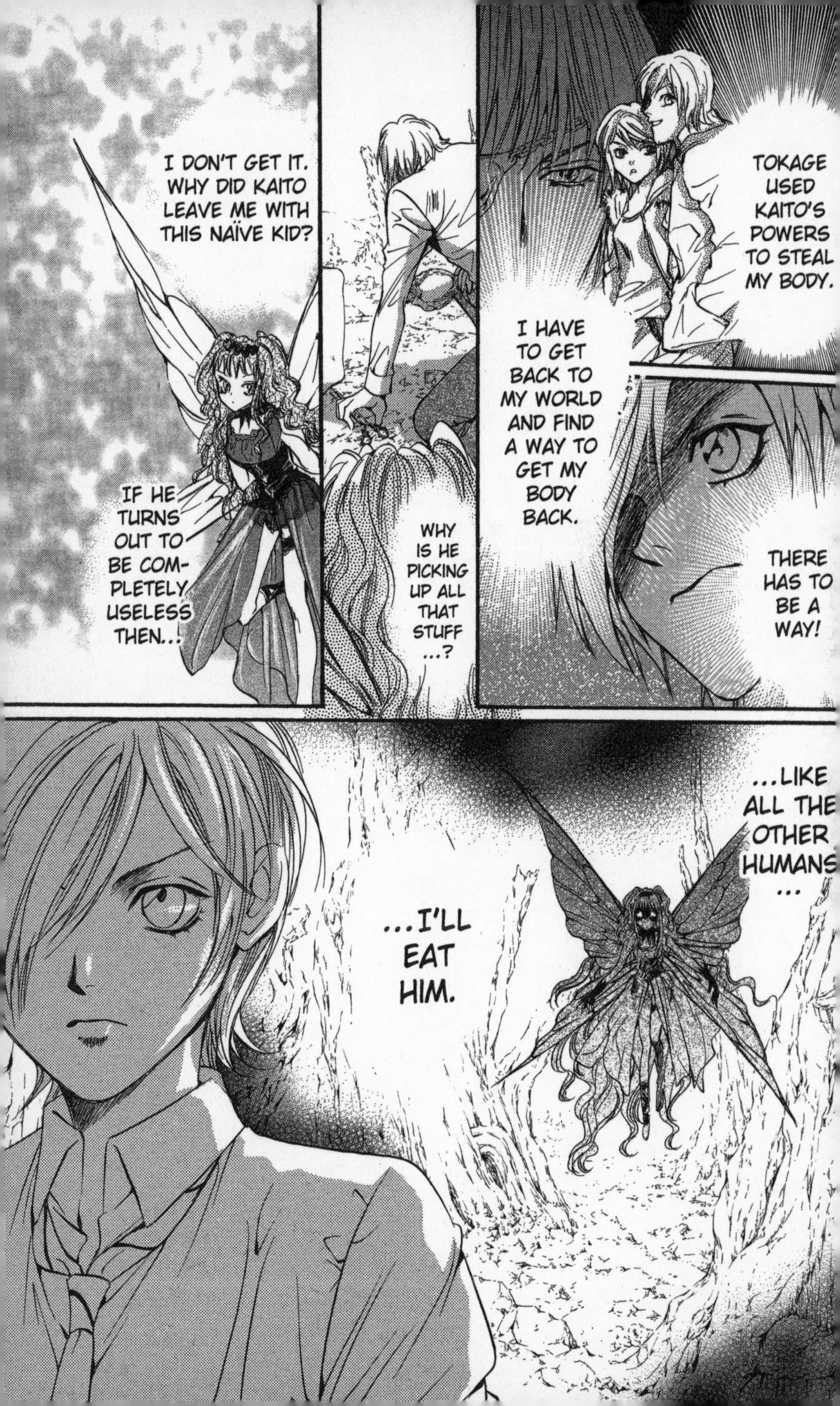
TOKAGE USED KAITO'S POWERS TO STEAL MY BODY.
I HAVE TO GET BACK TO MY WORLD AND FIND A WAY TO GET MY BODY BACK.
THERE HAS TO BE A WAY!
WHY IS HE PICKING UP ALL THAT STUFF ...?
I DON'T GET IT. WHY DID KAITO LEAVE ME WITH THIS NAÏVE KID?
IF HE TURNS OUT TO BE COM-PLETELY USELESS THEN...
...LIKE ALL THE OTHER HUMANS ...
...I'LL EAT HIM.

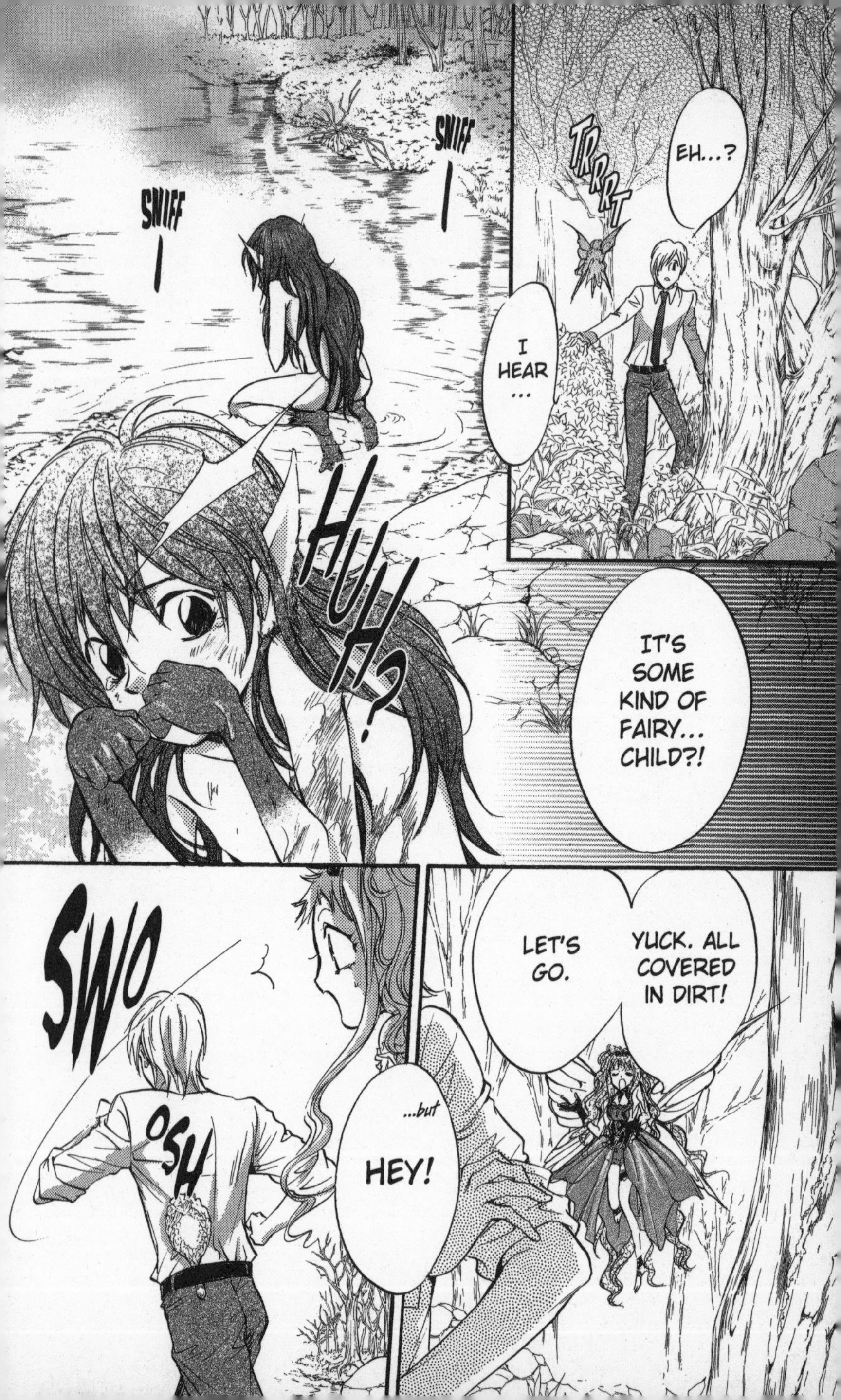

TRRRT
EH...?
I HEAR...
SNIFF
SNIFF
HUH?
IT'S SOME KIND OF FAIRY... CHILD?!
YUCK. ALL COVERED IN DIRT!
LET'S GO.
...but
HEY!
SWOOSH

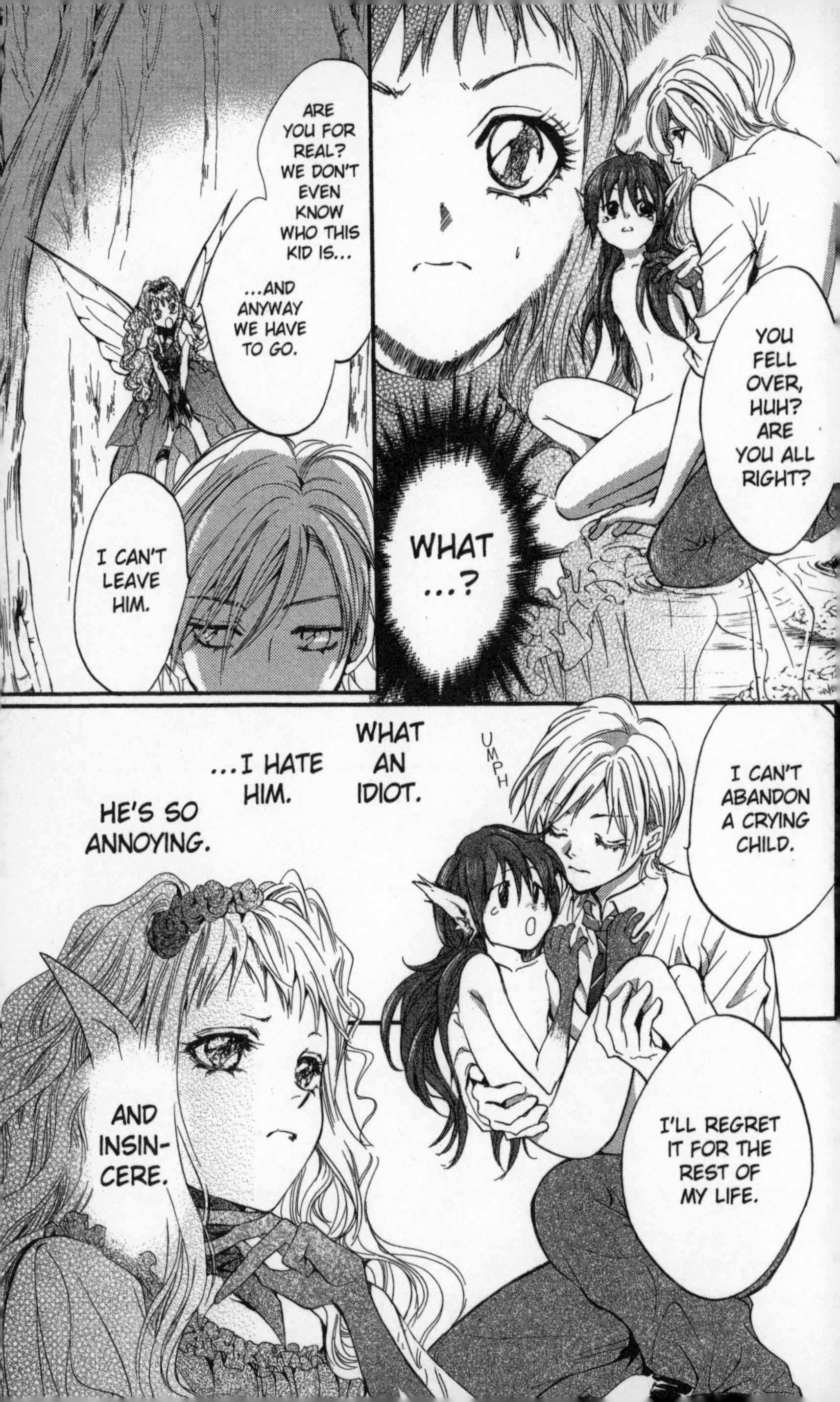
YOU FELL OVER, HUH? ARE YOU ALL RIGHT?
WHAT ...?
ARE YOU FOR REAL? WE DON'T EVEN KNOW WHO THIS KID IS...
...AND ANYWAY WE HAVE TO GO.
I CAN'T LEAVE HIM.
I CAN'T ABANDON A CRYING CHILD.
UMPH
WHAT AN IDIOT.
...I HATE HIM.
HE'S SO ANNOYING.
I'LL REGRET IT FOR THE REST OF MY LIFE.
AND INSINCERE.

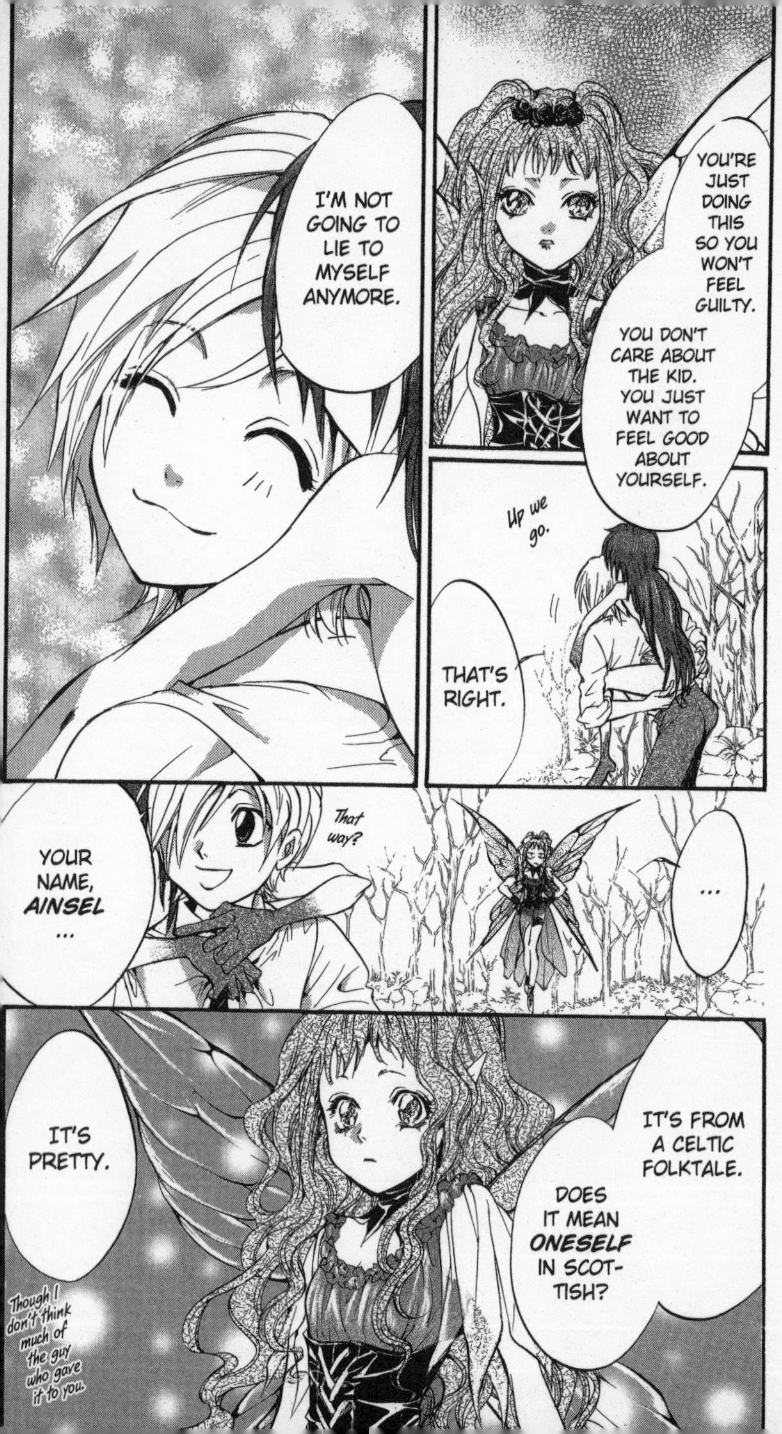
YOU'RE JUST DOING THIS SO YOU WON'T FEEL GUILTY.
YOU DON'T CARE ABOUT THE KID. YOU JUST WANT TO FEEL GOOD ABOUT YOURSELF.
Up we go.
THAT'S RIGHT.
I'M NOT GOING TO LIE TO MYSELF ANYMORE.
...
That way?
YOUR NAME, *AINSEL* ...
IT'S FROM A CELTIC FOLKTALE.
DOES IT MEAN *ONESELF* IN SCOT-TISH?
IT'S PRETTY.
Though I don't think much of the guy who gave it to you.

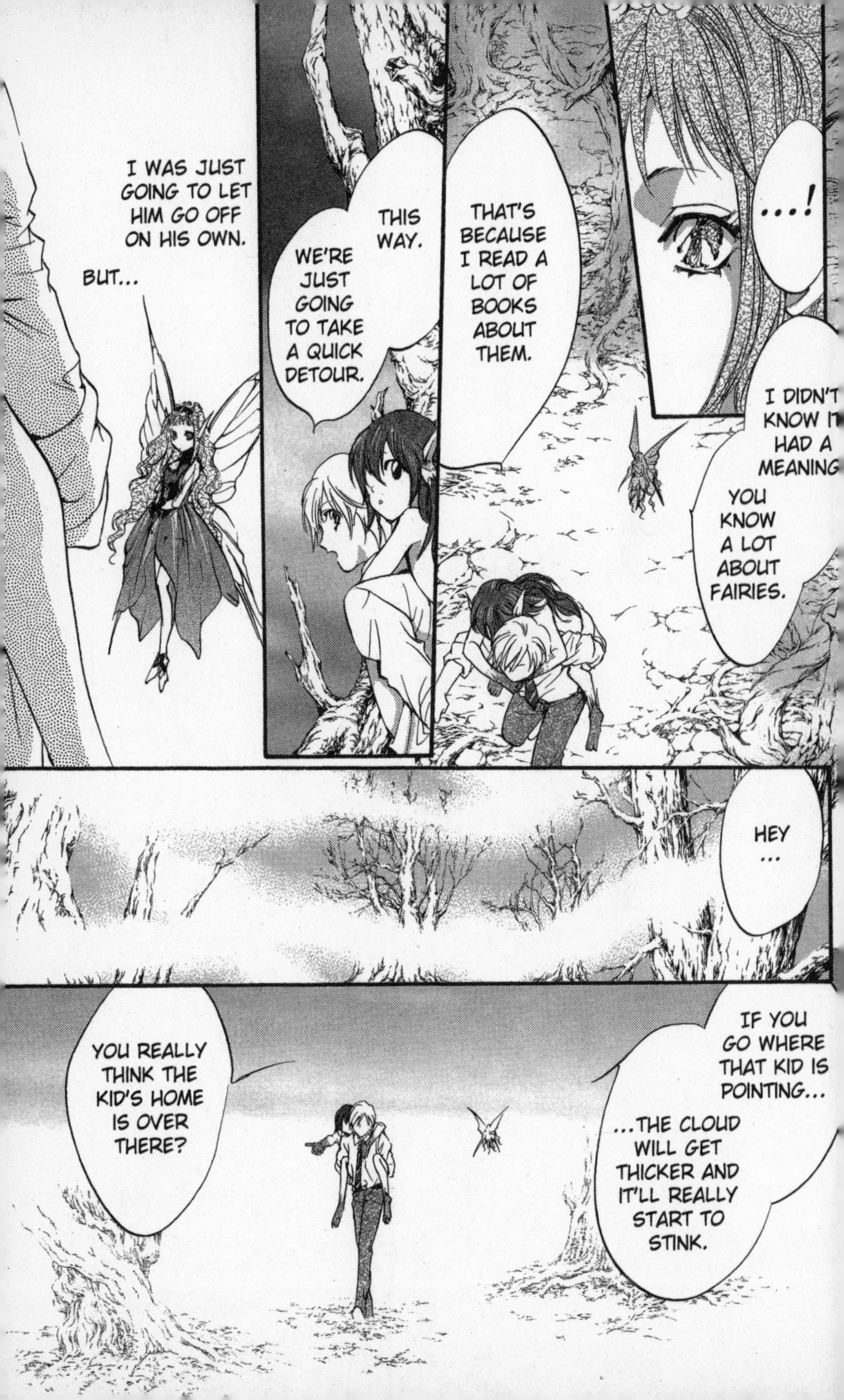
...!
I DIDN'T KNOW IT HAD A MEANING
YOU KNOW A LOT ABOUT FAIRIES.
THAT'S BECAUSE I READ A LOT OF BOOKS ABOUT THEM.
THIS WAY.
WE'RE JUST GOING TO TAKE A QUICK DETOUR.
I WAS JUST GOING TO LET HIM GO OFF ON HIS OWN.
BUT...
HEY...
IF YOU GO WHERE THAT KID IS POINTING...
...THE CLOUD WILL GET THICKER AND IT'LL REALLY START TO STINK.
YOU REALLY THINK THE KID'S HOME IS OVER THERE?

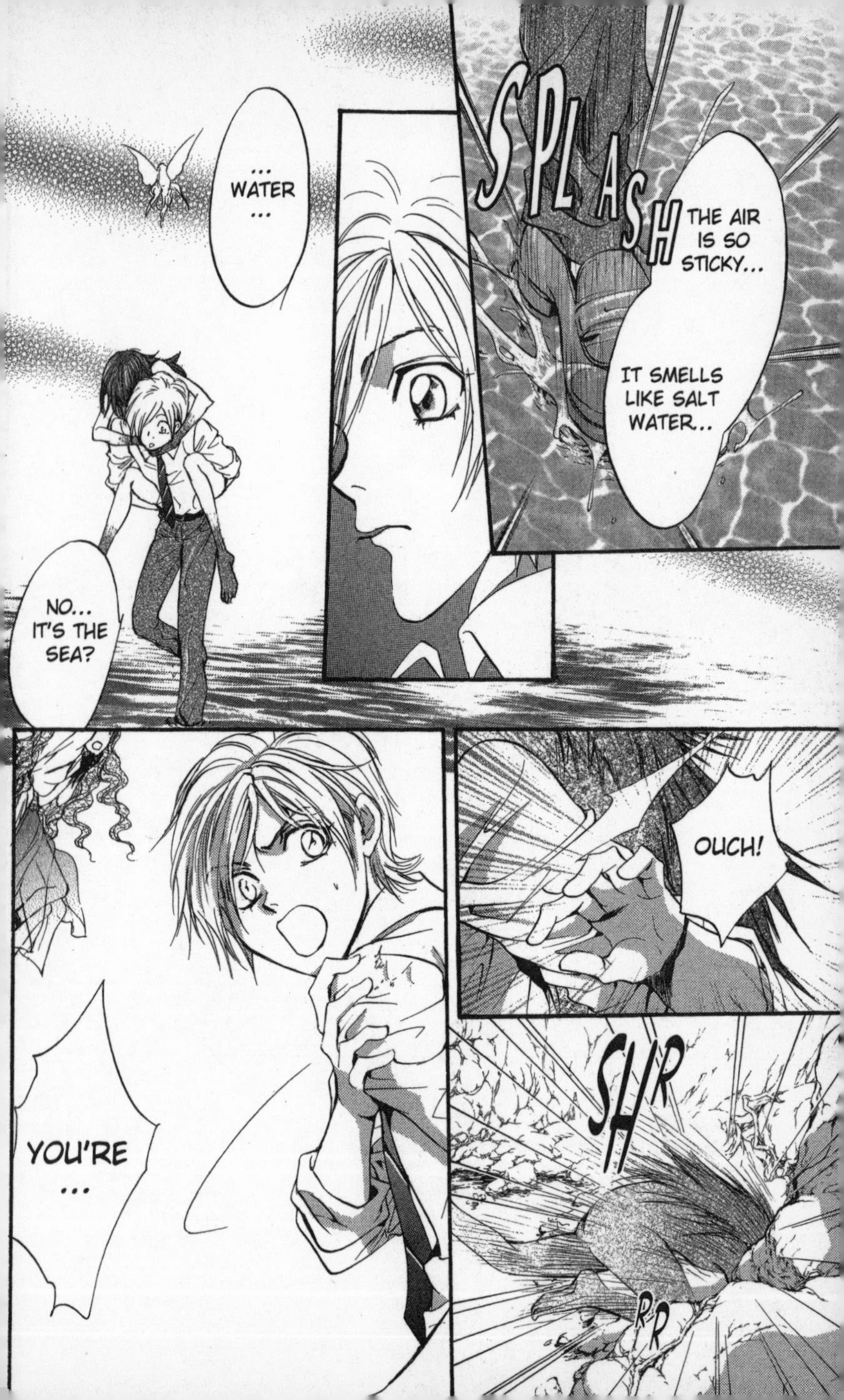
SPLASH
THE AIR IS SO STICKY...
IT SMELLS LIKE SALT WATER..
... WATER ...
NO... IT'S THE SEA?
OUCH!
SHRRR
YOU'RE ...

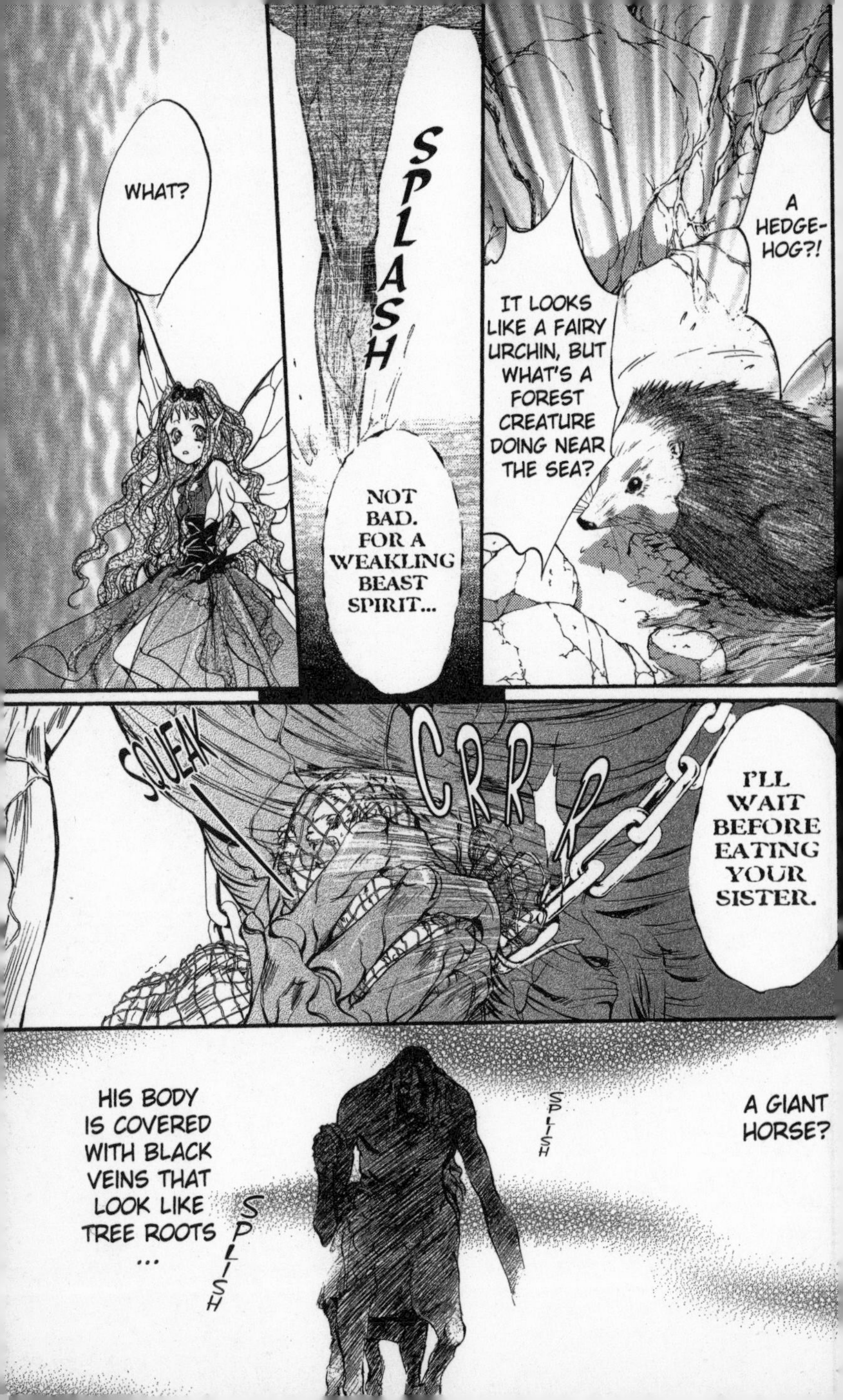
A HEDGE-HOG?!
IT LOOKS LIKE A FAIRY URCHIN, BUT WHAT'S A FOREST CREATURE DOING NEAR THE SEA?
SPLASH
NOT BAD. FOR A WEAKLING BEAST SPIRIT...
WHAT?
I'LL WAIT BEFORE EATING YOUR SISTER.
CRRR
SQUEAK
A GIANT HORSE?
SPLISH
SPLISH
HIS BODY IS COVERED WITH BLACK VEINS THAT LOOK LIKE TREE ROOTS ...

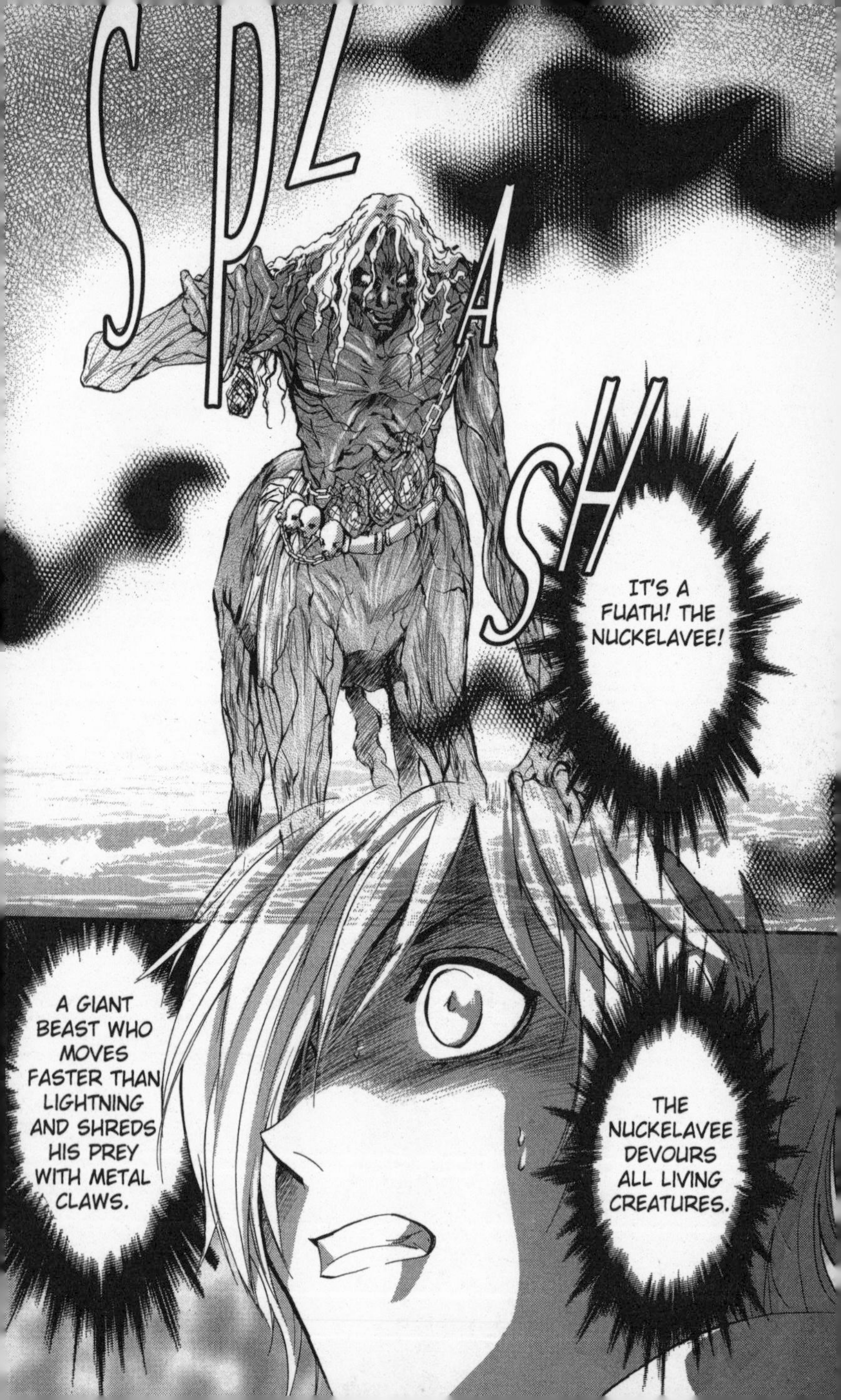
SPLASH
IT'S A FUATH! THE NUCKELAVEE!
THE NUCKELAVEE DEVOURS ALL LIVING CREATURES.
A GIANT BEAST WHO MOVES FASTER THAN LIGHTNING AND SHREDS HIS PREY WITH METAL CLAWS.

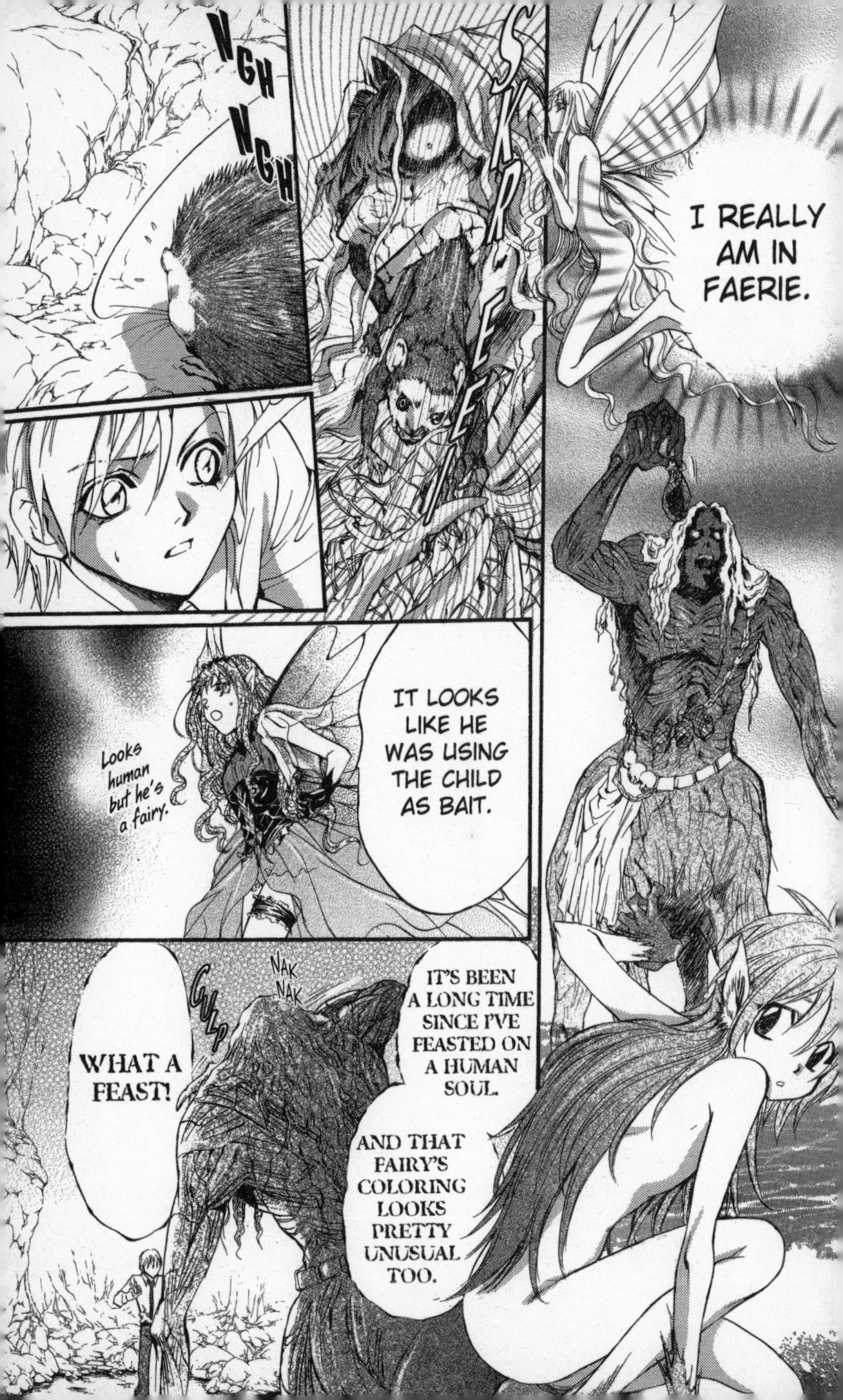
I REALLY AM IN FAERIE.
SKREEEE
NGH NGH
IT LOOKS LIKE HE WAS USING THE CHILD AS BAIT.
Looks human but he's a fairy.
IT'S BEEN A LONG TIME SINCE I'VE FEASTED ON A HUMAN SOUL.
AND THAT FAIRY'S COLORING LOOKS PRETTY UNUSUAL TOO.
NAK NAK
GULP
WHAT A FEAST!

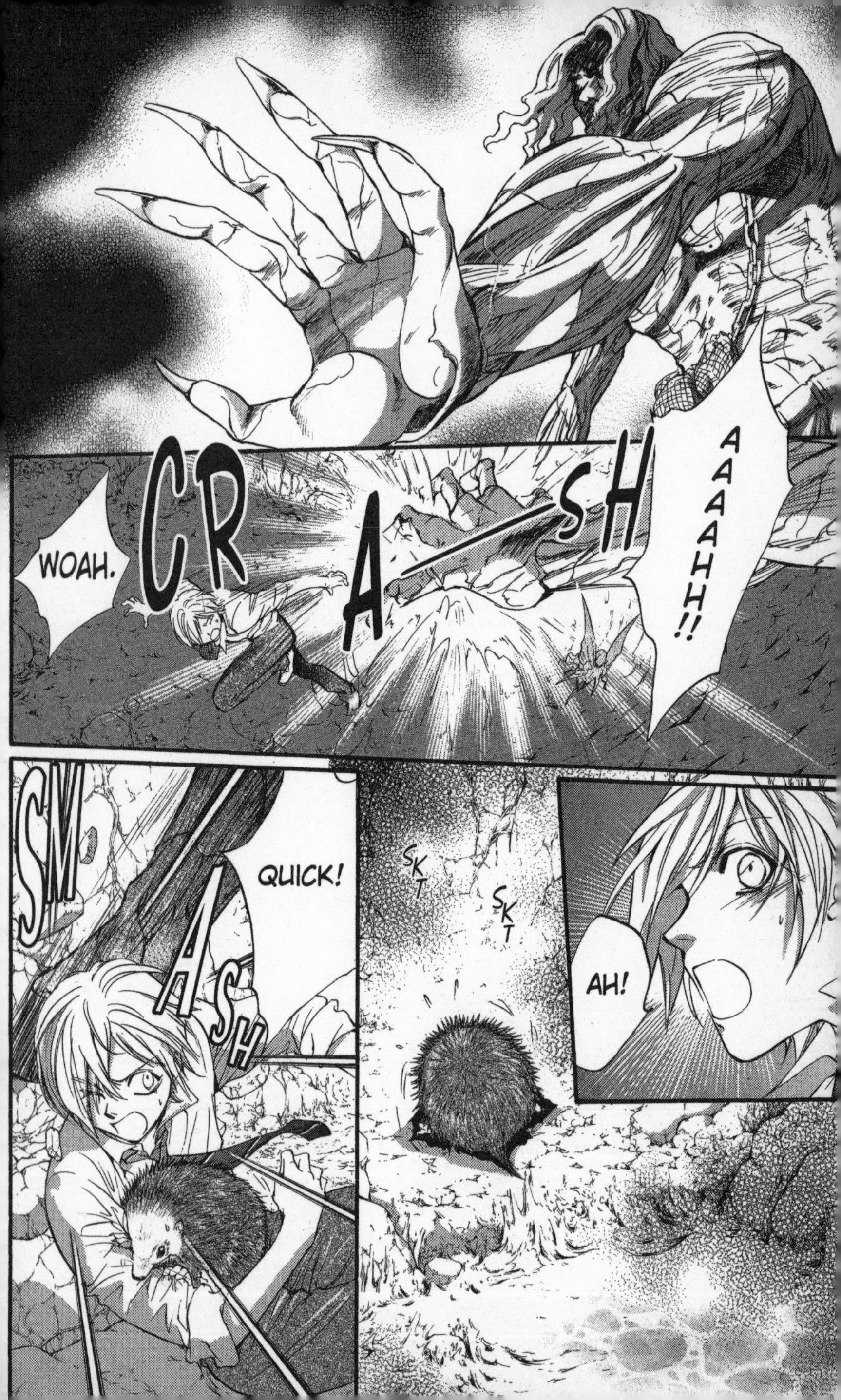
AAAAAHH!!
CRASH
WOAH.
AH!
SKT
SKT
SMASH
QUICK!

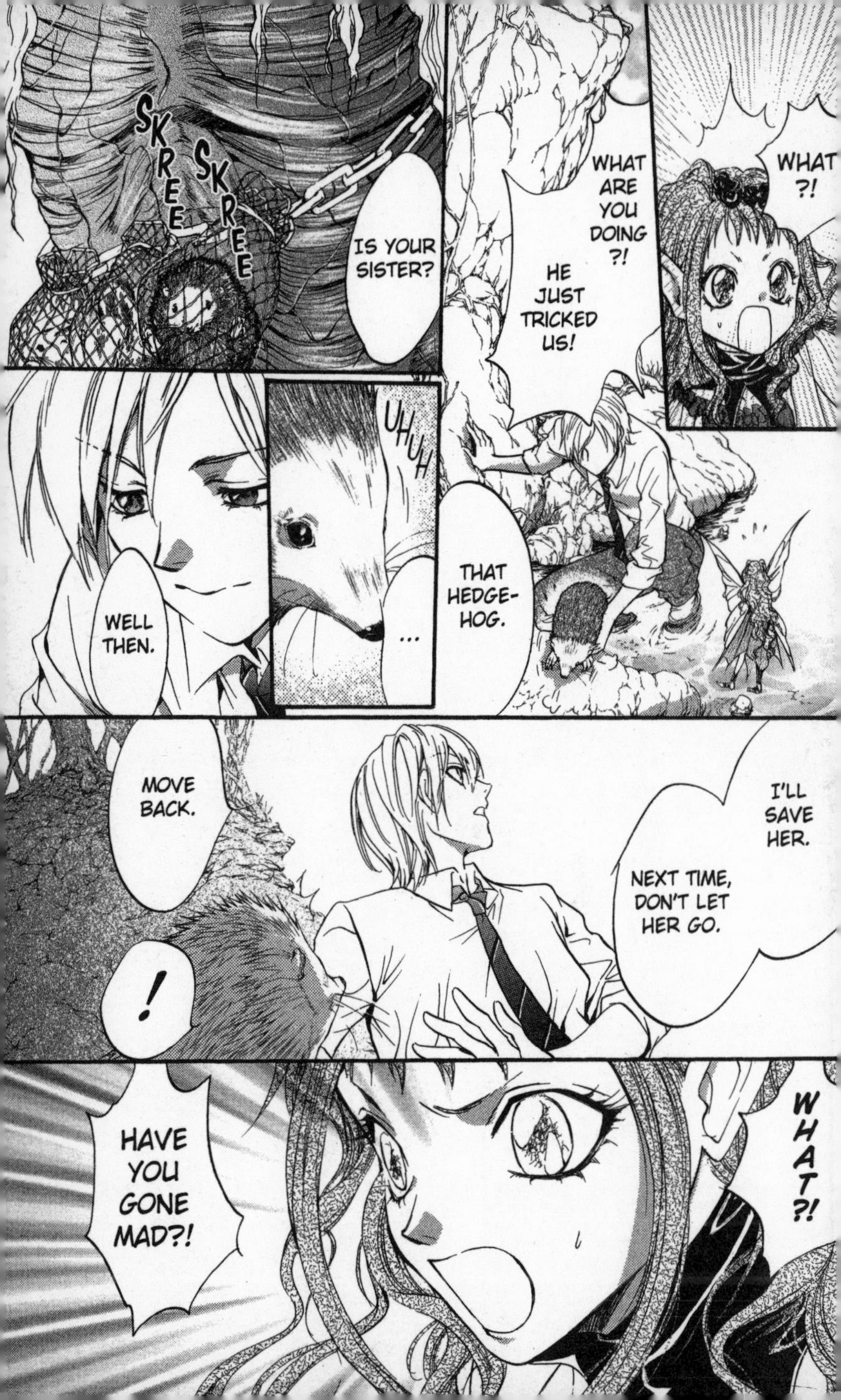
WHAT ?!
WHAT ARE YOU DOING ?!
HE JUST TRICKED US!
THAT HEDGE-HOG.
SKREE
SKREE
IS YOUR SISTER?
UHUH
...
WELL THEN.
I'LL SAVE HER.
NEXT TIME, DON'T LET HER GO.
MOVE BACK.
!
WHAT ?!
HAVE YOU GONE MAD?!

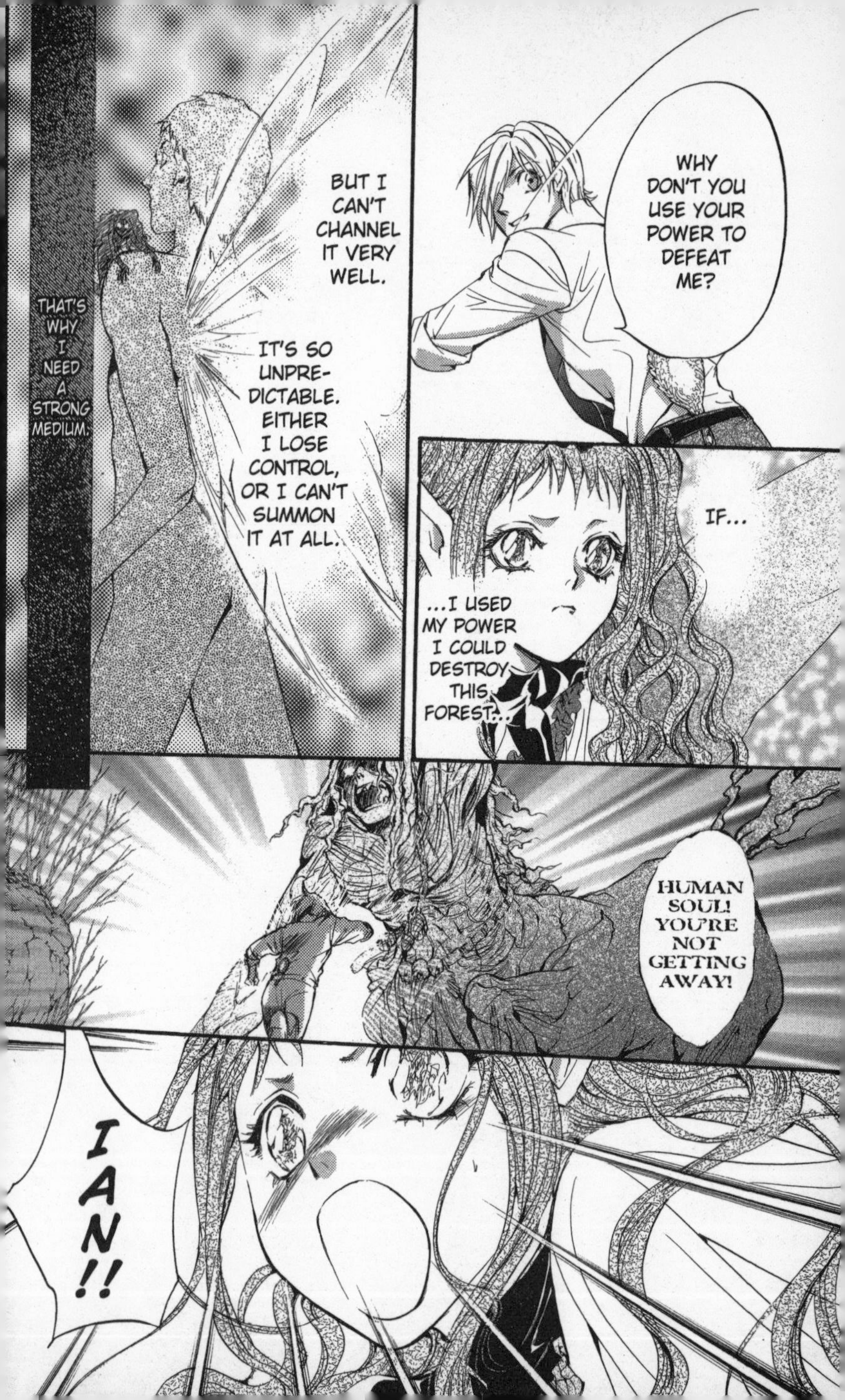

WHY DON'T YOU USE YOUR POWER TO DEFEAT ME?
IF...
...I USED MY POWER I COULD DESTROY THIS FOREST...
BUT I CAN'T CHANNEL IT VERY WELL.
IT'S SO UNPREDICTABLE. EITHER I LOSE CONTROL, OR I CAN'T SUMMON IT AT ALL.
THAT'S WHY I NEED A STRONG MEDIUM.
HUMAN SOUL! YOU'RE NOT GETTING AWAY!
IAN!!

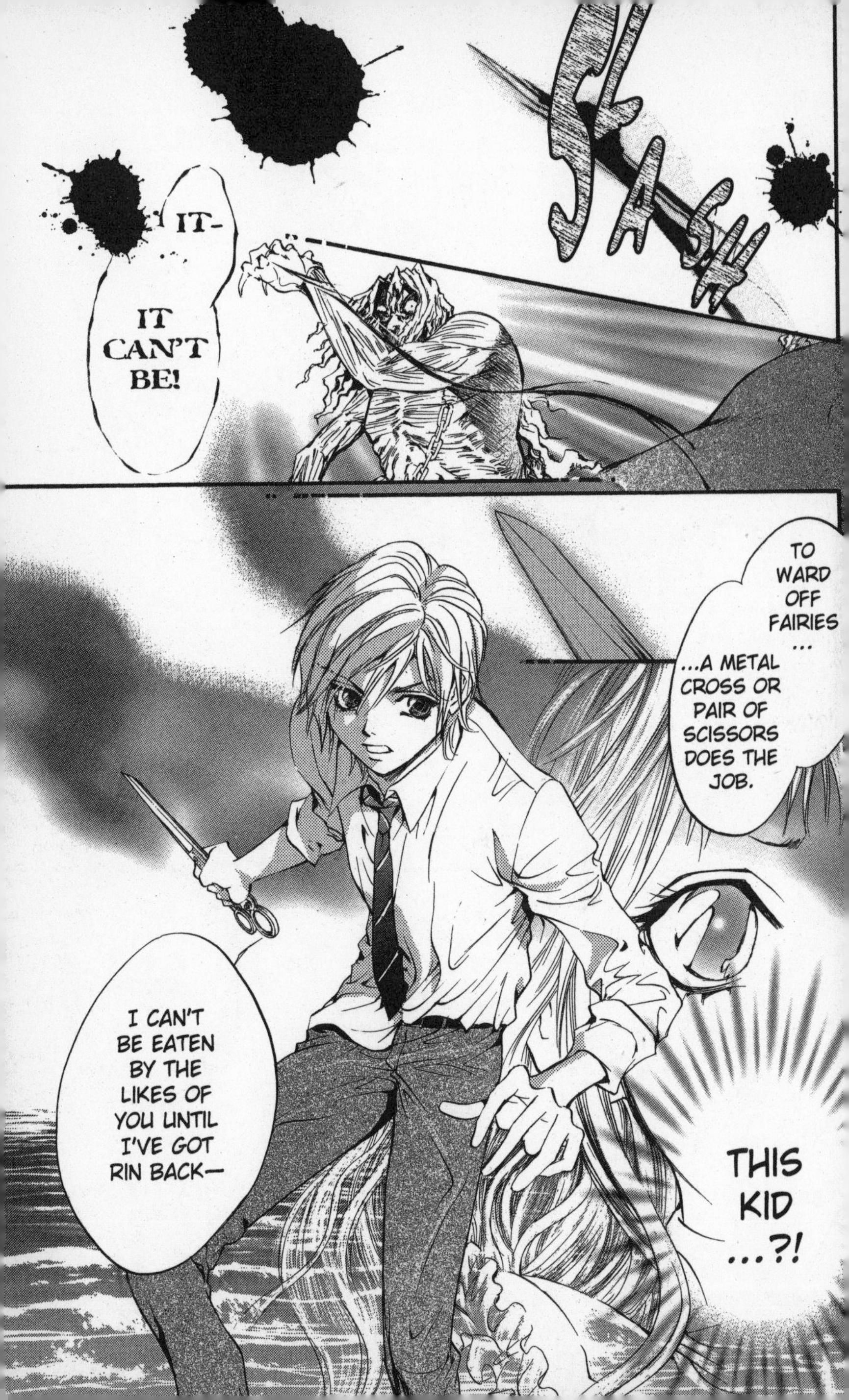
SLASH
IT-
IT CAN'T BE!
TO WARD OFF FAIRIES...
...A METAL CROSS OR PAIR OF SCISSORS DOES THE JOB.
I CAN'T BE EATEN BY THE LIKES OF YOU UNTIL I'VE GOT RIN BACK—
THIS KID...?!

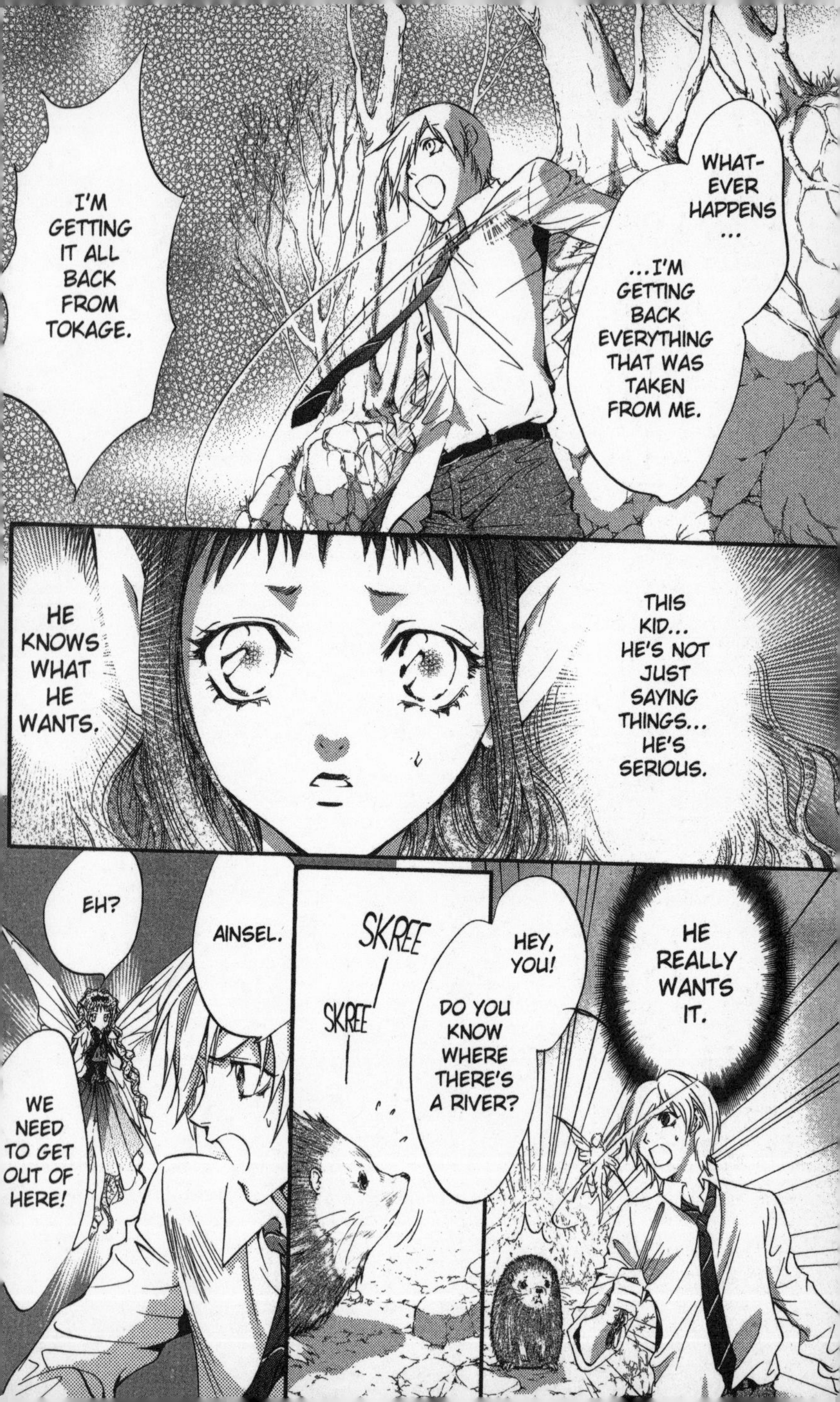
WHAT-EVER HAPPENS...
...I'M GETTING BACK EVERYTHING THAT WAS TAKEN FROM ME.
I'M GETTING IT ALL BACK FROM TOKAGE.
THIS KID... HE'S NOT JUST SAYING THINGS... HE'S SERIOUS.
HE KNOWS WHAT HE WANTS.
HE REALLY WANTS IT.
HEY, YOU!
DO YOU KNOW WHERE THERE'S A RIVER?
SKREE
SKREE
AINSEL.
EH?
WE NEED TO GET OUT OF HERE!

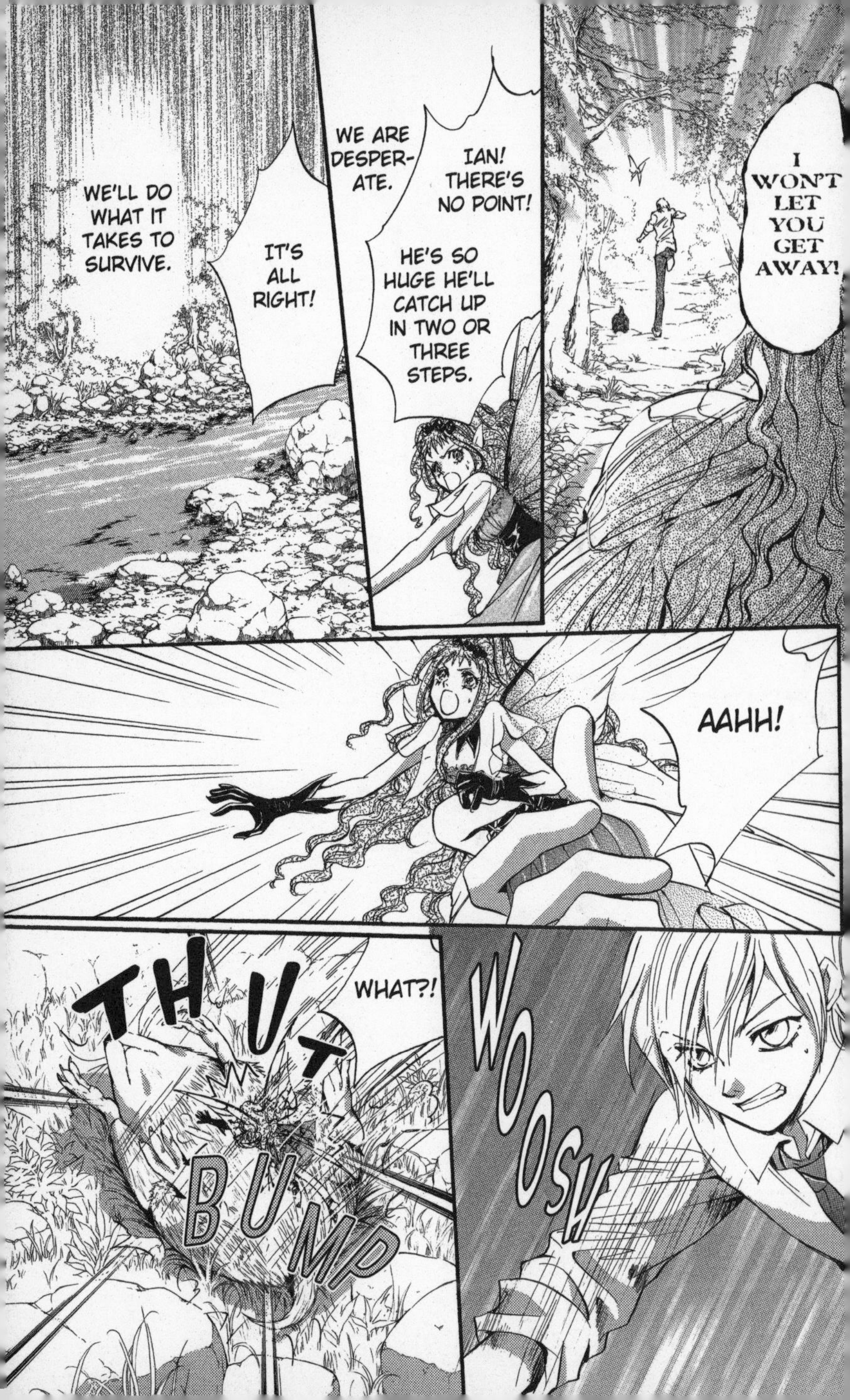
I WON'T LET YOU GET AWAY!
IAN! THERE'S NO POINT!
HE'S SO HUGE HE'LL CATCH UP IN TWO OR THREE STEPS.
WE ARE DESPER-ATE.
IT'S ALL RIGHT!
WE'LL DO WHAT IT TAKES TO SURVIVE.
AAHH!
WOOSH
WHAT?!
THUT
BUMP

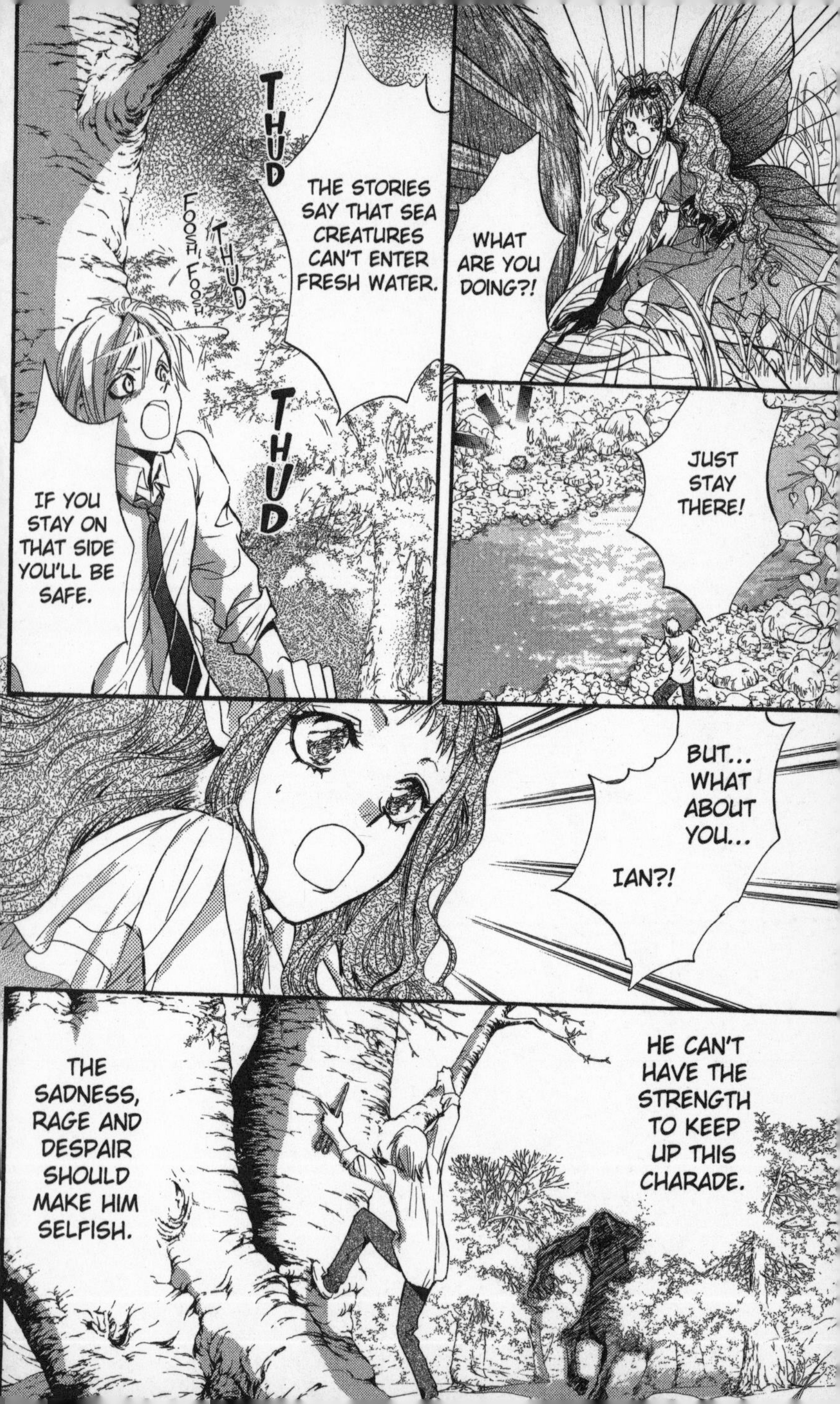
WHAT ARE YOU DOING?!
JUST STAY THERE!
THUD
THE STORIES SAY THAT SEA CREATURES CAN'T ENTER FRESH WATER.
THUD
FOOSH FOOSH
THUD
IF YOU STAY ON THAT SIDE YOU'LL BE SAFE.
BUT... WHAT ABOUT YOU...
IAN?!
HE CAN'T HAVE THE STRENGTH TO KEEP UP THIS CHARADE.
THE SADNESS, RAGE AND DESPAIR SHOULD MAKE HIM SELFISH.

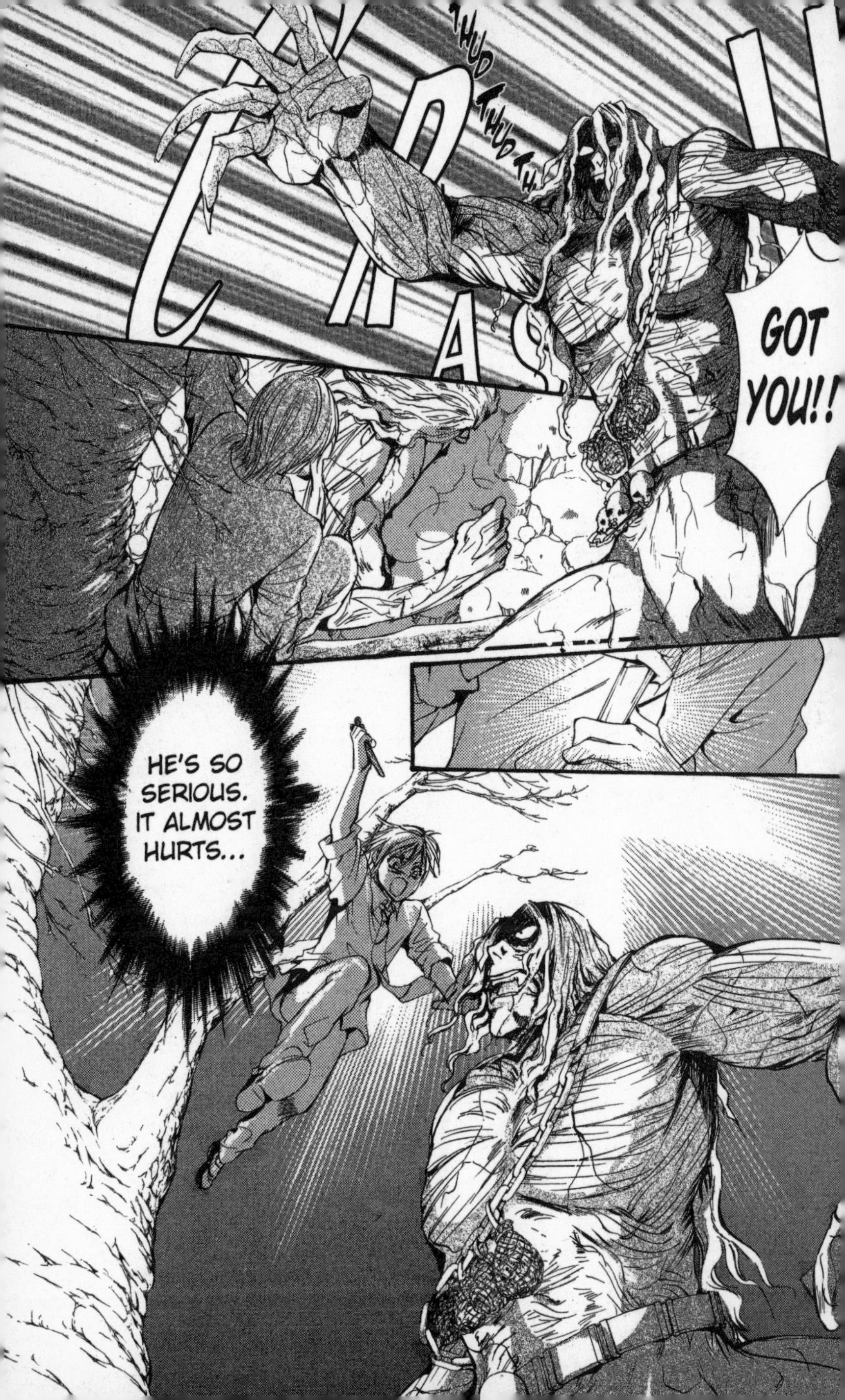
THUD THUD THUD THU
GOT YOU!!
HE'S SO SERIOUS. IT ALMOST HURTS...

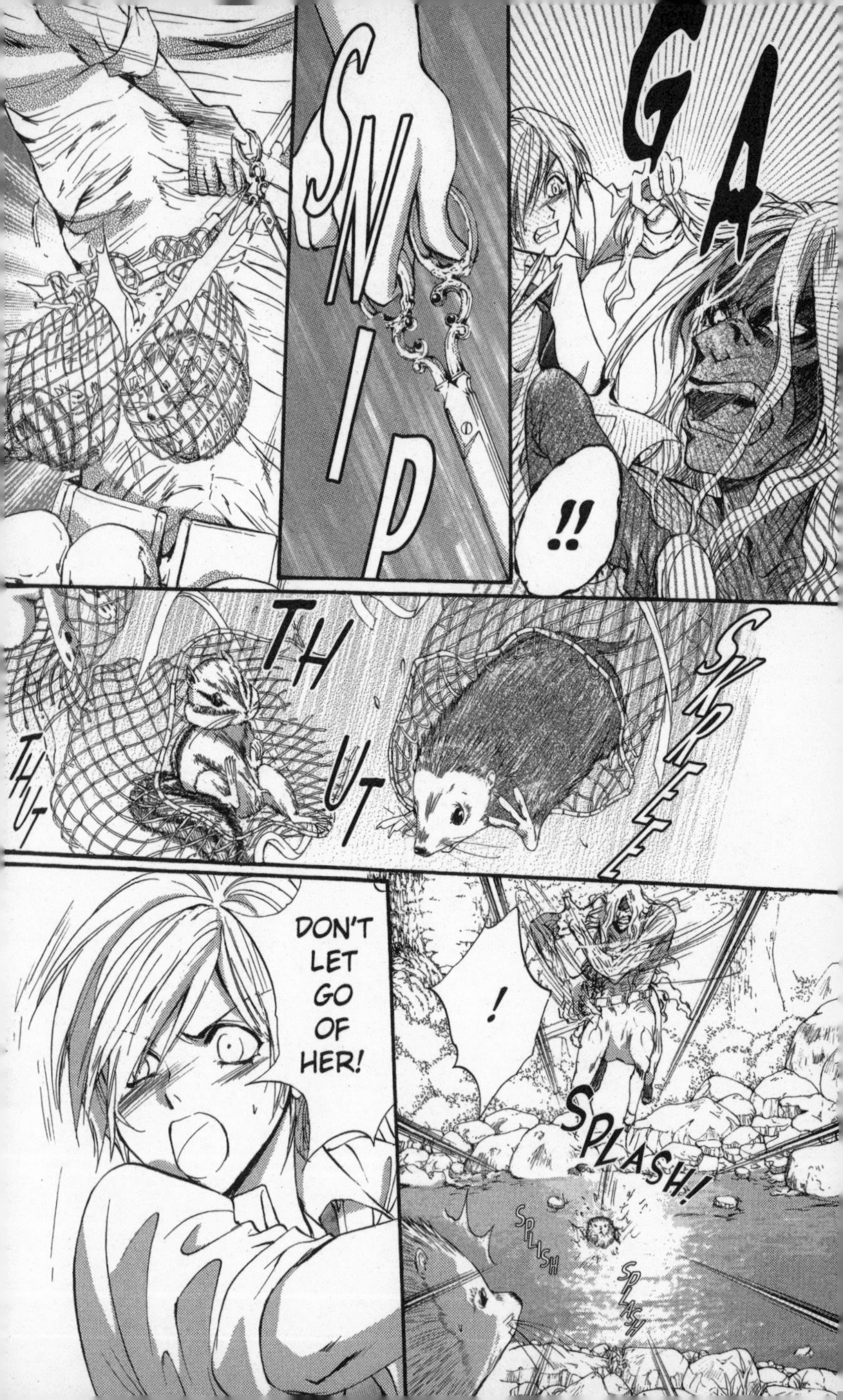

GA
!!
SNIP
SKREEE
THUT
THUT
!
SPLASH!
SPLISH
SPLASH
DON'T LET GO OF HER!

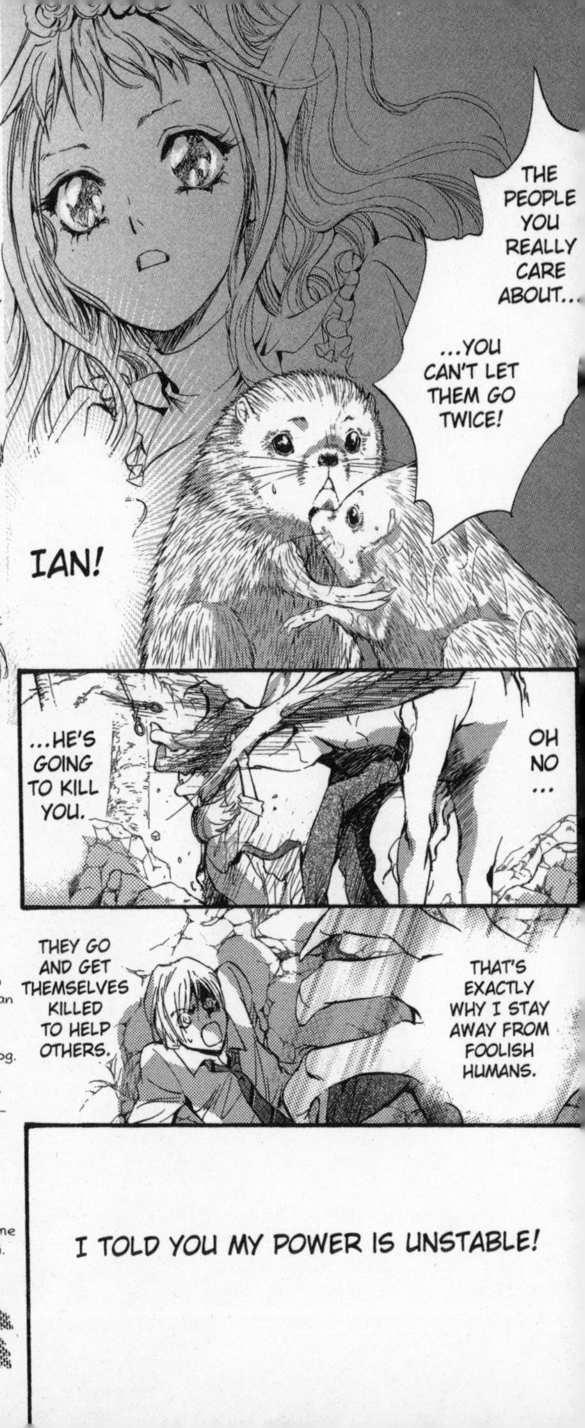
THE PEOPLE YOU REALLY CARE ABOUT...
...YOU CAN'T LET THEM GO TWICE!
IAN!
OH NO...
...HE'S GOING TO KILL YOU.
THEY GO AND GET THEMSELVES KILLED TO HELP OTHERS.
THAT'S EXACTLY WHY I STAY AWAY FROM FOOLISH HUMANS.
I TOLD YOU MY POWER IS UNSTABLE!

Nuckelavee:
A sea monster that's half horse, half human. Its huge, skinless body is muscular and full of veins. It's very scary.

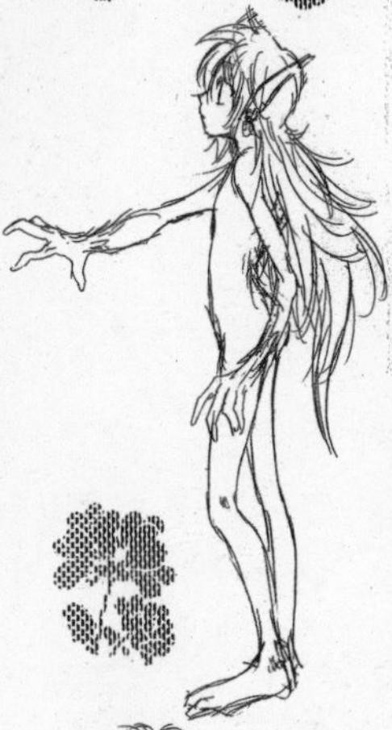

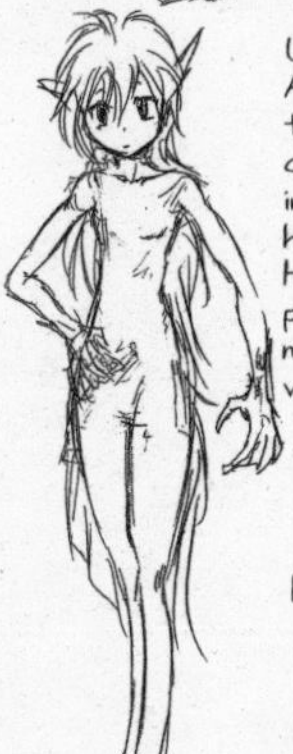

Urchin:
A goblin that can change into a hedgehog. He's pretty mischievous.

His name is Biki.

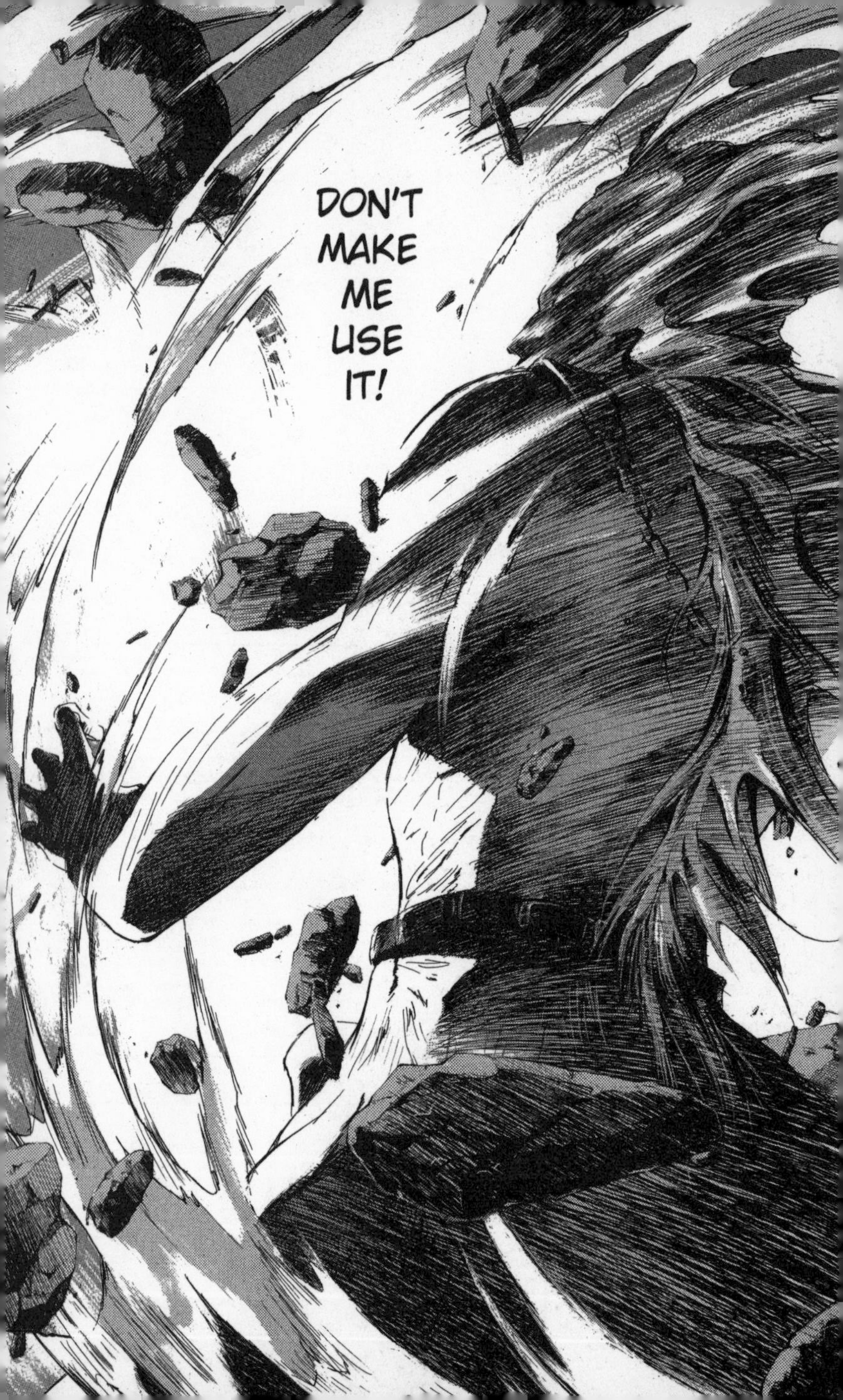
DON'T MAKE ME USE IT!

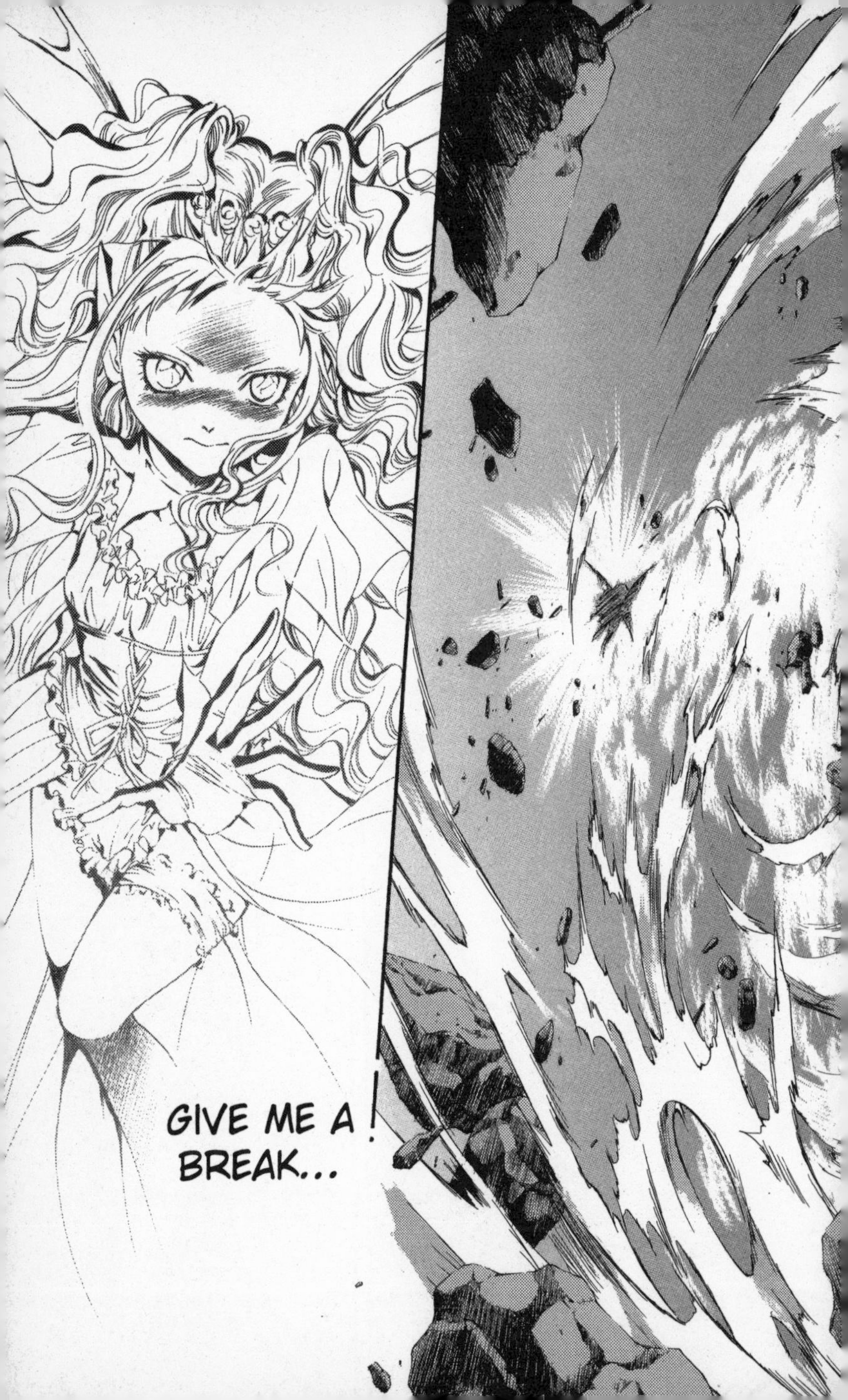
GIVE ME A BREAK...

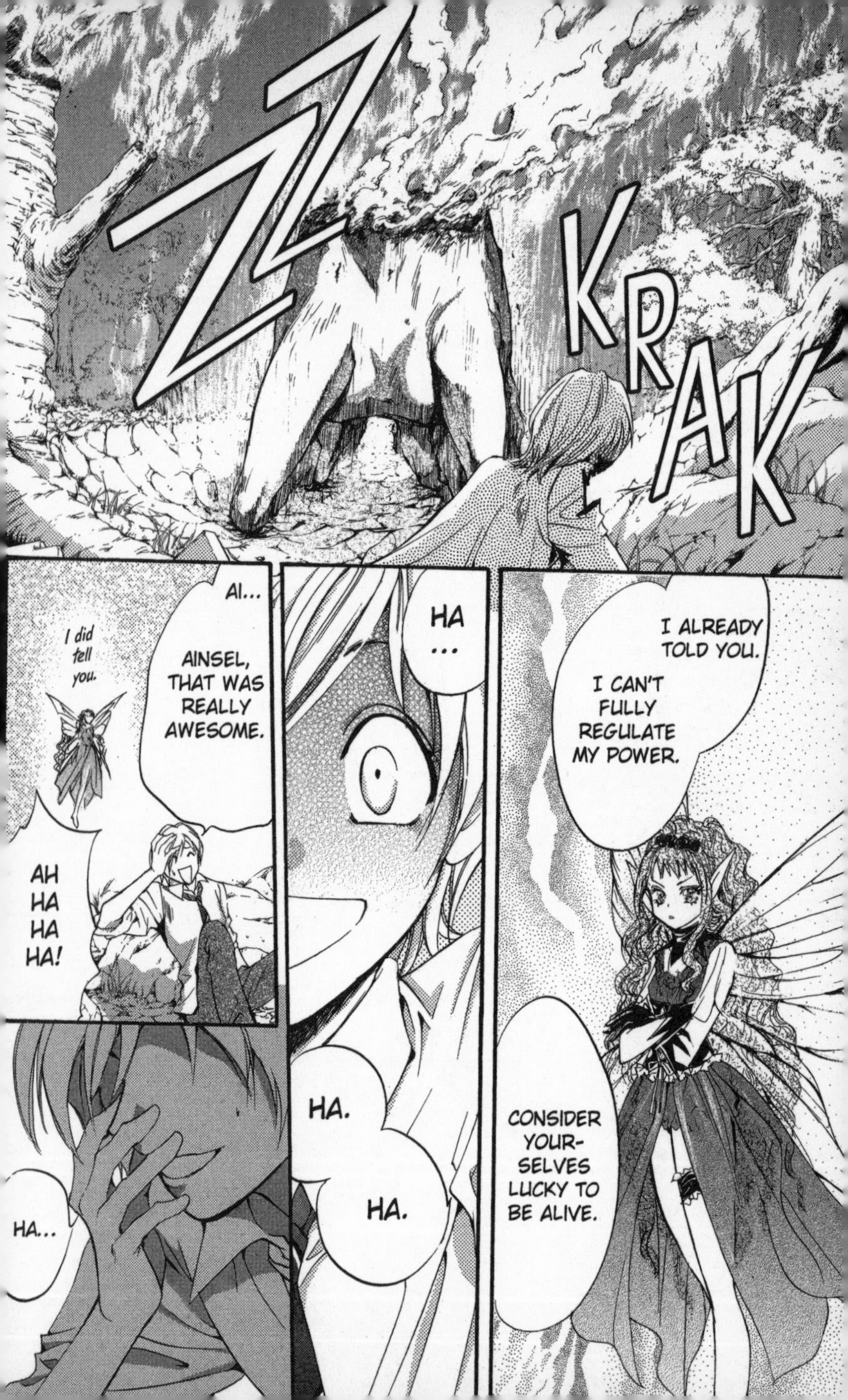
ZZ
KRAK
I ALREADY TOLD YOU.
I CAN'T FULLY REGULATE MY POWER.
CONSIDER YOUR-SELVES LUCKY TO BE ALIVE.
HA ...
HA.
HA.
AI...
AINSEL, THAT WAS REALLY AWESOME.
I did tell you.
AH HA HA HA!
HA...

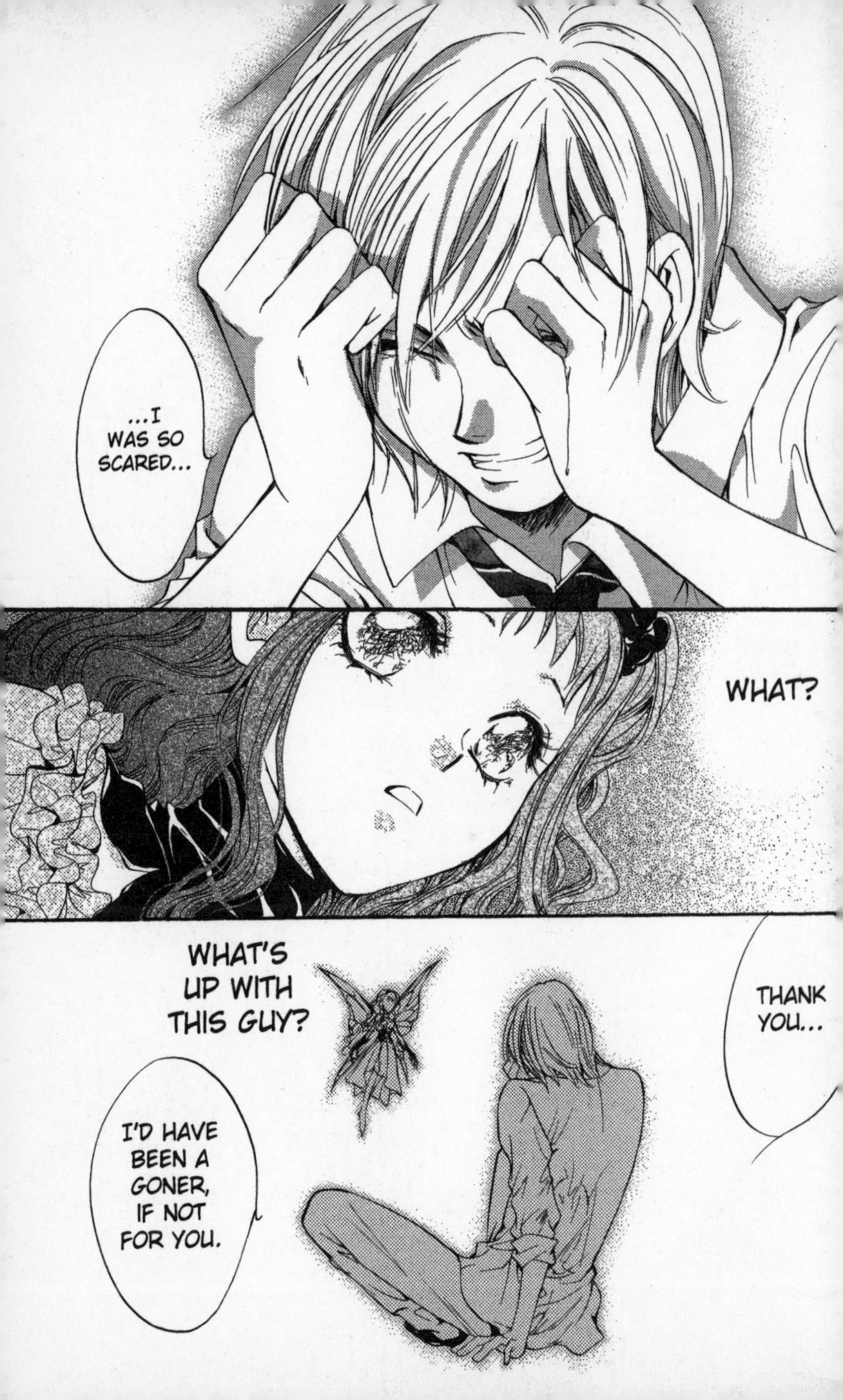
...I WAS SO SCARED...
WHAT?
THANK YOU...
WHAT'S UP WITH THIS GUY?
I'D HAVE BEEN A GONER, IF NOT FOR YOU.

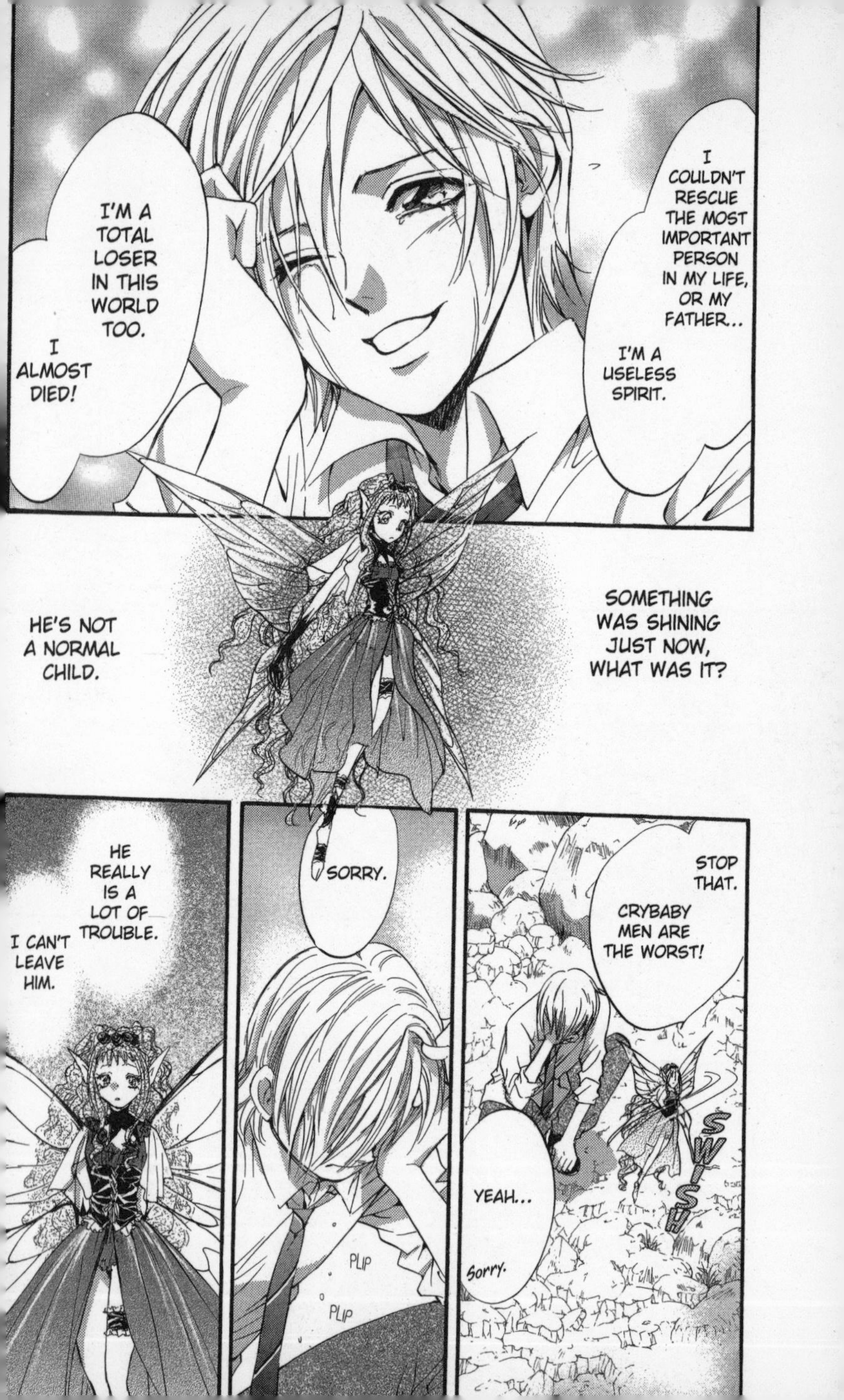
I COULDN'T RESCUE THE MOST IMPORTANT PERSON IN MY LIFE, OR MY FATHER...
I'M A USELESS SPIRIT.
I'M A TOTAL LOSER IN THIS WORLD TOO.
I ALMOST DIED!
SOMETHING WAS SHINING JUST NOW, WHAT WAS IT?
HE'S NOT A NORMAL CHILD.
STOP THAT.
CRYBABY MEN ARE THE WORST!
SWISH
YEAH...
Sorry.
SORRY.
PLIP
PLIP
HE REALLY IS A LOT OF TROUBLE.
I CAN'T LEAVE HIM.

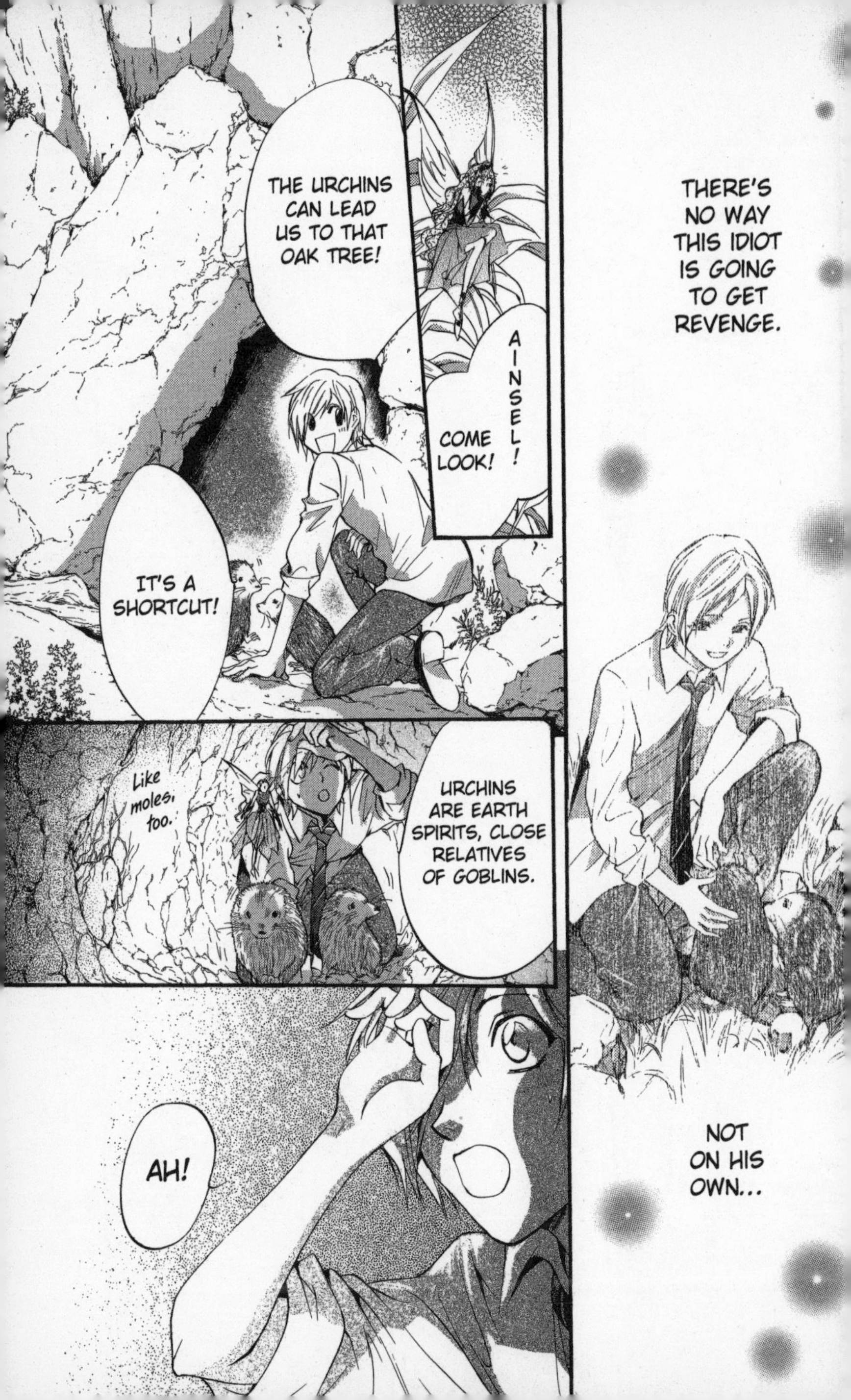
THERE'S NO WAY THIS IDIOT IS GOING TO GET REVENGE.
NOT ON HIS OWN...
AINSEL! COME LOOK!
THE URCHINS CAN LEAD US TO THAT OAK TREE!
IT'S A SHORTCUT!
URCHINS ARE EARTH SPIRITS, CLOSE RELATIVES OF GOBLINS.
Like moles, too.
AH!

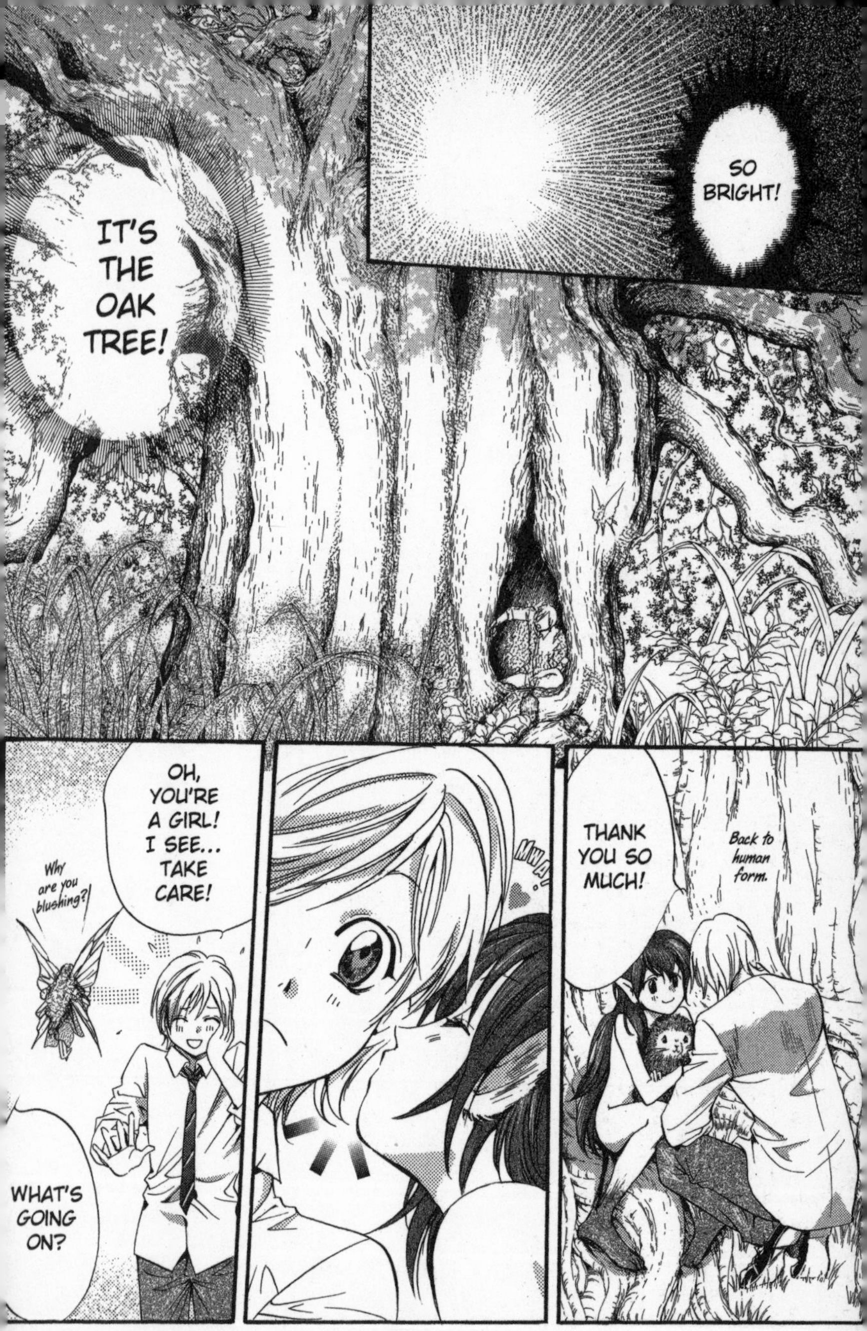
SO BRIGHT!
IT'S THE OAK TREE!
Back to human form.
THANK YOU SO MUCH!
MWA!
OH, YOU'RE A GIRL! I SEE... TAKE CARE!
Why are you blushing?
WHAT'S GOING ON?

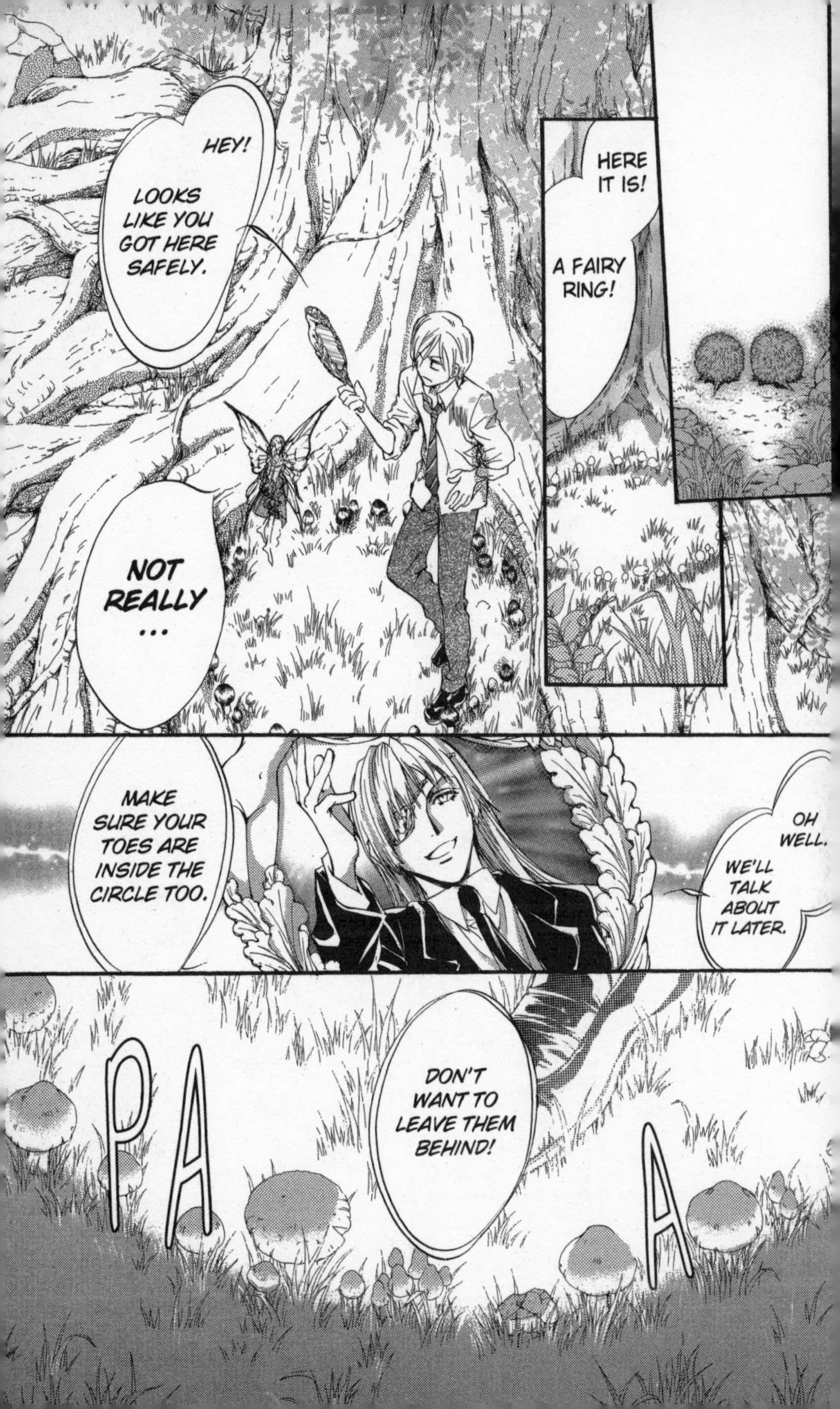
HERE IT IS!
A FAIRY RING!
HEY!
LOOKS LIKE YOU GOT HERE SAFELY.
NOT REALLY...
OH WELL.
WE'LL TALK ABOUT IT LATER.
MAKE SURE YOUR TOES ARE INSIDE THE CIRCLE TOO.
PA A
DON'T WANT TO LEAVE THEM BEHIND!

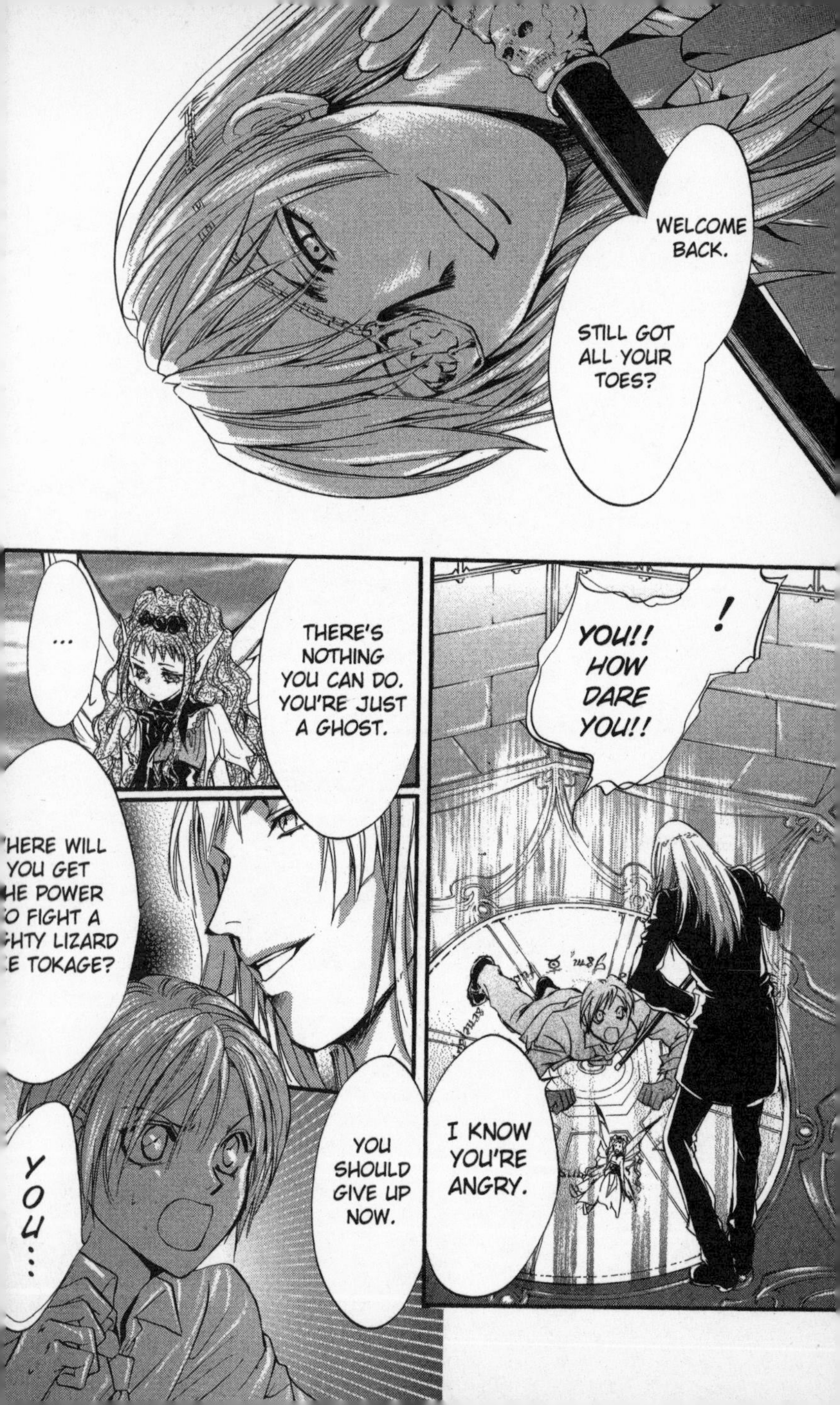
WELCOME BACK.
STILL GOT ALL YOUR TOES?
!
YOU!! HOW DARE YOU!!
I KNOW YOU'RE ANGRY.
THERE'S NOTHING YOU CAN DO. YOU'RE JUST A GHOST.
...
YOU SHOULD GIVE UP NOW.
HERE WILL YOU GET HE POWER O FIGHT A GHTY LIZARD E TOKAGE?
YOU...

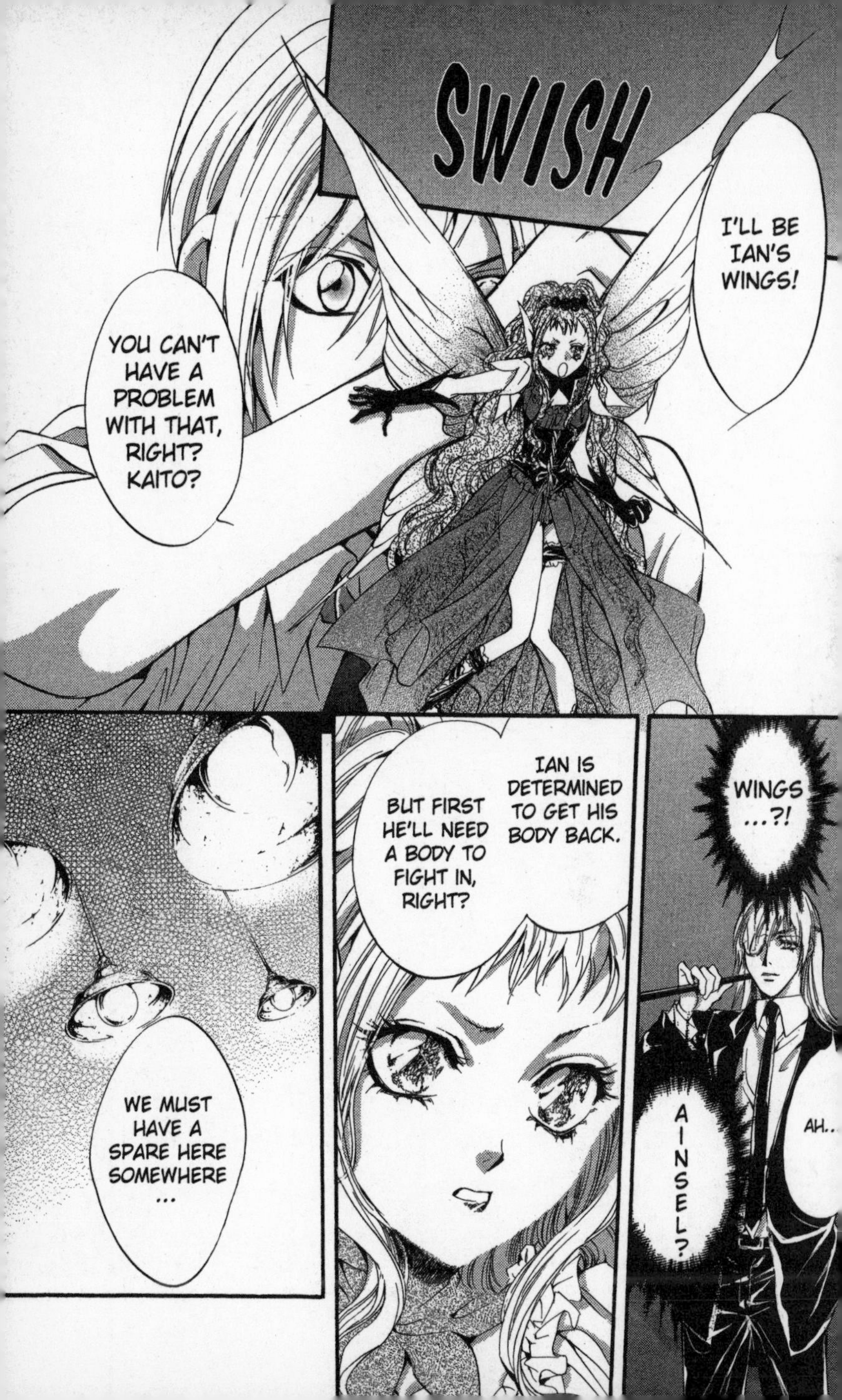
SWISH
I'LL BE IAN'S WINGS!
YOU CAN'T HAVE A PROBLEM WITH THAT, RIGHT? KAITO?
WINGS ...?!
AH..
AINSEL?
IAN IS DETERMINED TO GET HIS BODY BACK.
BUT FIRST HE'LL NEED A BODY TO FIGHT IN, RIGHT?
WE MUST HAVE A SPARE HERE SOMEWHERE ...

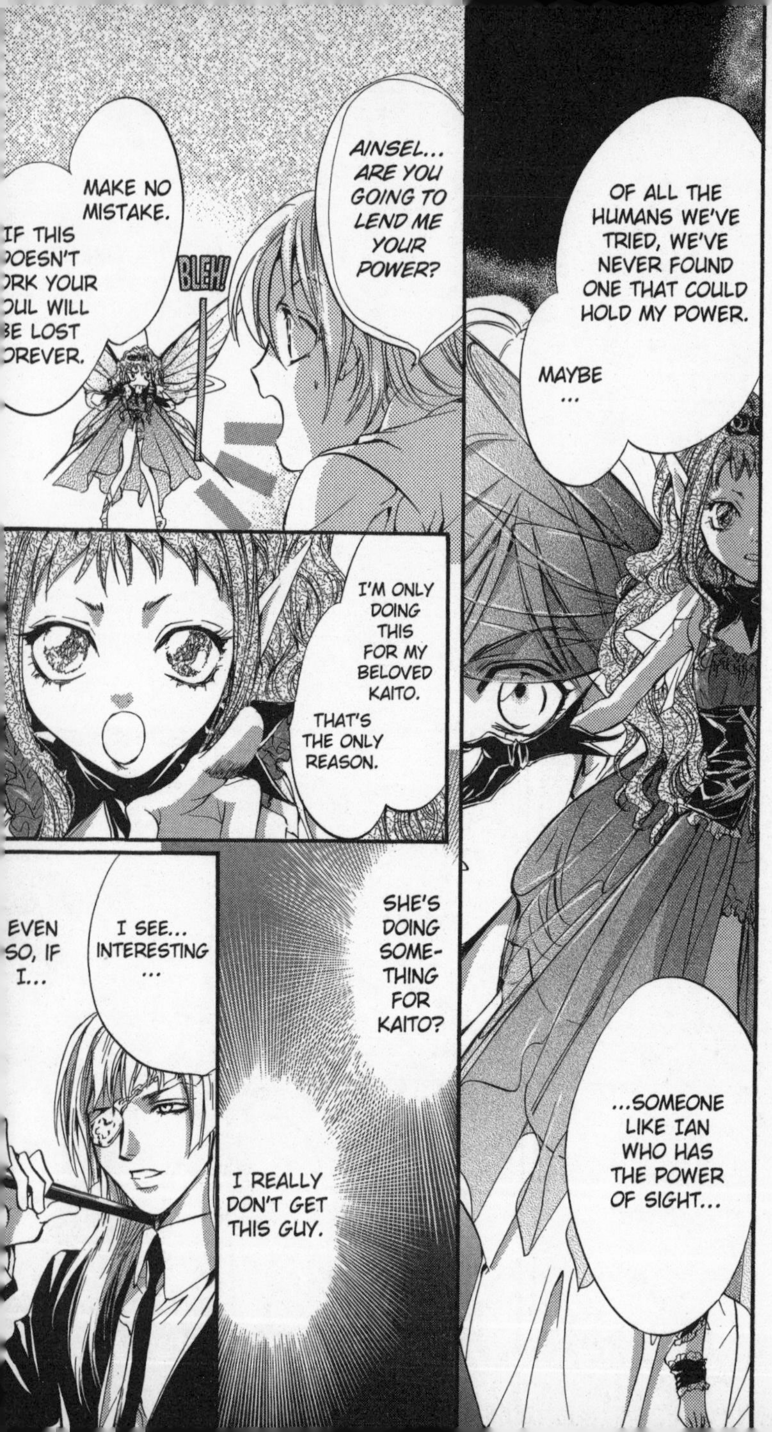
OF ALL THE HUMANS WE'VE TRIED, WE'VE NEVER FOUND ONE THAT COULD HOLD MY POWER.
MAYBE ...
...SOMEONE LIKE IAN WHO HAS THE POWER OF SIGHT...
AINSEL... ARE YOU GOING TO LEND ME YOUR POWER?
BLEH!
MAKE NO MISTAKE.
IF THIS OESN'T ORK YOUR OUL WILL E LOST OREVER.
I'M ONLY DOING THIS FOR MY BELOVED KAITO.
THAT'S THE ONLY REASON.
SHE'S DOING SOME-THING FOR KAITO?
I SEE... INTERESTING ...
EVEN SO, IF I...
I REALLY DON'T GET THIS GUY.

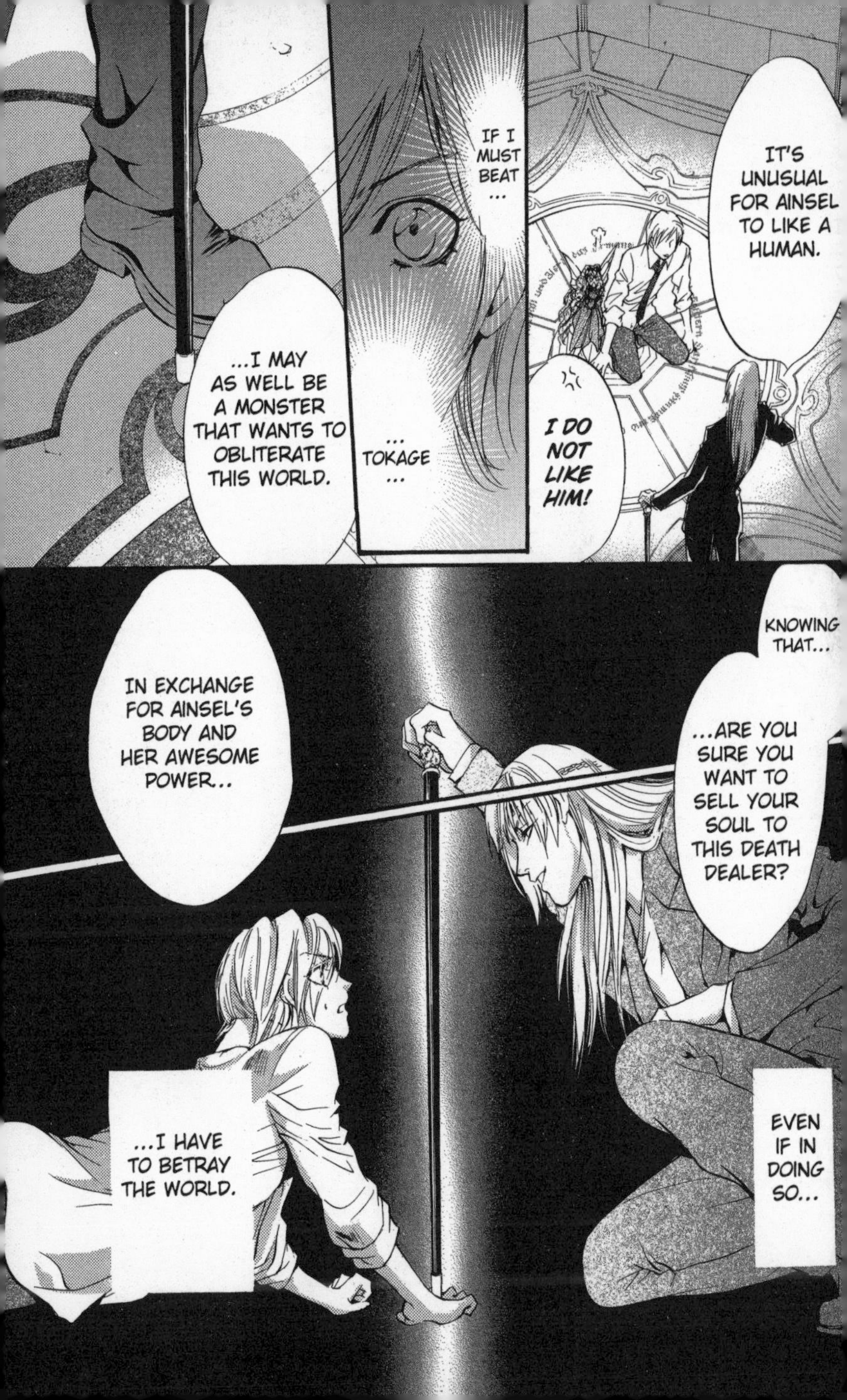
IT'S UNUSUAL FOR AINSEL TO LIKE A HUMAN.
I DO NOT LIKE HIM!
IF I MUST BEAT ...
... TOKAGE ...
...I MAY AS WELL BE A MONSTER THAT WANTS TO OBLITERATE THIS WORLD.
KNOWING THAT...
...ARE YOU SURE YOU WANT TO SELL YOUR SOUL TO THIS DEATH DEALER?
IN EXCHANGE FOR AINSEL'S BODY AND HER AWESOME POWER...
EVEN IF IN DOING SO...
...I HAVE TO BETRAY THE WORLD.

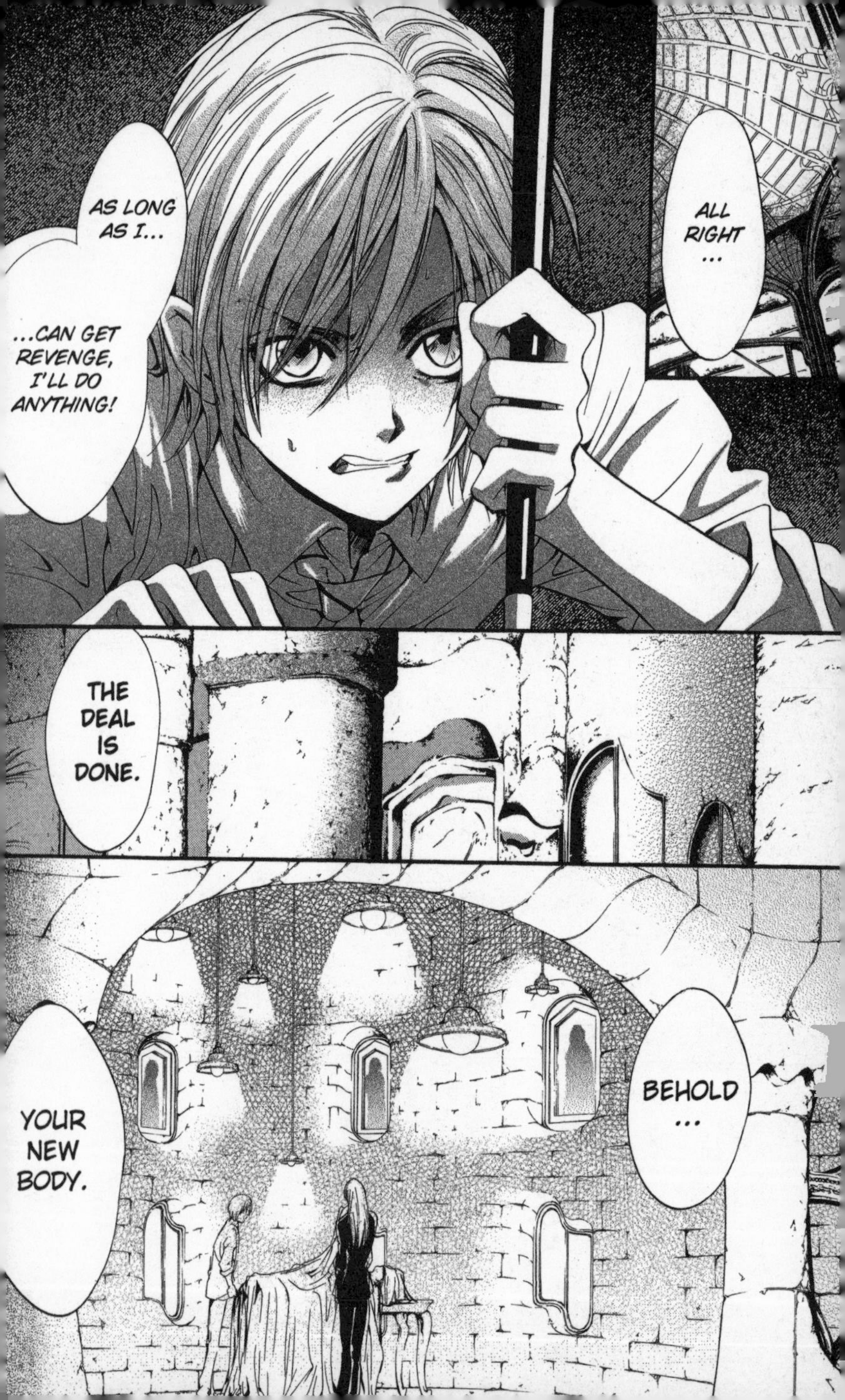
ALL RIGHT ...
AS LONG AS I...
...CAN GET REVENGE, I'LL DO ANYTHING!
THE DEAL IS DONE.
BEHOLD ...
YOUR NEW BODY.

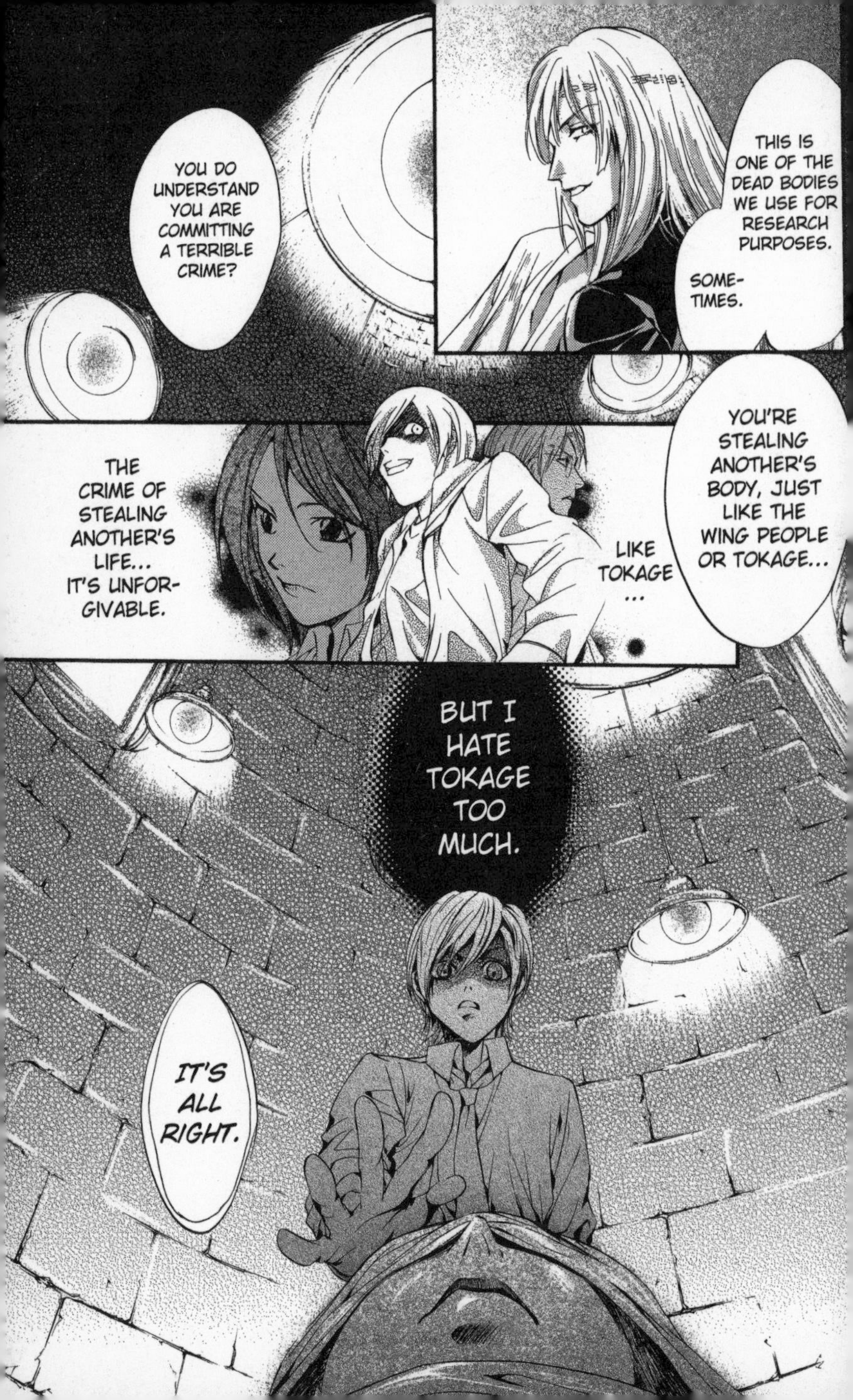
THIS IS ONE OF THE DEAD BODIES WE USE FOR RESEARCH PURPOSES.
SOME-TIMES.
YOU DO UNDERSTAND YOU ARE COMMITTING A TERRIBLE CRIME?
YOU'RE STEALING ANOTHER'S BODY, JUST LIKE THE WING PEOPLE OR TOKAGE...
LIKE TOKAGE ...
THE CRIME OF STEALING ANOTHER'S LIFE... IT'S UNFOR-GIVABLE.
BUT I HATE TOKAGE TOO MUCH.
IT'S ALL RIGHT.

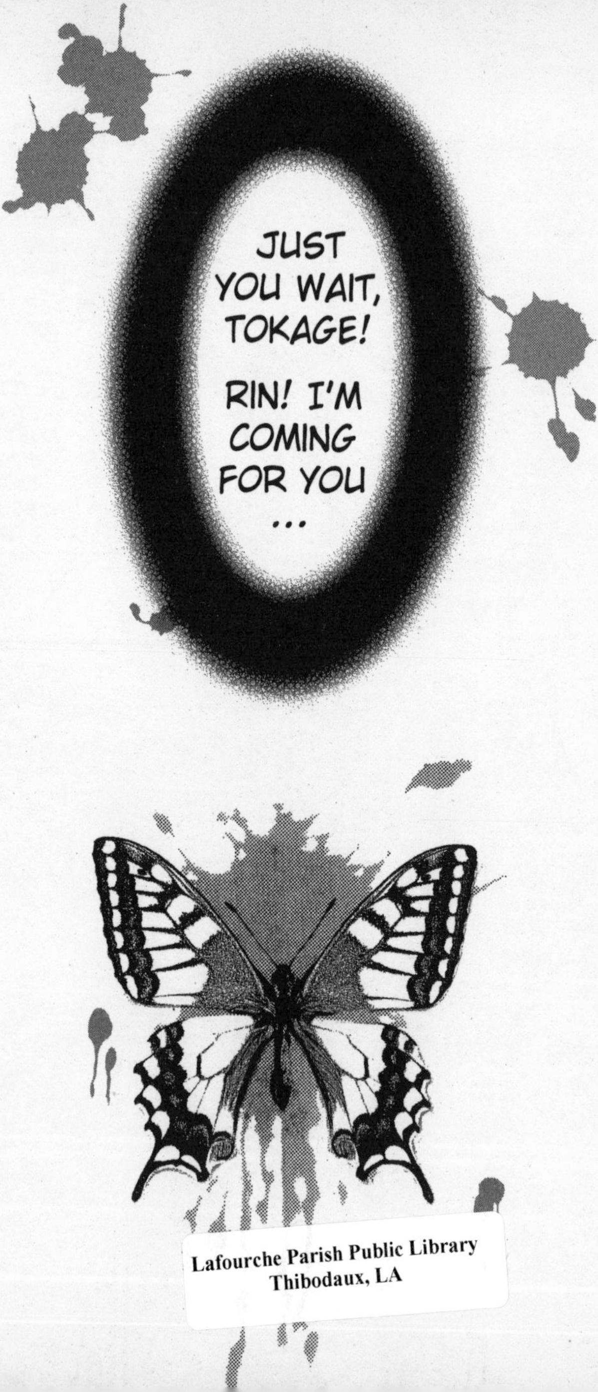
JUST YOU WAIT, TOKAGE!
RIN! I'M COMING FOR YOU ...

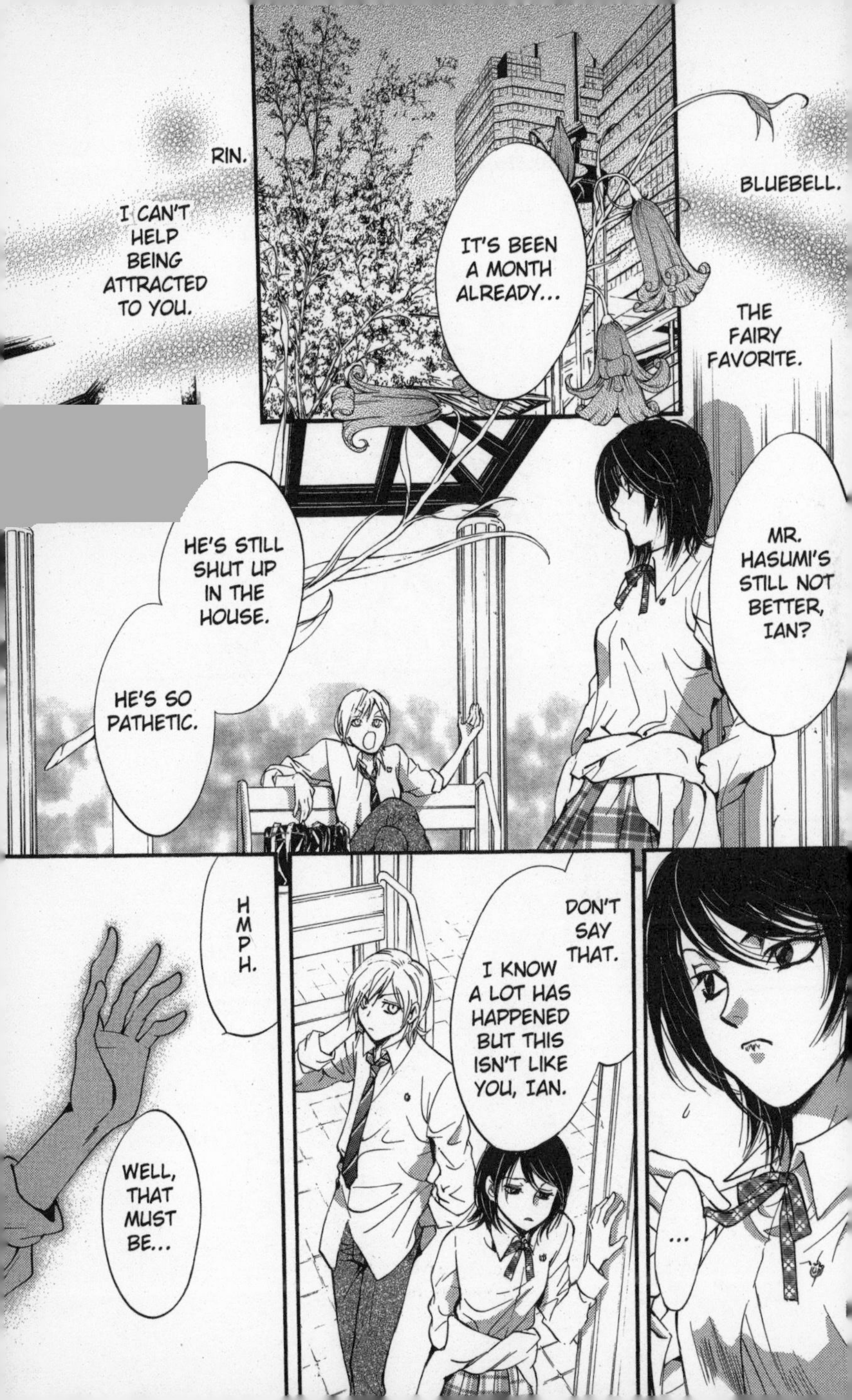
BLUEBELL.
THE FAIRY FAVORITE.
IT'S BEEN A MONTH ALREADY...
RIN.
I CAN'T HELP BEING ATTRACTED TO YOU.
MR. HASUMI'S STILL NOT BETTER, IAN?
HE'S STILL SHUT UP IN THE HOUSE.
HE'S SO PATHETIC.
...
DON'T SAY THAT.
I KNOW A LOT HAS HAPPENED BUT THIS ISN'T LIKE YOU, IAN.
HMPH.
WELL, THAT MUST BE...

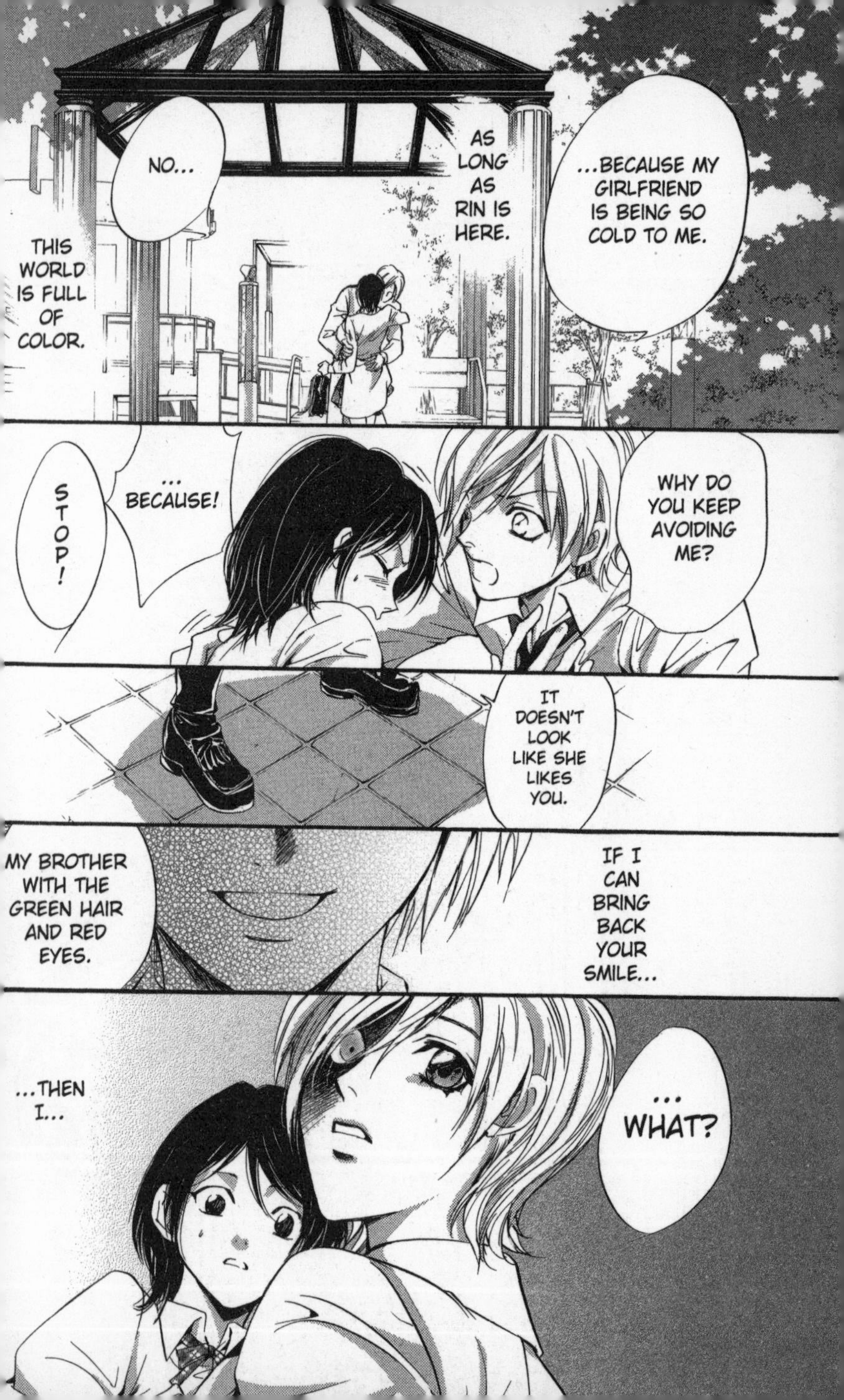
...BECAUSE MY GIRLFRIEND IS BEING SO COLD TO ME.
AS LONG AS RIN IS HERE.
NO...
THIS WORLD IS FULL OF COLOR.
WHY DO YOU KEEP AVOIDING ME?
...BECAUSE!
STOP!
IT DOESN'T LOOK LIKE SHE LIKES YOU.
IF I CAN BRING BACK YOUR SMILE...
MY BROTHER WITH THE GREEN HAIR AND RED EYES.
...WHAT?
...THEN I...

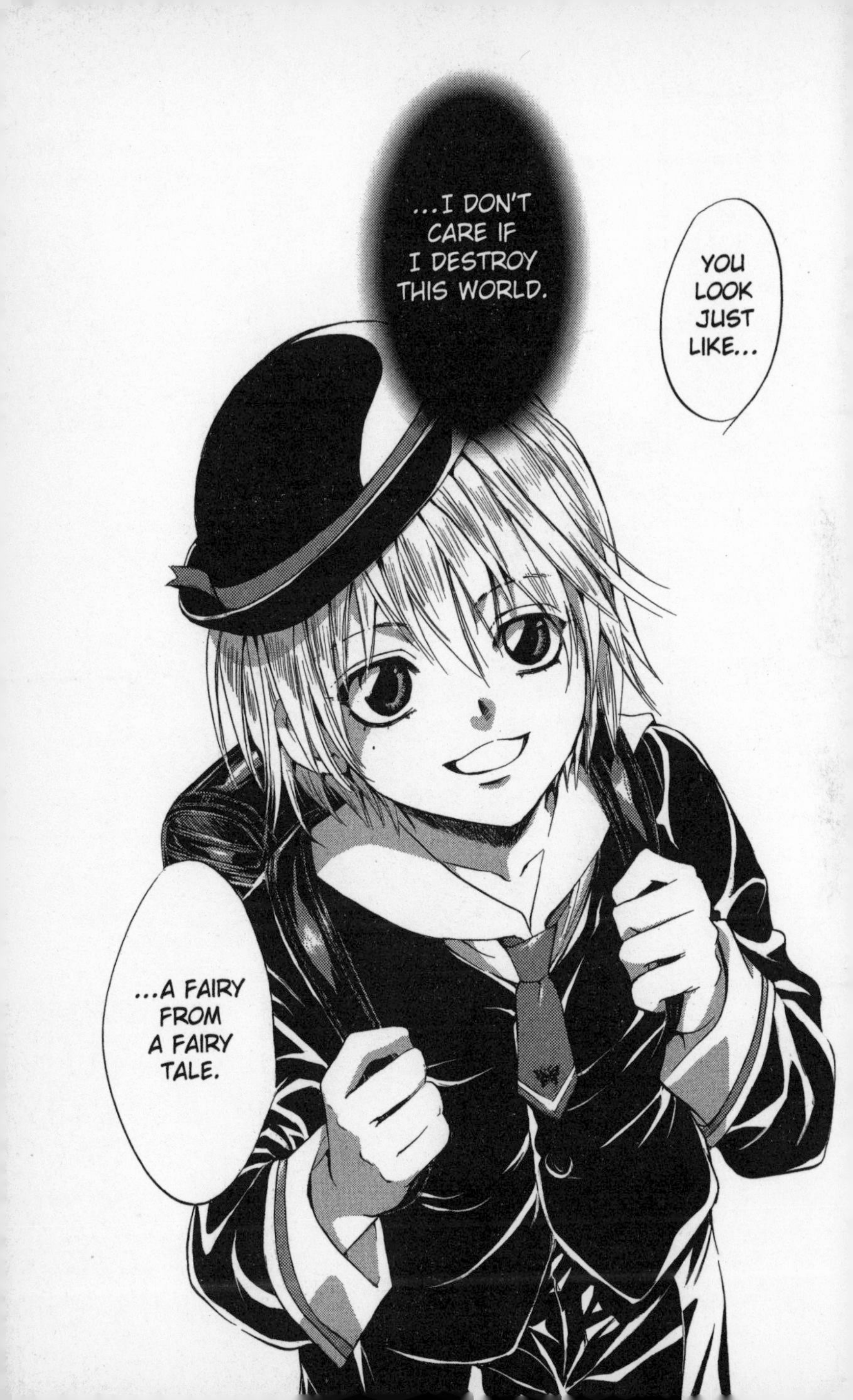
...I DON'T CARE IF I DESTROY THIS WORLD.
YOU LOOK JUST LIKE...
...A FAIRY FROM A FAIRY TALE.

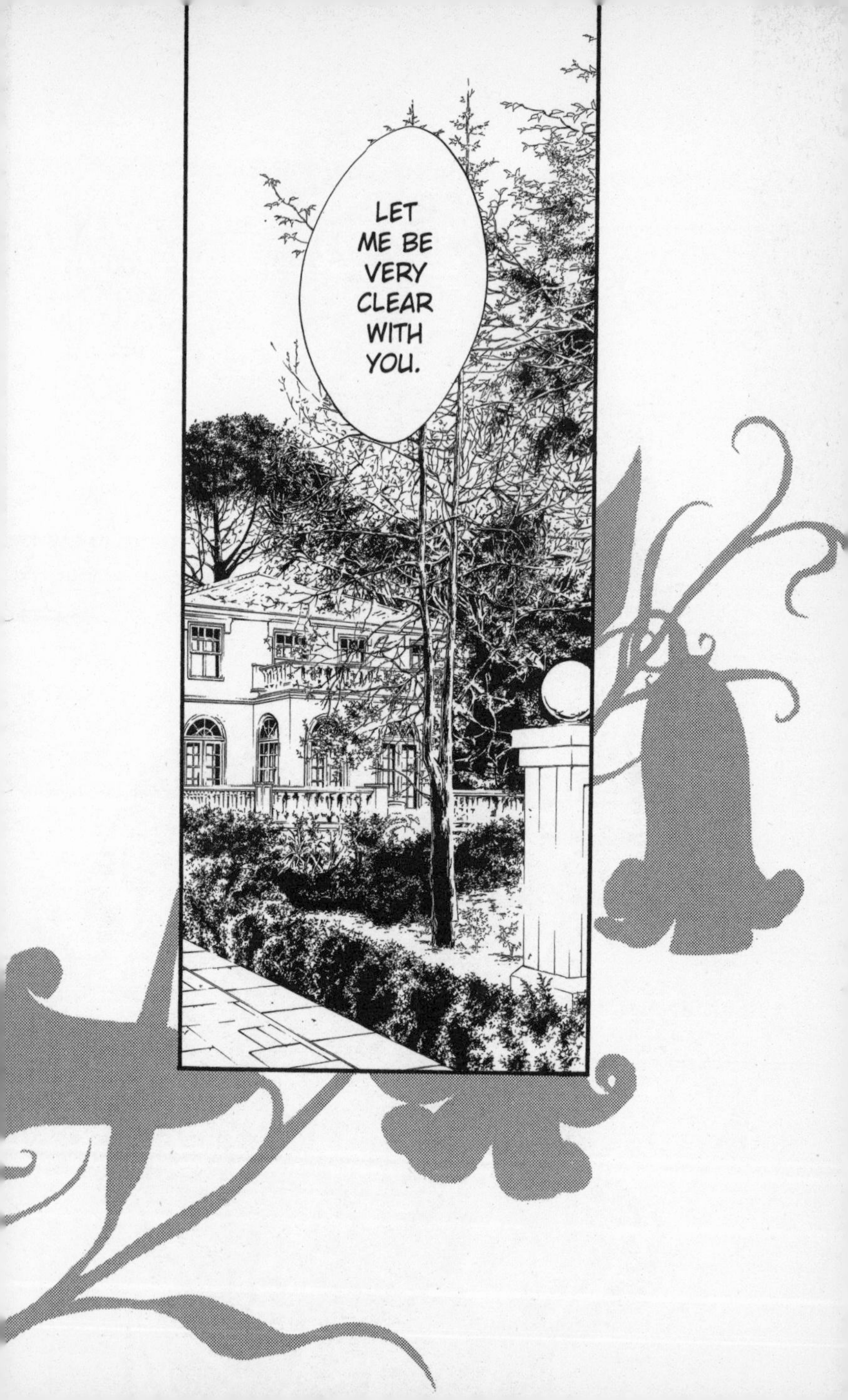
LET ME BE VERY CLEAR WITH YOU.

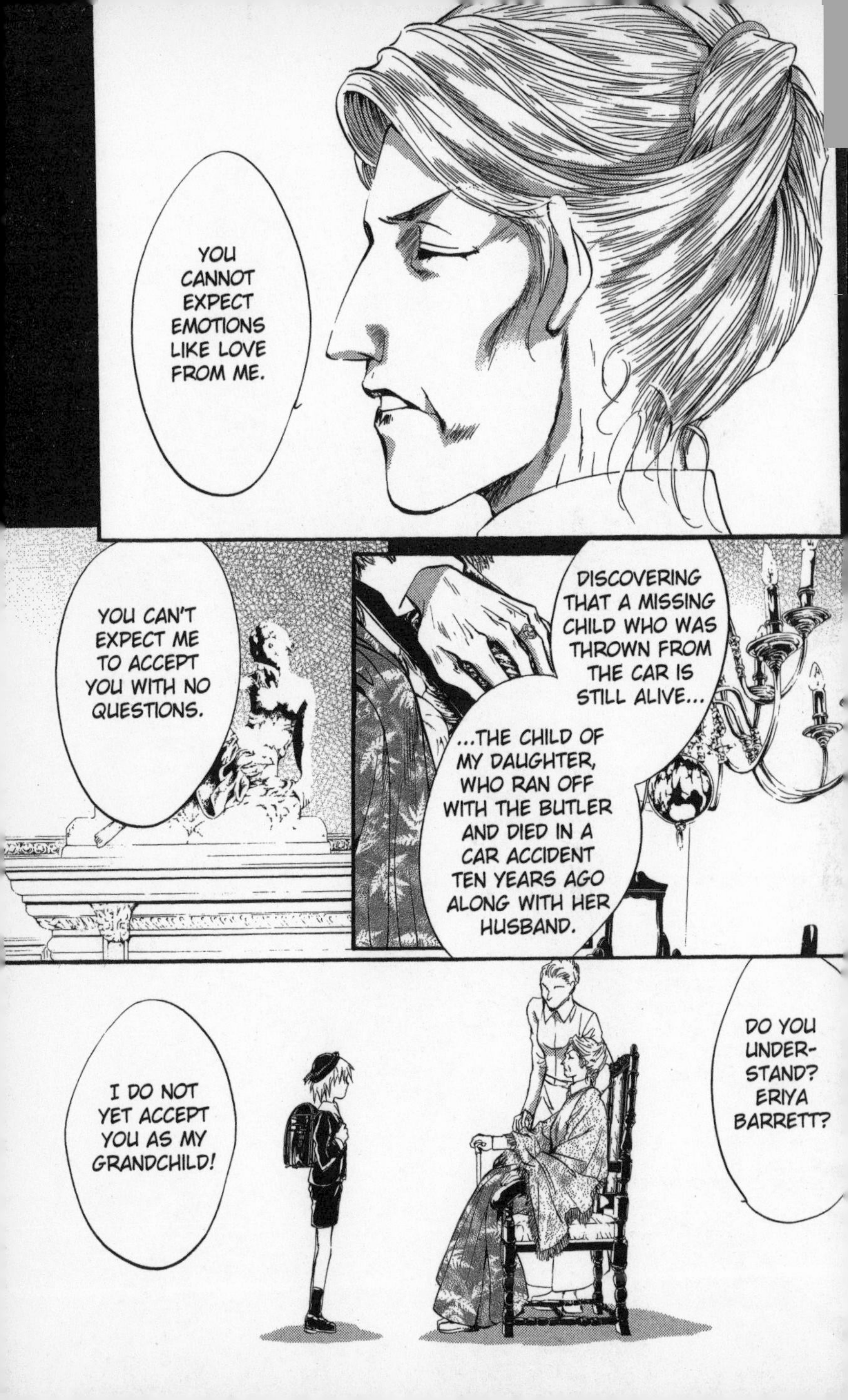
YOU CANNOT EXPECT EMOTIONS LIKE LOVE FROM ME.
DISCOVERING THAT A MISSING CHILD WHO WAS THROWN FROM THE CAR IS STILL ALIVE...
...THE CHILD OF MY DAUGHTER, WHO RAN OFF WITH THE BUTLER AND DIED IN A CAR ACCIDENT TEN YEARS AGO ALONG WITH HER HUSBAND.
YOU CAN'T EXPECT ME TO ACCEPT YOU WITH NO QUESTIONS.
DO YOU UNDER-STAND? ERIYA BARRETT?
I DO NOT YET ACCEPT YOU AS MY GRANDCHILD!

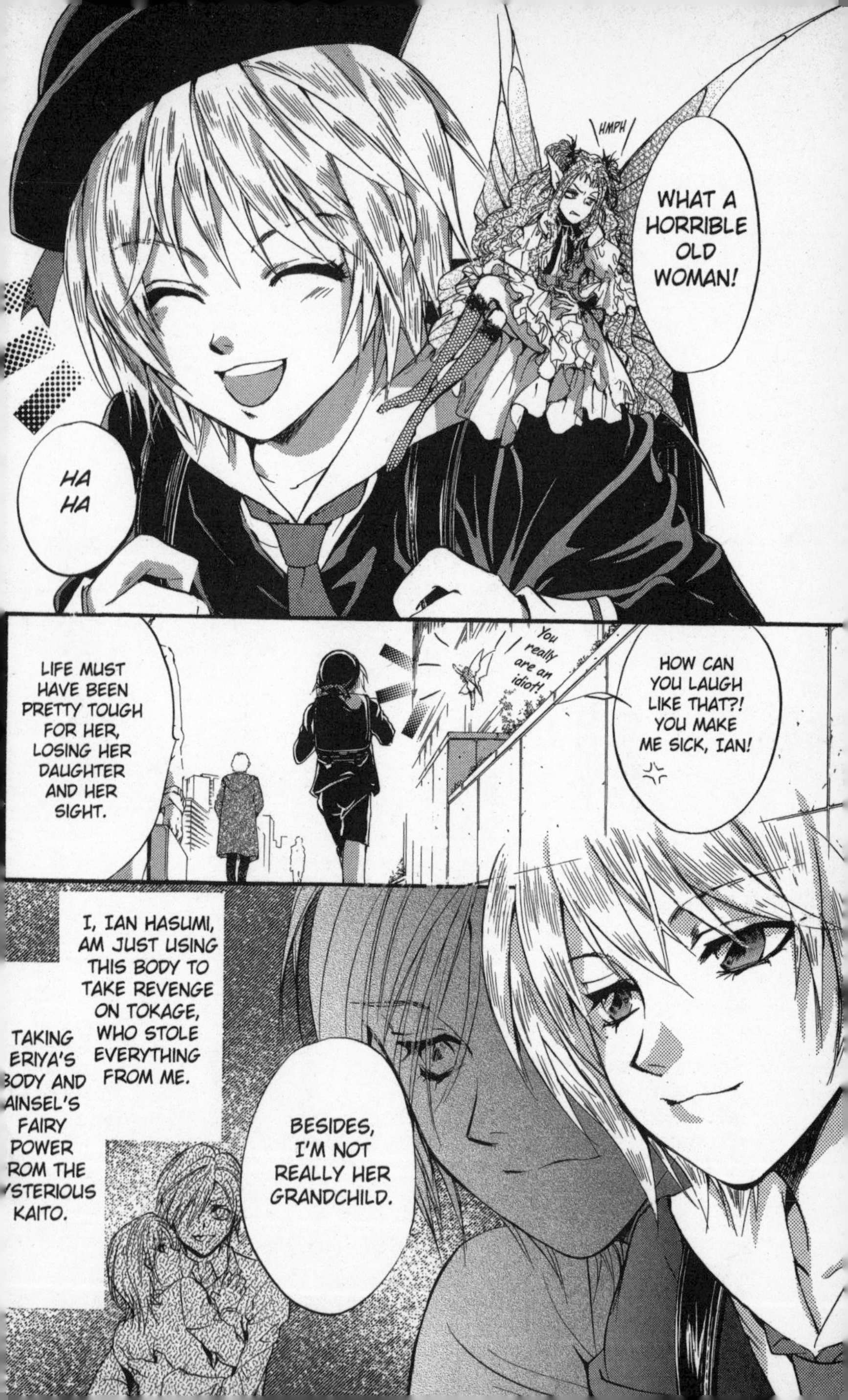
HMPH
WHAT A HORRIBLE OLD WOMAN!
HA HA
HOW CAN YOU LAUGH LIKE THAT?! YOU MAKE ME SICK, IAN!
You really are an idiot!
LIFE MUST HAVE BEEN PRETTY TOUGH FOR HER, LOSING HER DAUGHTER AND HER SIGHT.
I, IAN HASUMI, AM JUST USING THIS BODY TO TAKE REVENGE ON TOKAGE, WHO STOLE EVERYTHING FROM ME.
TAKING ERIYA'S BODY AND AINSEL'S FAIRY POWER ROM THE YSTERIOUS KAITO.
BESIDES, I'M NOT REALLY HER GRANDCHILD.

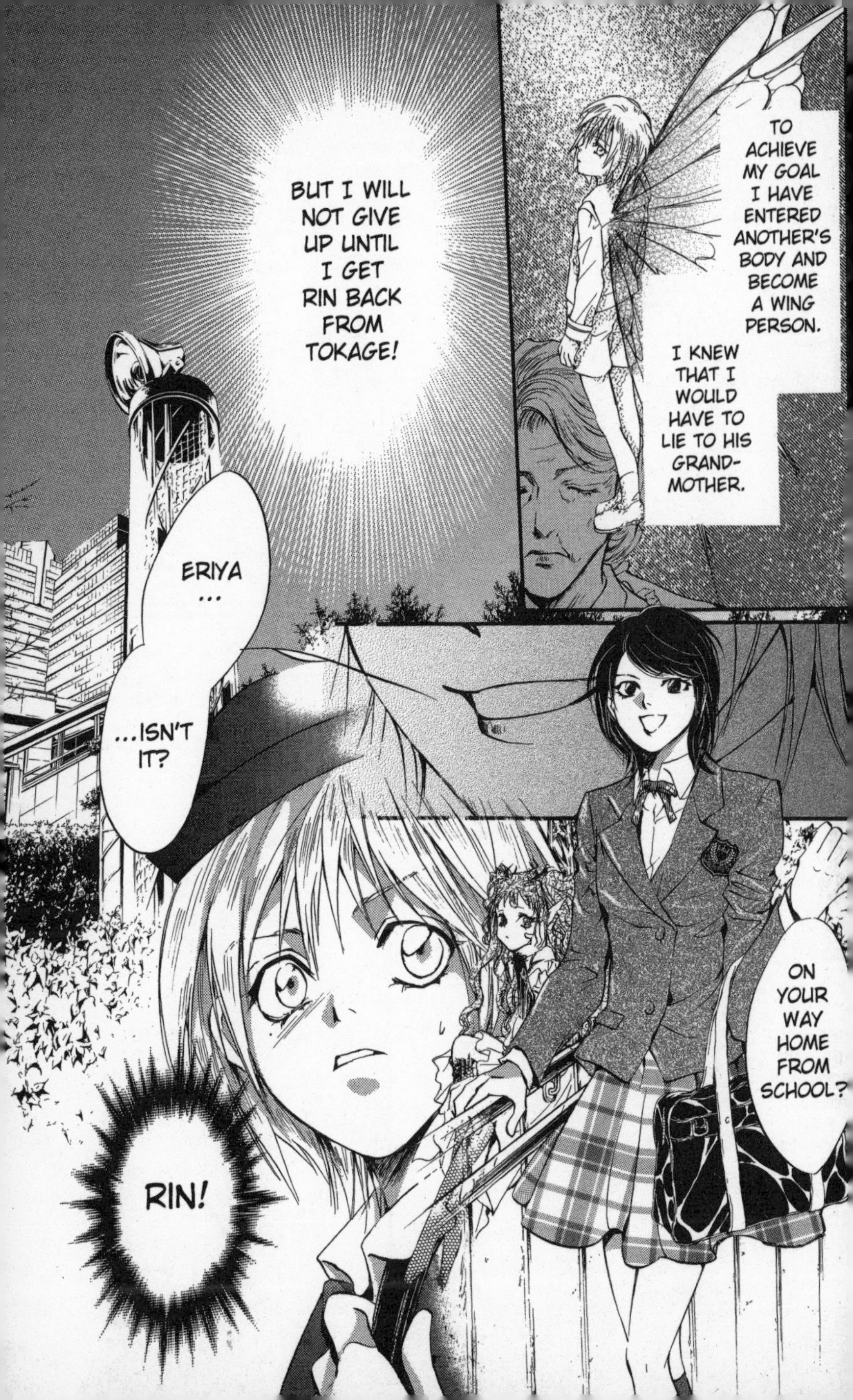
TO ACHIEVE MY GOAL I HAVE ENTERED ANOTHER'S BODY AND BECOME A WING PERSON.
I KNEW THAT I WOULD HAVE TO LIE TO HIS GRAND-MOTHER.
BUT I WILL NOT GIVE UP UNTIL I GET RIN BACK FROM TOKAGE!
ERIYA...
...ISN'T IT?
ON YOUR WAY HOME FROM SCHOOL?
RIN!

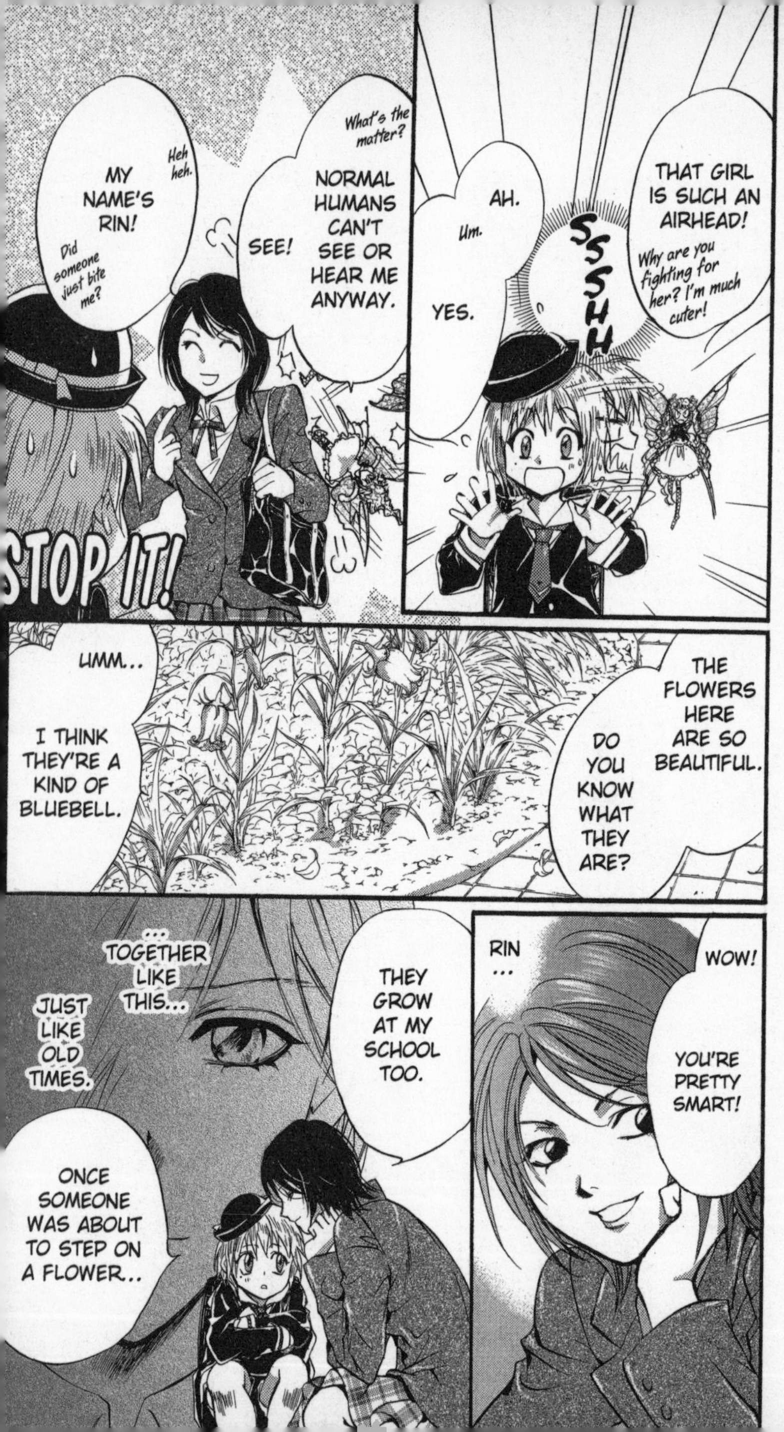
THAT GIRL IS SUCH AN AIRHEAD!
Why are you fighting for her? I'm much cuter!
SSSHH
AH.
Um.
YES.
What's the matter?
NORMAL HUMANS CAN'T SEE OR HEAR ME ANYWAY.
SEE!
Heh heh.
MY NAME'S RIN!
Did someone just bite me?
STOP IT!
THE FLOWERS HERE ARE SO BEAUTIFUL.
DO YOU KNOW WHAT THEY ARE?
UMM...
I THINK THEY'RE A KIND OF BLUEBELL.
WOW!
YOU'RE PRETTY SMART!
RIN...
THEY GROW AT MY SCHOOL TOO.
...TOGETHER LIKE THIS...
JUST LIKE OLD TIMES.
ONCE SOMEONE WAS ABOUT TO STEP ON A FLOWER...

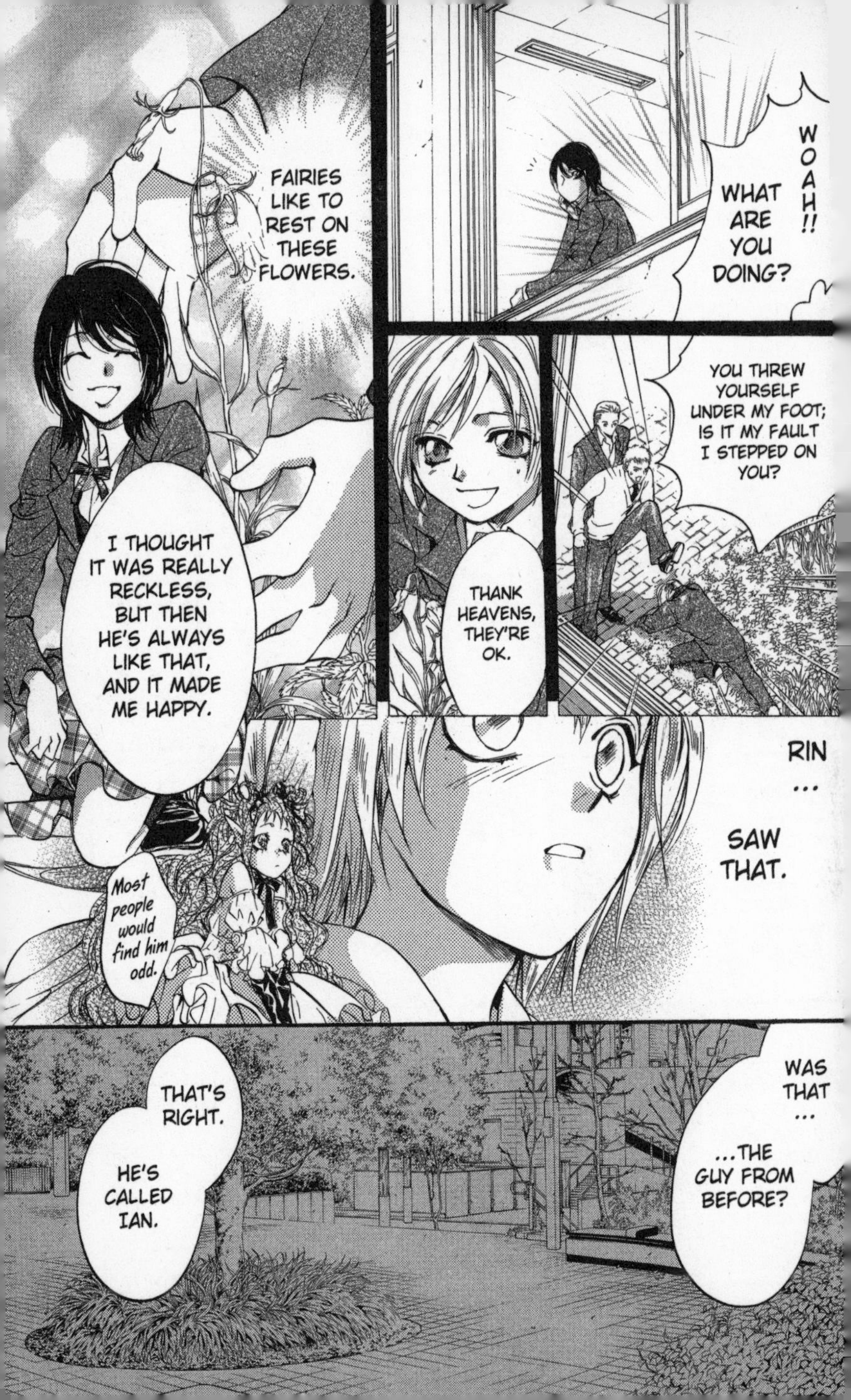
WOAH!!
WHAT ARE YOU DOING?
YOU THREW YOURSELF UNDER MY FOOT; IS IT MY FAULT I STEPPED ON YOU?
THANK HEAVENS, THEY'RE OK.
RIN ...
SAW THAT.
FAIRIES LIKE TO REST ON THESE FLOWERS.
I THOUGHT IT WAS REALLY RECKLESS, BUT THEN HE'S ALWAYS LIKE THAT, AND IT MADE ME HAPPY.
Most people would find him odd.
WAS THAT ...
...THE GUY FROM BEFORE?
THAT'S RIGHT.
HE'S CALLED IAN.

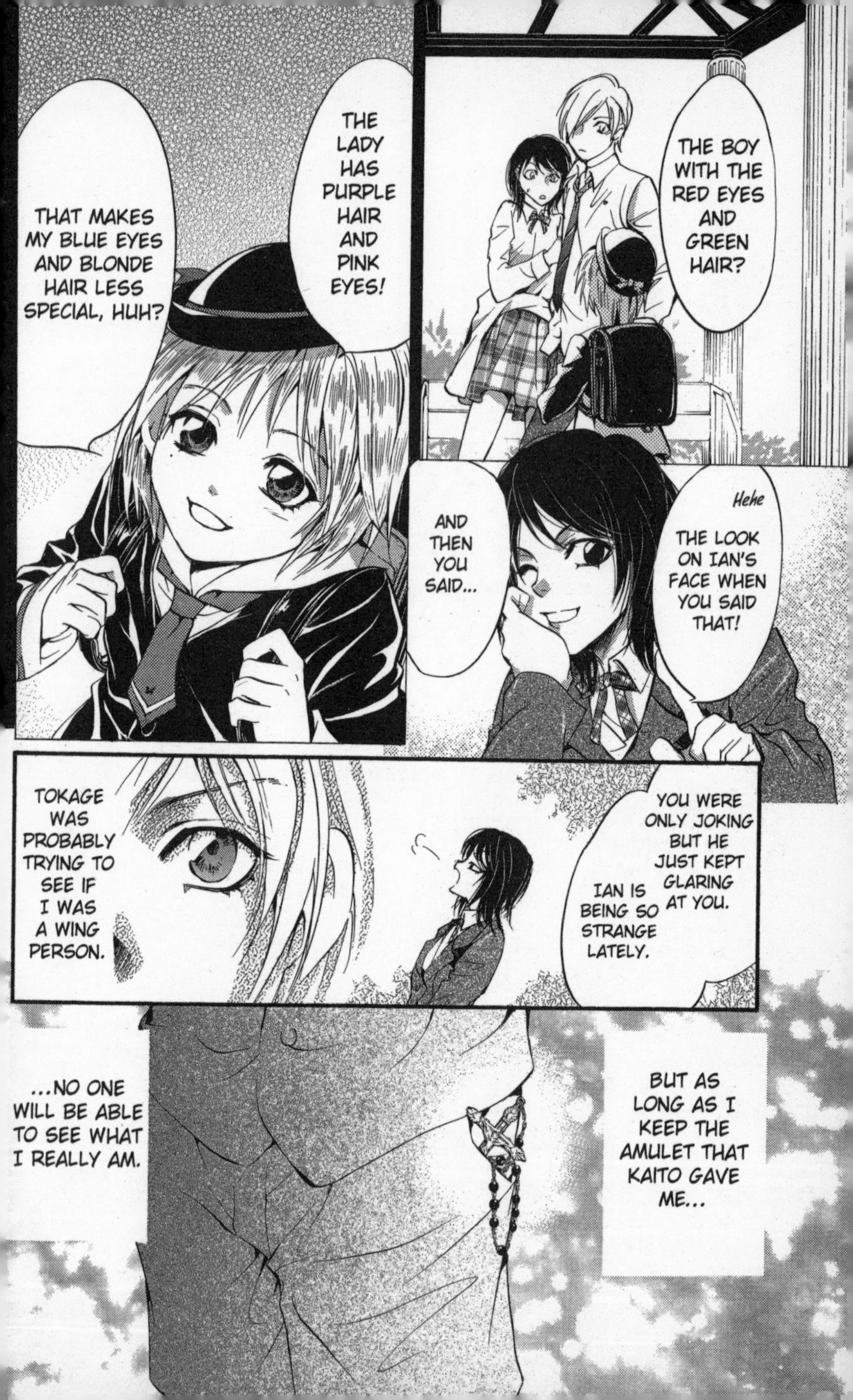
THE BOY WITH THE RED EYES AND GREEN HAIR?
Hehe
THE LOOK ON IAN'S FACE WHEN YOU SAID THAT!
AND THEN YOU SAID...
THE LADY HAS PURPLE HAIR AND PINK EYES!
THAT MAKES MY BLUE EYES AND BLONDE HAIR LESS SPECIAL, HUH?
YOU WERE ONLY JOKING BUT HE JUST KEPT GLARING AT YOU.
IAN IS BEING SO STRANGE LATELY.
TOKAGE WAS PROBABLY TRYING TO SEE IF I WAS A WING PERSON.
BUT AS LONG AS I KEEP THE AMULET THAT KAITO GAVE ME...
...NO ONE WILL BE ABLE TO SEE WHAT I REALLY AM.

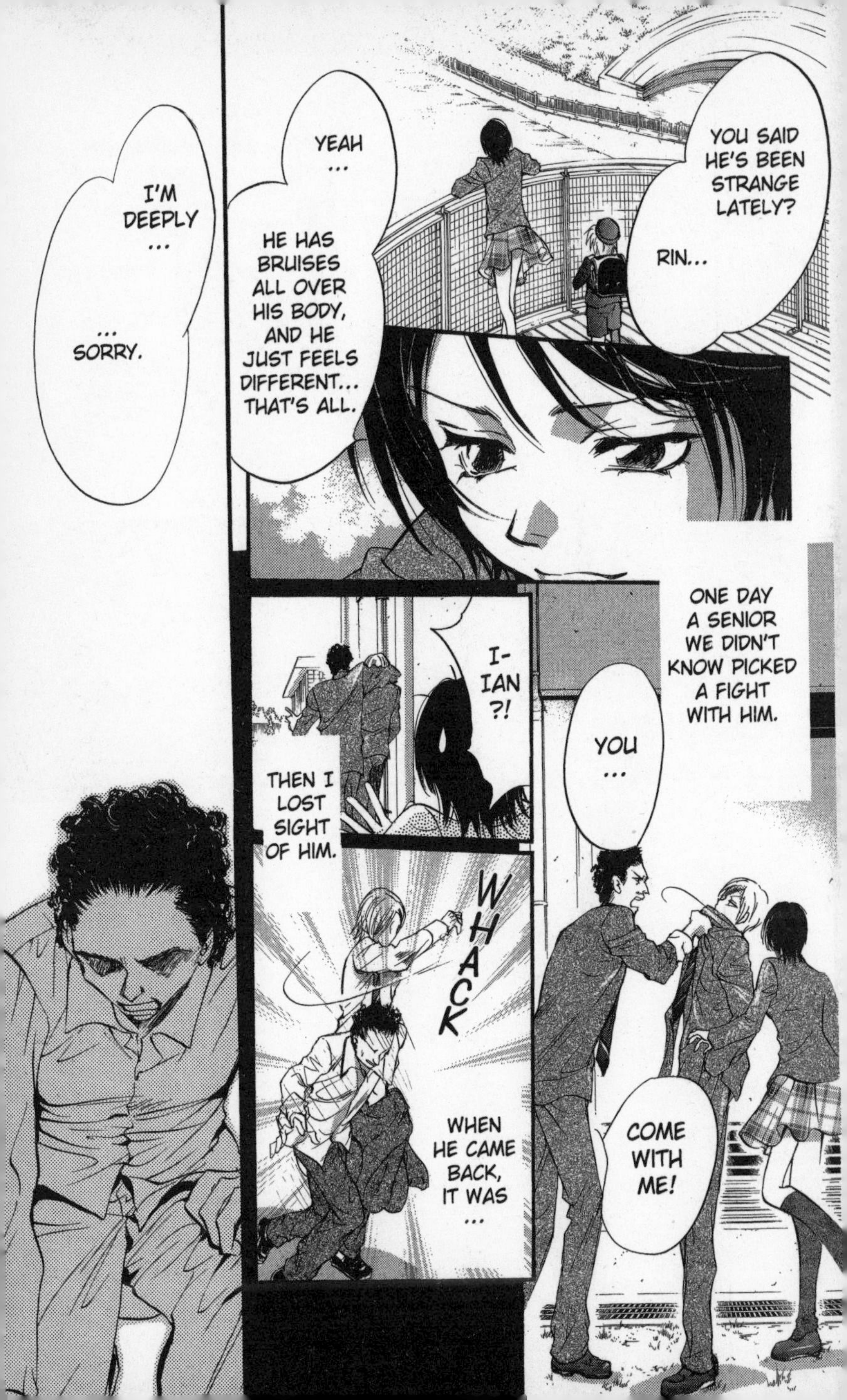
YOU SAID HE'S BEEN STRANGE LATELY?
RIN...
YEAH ...
HE HAS BRUISES ALL OVER HIS BODY, AND HE JUST FEELS DIFFERENT... THAT'S ALL.
ONE DAY A SENIOR WE DIDN'T KNOW PICKED A FIGHT WITH HIM.
YOU ...
COME WITH ME!
I-IAN ?!
THEN I LOST SIGHT OF HIM.
WHACK
WHEN HE CAME BACK, IT WAS ...
I'M DEEPLY ...
... SORRY.

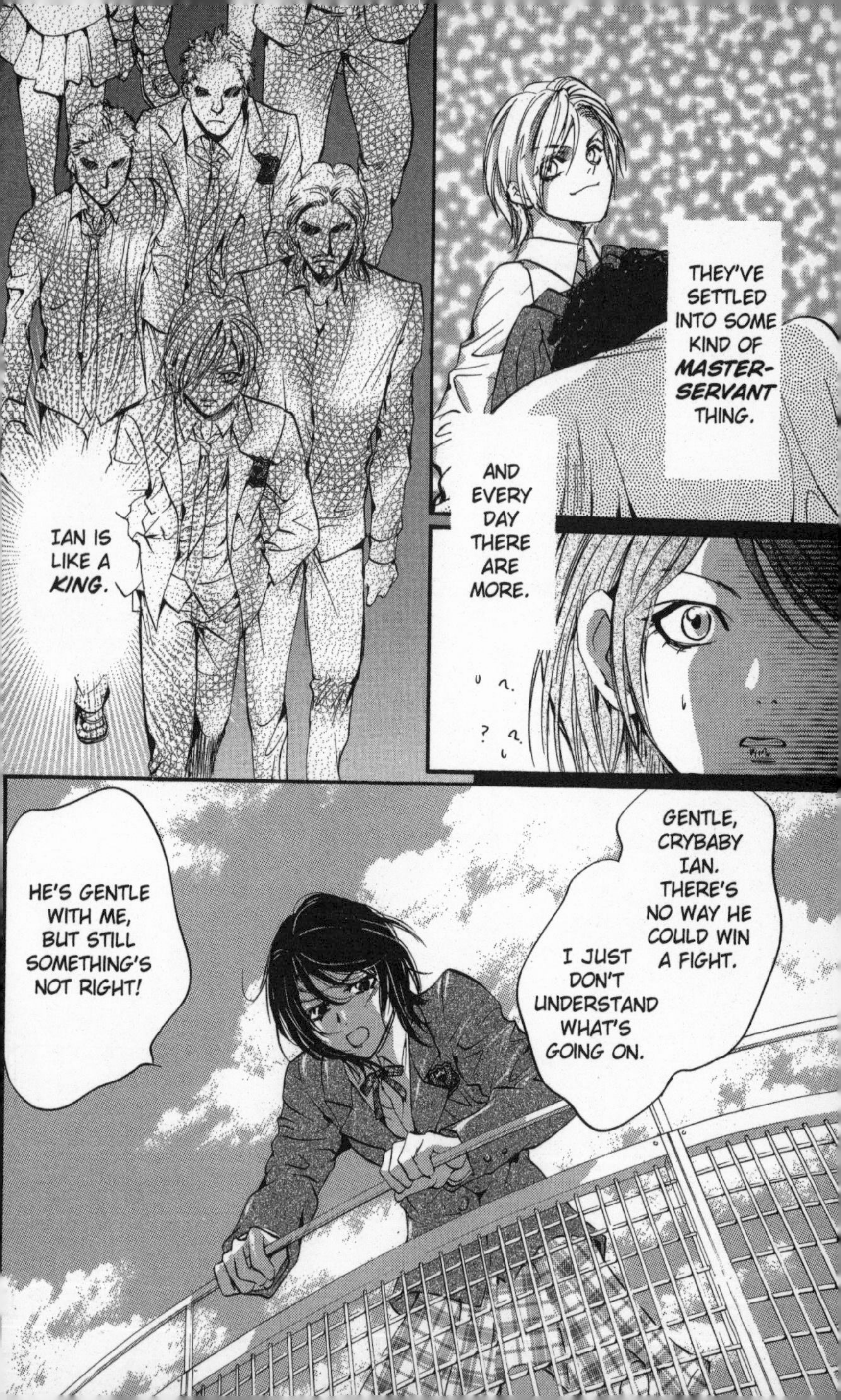
THEY'VE SETTLED INTO SOME KIND OF MASTER-SERVANT THING.
AND EVERY DAY THERE ARE MORE.
IAN IS LIKE A KING.
GENTLE, CRYBABY IAN. THERE'S NO WAY HE COULD WIN A FIGHT.
I JUST DON'T UNDERSTAND WHAT'S GOING ON.
HE'S GENTLE WITH ME, BUT STILL SOMETHING'S NOT RIGHT!

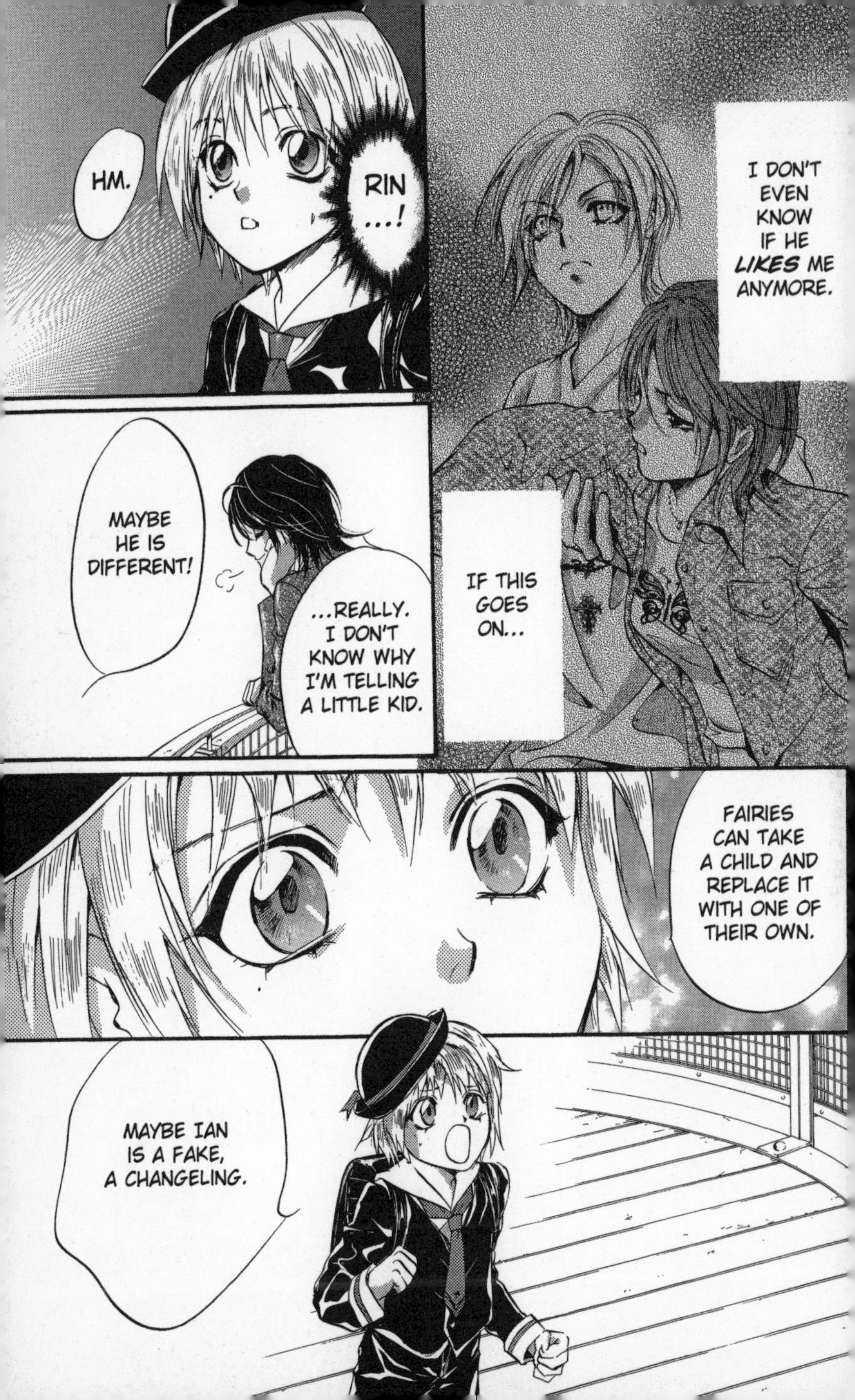
I DON'T EVEN KNOW IF HE *LIKES* ME ANYMORE.
IF THIS GOES ON...
RIN ...!
HM.
MAYBE HE IS DIFFERENT!
...REALLY. I DON'T KNOW WHY I'M TELLING A LITTLE KID.
FAIRIES CAN TAKE A CHILD AND REPLACE IT WITH ONE OF THEIR OWN.
MAYBE IAN IS A FAKE, A CHANGELING.

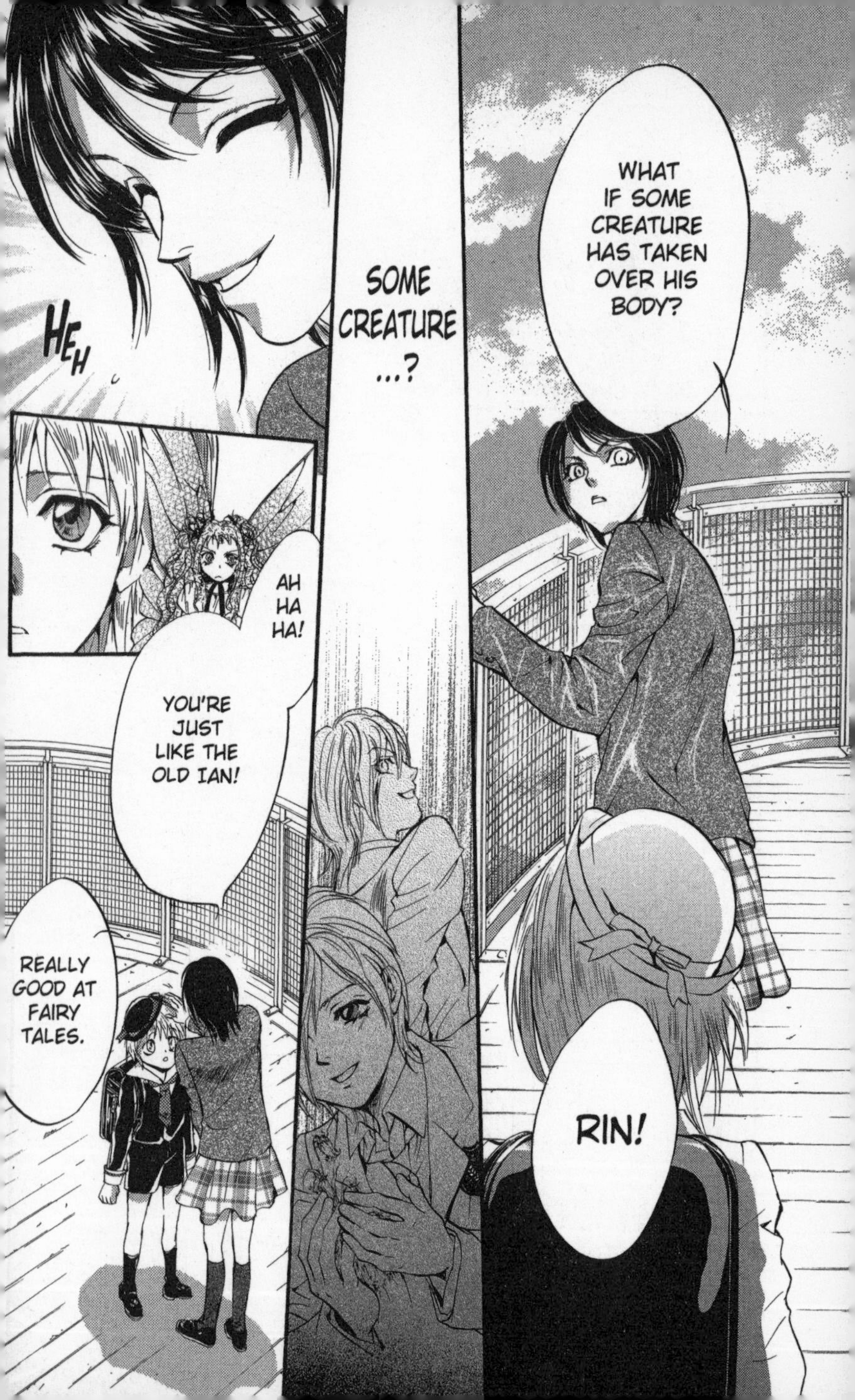
WHAT IF SOME CREATURE HAS TAKEN OVER HIS BODY?
RIN!
SOME CREATURE ...?
HEH
AH HA HA!
YOU'RE JUST LIKE THE OLD IAN!
REALLY GOOD AT FAIRY TALES.

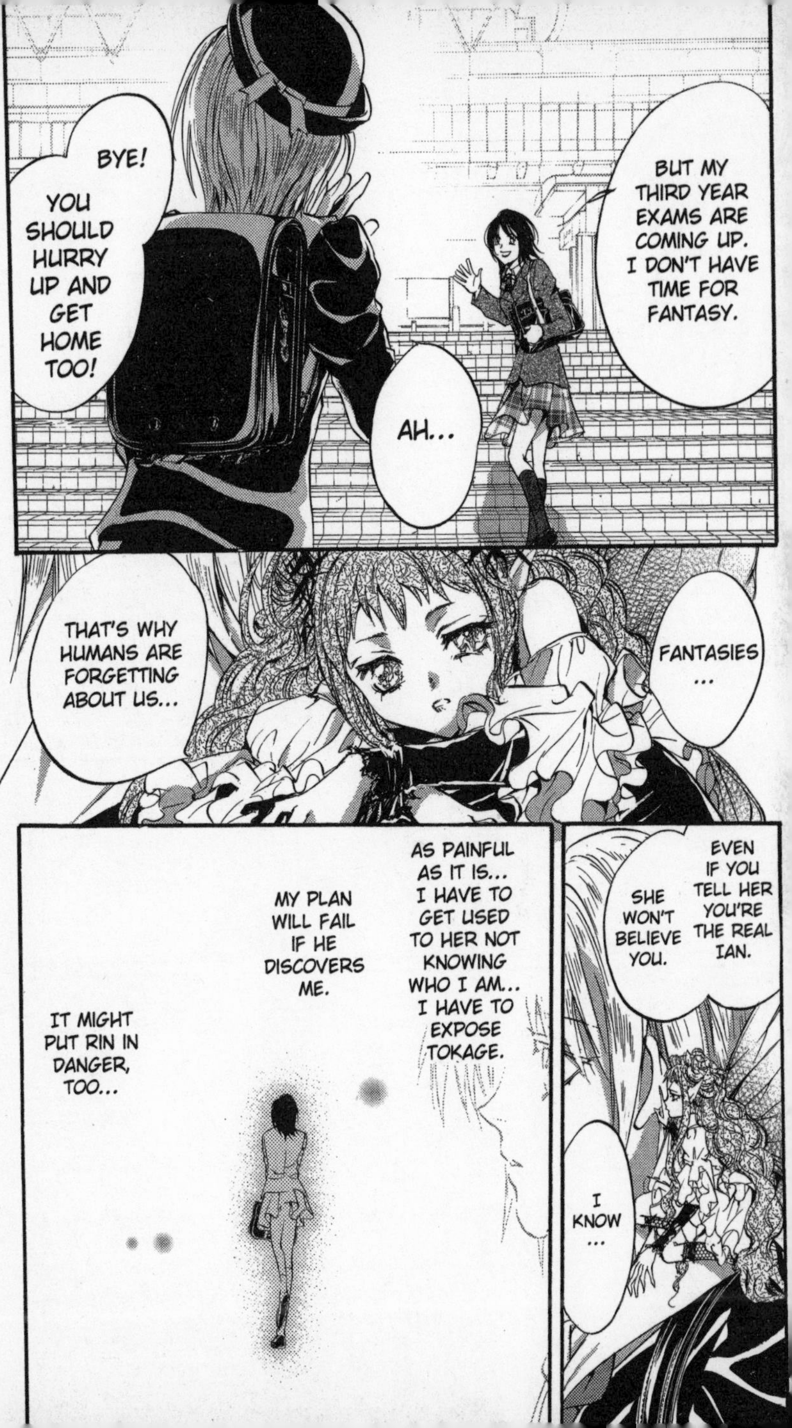
BUT MY THIRD YEAR EXAMS ARE COMING UP. I DON'T HAVE TIME FOR FANTASY.
BYE!
YOU SHOULD HURRY UP AND GET HOME TOO!
AH...
FANTASIES...
THAT'S WHY HUMANS ARE FORGETTING ABOUT US...
EVEN IF YOU TELL HER YOU'RE THE REAL IAN.
SHE WON'T BELIEVE YOU.
I KNOW...
AS PAINFUL AS IT IS... I HAVE TO GET USED TO HER NOT KNOWING WHO I AM... I HAVE TO EXPOSE TOKAGE.
MY PLAN WILL FAIL IF HE DISCOVERS ME.
IT MIGHT PUT RIN IN DANGER, TOO...

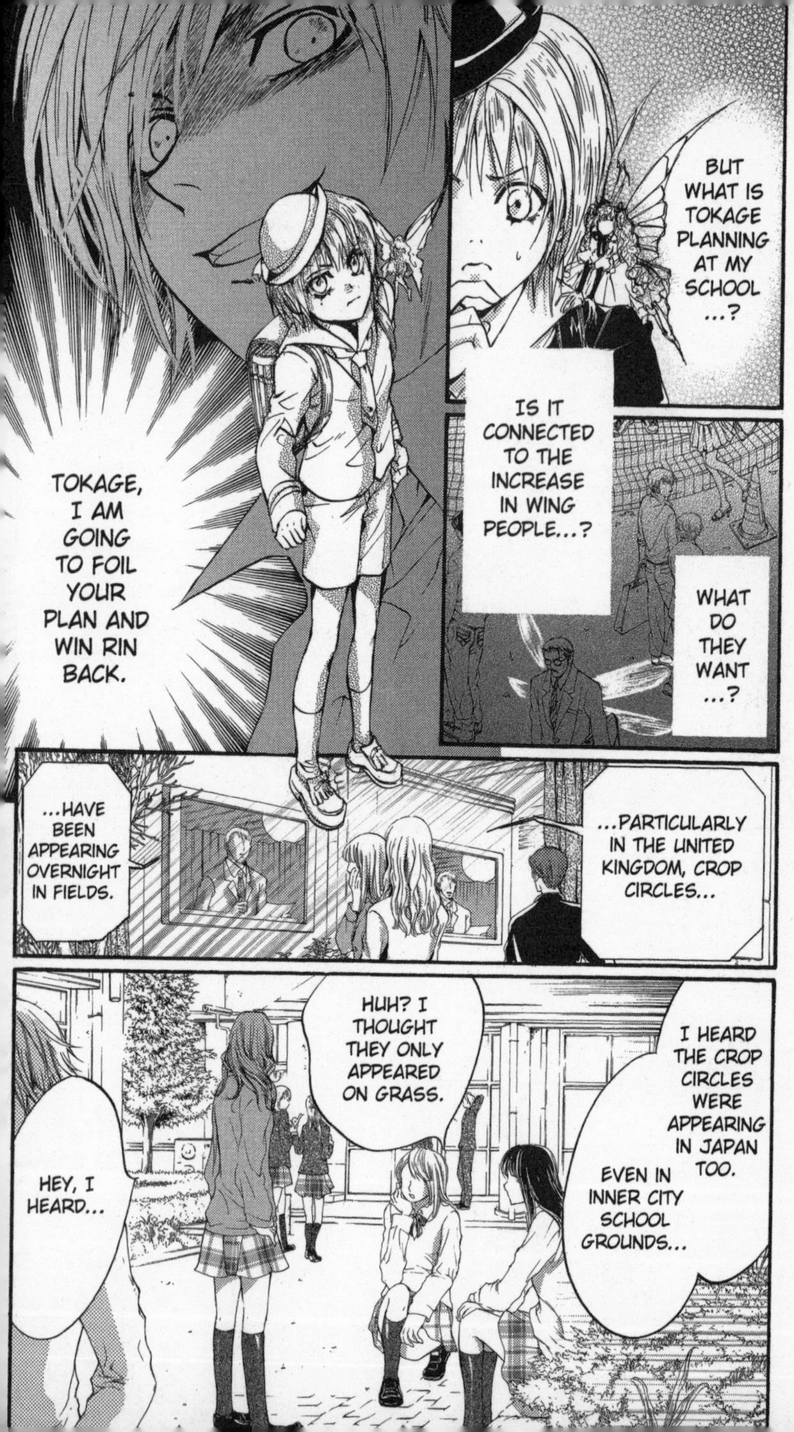
BUT WHAT IS TOKAGE PLANNING AT MY SCHOOL...?
IS IT CONNECTED TO THE INCREASE IN WING PEOPLE...?
WHAT DO THEY WANT...?
TOKAGE, I AM GOING TO FOIL YOUR PLAN AND WIN RIN BACK.
...PARTICULARLY IN THE UNITED KINGDOM, CROP CIRCLES...
...HAVE BEEN APPEARING OVERNIGHT IN FIELDS.
I HEARD THE CROP CIRCLES WERE APPEARING IN JAPAN TOO.
EVEN IN INNER CITY SCHOOL GROUNDS...
HUH? I THOUGHT THEY ONLY APPEARED ON GRASS.
HEY, I HEARD...

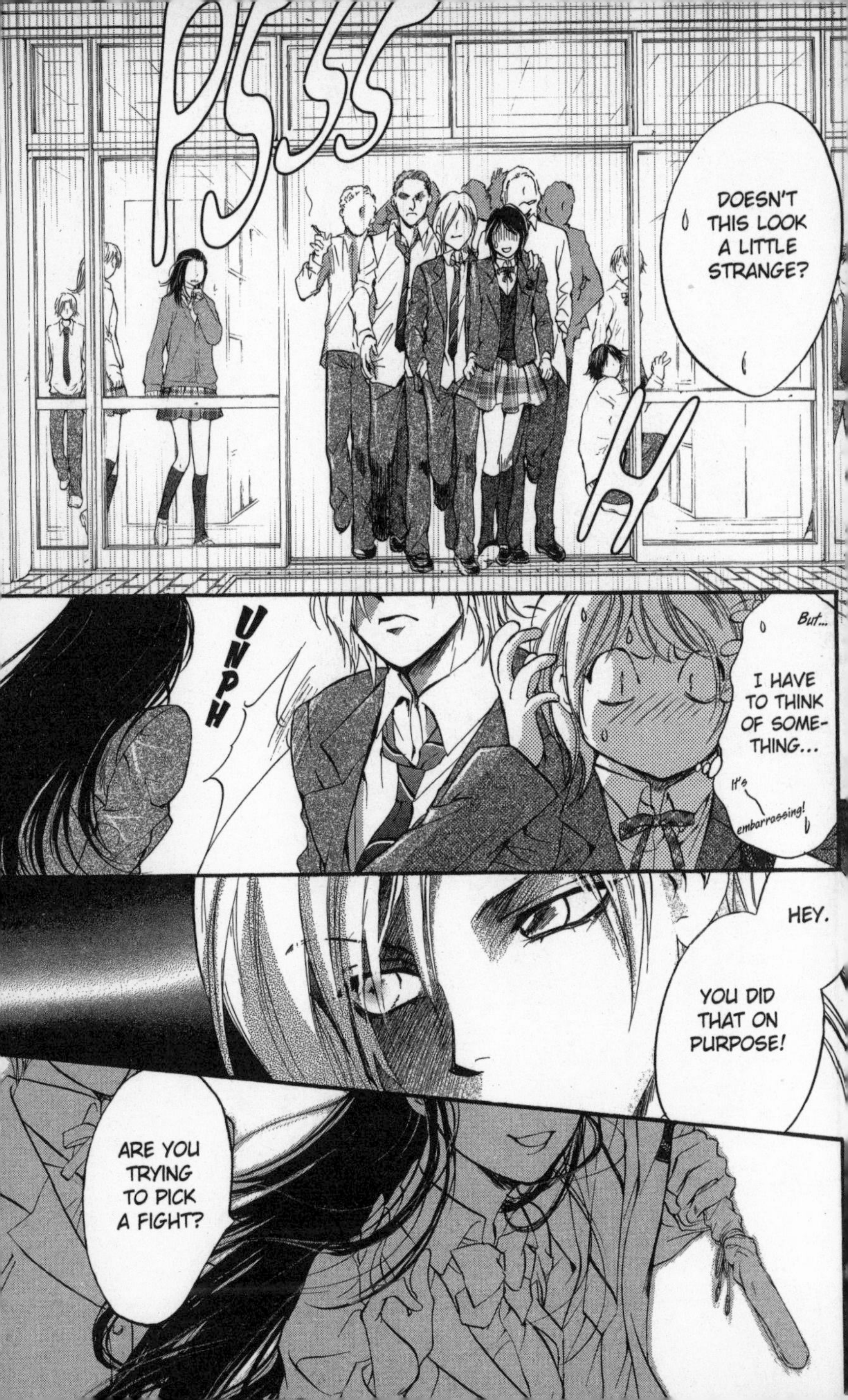
PSSS
DOESN'T THIS LOOK A LITTLE STRANGE?
H
But...
I HAVE TO THINK OF SOME-THING...
It's embarrassing!
UNPH
HEY.
YOU DID THAT ON PURPOSE!
ARE YOU TRYING TO PICK A FIGHT?

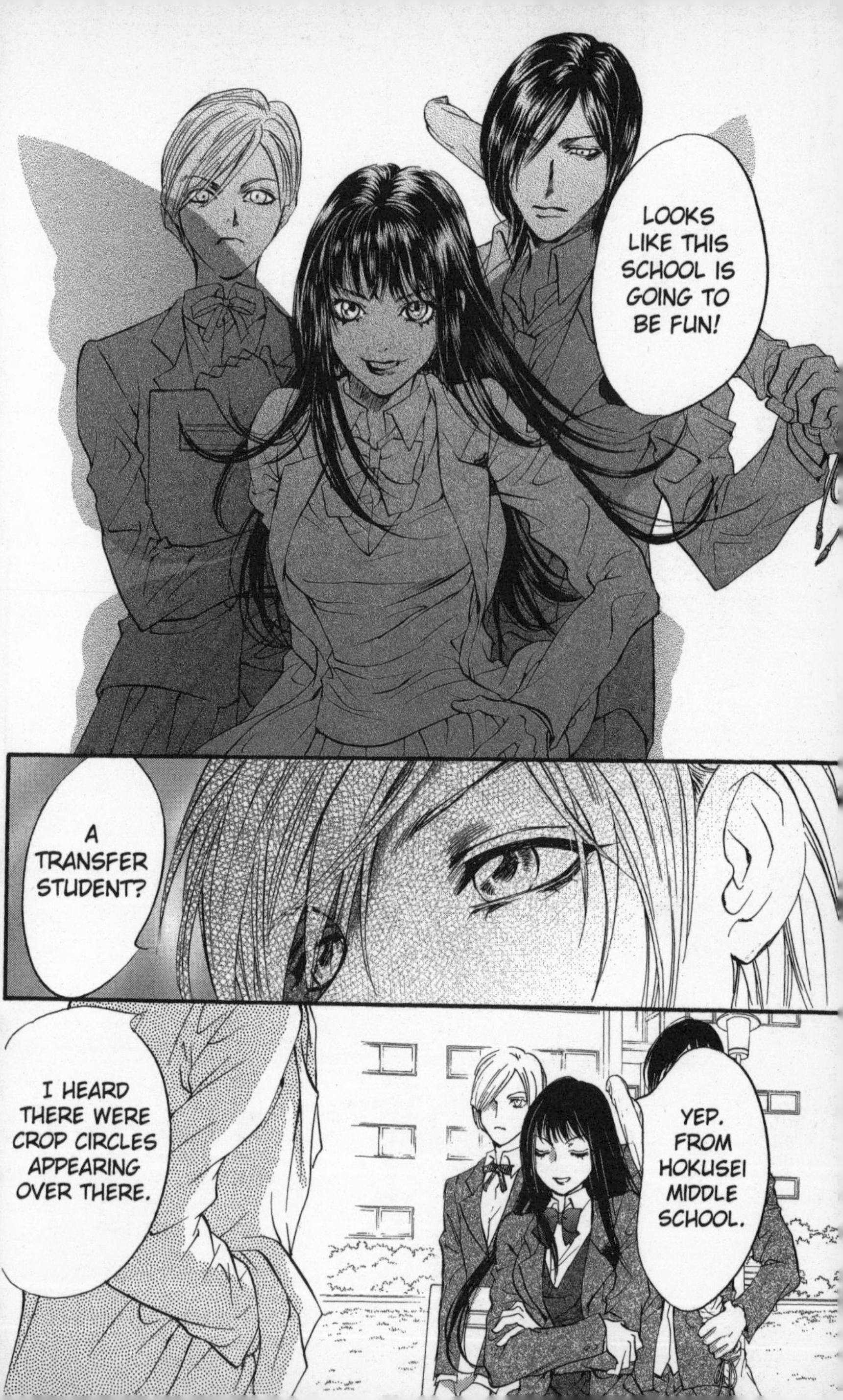
LOOKS LIKE THIS SCHOOL IS GOING TO BE FUN!
A TRANSFER STUDENT?
YEP. FROM HOKUSEI MIDDLE SCHOOL.
I HEARD THERE WERE CROP CIRCLES APPEARING OVER THERE.

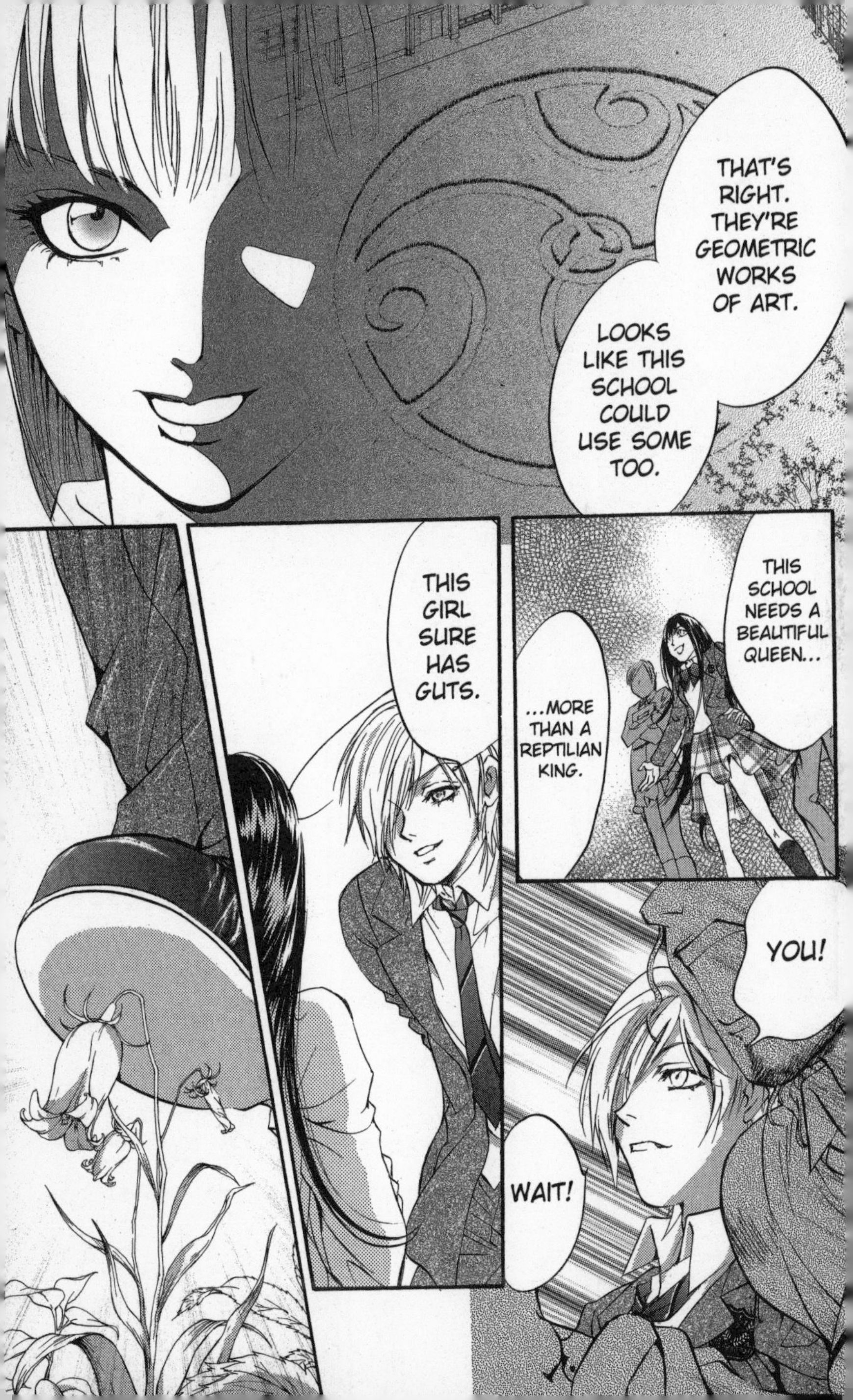
THAT'S RIGHT. THEY'RE GEOMETRIC WORKS OF ART.
LOOKS LIKE THIS SCHOOL COULD USE SOME TOO.
THIS SCHOOL NEEDS A BEAUTIFUL QUEEN...
...MORE THAN A REPTILIAN KING.
YOU!
WAIT!
THIS GIRL SURE HAS GUTS.

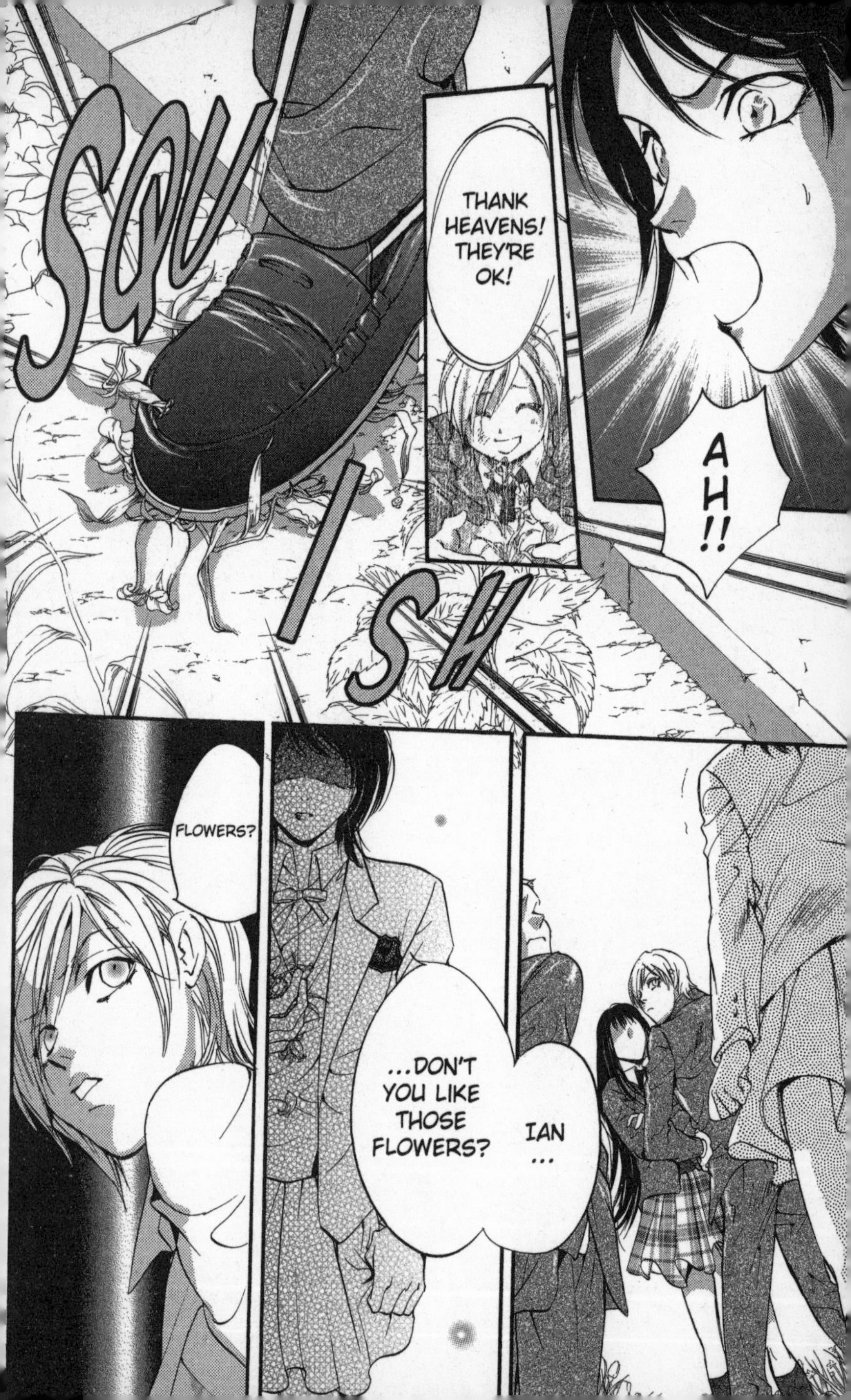
AH!!
THANK HEAVENS! THEY'RE OK!
SQU
ISH
IAN ...
...DON'T YOU LIKE THOSE FLOWERS?
FLOWERS?

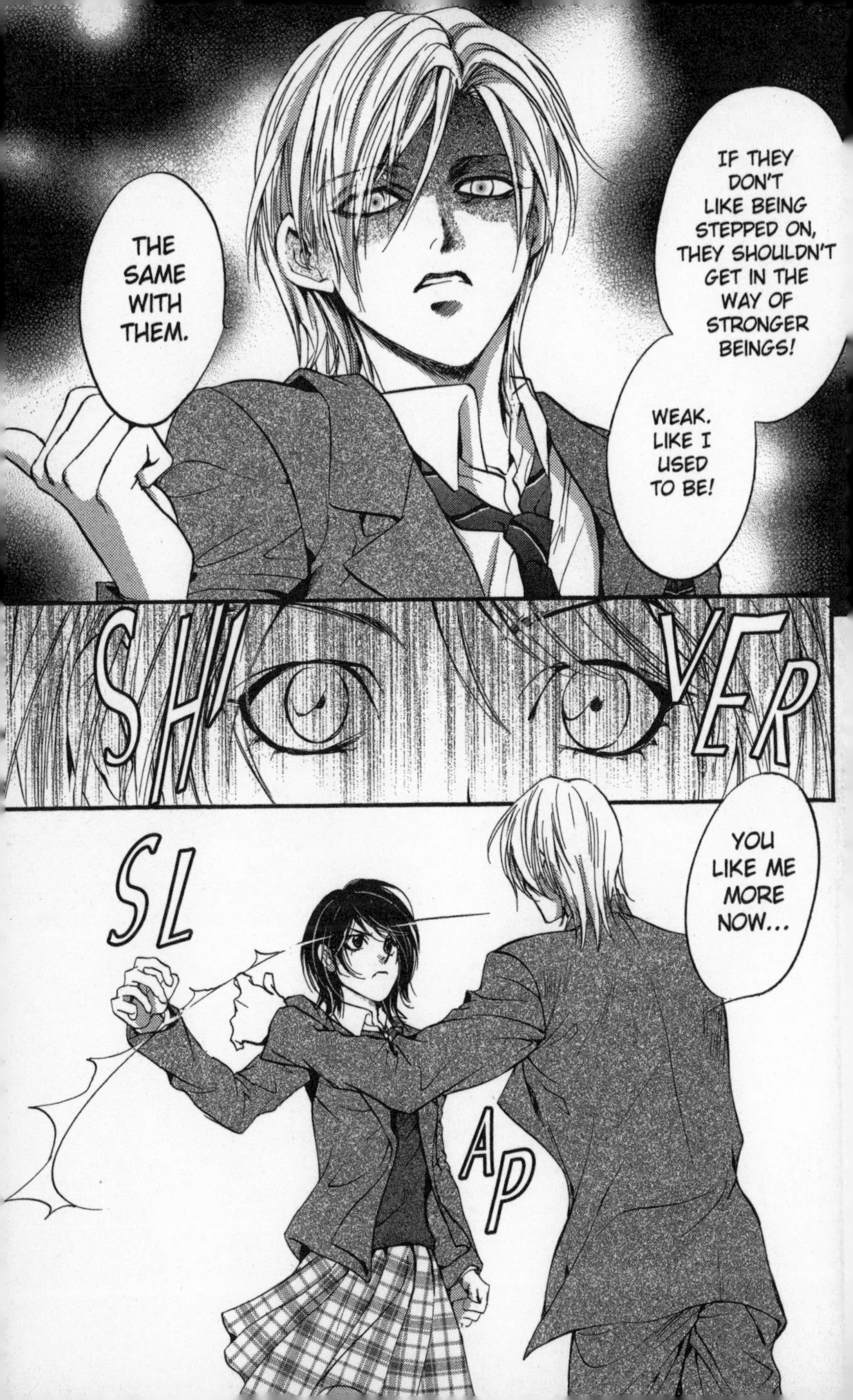
IF THEY DON'T LIKE BEING STEPPED ON, THEY SHOULDN'T GET IN THE WAY OF STRONGER BEINGS!
WEAK. LIKE I USED TO BE!
THE SAME WITH THEM.
SHI
VER
YOU LIKE ME MORE NOW...
SL
AP

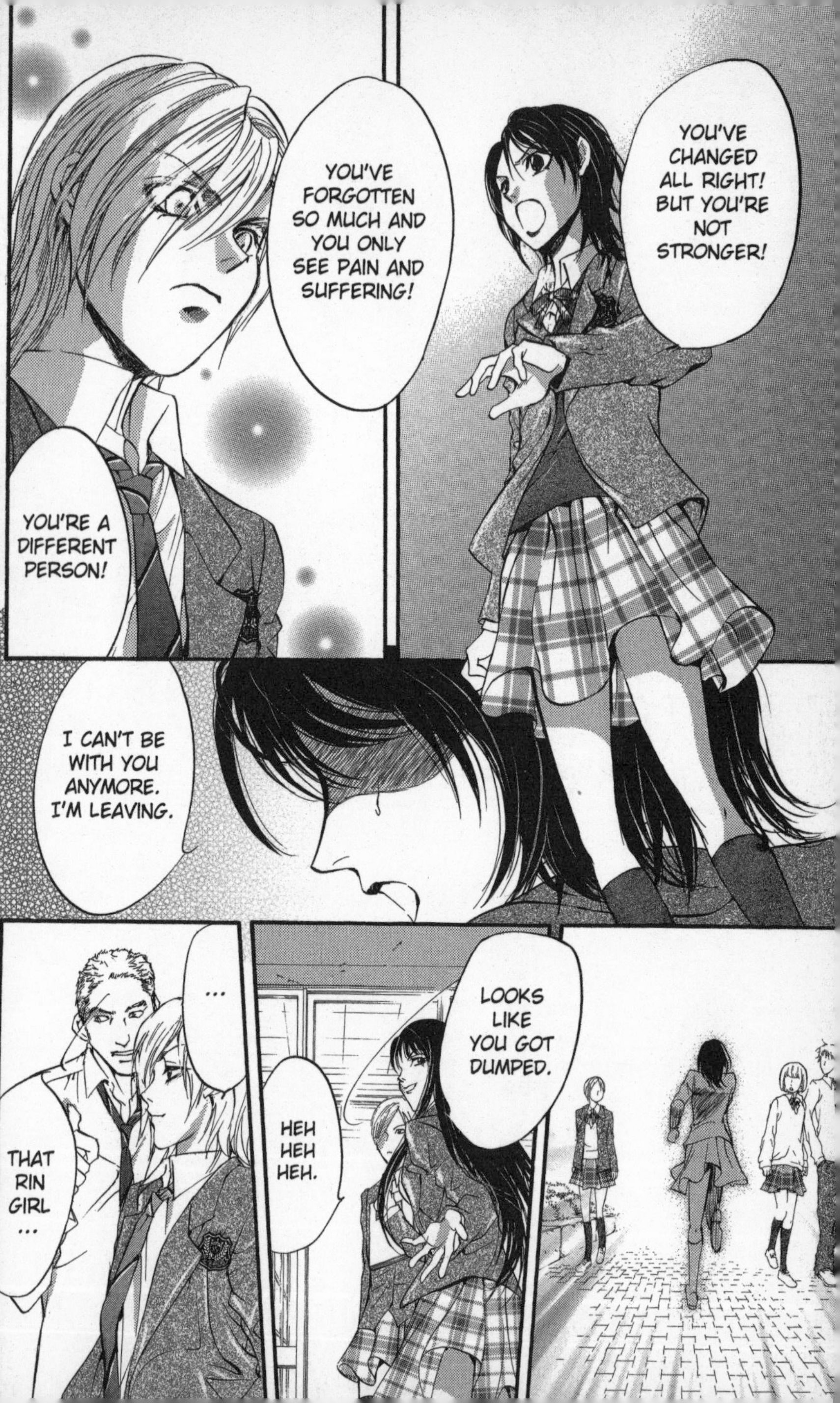
YOU'VE CHANGED ALL RIGHT! BUT YOU'RE NOT STRONGER!
YOU'VE FORGOTTEN SO MUCH AND YOU ONLY SEE PAIN AND SUFFERING!
YOU'RE A DIFFERENT PERSON!
I CAN'T BE WITH YOU ANYMORE. I'M LEAVING.
LOOKS LIKE YOU GOT DUMPED.
HEH HEH HEH.
...
THAT RIN GIRL ...

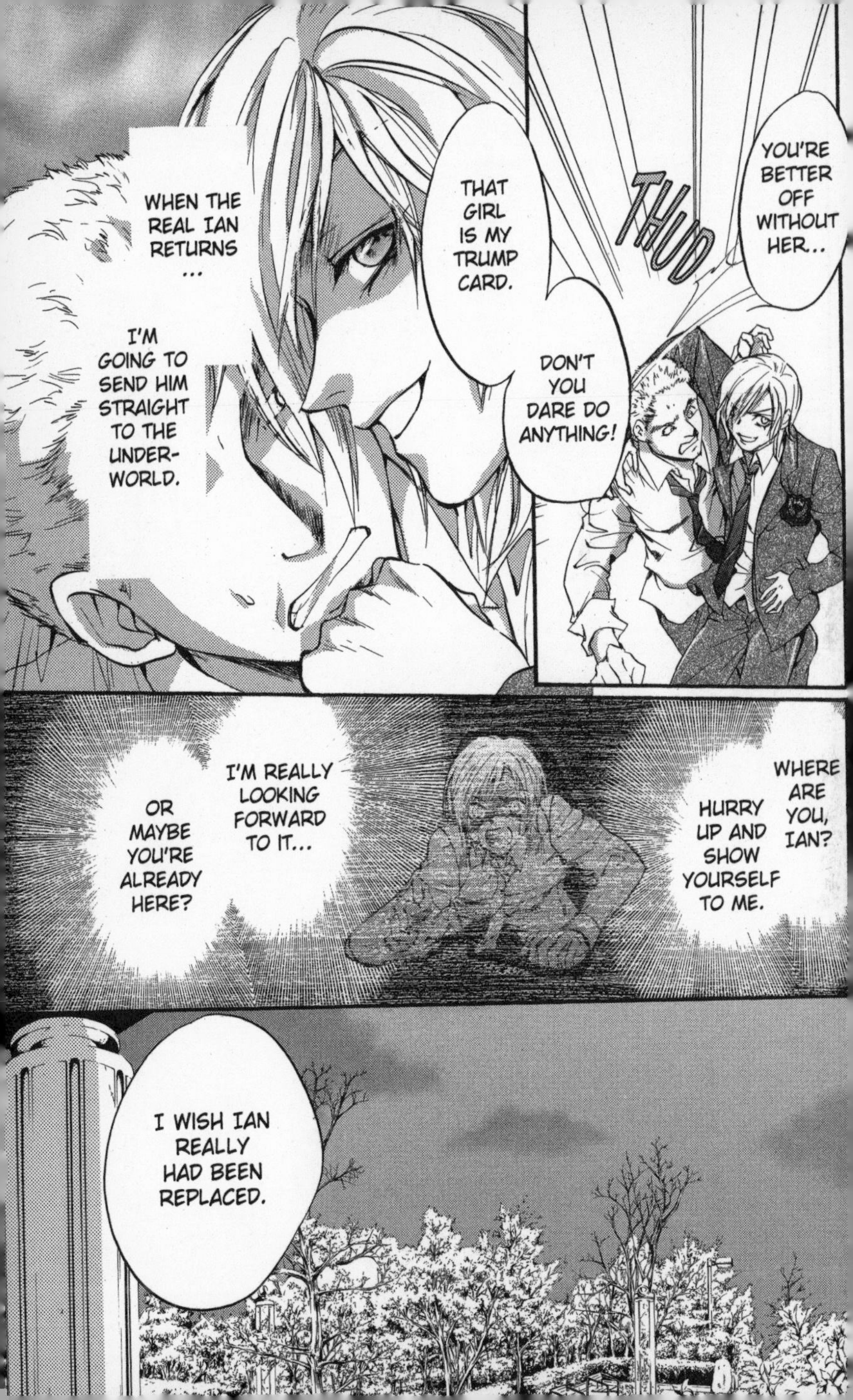
YOU'RE BETTER OFF WITHOUT HER...
THUD
DON'T YOU DARE DO ANYTHING!
THAT GIRL IS MY TRUMP CARD.
WHEN THE REAL IAN RETURNS...
I'M GOING TO SEND HIM STRAIGHT TO THE UNDER-WORLD.
WHERE ARE YOU, IAN?
HURRY UP AND SHOW YOURSELF TO ME.
I'M REALLY LOOKING FORWARD TO IT...
OR MAYBE YOU'RE ALREADY HERE?
I WISH IAN REALLY HAD BEEN REPLACED.

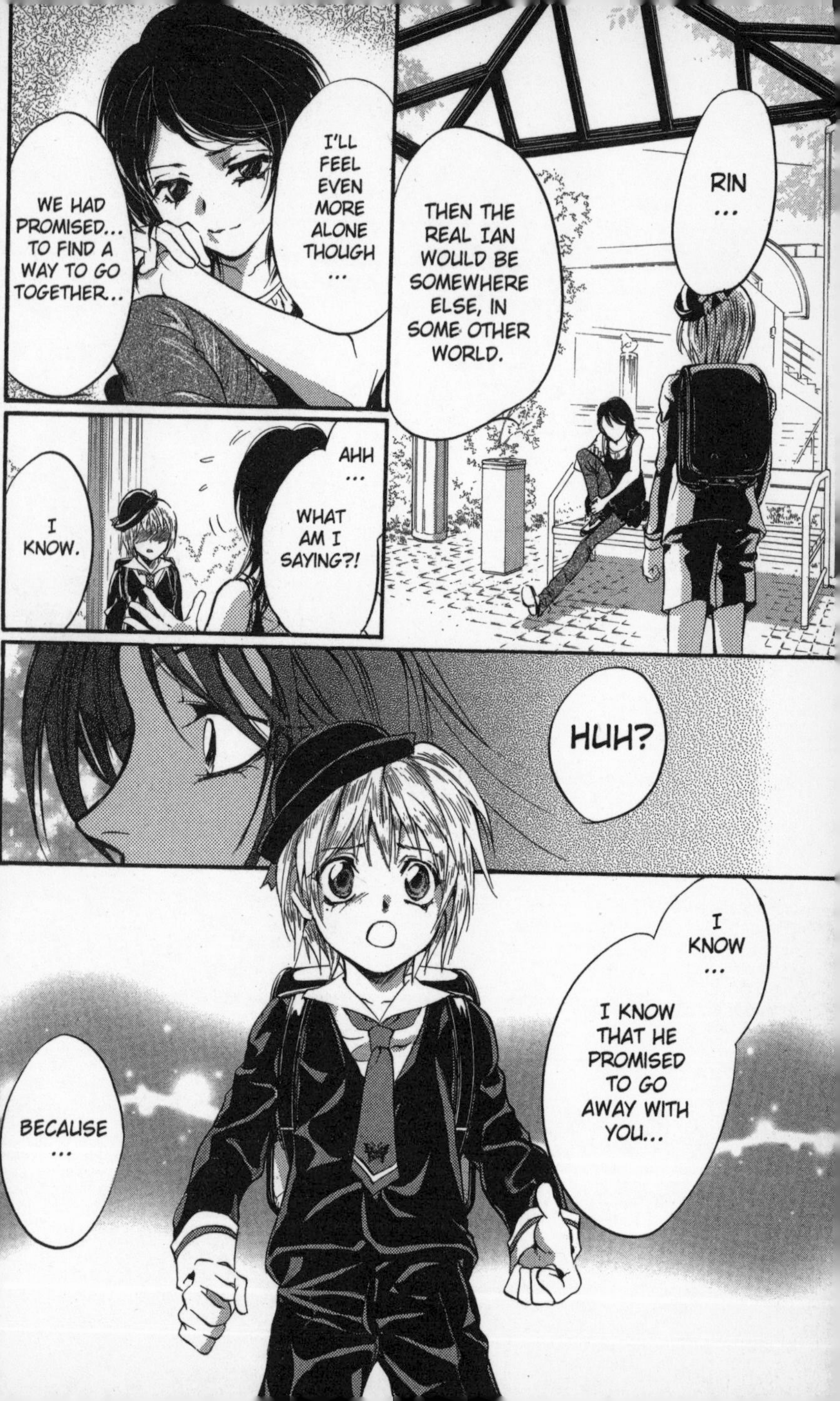
RIN ...
THEN THE REAL IAN WOULD BE SOMEWHERE ELSE, IN SOME OTHER WORLD.
I'LL FEEL EVEN MORE ALONE THOUGH ...
WE HAD PROMISED... TO FIND A WAY TO GO TOGETHER...
AHH ... WHAT AM I SAYING?!
I KNOW.
HUH?
I KNOW ...
I KNOW THAT HE PROMISED TO GO AWAY WITH YOU...
BECAUSE ...

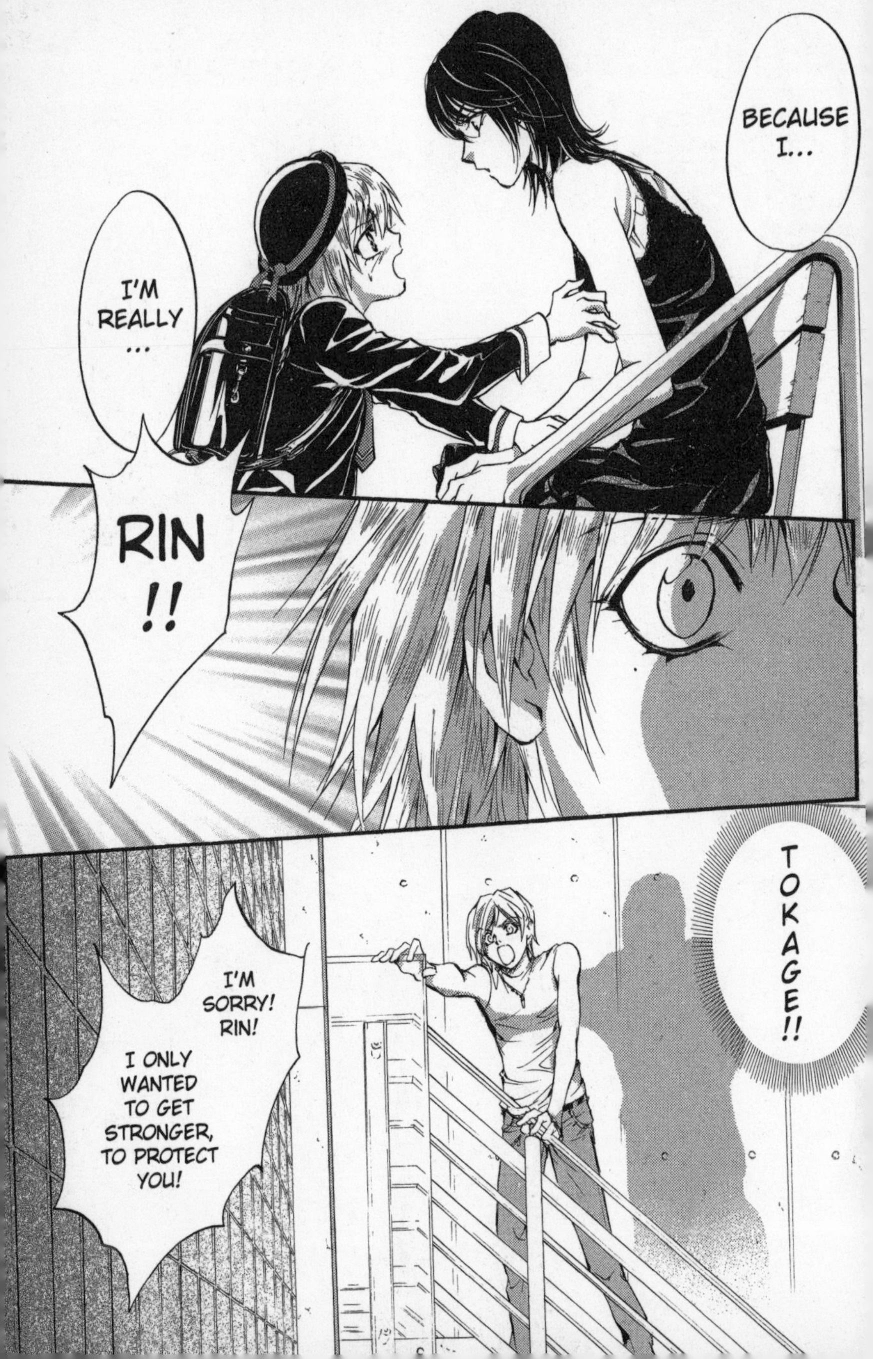
BECAUSE I...
I'M REALLY ...
RIN!!
TOKAGE!!
I'M SORRY! RIN!
I ONLY WANTED TO GET STRONGER, TO PROTECT YOU!

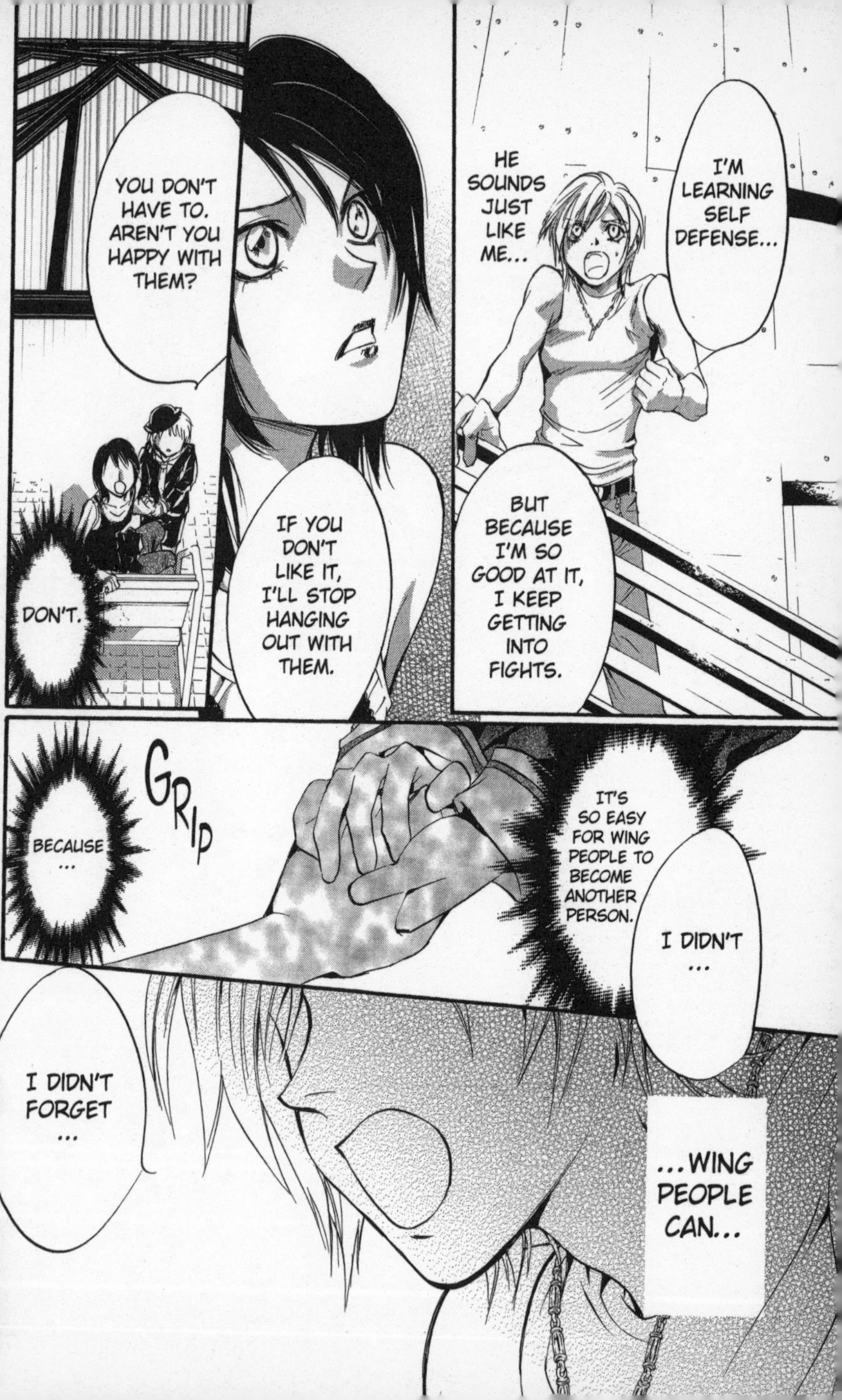
I'M LEARNING SELF DEFENSE...
HE SOUNDS JUST LIKE ME...
BUT BECAUSE I'M SO GOOD AT IT, I KEEP GETTING INTO FIGHTS.
IF YOU DON'T LIKE IT, I'LL STOP HANGING OUT WITH THEM.
YOU DON'T HAVE TO. AREN'T YOU HAPPY WITH THEM?
DON'T.
IT'S SO EASY FOR WING PEOPLE TO BECOME ANOTHER PERSON.
GRIP
BECAUSE ...
I DIDN'T ...
...WING PEOPLE CAN...
I DIDN'T FORGET ...

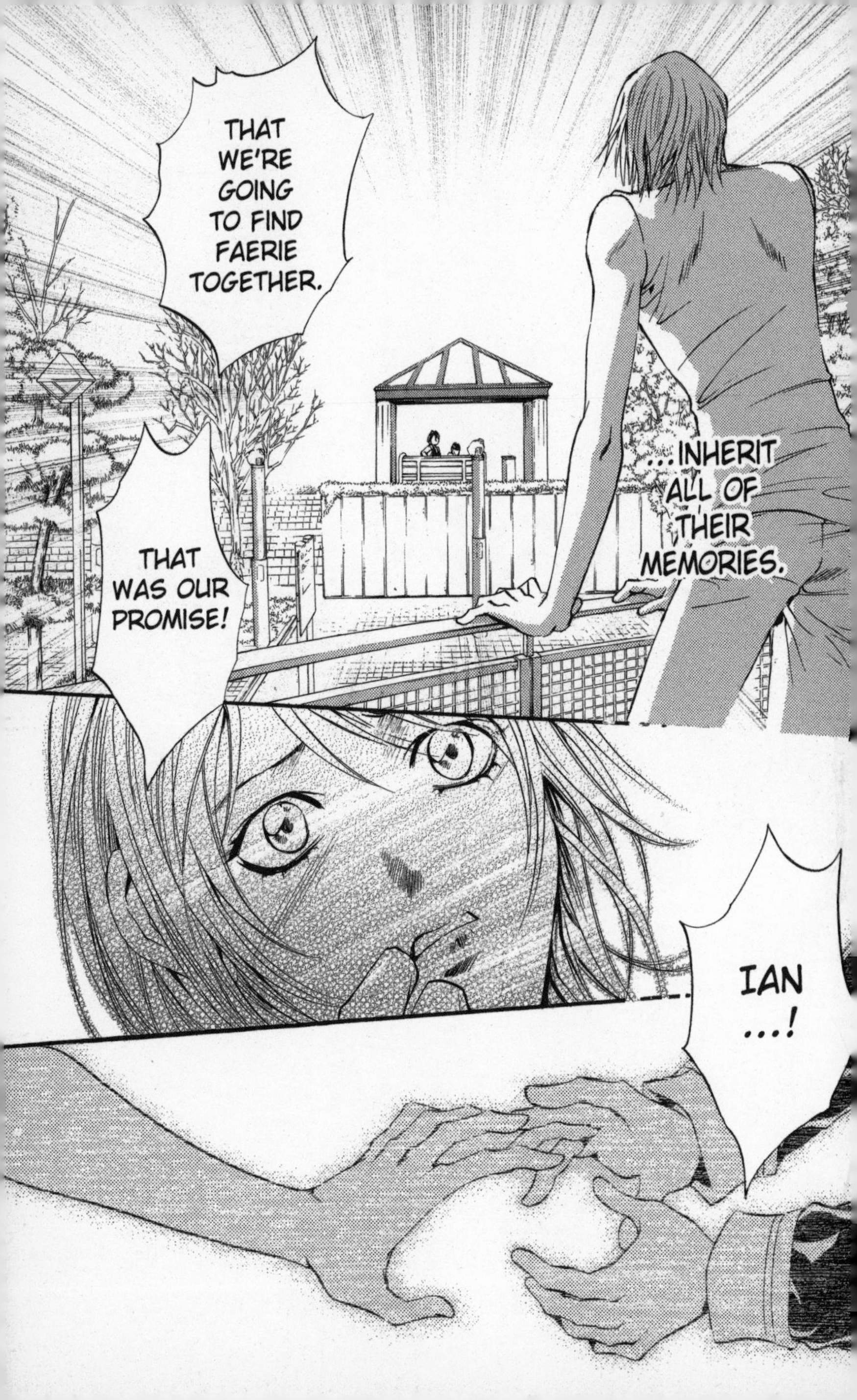
...INHERIT ALL OF THEIR MEMORIES.
THAT WE'RE GOING TO FIND FAERIE TOGETHER.
THAT WAS OUR PROMISE!
IAN ...!

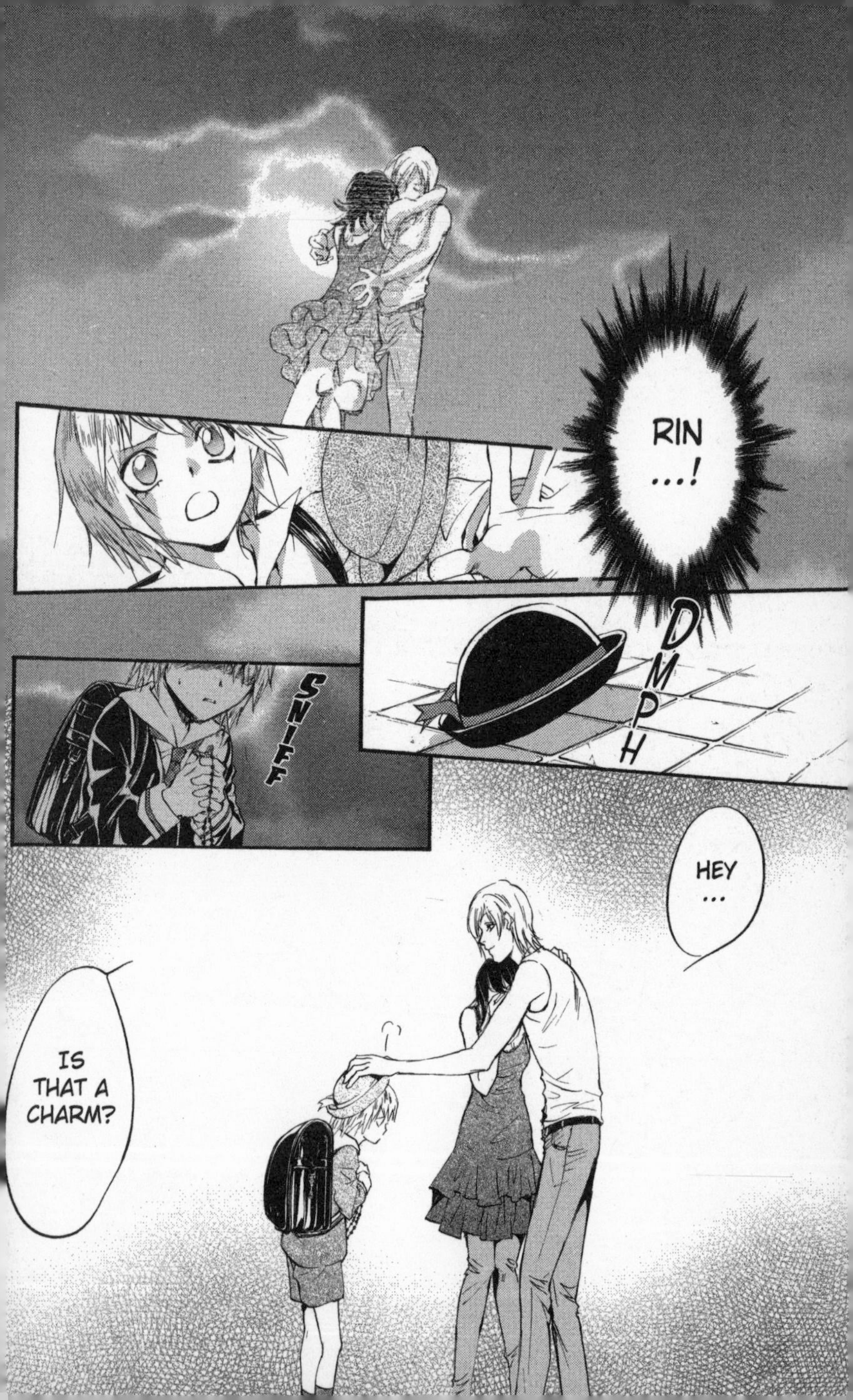
RIN ...!
DMPH
SNIFF
HEY ...
IS THAT A CHARM?

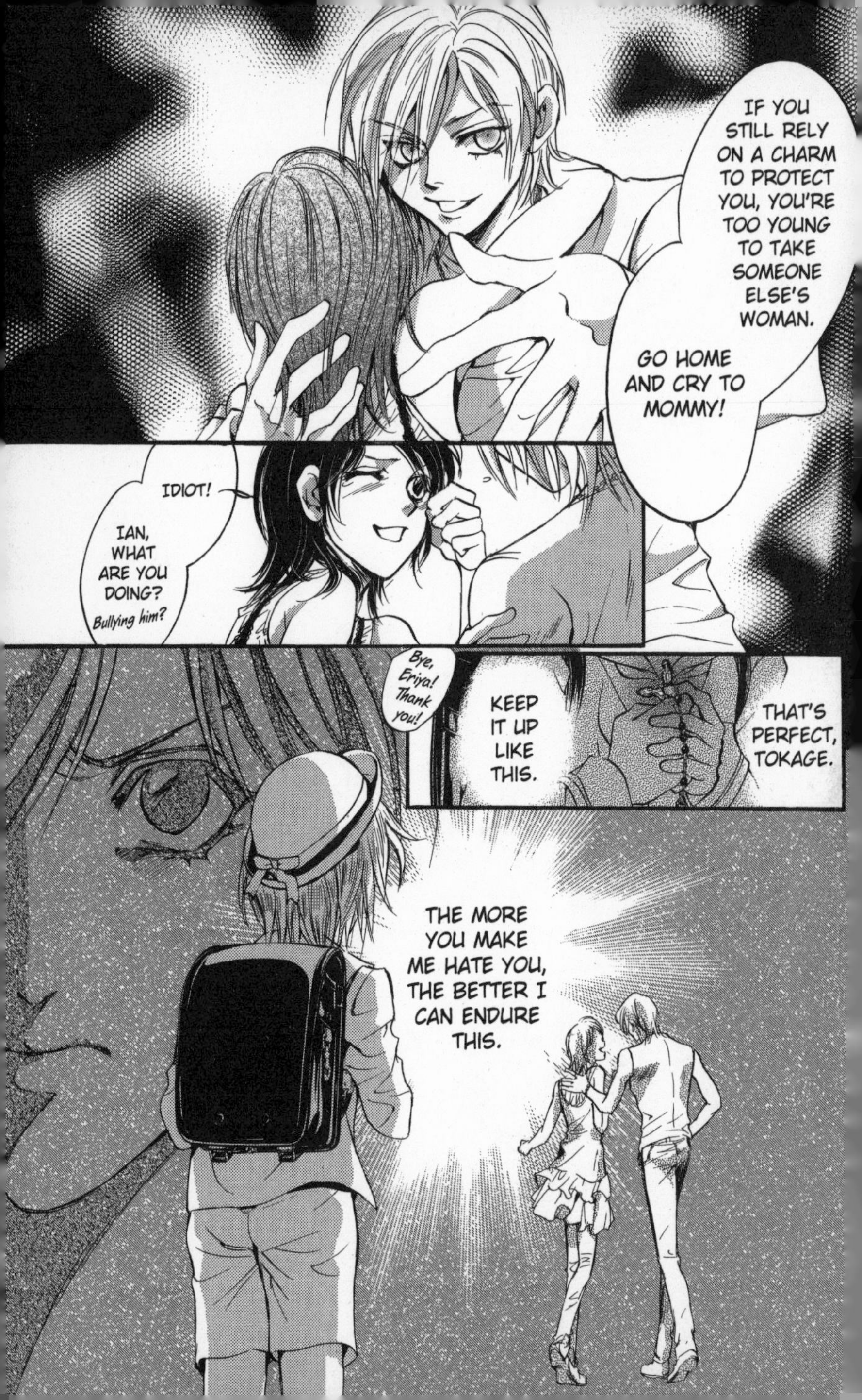

IF YOU STILL RELY ON A CHARM TO PROTECT YOU, YOU'RE TOO YOUNG TO TAKE SOMEONE ELSE'S WOMAN.
GO HOME AND CRY TO MOMMY!
IDIOT!
IAN, WHAT ARE YOU DOING?
Bullying him?
THAT'S PERFECT, TOKAGE.
KEEP IT UP LIKE THIS.
Bye, Eriya! Thank you!
THE MORE YOU MAKE ME HATE YOU, THE BETTER I CAN ENDURE THIS.

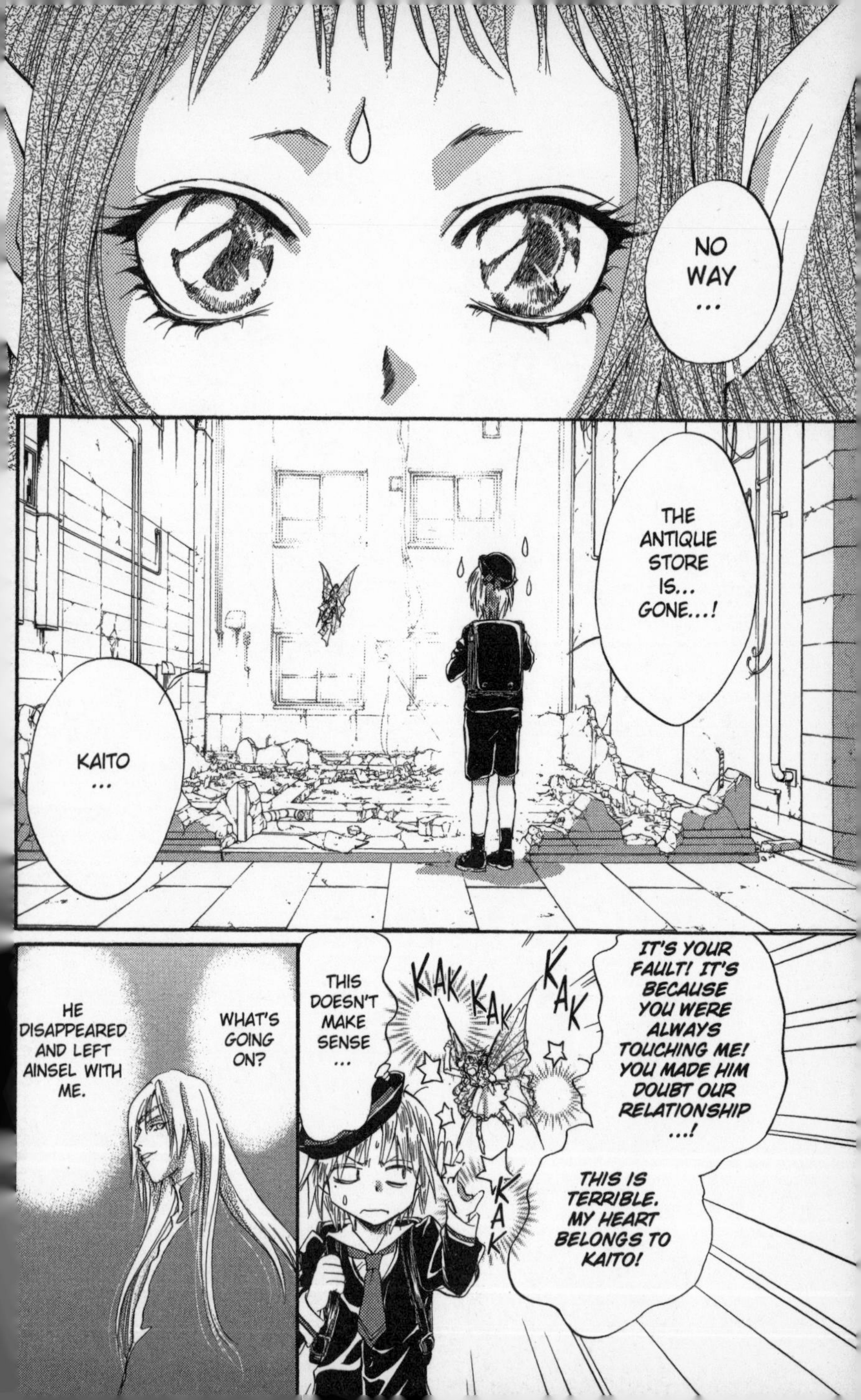

NO WAY ...
THE ANTIQUE STORE IS... GONE...!
KAITO ...
IT'S YOUR FAULT! IT'S BECAUSE YOU WERE ALWAYS TOUCHING ME! YOU MADE HIM DOUBT OUR RELATIONSHIP ...!
KAK KAK KAK
THIS IS TERRIBLE. MY HEART BELONGS TO KAITO!
KAK
THIS DOESN'T MAKE SENSE ...
WHAT'S GOING ON?
HE DISAPPEARED AND LEFT AINSEL WITH ME.

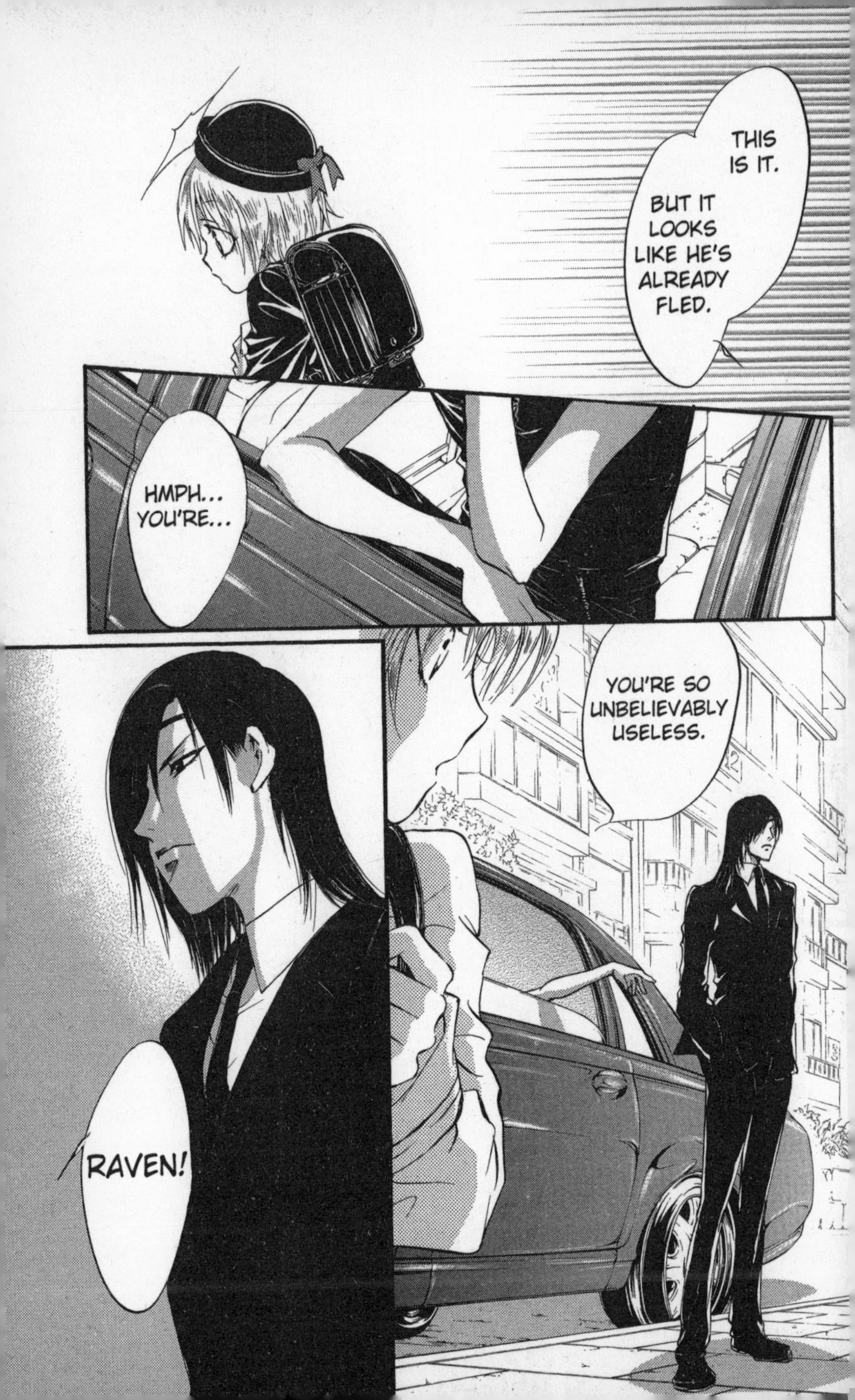
THIS IS IT.
BUT IT LOOKS LIKE HE'S ALREADY FLED.
HMPH... YOU'RE...
YOU'RE SO UNBELIEVABLY USELESS.
RAVEN!

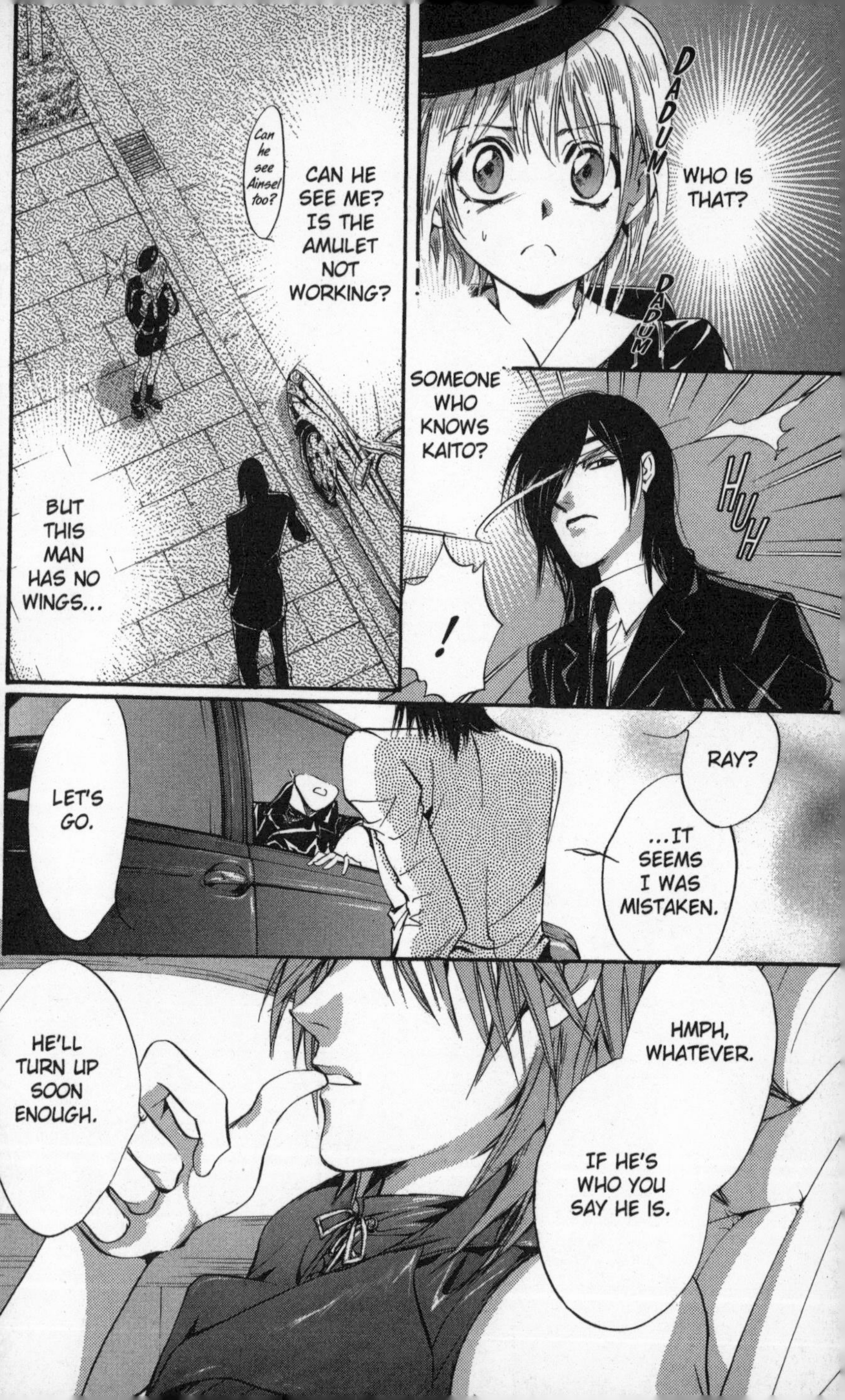
DADUM
WHO IS THAT?
DADUM
SOMEONE WHO KNOWS KAITO?
HUH
!
Can he see Ainsel too?
CAN HE SEE ME? IS THE AMULET NOT WORKING?
BUT THIS MAN HAS NO WINGS...
RAY?
...IT SEEMS I WAS MISTAKEN.
LET'S GO.
HMPH, WHATEVER.
IF HE'S WHO YOU SAY HE IS.
HE'LL TURN UP SOON ENOUGH.

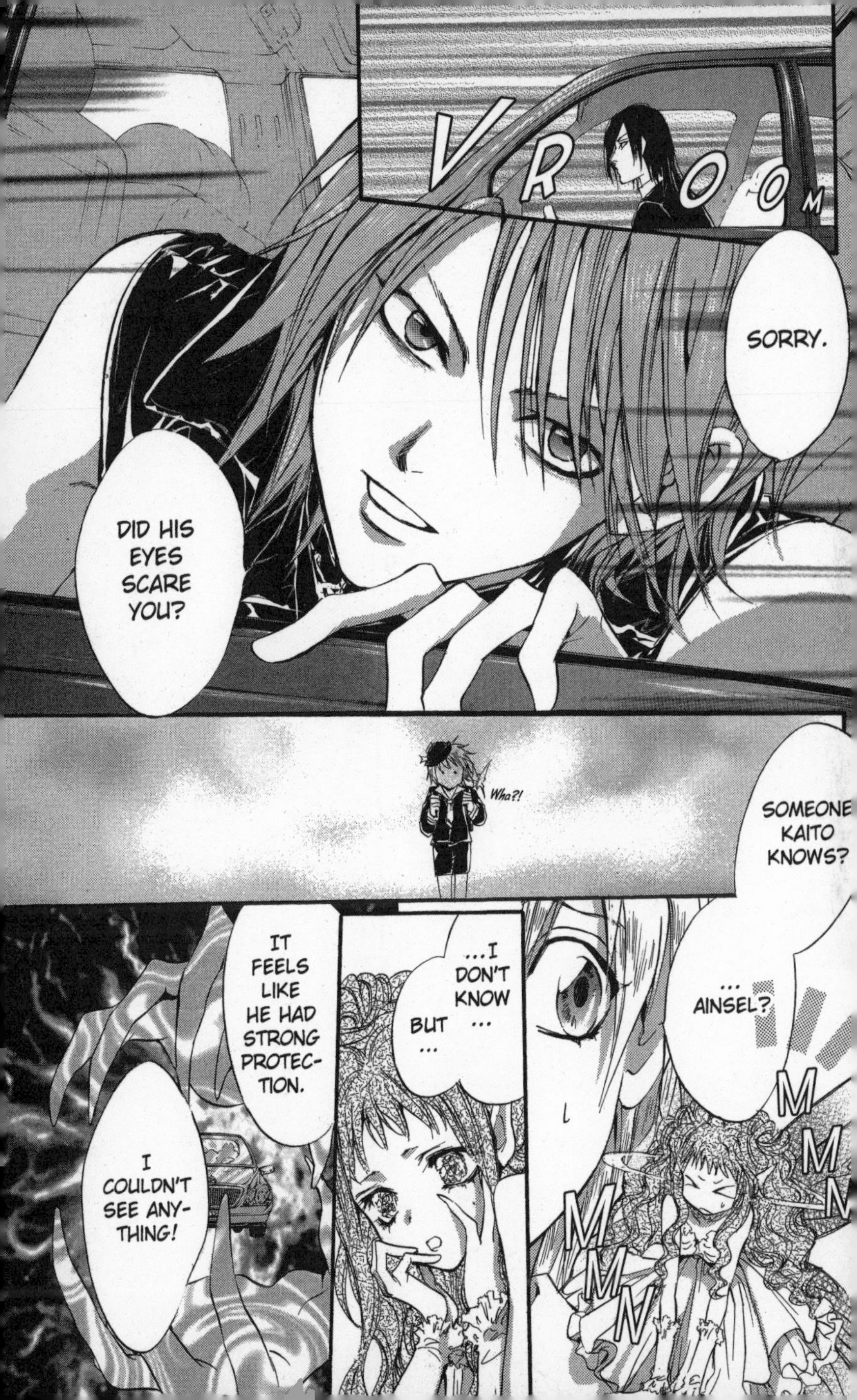
VROOOM
SORRY.
DID HIS EYES SCARE YOU?
SOMEONE KAITO KNOWS?
Wha?!
...AINSEL?
MMMM
MMMN
...I DON'T KNOW...
BUT...
IT FEELS LIKE HE HAD STRONG PROTECTION.
I COULDN'T SEE ANY-THING!

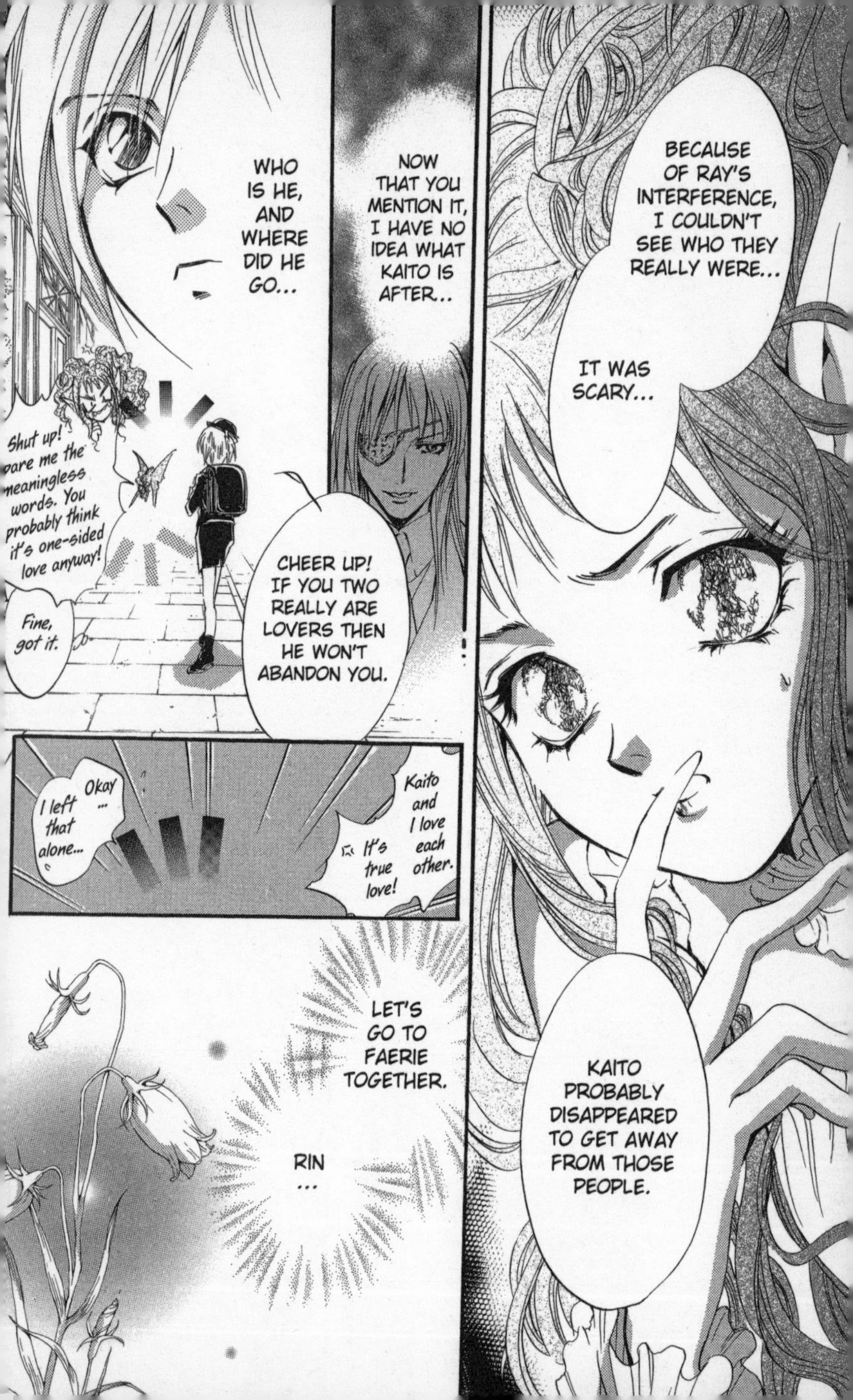
BECAUSE OF RAY'S INTERFERENCE, I COULDN'T SEE WHO THEY REALLY WERE...
IT WAS SCARY...
KAITO PROBABLY DISAPPEARED TO GET AWAY FROM THOSE PEOPLE.
NOW THAT YOU MENTION IT, I HAVE NO IDEA WHAT KAITO IS AFTER...
CHEER UP! IF YOU TWO REALLY ARE LOVERS THEN HE WON'T ABANDON YOU.
WHO IS HE, AND WHERE DID HE GO...
Shut up! pare me the neaningless words. You probably think it's one-sided love anyway!
Fine, got it.
Kaito and I love each other.
It's true love!
Okay...
I left that alone...
LET'S GO TO FAERIE TOGETHER.
RIN...

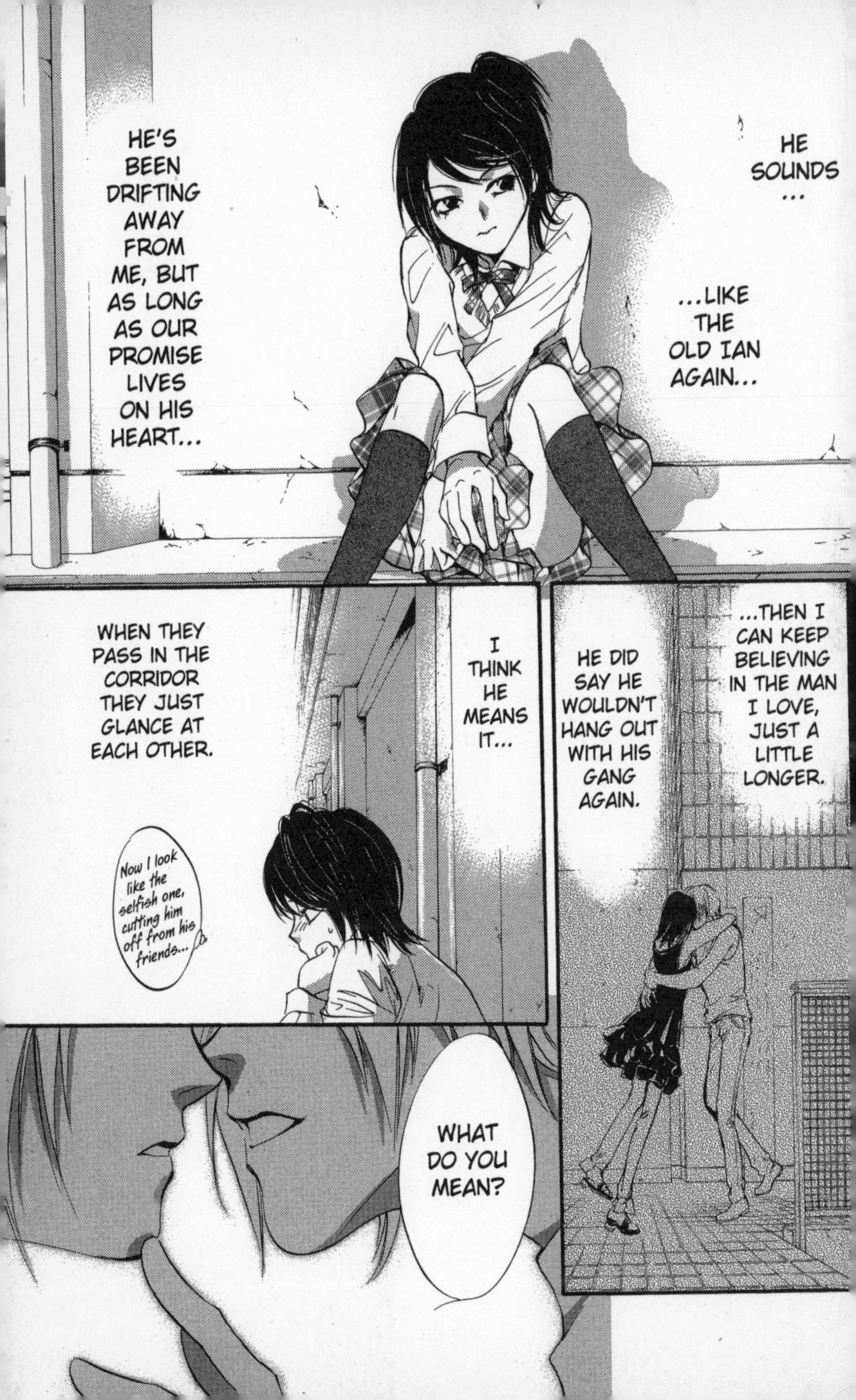
HE SOUNDS ...
...LIKE THE OLD IAN AGAIN...
HE'S BEEN DRIFTING AWAY FROM ME, BUT AS LONG AS OUR PROMISE LIVES ON HIS HEART...
...THEN I CAN KEEP BELIEVING IN THE MAN I LOVE, JUST A LITTLE LONGER.
HE DID SAY HE WOULDN'T HANG OUT WITH HIS GANG AGAIN.
I THINK HE MEANS IT...
WHEN THEY PASS IN THE CORRIDOR THEY JUST GLANCE AT EACH OTHER.
Now I look like the selfish one, cutting him off from his friends...
WHAT DO YOU MEAN?

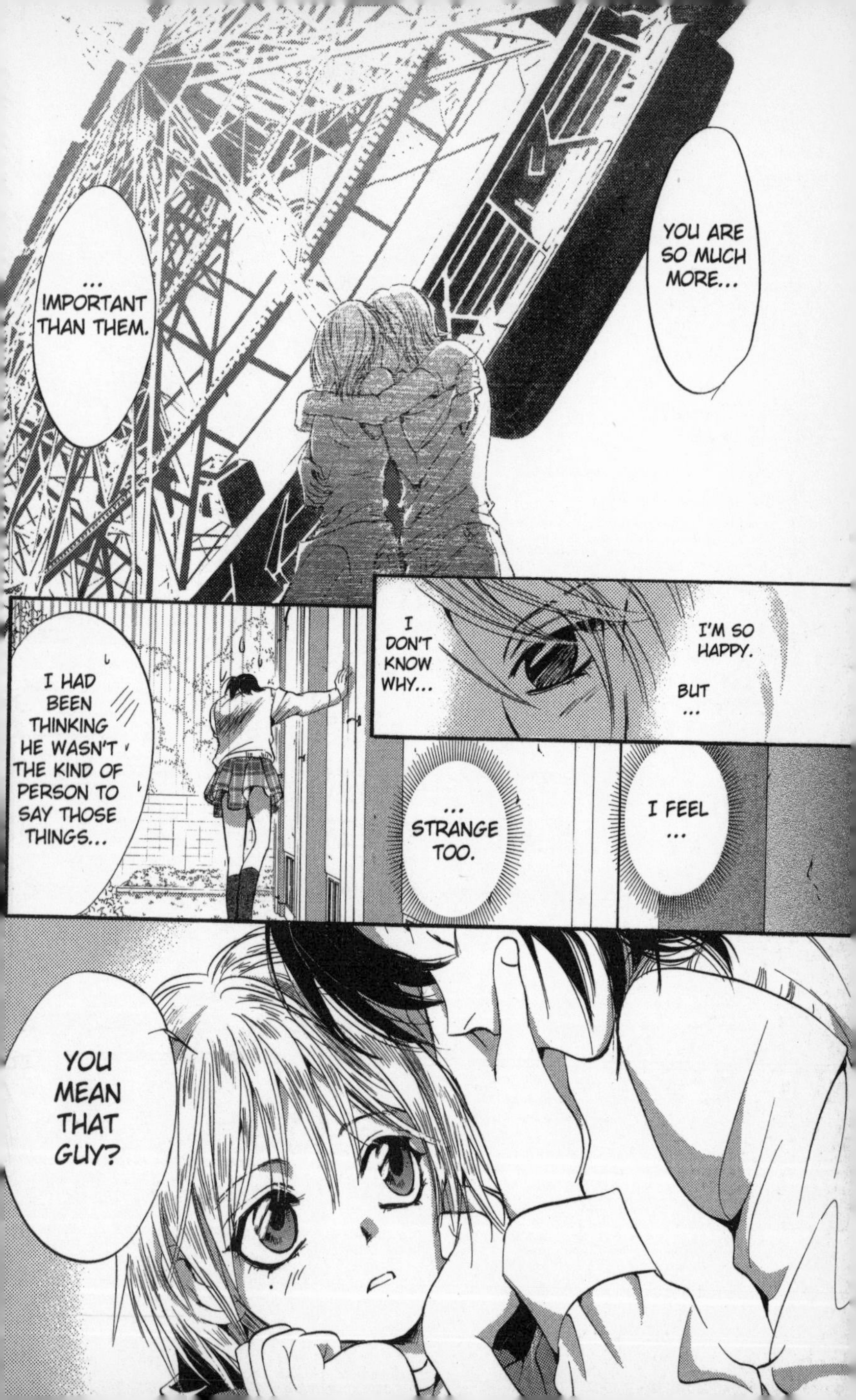

YOU ARE SO MUCH MORE...
... IMPORTANT THAN THEM.
I'M SO HAPPY.
BUT ...
I DON'T KNOW WHY...
I FEEL ...
... STRANGE TOO.
I HAD BEEN THINKING HE WASN'T THE KIND OF PERSON TO SAY THOSE THINGS...
YOU MEAN THAT GUY?

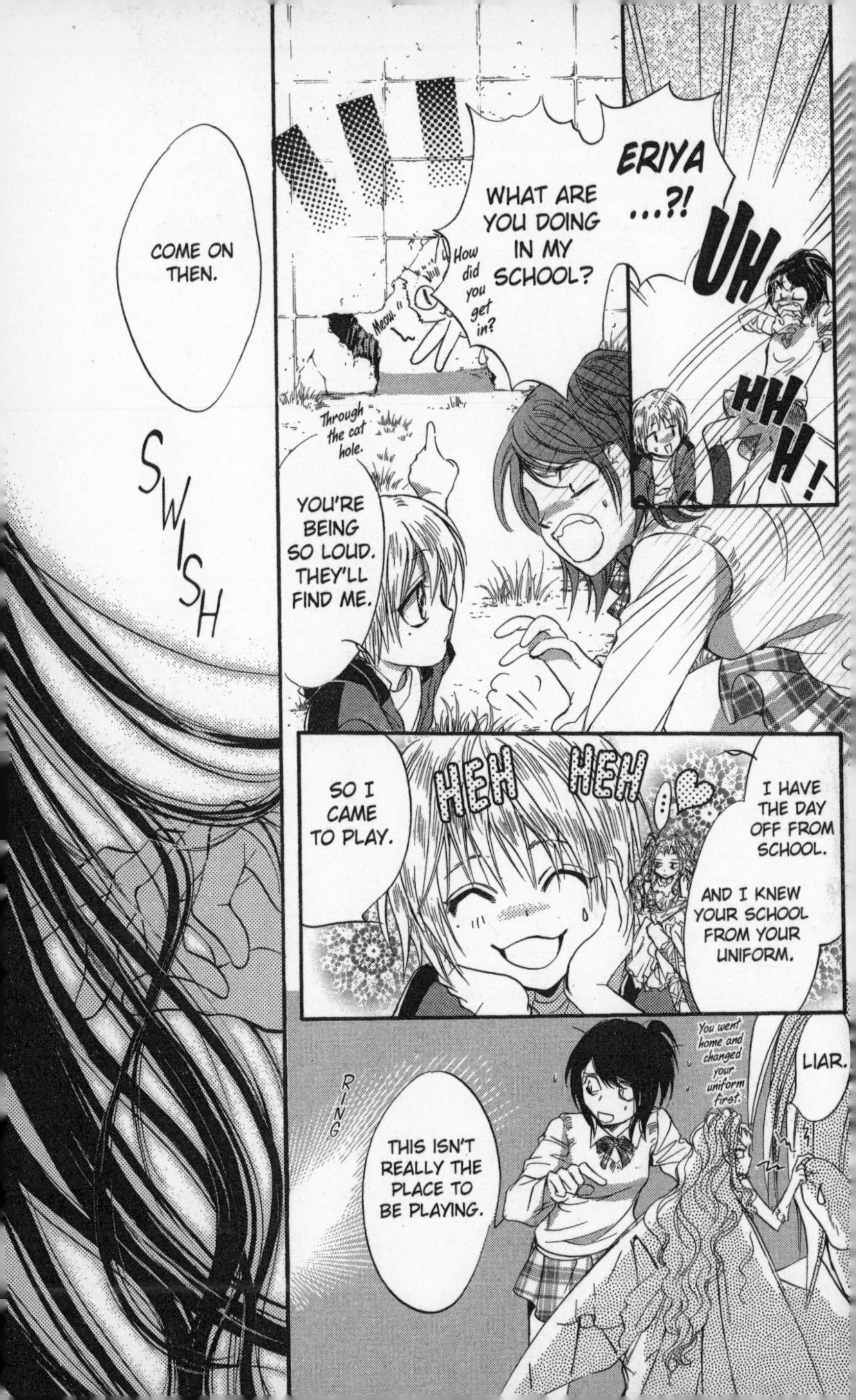
ERIYA ...?!
UHHHHH!
WHAT ARE YOU DOING IN MY SCHOOL?
How did you get in?
Meow.
Through the cat hole.
YOU'RE BEING SO LOUD. THEY'LL FIND ME.
I HAVE THE DAY OFF FROM SCHOOL.
AND I KNEW YOUR SCHOOL FROM YOUR UNIFORM.
HEH HEH
SO I CAME TO PLAY.
LIAR.
You went home and changed your uniform first.
RING
THIS ISN'T REALLY THE PLACE TO BE PLAYING.
COME ON THEN.
SWISH

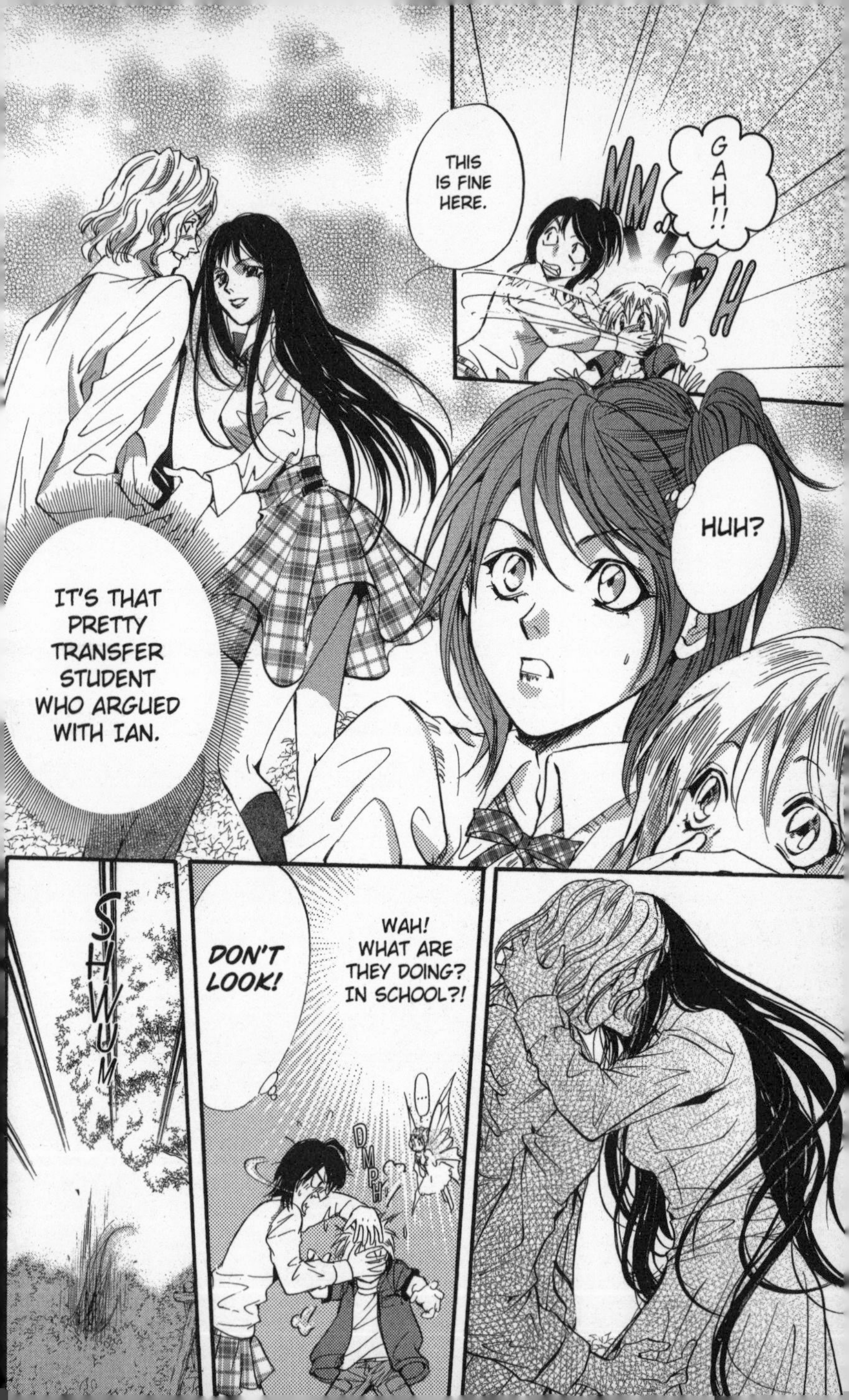
THIS IS FINE HERE.
MMPH
GAH!!
HUH?
IT'S THAT PRETTY TRANSFER STUDENT WHO ARGUED WITH IAN.
WAH! WHAT ARE THEY DOING? IN SCHOOL?!
DON'T LOOK!
DMPH
...
SHWUM

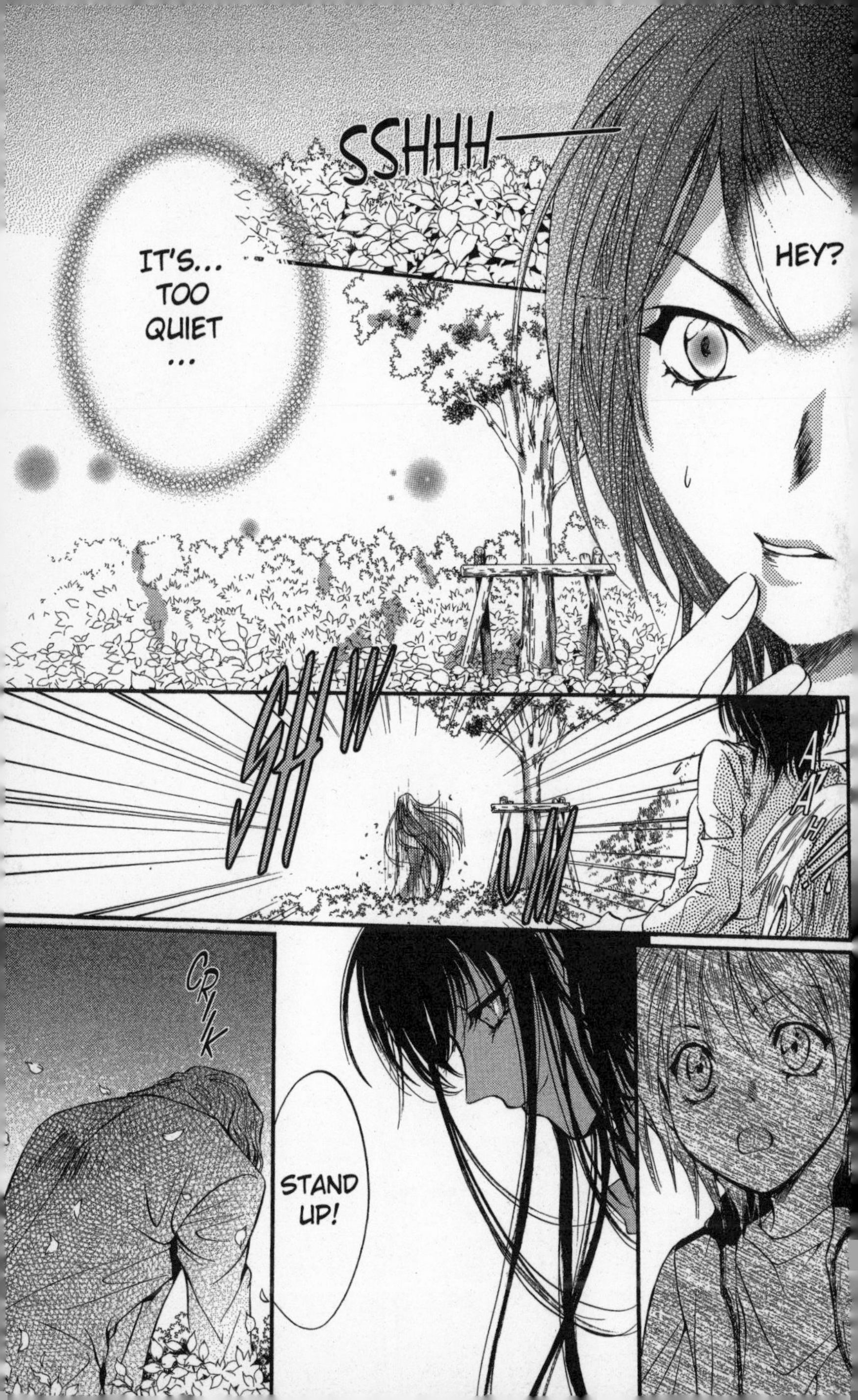
SSHHH
HEY?
IT'S... TOO QUIET...
AAAH
SHW
UM
CRIK
STAND UP!

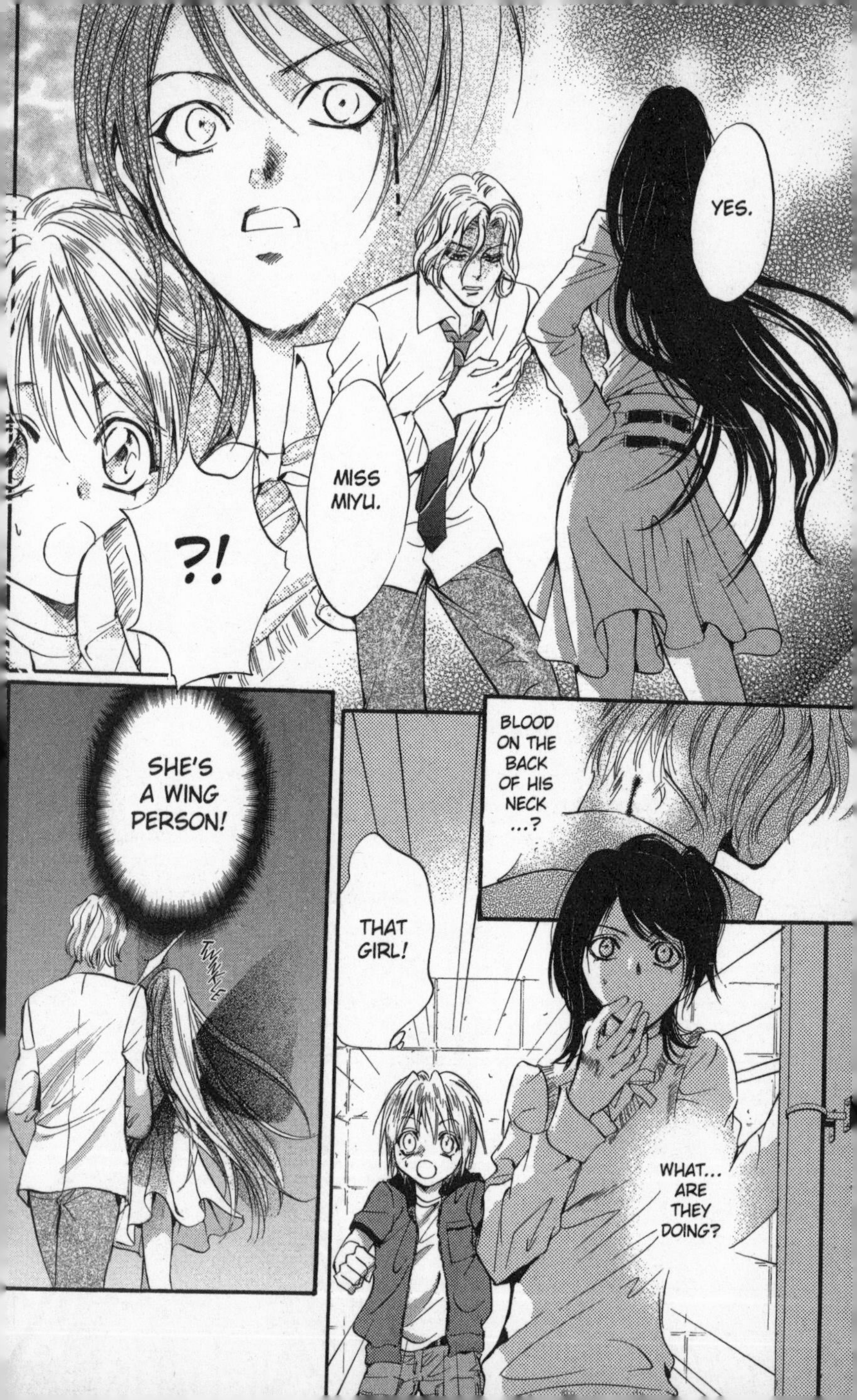
YES.
MISS MIYU.
?!
BLOOD ON THE BACK OF HIS NECK ...?
THAT GIRL!
WHAT... ARE THEY DOING?
SHE'S A WING PERSON!
TWINKLE

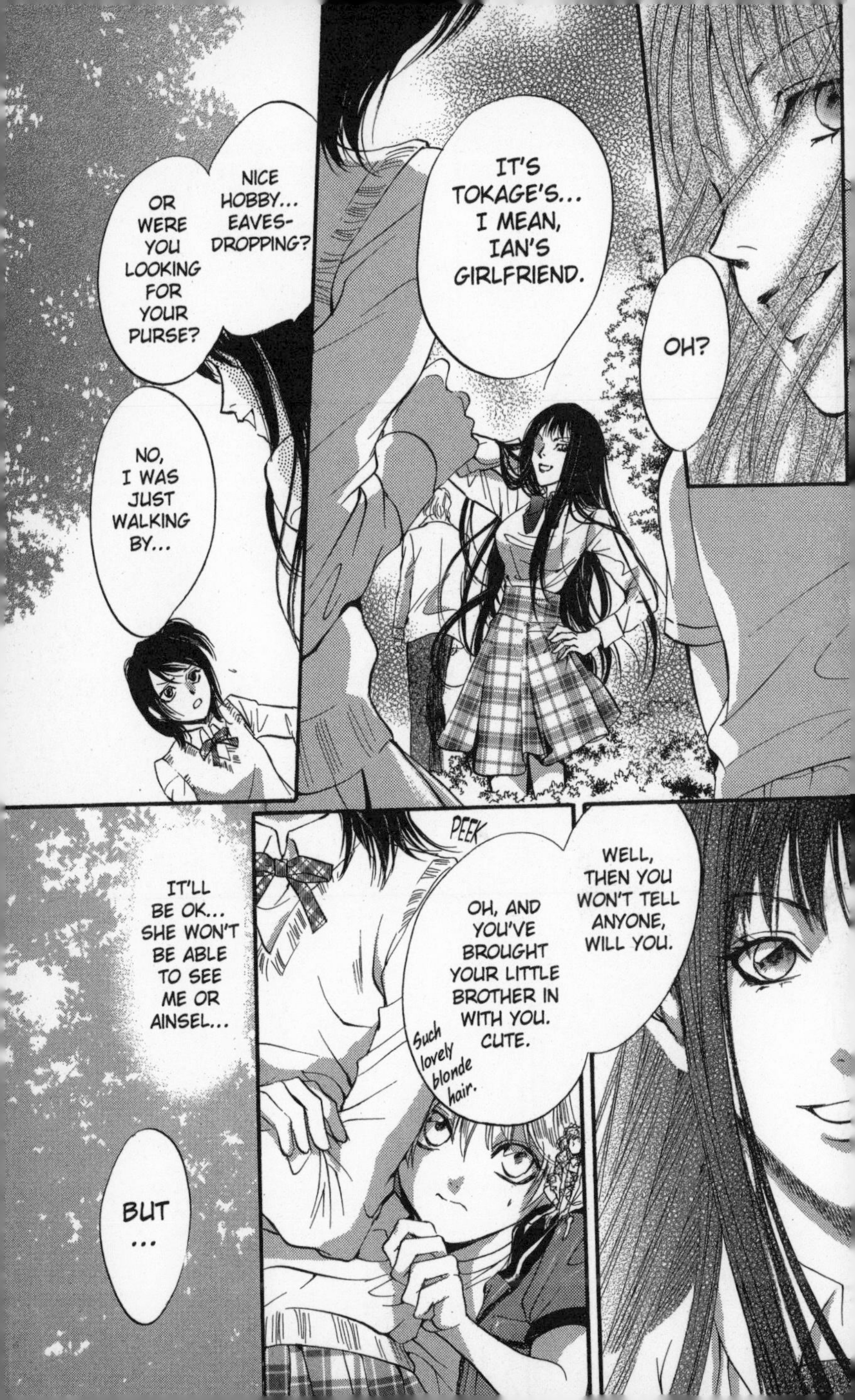
OH?
IT'S TOKAGE'S... I MEAN, IAN'S GIRLFRIEND.
NICE HOBBY... EAVES-DROPPING?
OR WERE YOU LOOKING FOR YOUR PURSE?
NO, I WAS JUST WALKING BY...
WELL, THEN YOU WON'T TELL ANYONE, WILL YOU.
PEEK
OH, AND YOU'VE BROUGHT YOUR LITTLE BROTHER IN WITH YOU. CUTE.
Such lovely blonde hair.
IT'LL BE OK... SHE WON'T BE ABLE TO SEE ME OR AINSEL...
BUT ...

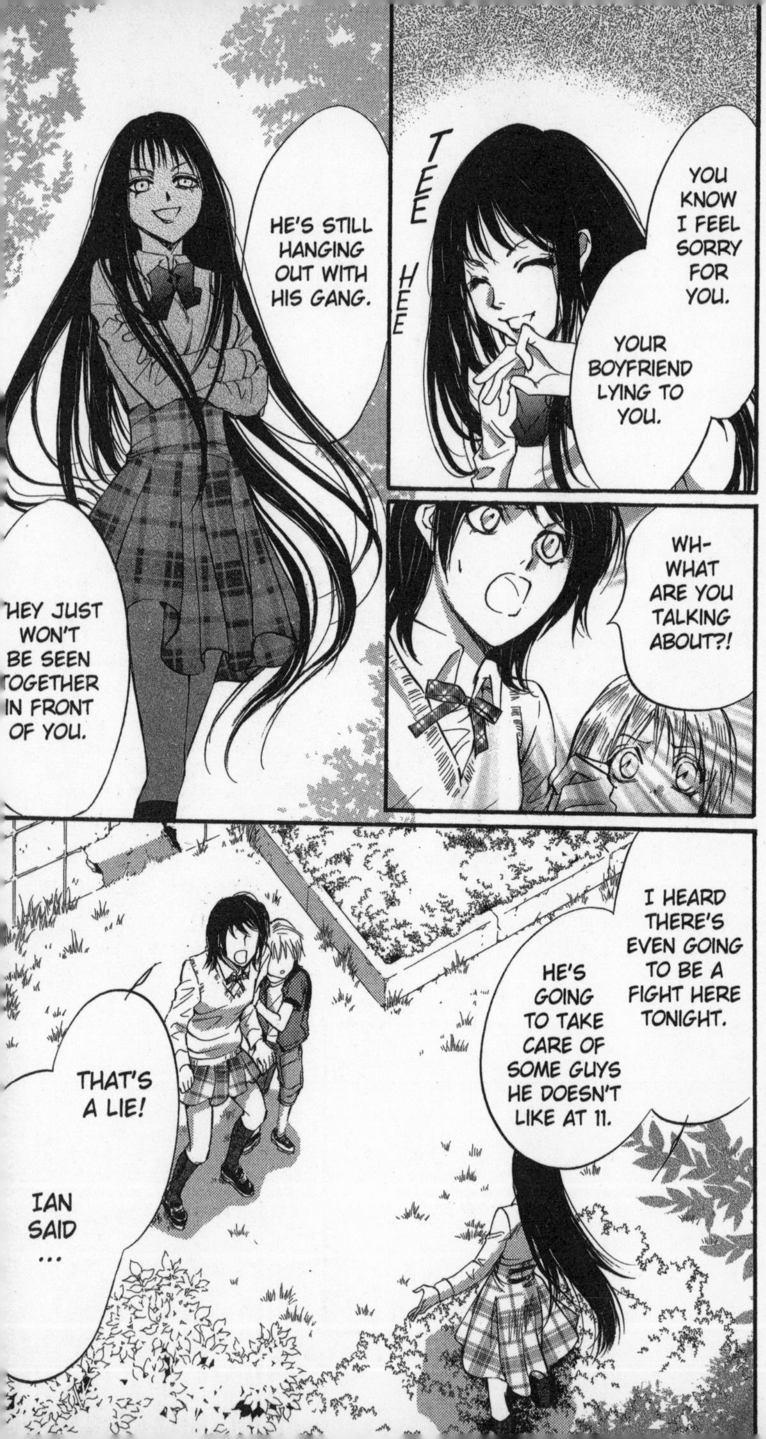
TEE HEE
YOU KNOW I FEEL SORRY FOR YOU.
YOUR BOYFRIEND LYING TO YOU.
WH- WHAT ARE YOU TALKING ABOUT?!
HE'S STILL HANGING OUT WITH HIS GANG.
THEY JUST WON'T BE SEEN TOGETHER IN FRONT OF YOU.
I HEARD THERE'S EVEN GOING TO BE A FIGHT HERE TONIGHT.
HE'S GOING TO TAKE CARE OF SOME GUYS HE DOESN'T LIKE AT 11.
THAT'S A LIE!
IAN SAID ...

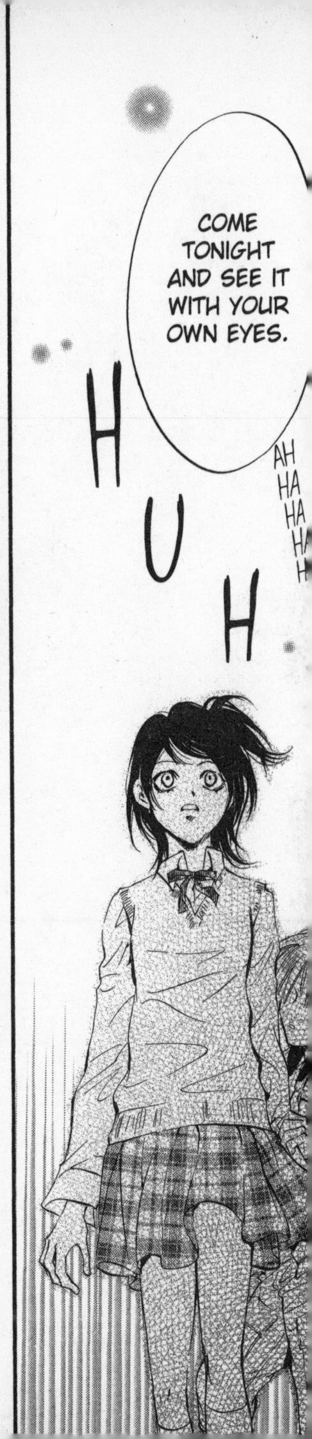
COME TONIGHT AND SEE IT WITH YOUR OWN EYES.
HUH
AH HA HA HA H

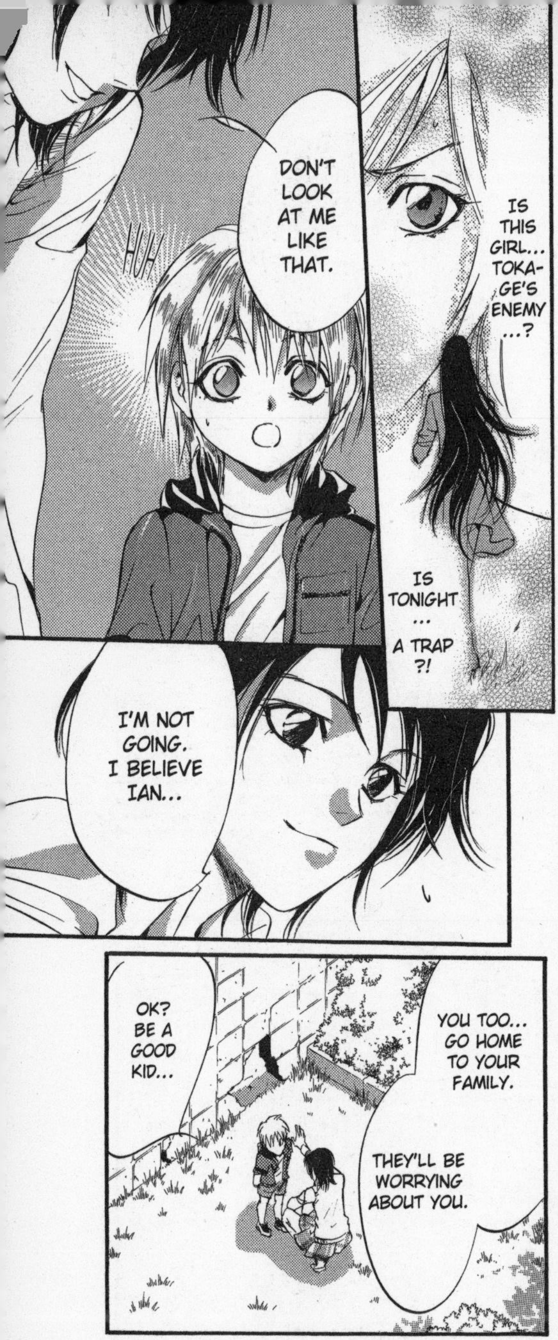
IS THIS GIRL... TOKA-GE'S ENEMY ...?
IS TONIGHT ... A TRAP ?!
DON'T LOOK AT ME LIKE THAT.
HUH
I'M NOT GOING. I BELIEVE IAN...
YOU TOO... GO HOME TO YOUR FAMILY.
THEY'LL BE WORRYING ABOUT YOU.
OK? BE A GOOD KID...

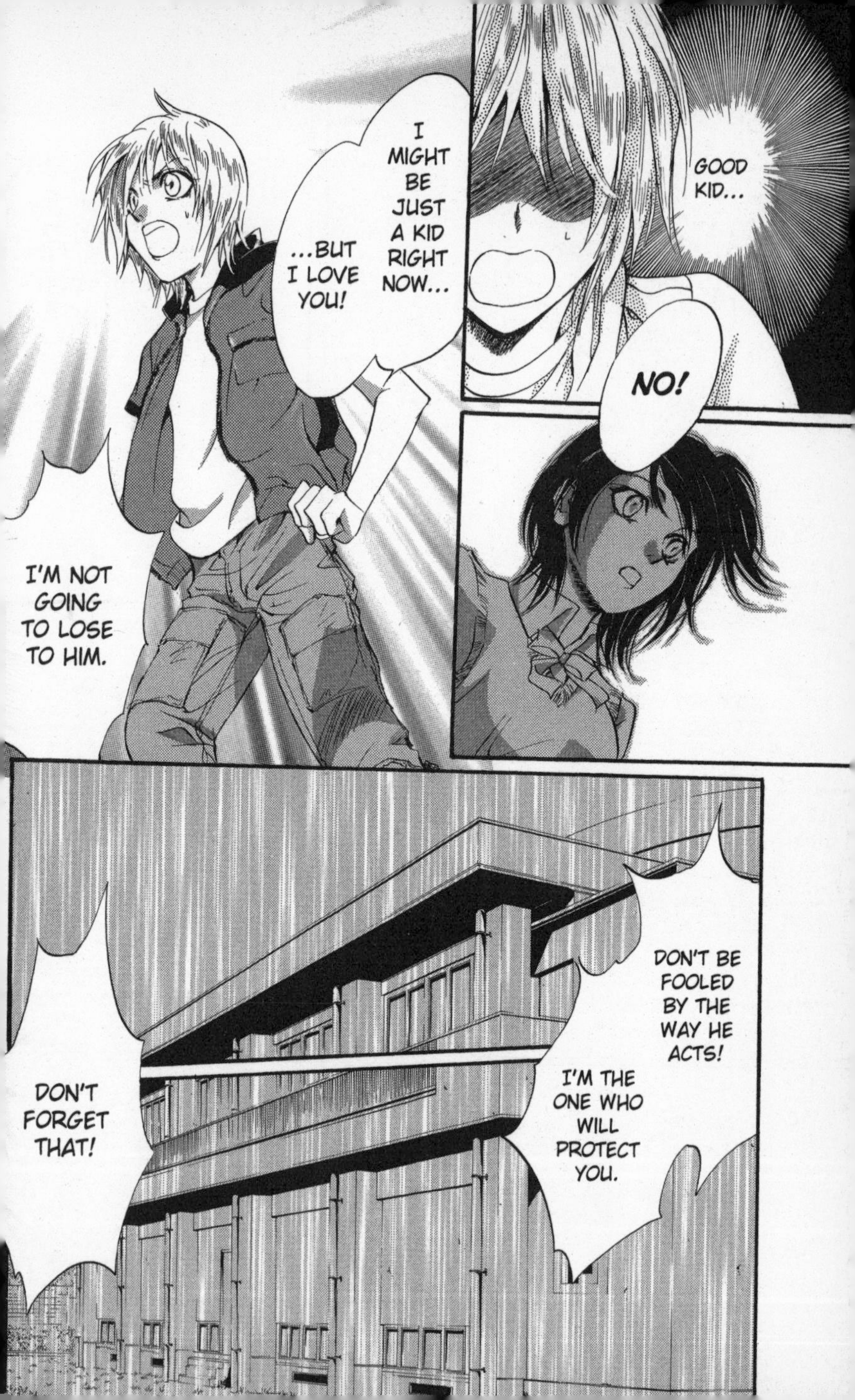
GOOD KID...
NO!
I MIGHT BE JUST A KID RIGHT NOW...
...BUT I LOVE YOU!
I'M NOT GOING TO LOSE TO HIM.
DON'T BE FOOLED BY THE WAY HE ACTS!
I'M THE ONE WHO WILL PROTECT YOU.
DON'T FORGET THAT!

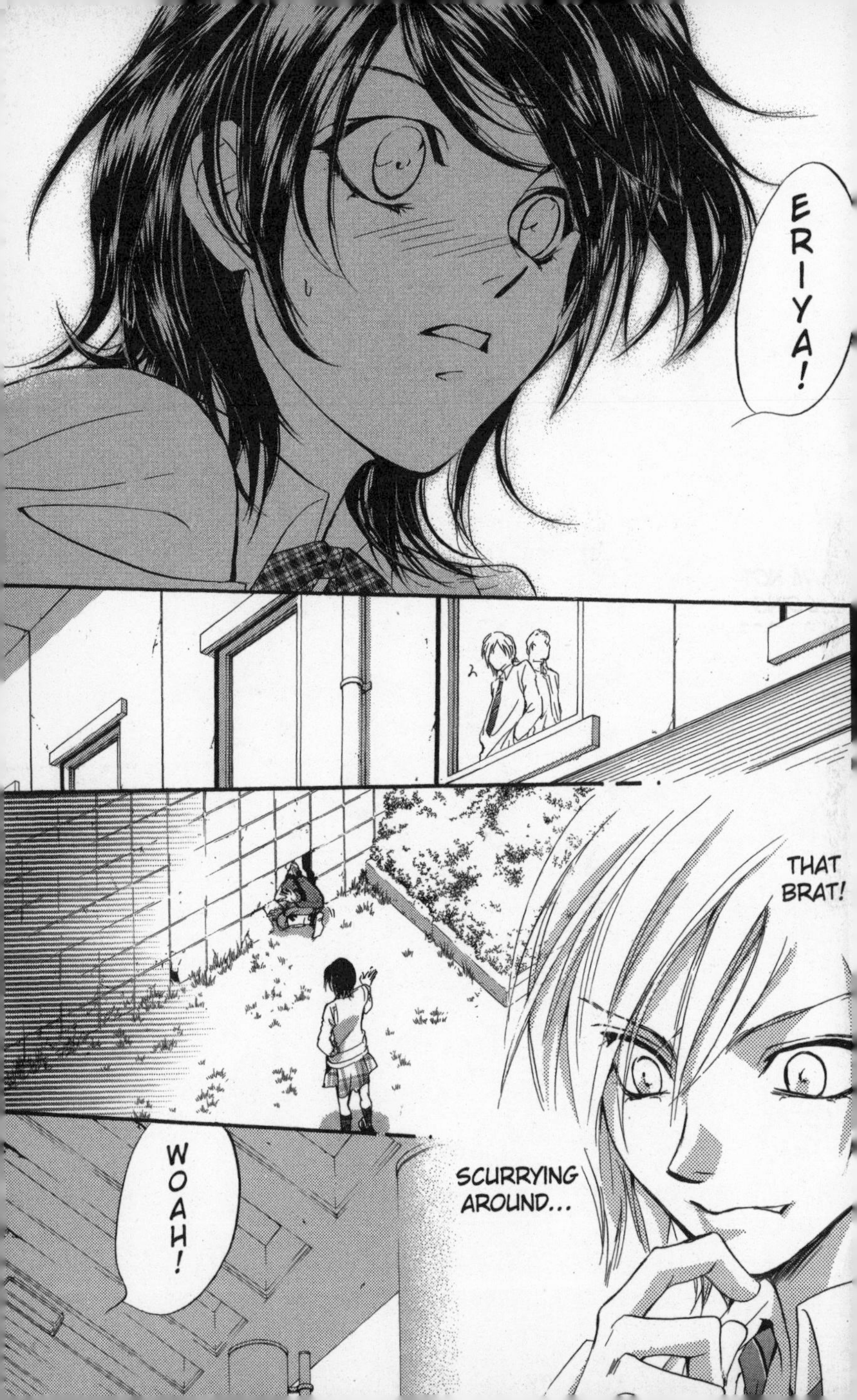
ERIYA!
THAT BRAT!
SCURRYING AROUND...
WOAH!

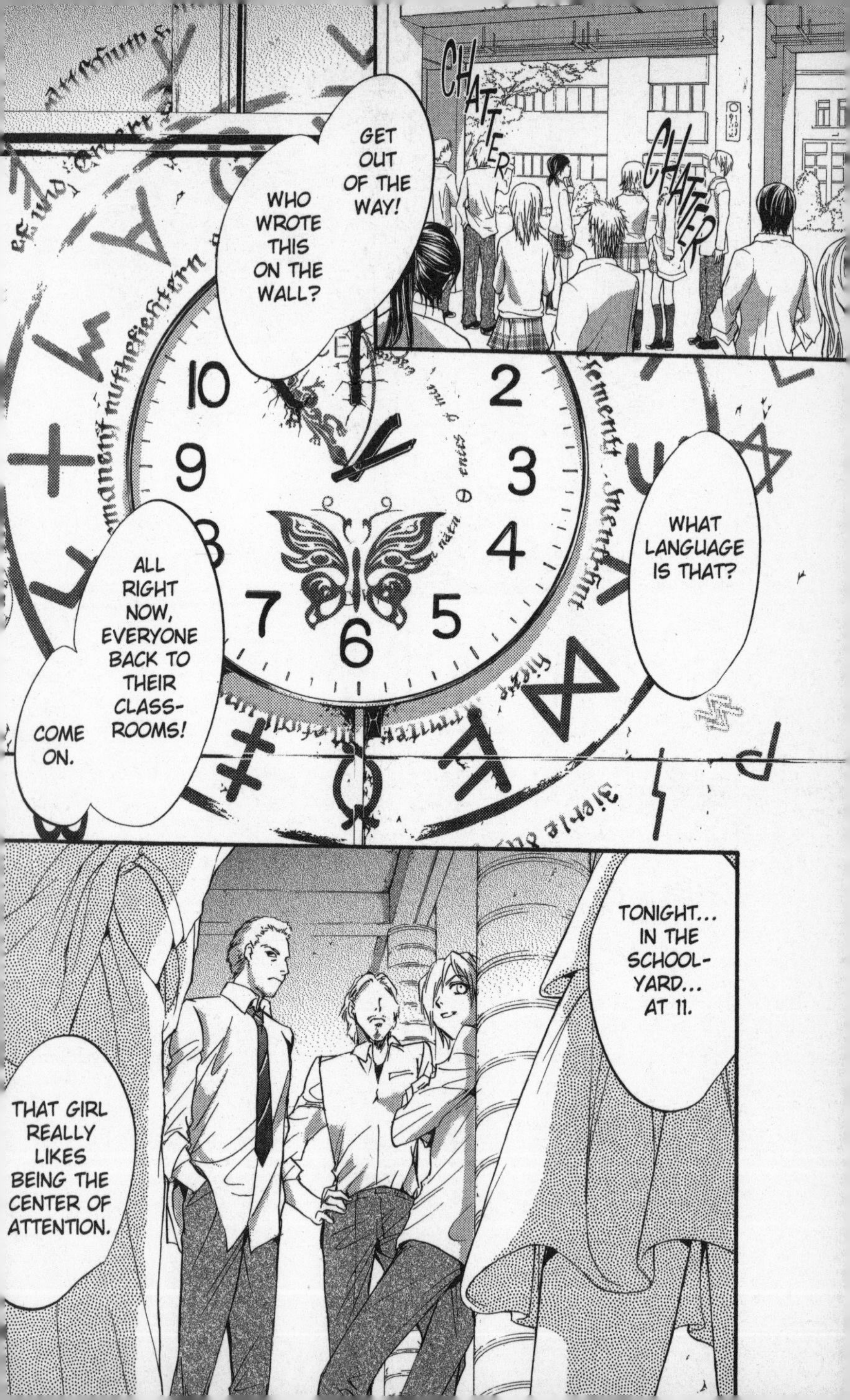
CHATTER
CHATTER
GET OUT OF THE WAY!
WHO WROTE THIS ON THE WALL?
WHAT LANGUAGE IS THAT?
ALL RIGHT NOW, EVERYONE BACK TO THEIR CLASS-ROOMS!
COME ON.
TONIGHT... IN THE SCHOOL-YARD... AT 11.
THAT GIRL REALLY LIKES BEING THE CENTER OF ATTENTION.

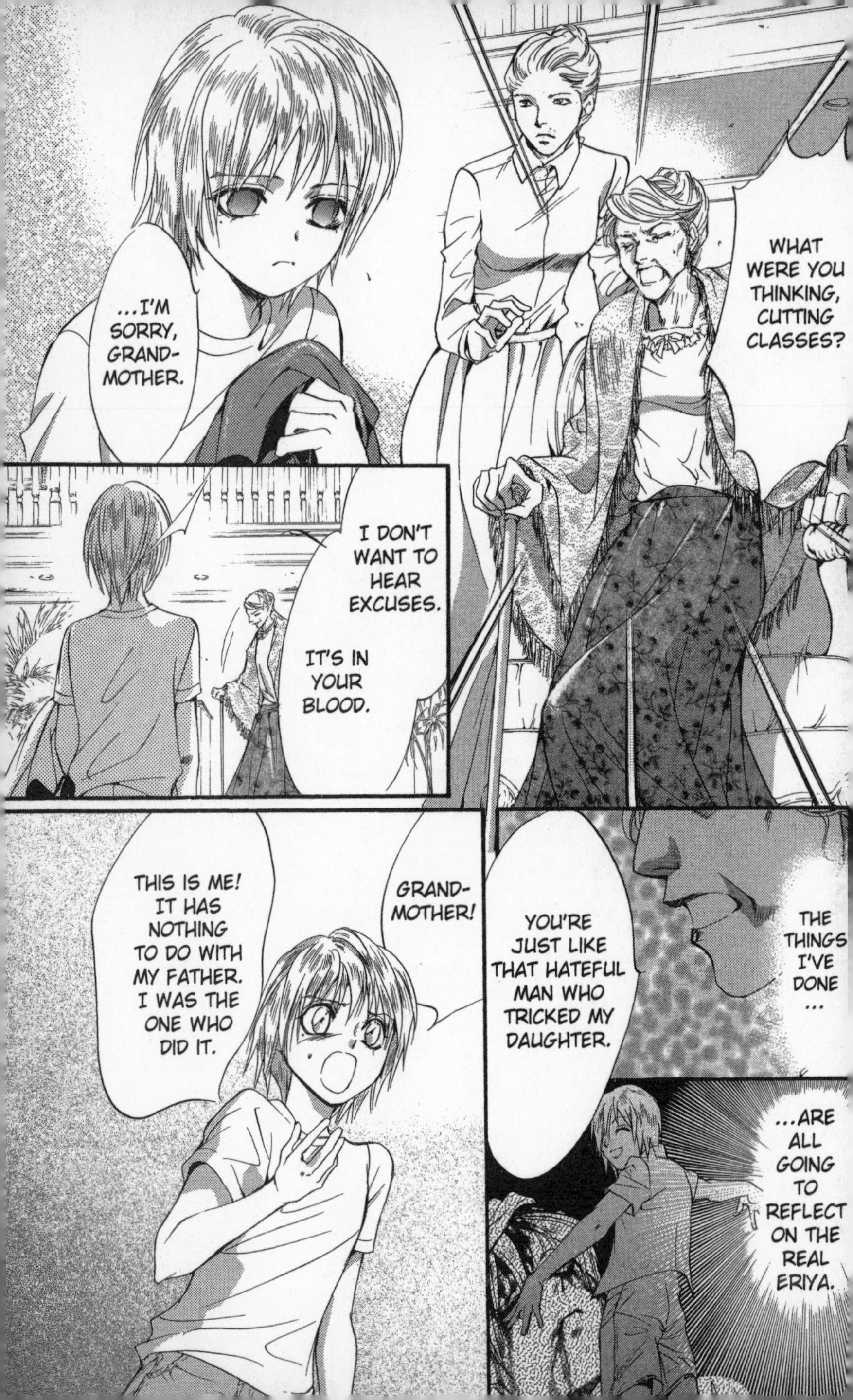
WHAT WERE YOU THINKING, CUTTING CLASSES?
...I'M SORRY, GRAND-MOTHER.
I DON'T WANT TO HEAR EXCUSES.
IT'S IN YOUR BLOOD.
YOU'RE JUST LIKE THAT HATEFUL MAN WHO TRICKED MY DAUGHTER.
THE THINGS I'VE DONE...
...ARE ALL GOING TO REFLECT ON THE REAL ERIYA.
GRAND-MOTHER!
THIS IS ME! IT HAS NOTHING TO DO WITH MY FATHER. I WAS THE ONE WHO DID IT.

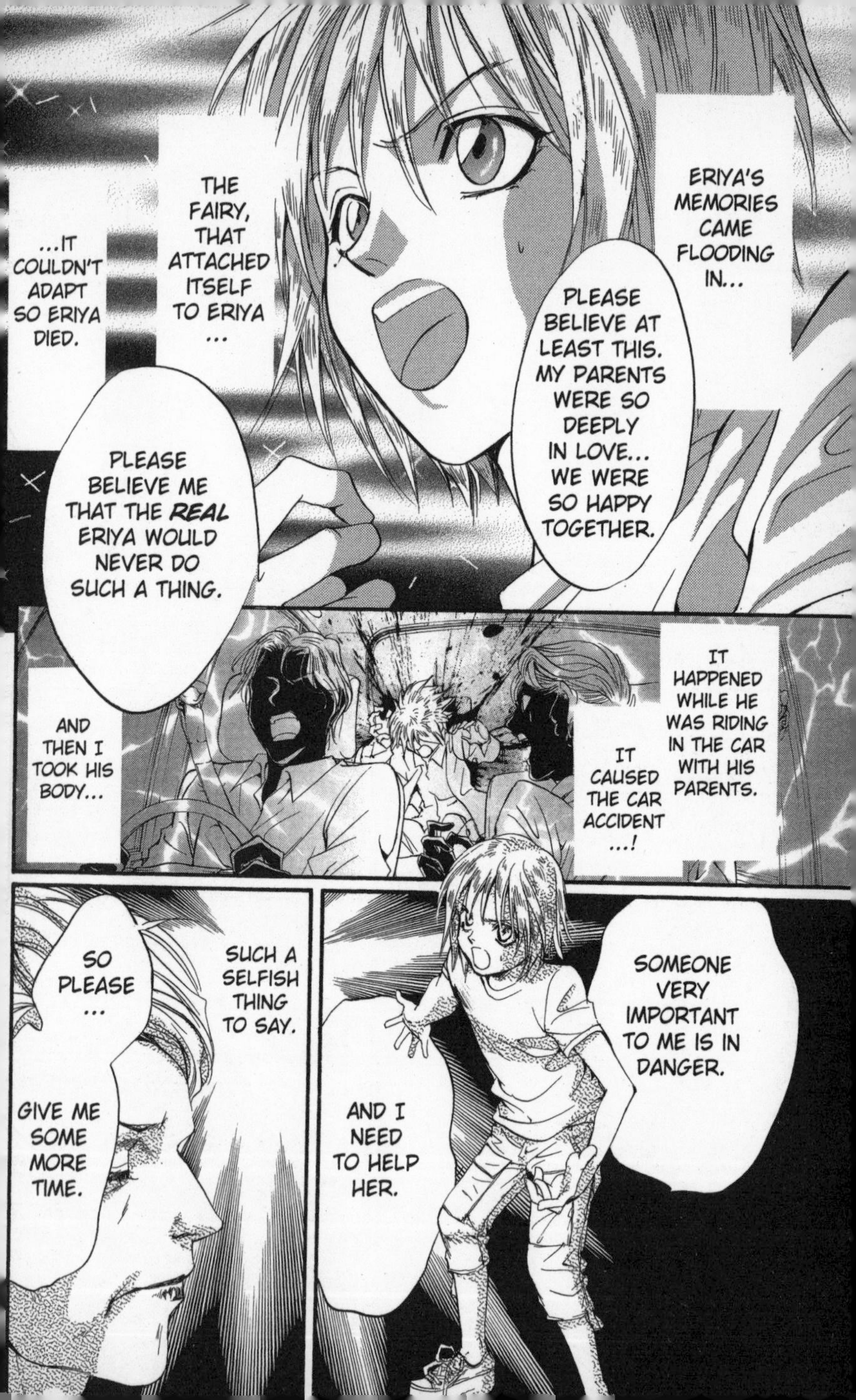
ERIYA'S MEMORIES CAME FLOODING IN...
PLEASE BELIEVE AT LEAST THIS. MY PARENTS WERE SO DEEPLY IN LOVE... WE WERE SO HAPPY TOGETHER.
THE FAIRY, THAT ATTACHED ITSELF TO ERIYA...
...IT COULDN'T ADAPT SO ERIYA DIED.
PLEASE BELIEVE ME THAT THE *REAL* ERIYA WOULD NEVER DO SUCH A THING.
IT HAPPENED WHILE HE WAS RIDING IN THE CAR WITH HIS PARENTS.
IT CAUSED THE CAR ACCIDENT...!
AND THEN I TOOK HIS BODY...
SOMEONE VERY IMPORTANT TO ME IS IN DANGER.
AND I NEED TO HELP HER.
SUCH A SELFISH THING TO SAY.
SO PLEASE...
GIVE ME SOME MORE TIME.

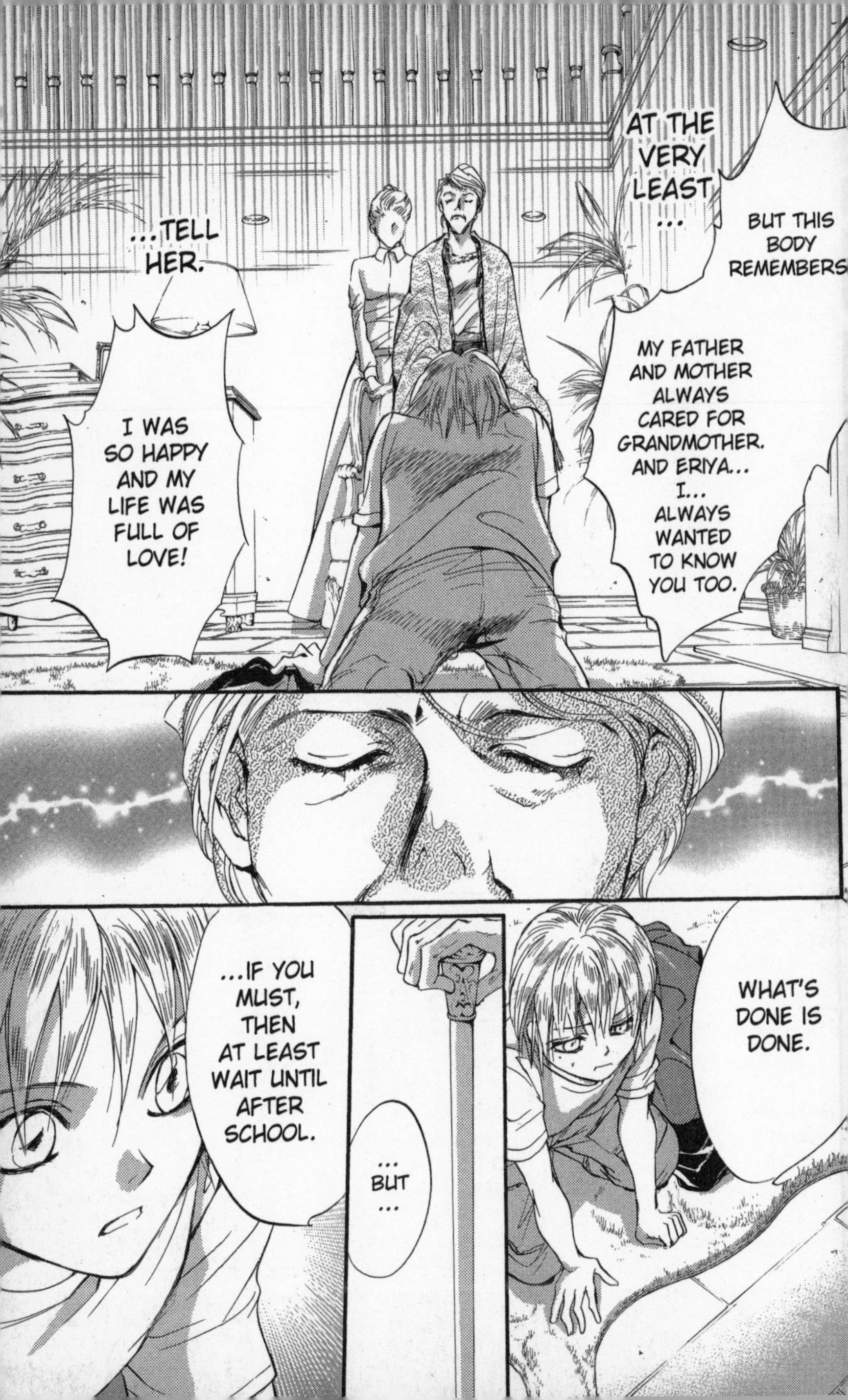
AT THE VERY LEAST...
BUT THIS BODY REMEMBERS
MY FATHER AND MOTHER ALWAYS CARED FOR GRANDMOTHER. AND ERIYA... I... ALWAYS WANTED TO KNOW YOU TOO.
...TELL HER.
I WAS SO HAPPY AND MY LIFE WAS FULL OF LOVE!
WHAT'S DONE IS DONE.
...BUT...
...IF YOU MUST, THEN AT LEAST WAIT UNTIL AFTER SCHOOL.

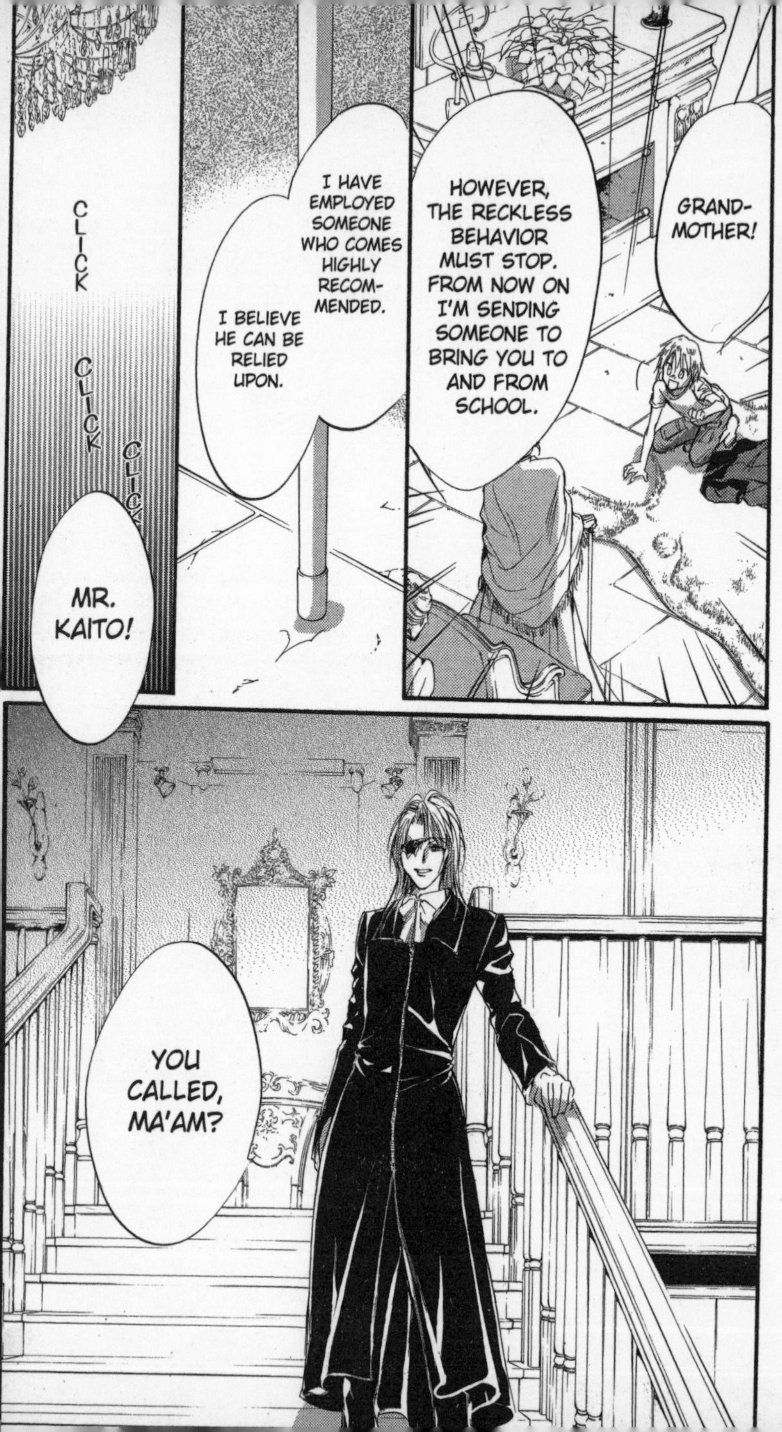
GRAND-MOTHER!
HOWEVER, THE RECKLESS BEHAVIOR MUST STOP. FROM NOW ON I'M SENDING SOMEONE TO BRING YOU TO AND FROM SCHOOL.
I HAVE EMPLOYED SOMEONE WHO COMES HIGHLY RECOM-MENDED.
I BELIEVE HE CAN BE RELIED UPON.
CLICK
CLICK
CLICK
MR. KAITO!
YOU CALLED, MA'AM?

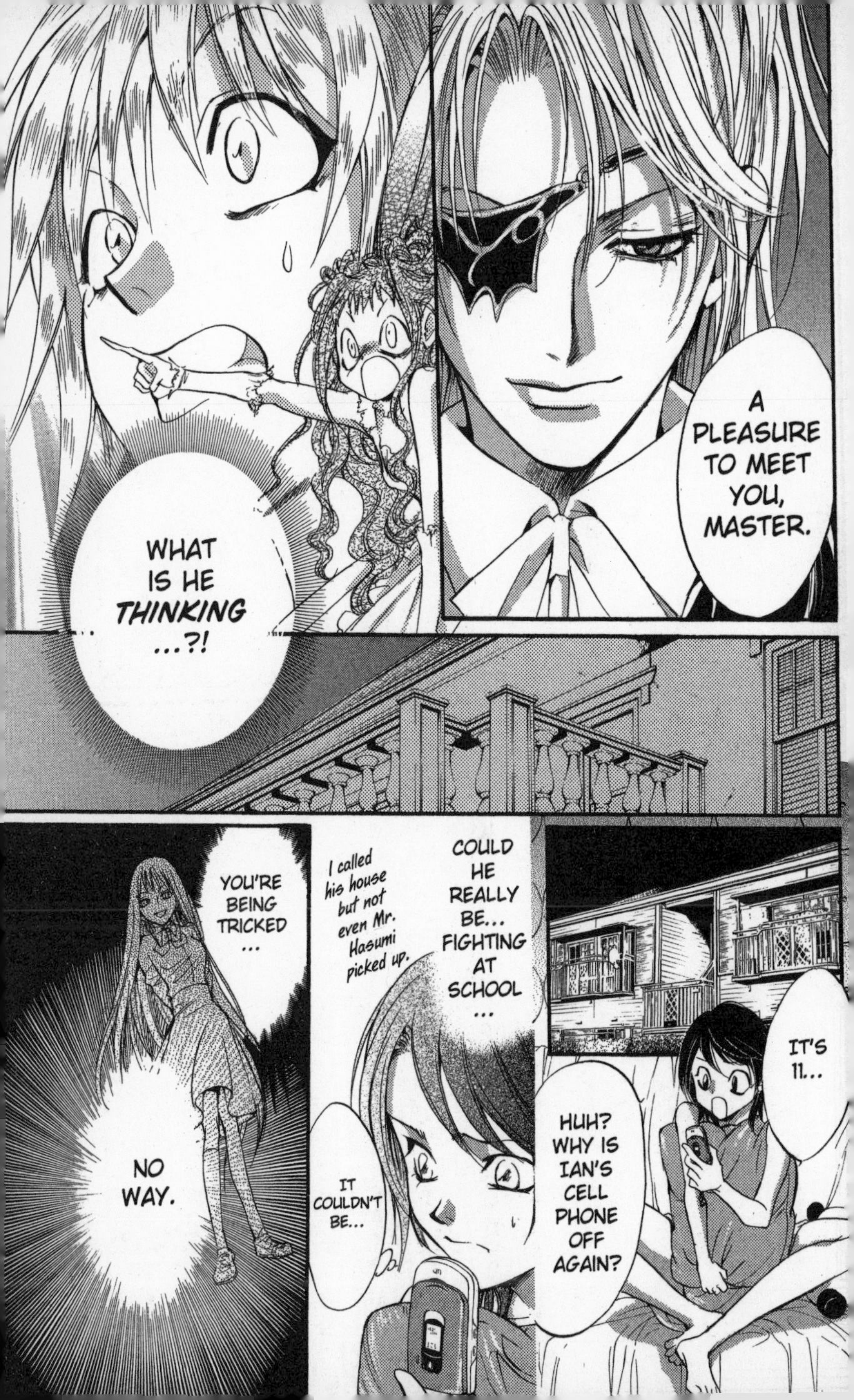
A PLEASURE TO MEET YOU, MASTER.
WHAT IS HE THINKING ...?!
IT'S 11...
HUH? WHY IS IAN'S CELL PHONE OFF AGAIN?
COULD HE REALLY BE... FIGHTING AT SCHOOL ...
I called his house but not even Mr. Hasumi picked up.
IT COULDN'T BE...
YOU'RE BEING TRICKED ...
NO WAY.

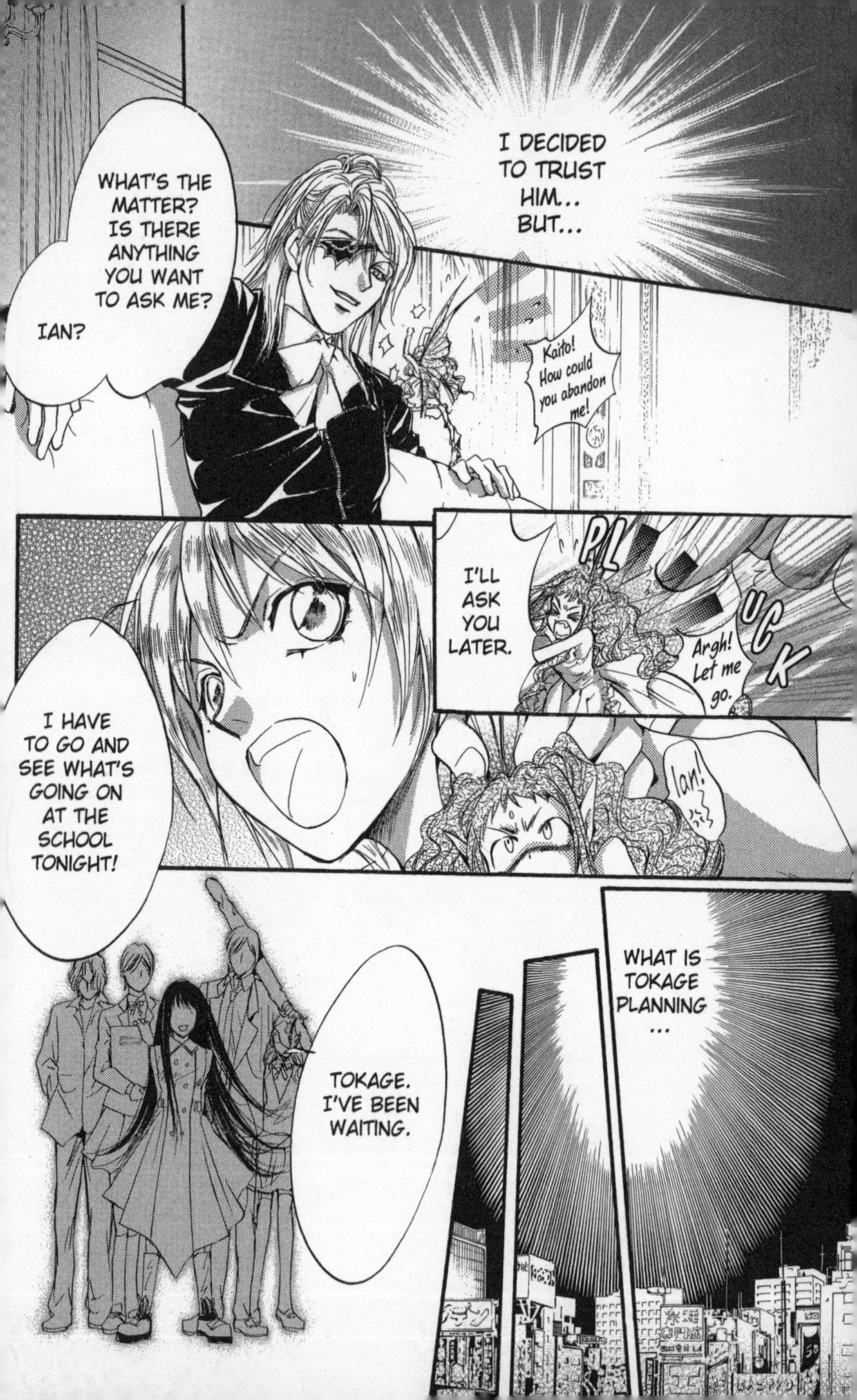
I DECIDED TO TRUST HIM... BUT...
WHAT'S THE MATTER? IS THERE ANYTHING YOU WANT TO ASK ME?
IAN?
Kaito! How could you abandon me!
PLUCK
I'LL ASK YOU LATER.
Argh! Let me go.
Ian!
I HAVE TO GO AND SEE WHAT'S GOING ON AT THE SCHOOL TONIGHT!
WHAT IS TOKAGE PLANNING...
TOKAGE. I'VE BEEN WAITING.

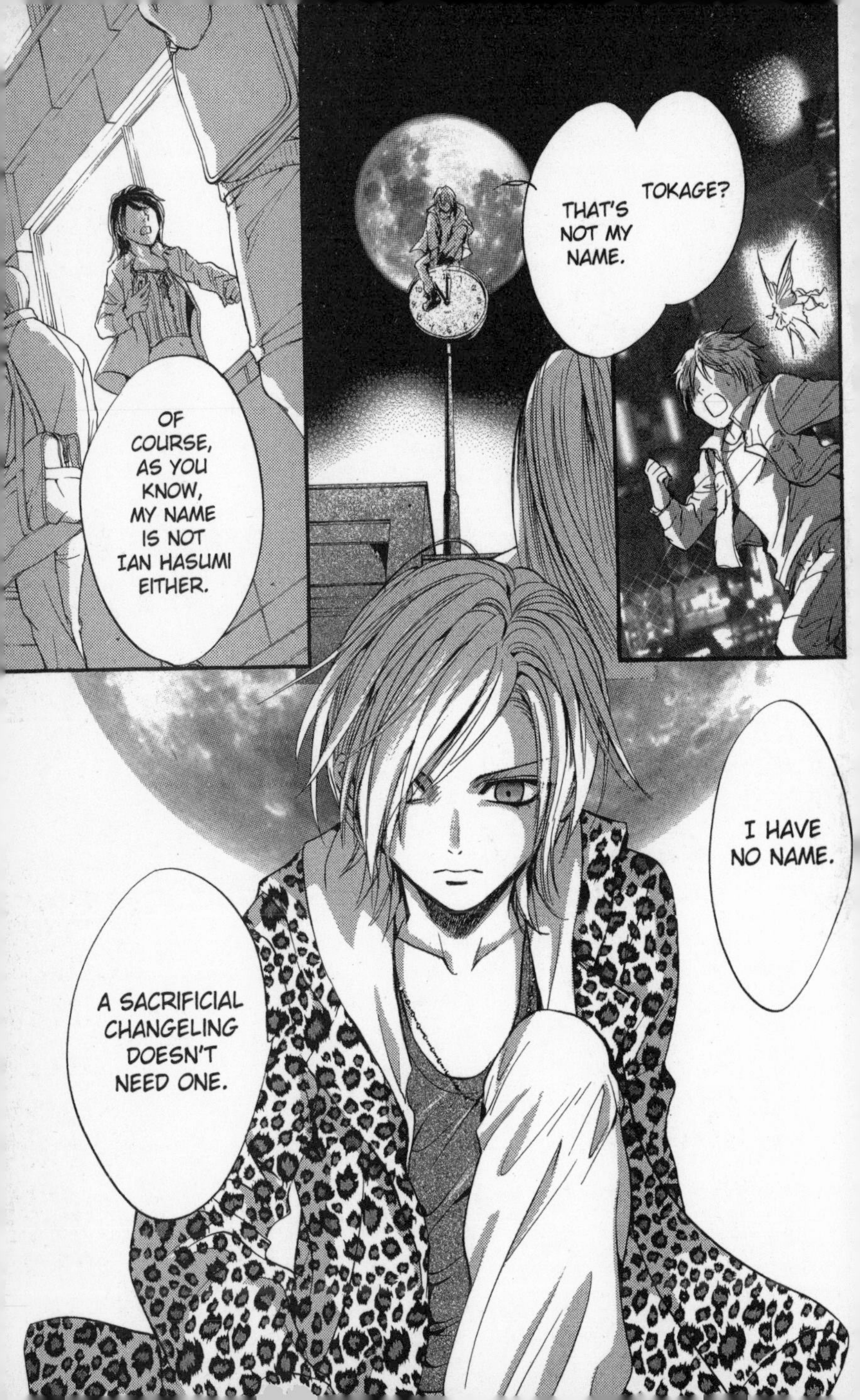
TOKAGE?
THAT'S NOT MY NAME.
OF COURSE, AS YOU KNOW, MY NAME IS NOT IAN HASUMI EITHER.
I HAVE NO NAME.
A SACRIFICIAL CHANGELING DOESN'T NEED ONE.

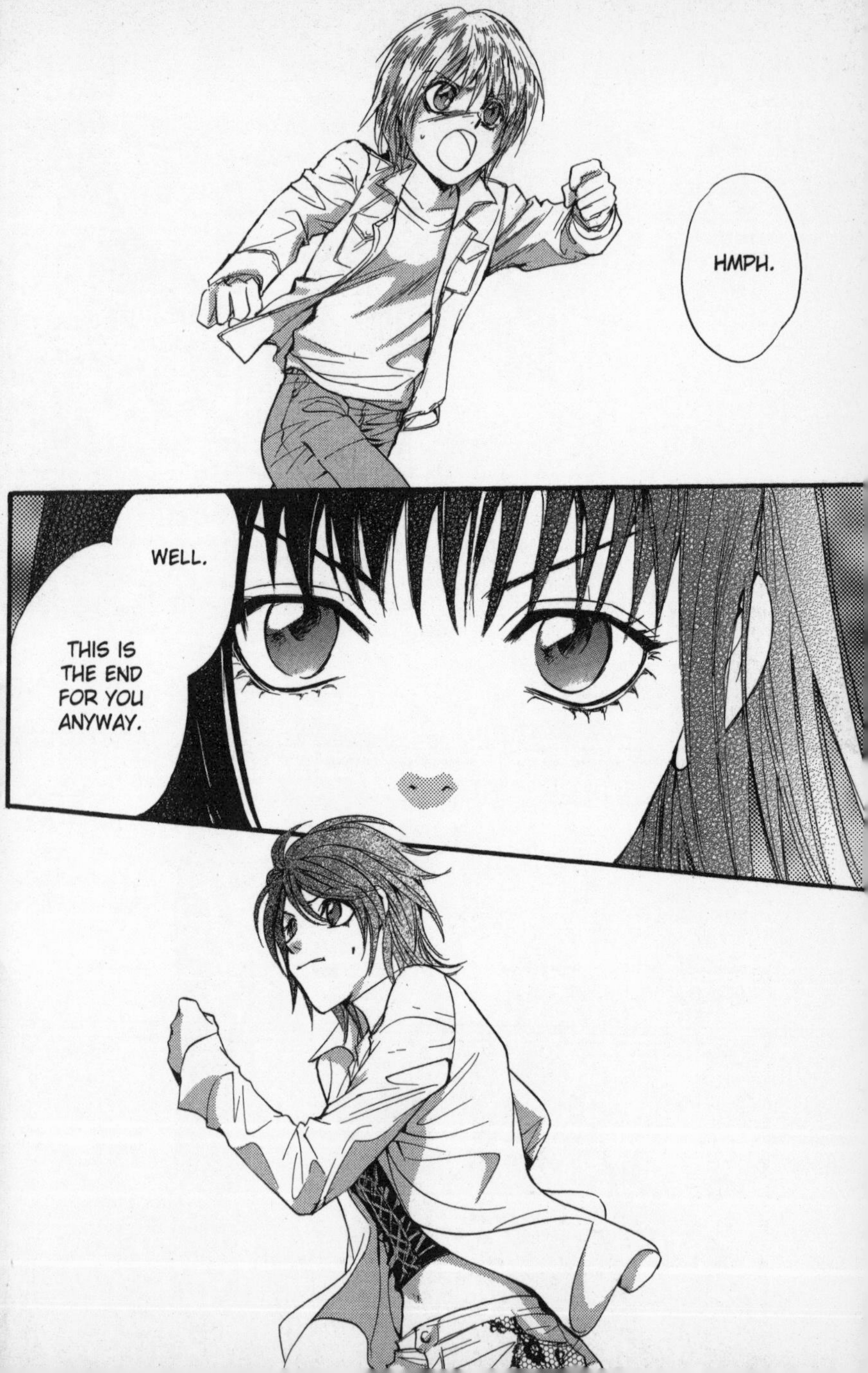
HMPH.
WELL.
THIS IS THE END FOR YOU ANYWAY.

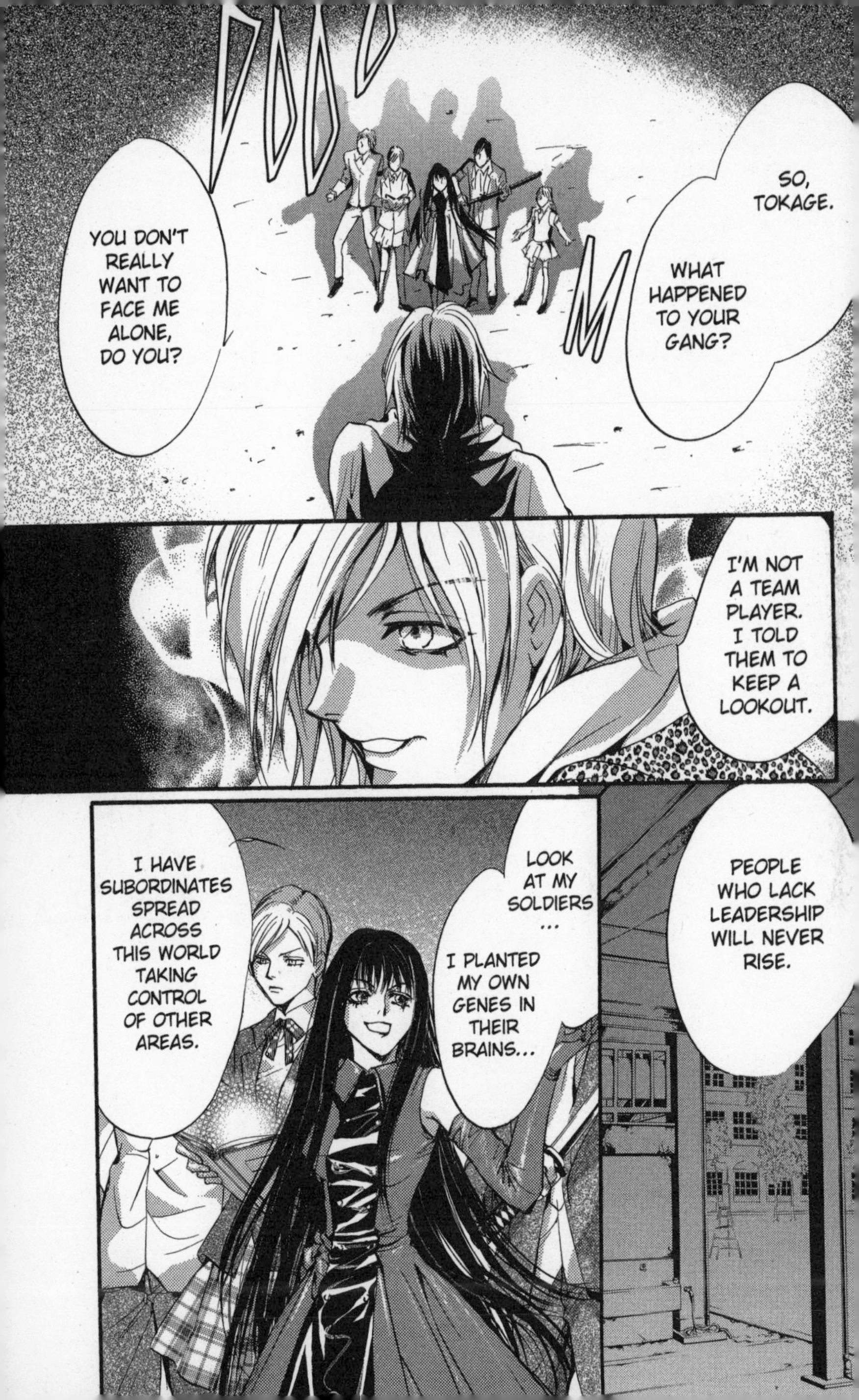
SO, TOKAGE.
WHAT HAPPENED TO YOUR GANG?
YOU DON'T REALLY WANT TO FACE ME ALONE, DO YOU?
I'M NOT A TEAM PLAYER. I TOLD THEM TO KEEP A LOOKOUT.
PEOPLE WHO LACK LEADERSHIP WILL NEVER RISE.
LOOK AT MY SOLDIERS...
I PLANTED MY OWN GENES IN THEIR BRAINS...
I HAVE SUBORDINATES SPREAD ACROSS THIS WORLD TAKING CONTROL OF OTHER AREAS.

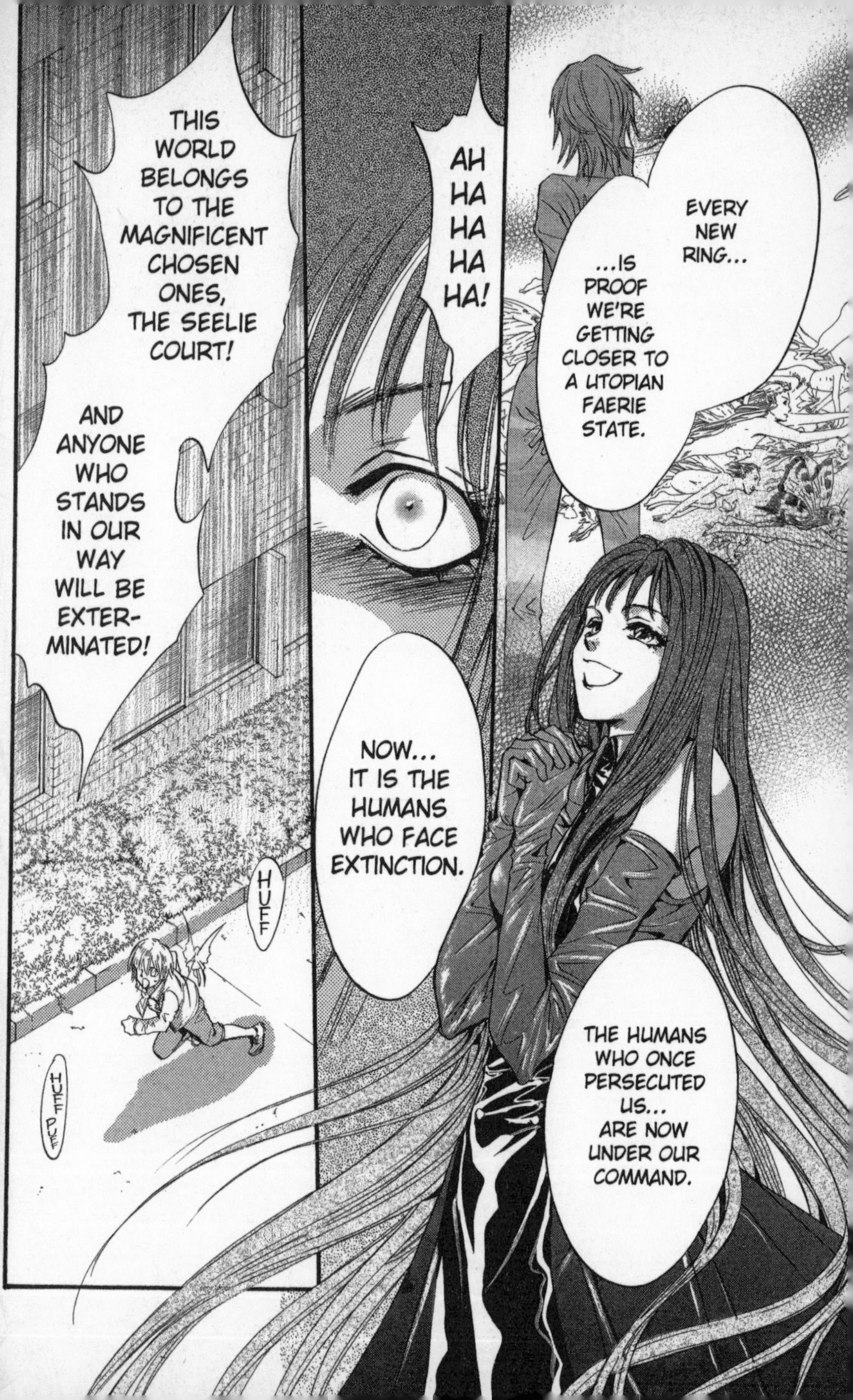
EVERY NEW RING...
...IS PROOF WE'RE GETTING CLOSER TO A UTOPIAN FAERIE STATE.
NOW... IT IS THE HUMANS WHO FACE EXTINCTION.
THE HUMANS WHO ONCE PERSECUTED US... ARE NOW UNDER OUR COMMAND.
AH HA HA HA HA!
THIS WORLD BELONGS TO THE MAGNIFICENT CHOSEN ONES, THE SEELIE COURT!
AND ANYONE WHO STANDS IN OUR WAY WILL BE EXTERMINATED!
HUFF
HUFF PUFF

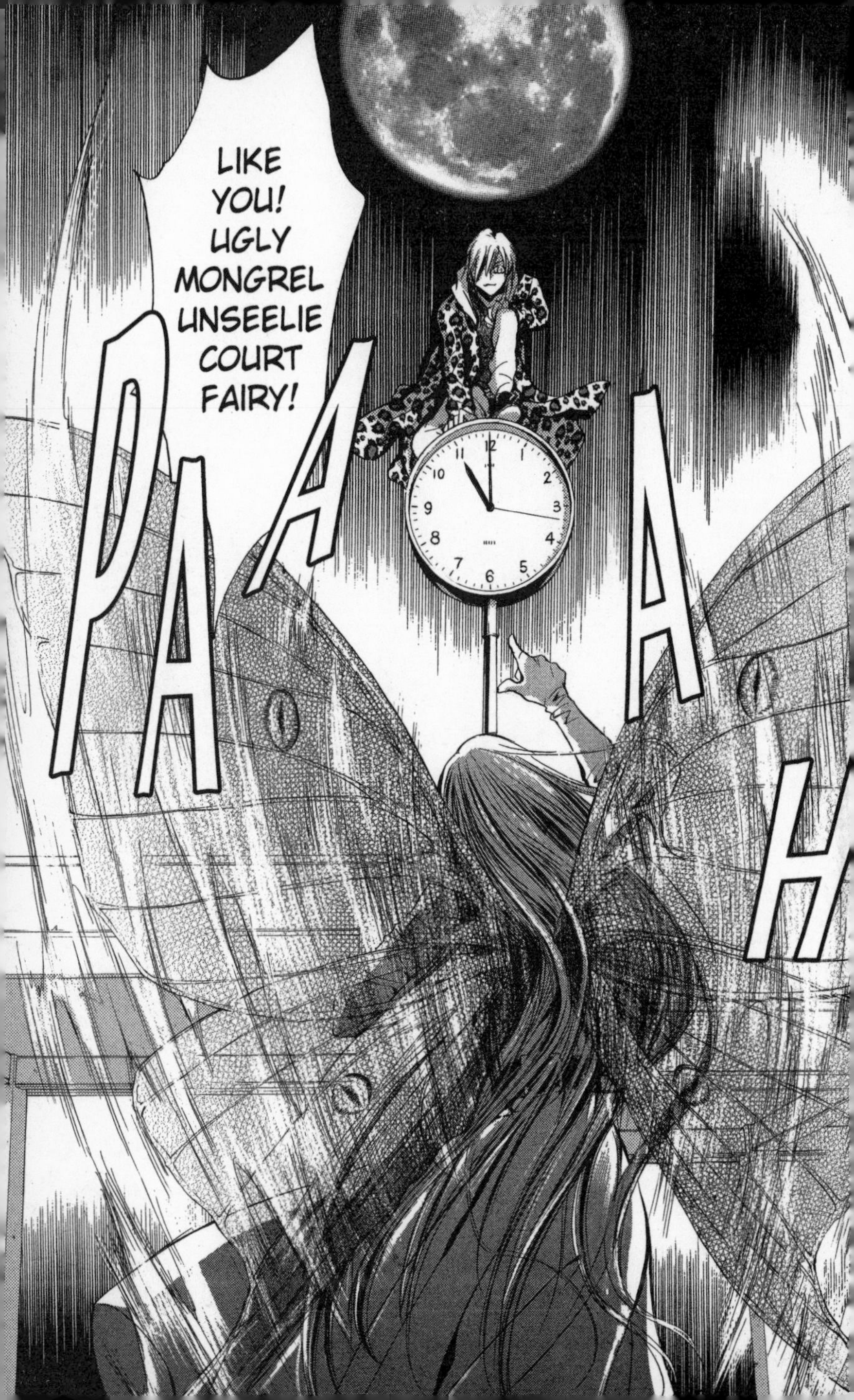
LIKE YOU! UGLY MONGREL UNSEELIE COURT FAIRY!
PAAAH

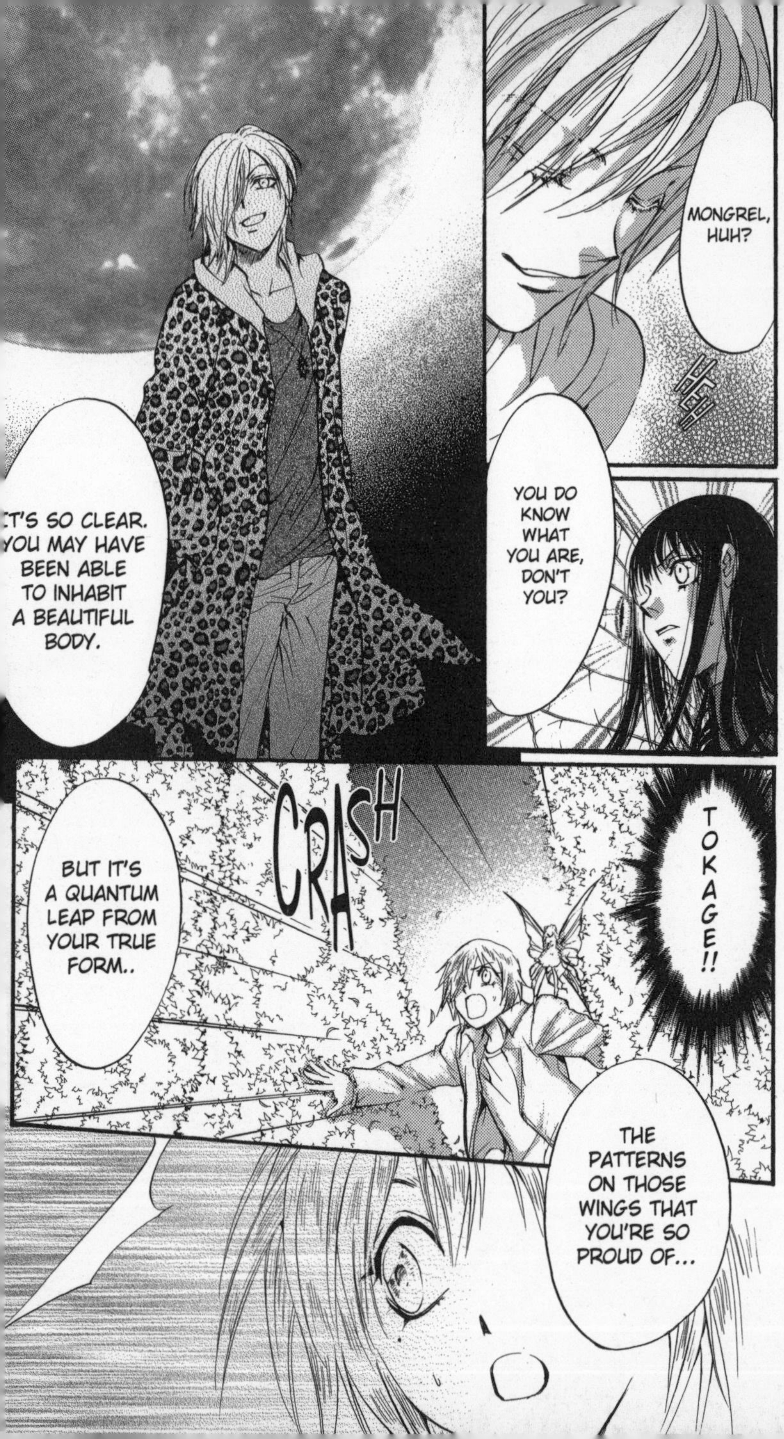
MONGREL, HUH?
HEH
YOU DO KNOW WHAT YOU ARE, DON'T YOU?
IT'S SO CLEAR. YOU MAY HAVE BEEN ABLE TO INHABIT A BEAUTIFUL BODY.
TOKAGE!!
CRASH
BUT IT'S A QUANTUM LEAP FROM YOUR TRUE FORM..
THE PATTERNS ON THOSE WINGS THAT YOU'RE SO PROUD OF...

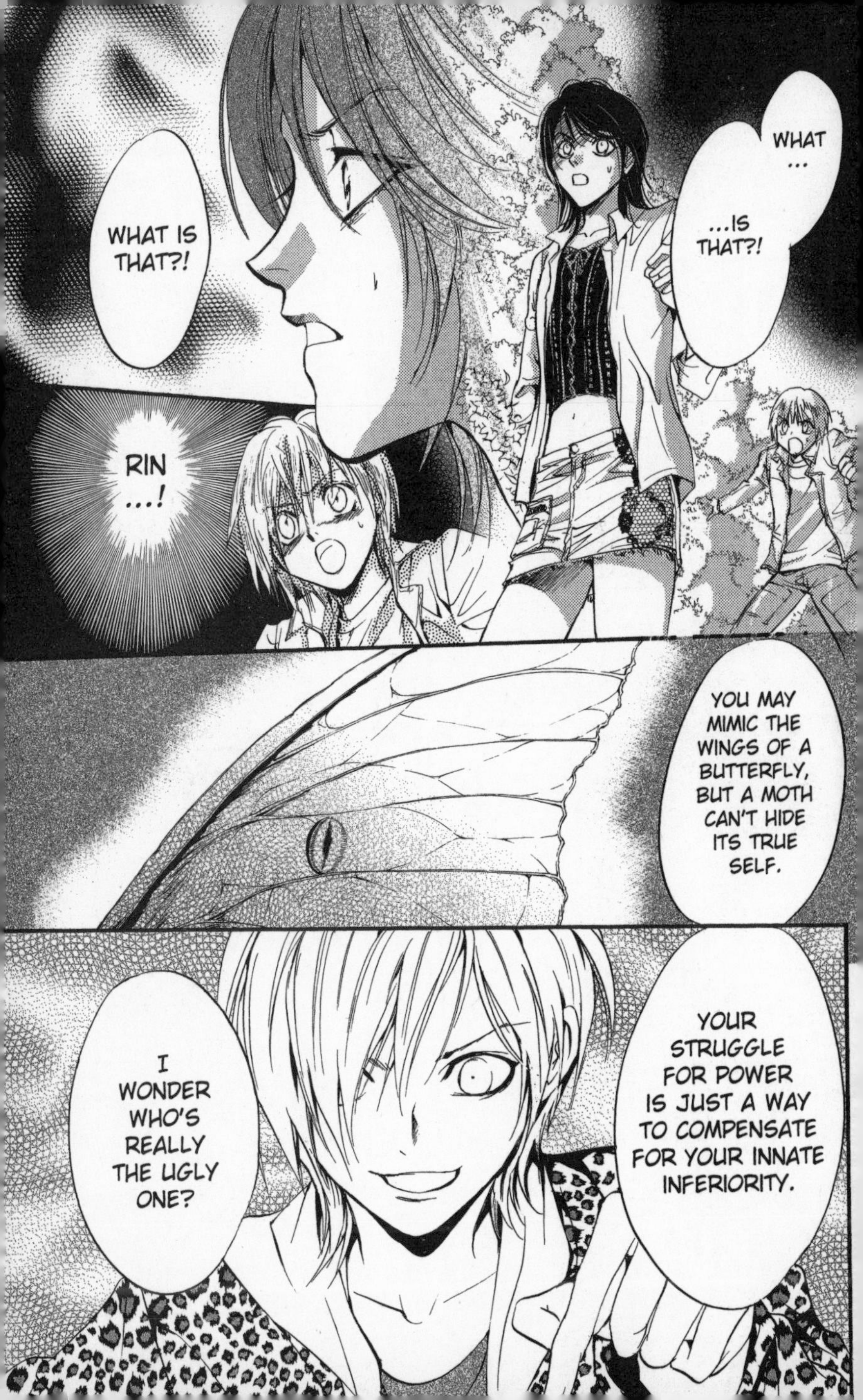
WHAT ... ...IS THAT?!
WHAT IS THAT?!
RIN ...!
YOU MAY MIMIC THE WINGS OF A BUTTERFLY, BUT A MOTH CAN'T HIDE ITS TRUE SELF.
YOUR STRUGGLE FOR POWER IS JUST A WAY TO COMPENSATE FOR YOUR INNATE INFERIORITY.
I WONDER WHO'S REALLY THE UGLY ONE?

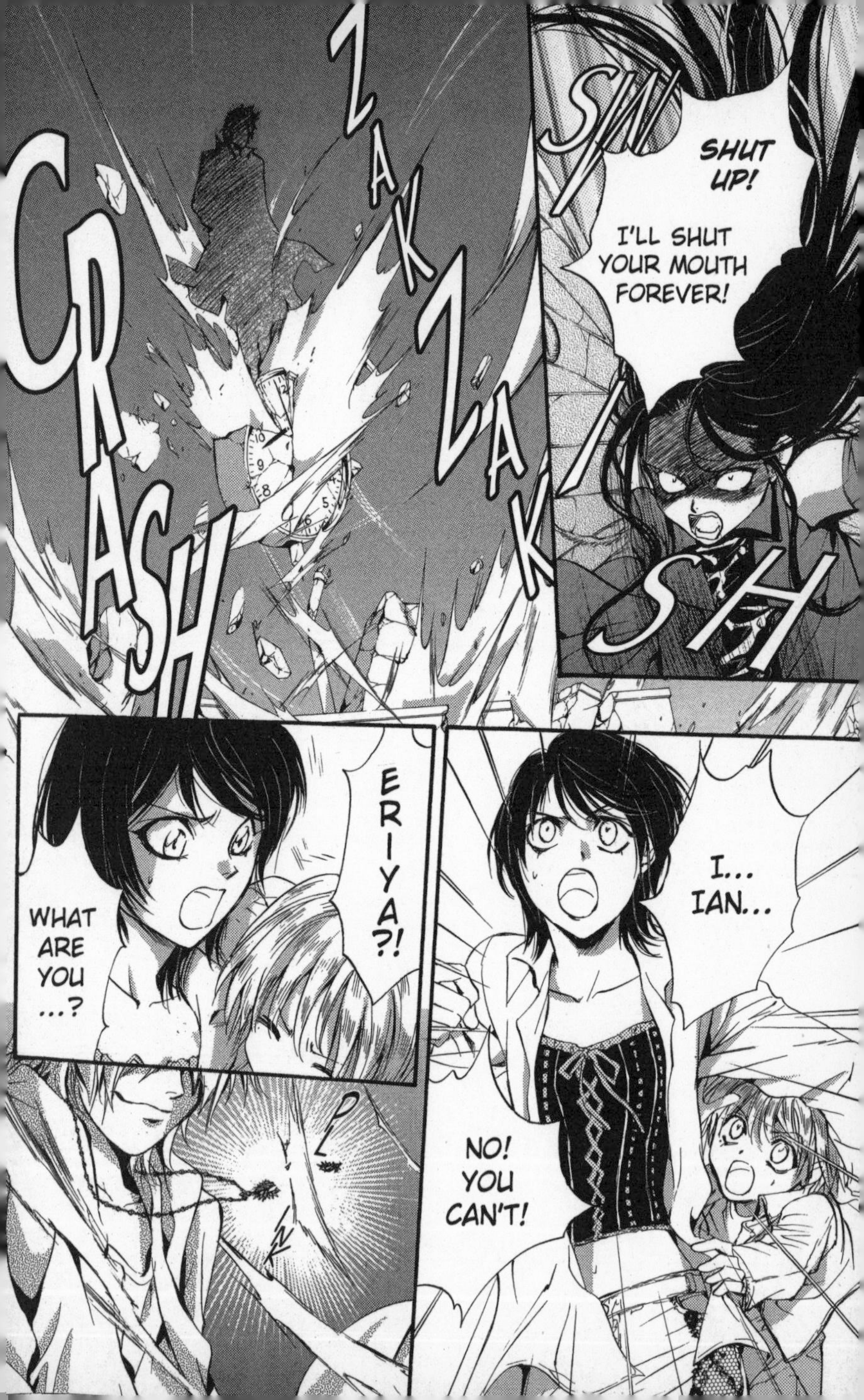
SHUT UP!
I'LL SHUT YOUR MOUTH FOREVER!
SWISH
CRASH
ZAK
ZAK
I... IAN...
NO! YOU CAN'T!
ERIYA?!
WHAT ARE YOU ...?
PLINK

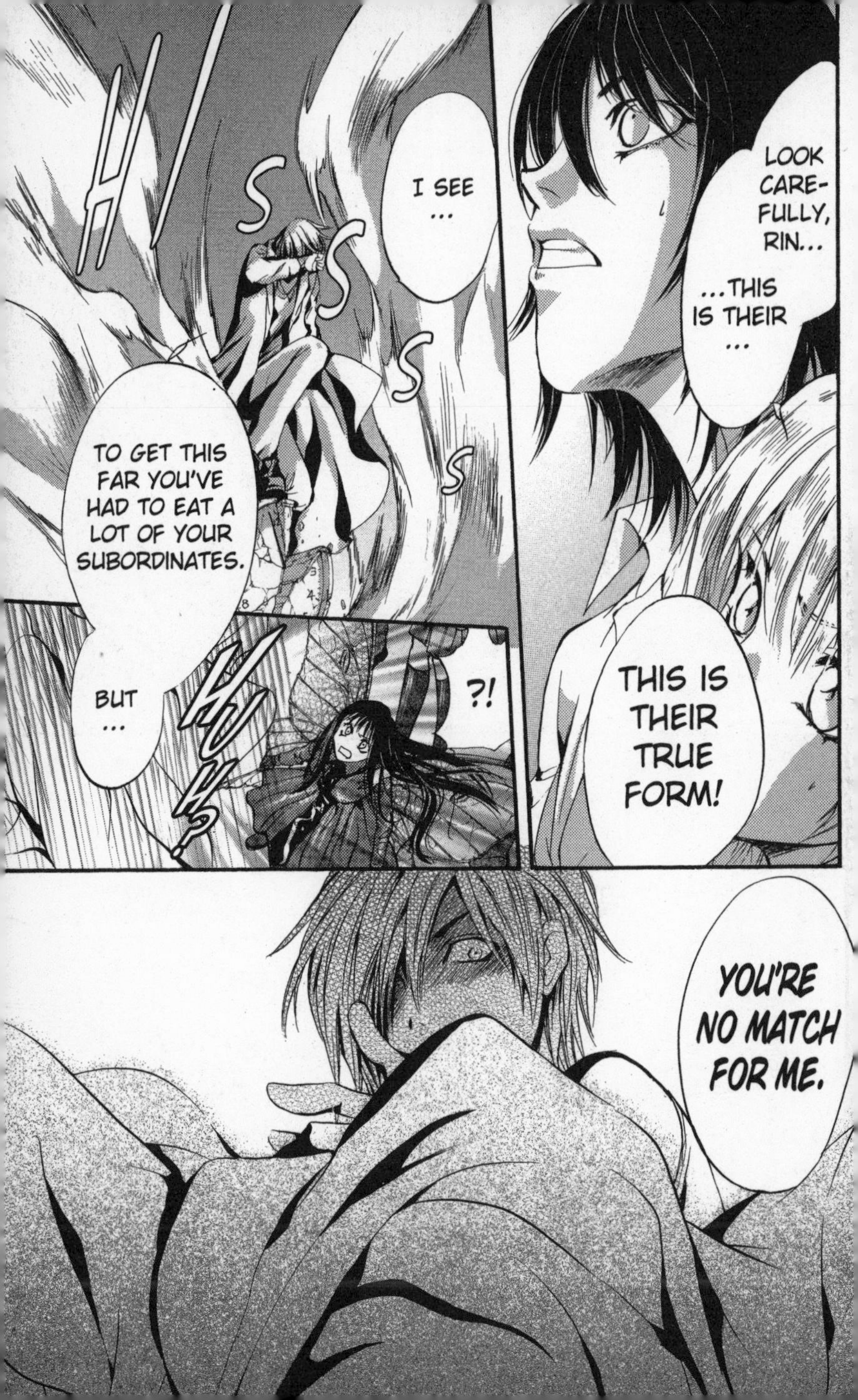
LOOK CARE-FULLY, RIN...
...THIS IS THEIR...
THIS IS THEIR TRUE FORM!
HISSSS
I SEE...
TO GET THIS FAR YOU'VE HAD TO EAT A LOT OF YOUR SUBORDINATES.
BUT...
?!
YOU'RE NO MATCH FOR ME.

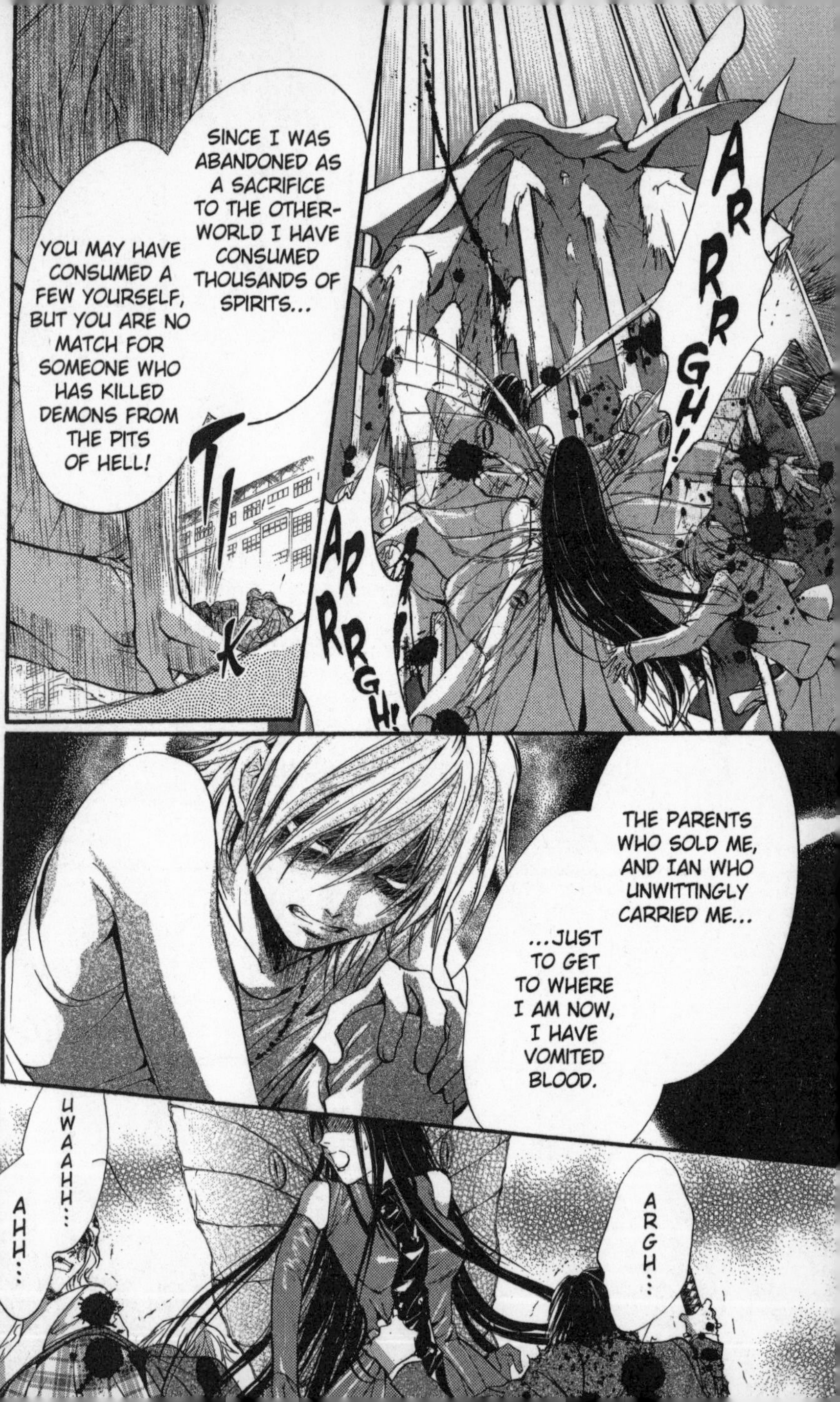
ARRRRGH!
ARRRGH!
SINCE I WAS ABANDONED AS A SACRIFICE TO THE OTHER-WORLD I HAVE CONSUMED THOUSANDS OF SPIRITS...
YOU MAY HAVE CONSUMED A FEW YOURSELF, BUT YOU ARE NO MATCH FOR SOMEONE WHO HAS KILLED DEMONS FROM THE PITS OF HELL!
TIK
THE PARENTS WHO SOLD ME, AND IAN WHO UNWITTINGLY CARRIED ME...
...JUST TO GET TO WHERE I AM NOW, I HAVE VOMITED BLOOD.
ARGH...
UWAAHH...
AHH...

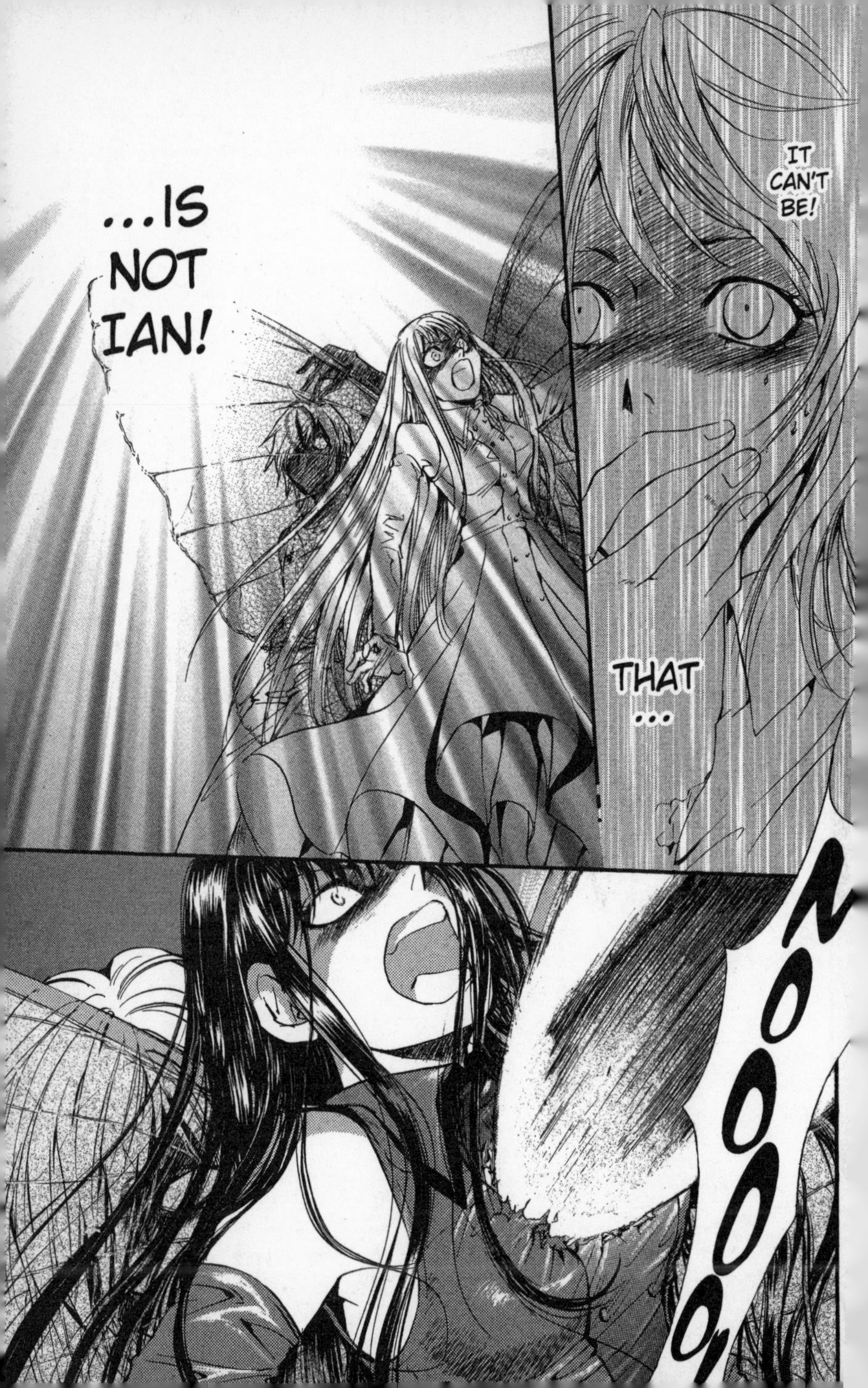
IT CAN'T BE!
THAT ...
...IS NOT IAN!
NOOOOO

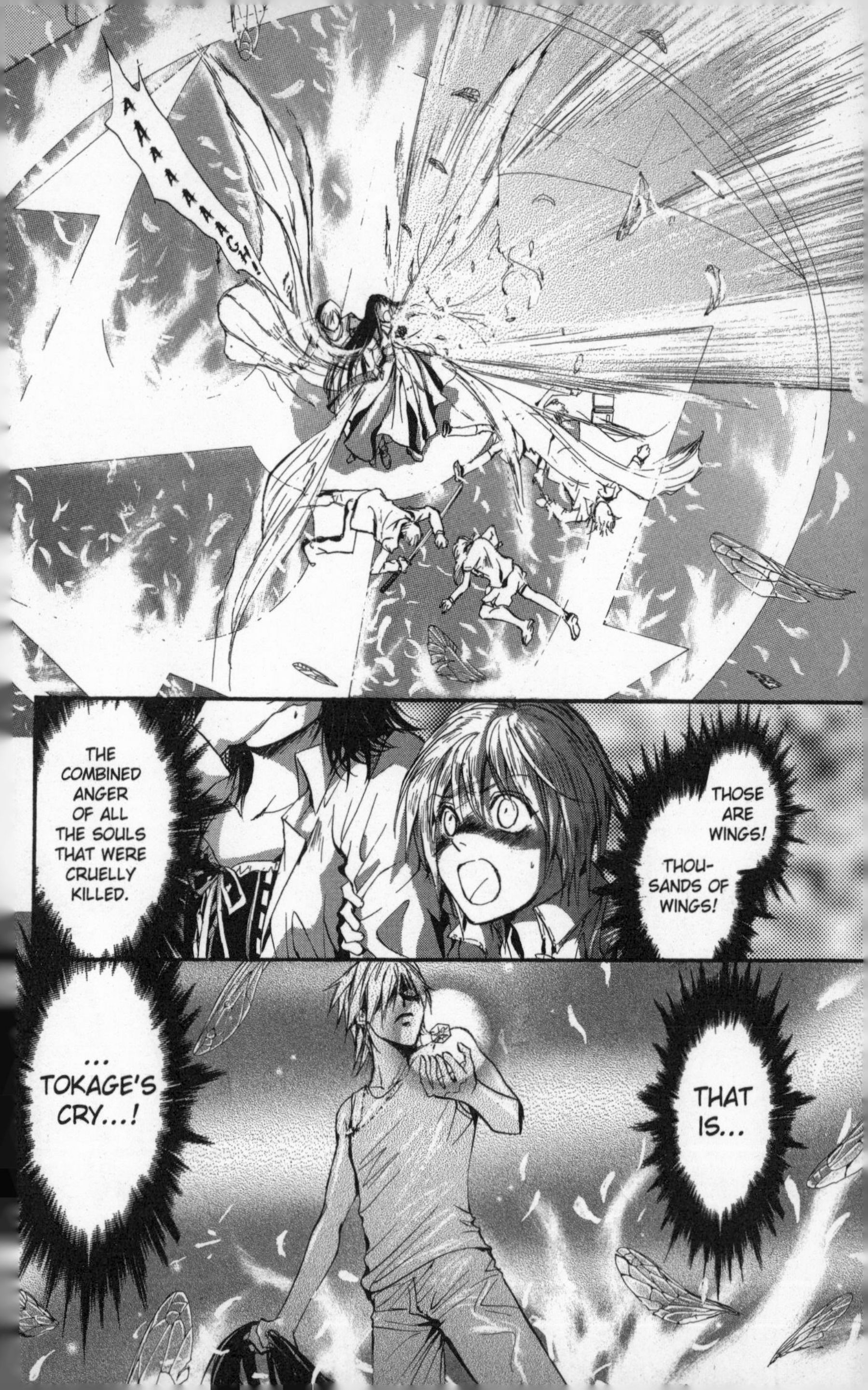
AAAAAAAAAGH!
THOSE ARE WINGS!
THOUSANDS OF WINGS!
THE COMBINED ANGER OF ALL THE SOULS THAT WERE CRUELLY KILLED.
THAT IS...
...TOKAGE'S CRY...!

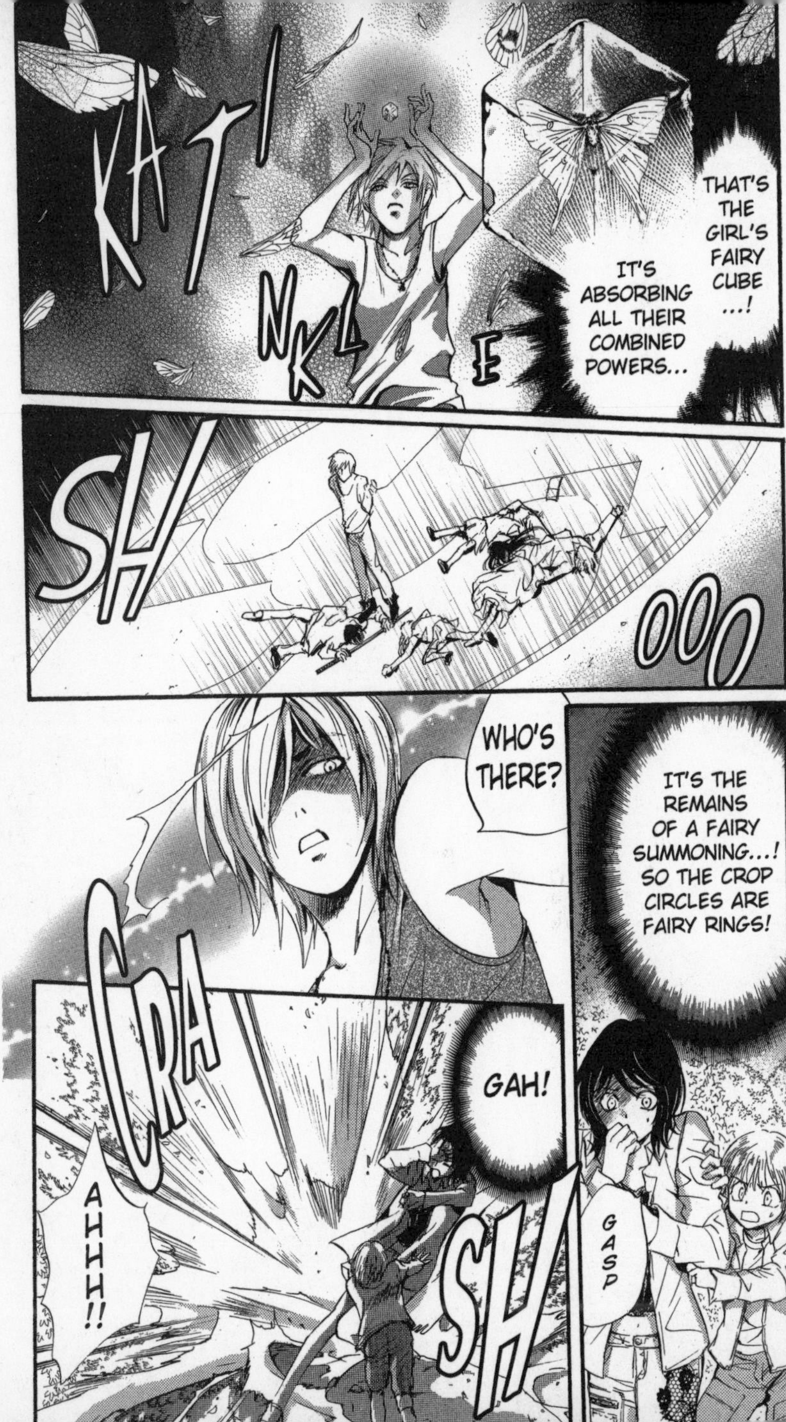
THAT'S THE GIRL'S FAIRY CUBE ...!
IT'S ABSORBING ALL THEIR COMBINED POWERS...
KATINKLE
SHOOO
IT'S THE REMAINS OF A FAIRY SUMMONING...! SO THE CROP CIRCLES ARE FAIRY RINGS!
WHO'S THERE?
CRA
GAH!
GASP
SHA
AHHH!!

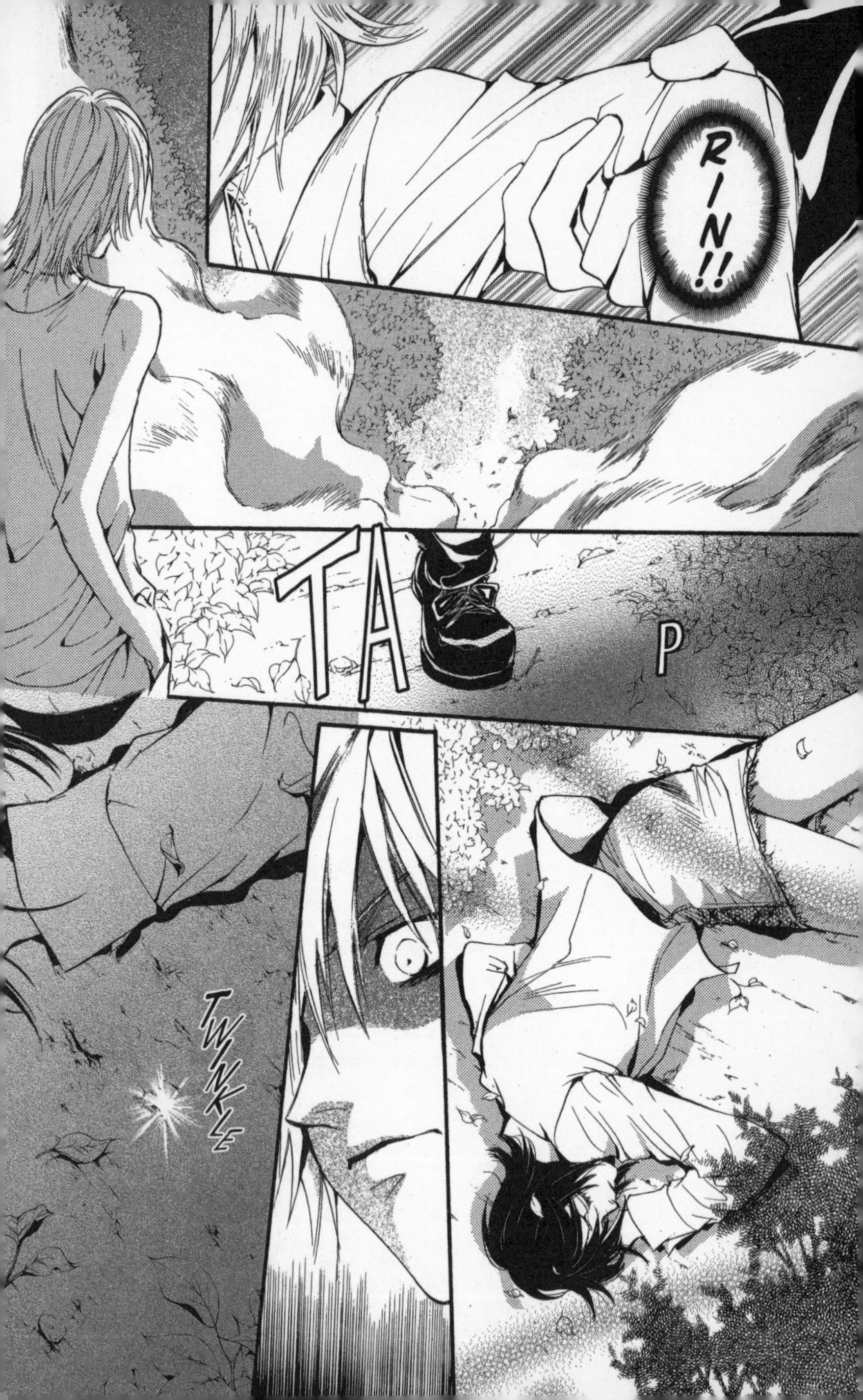
RIN!!
TA P
TWINKLE

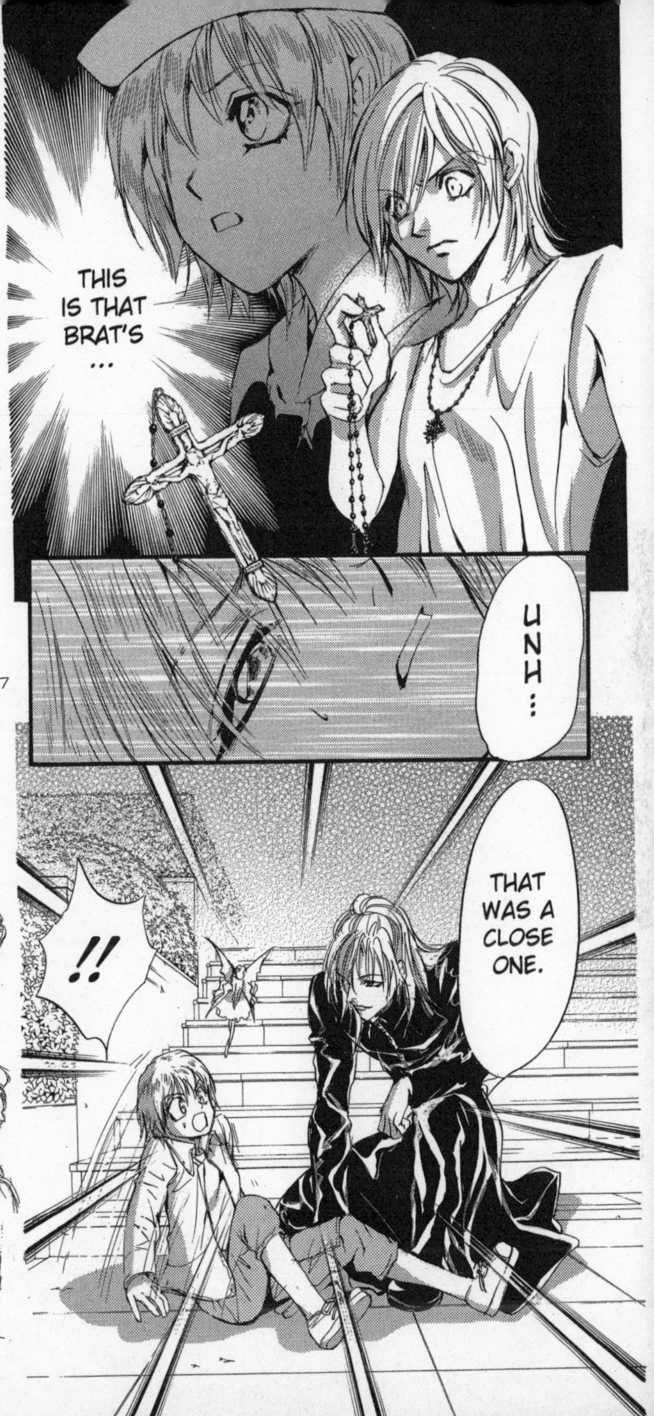
THIS IS THAT BRAT'S ...
UNH...
THAT WAS A CLOSE ONE.
!!

My favorite character has to be Rin. She's an unusually deep heroine. I really hate it when women get beaten up, though. Sorry, Rin.

I also really enjoy drawing Ainsel!

I've been working really hard so please let me know what you think! I look forward to hearing from you! ♡

See you in the next volume!

Kaori Yuki
Fairy Cube
Shojo Beat/Fairy Cube
c/o VIZ Media, LLC
P.O. Box 77010
San Francisco, CA 94107

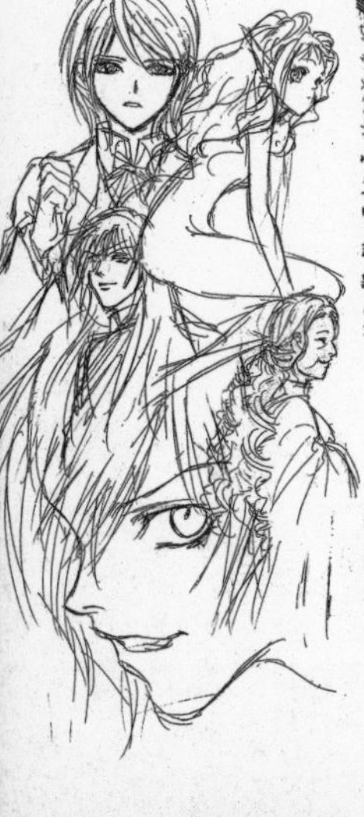

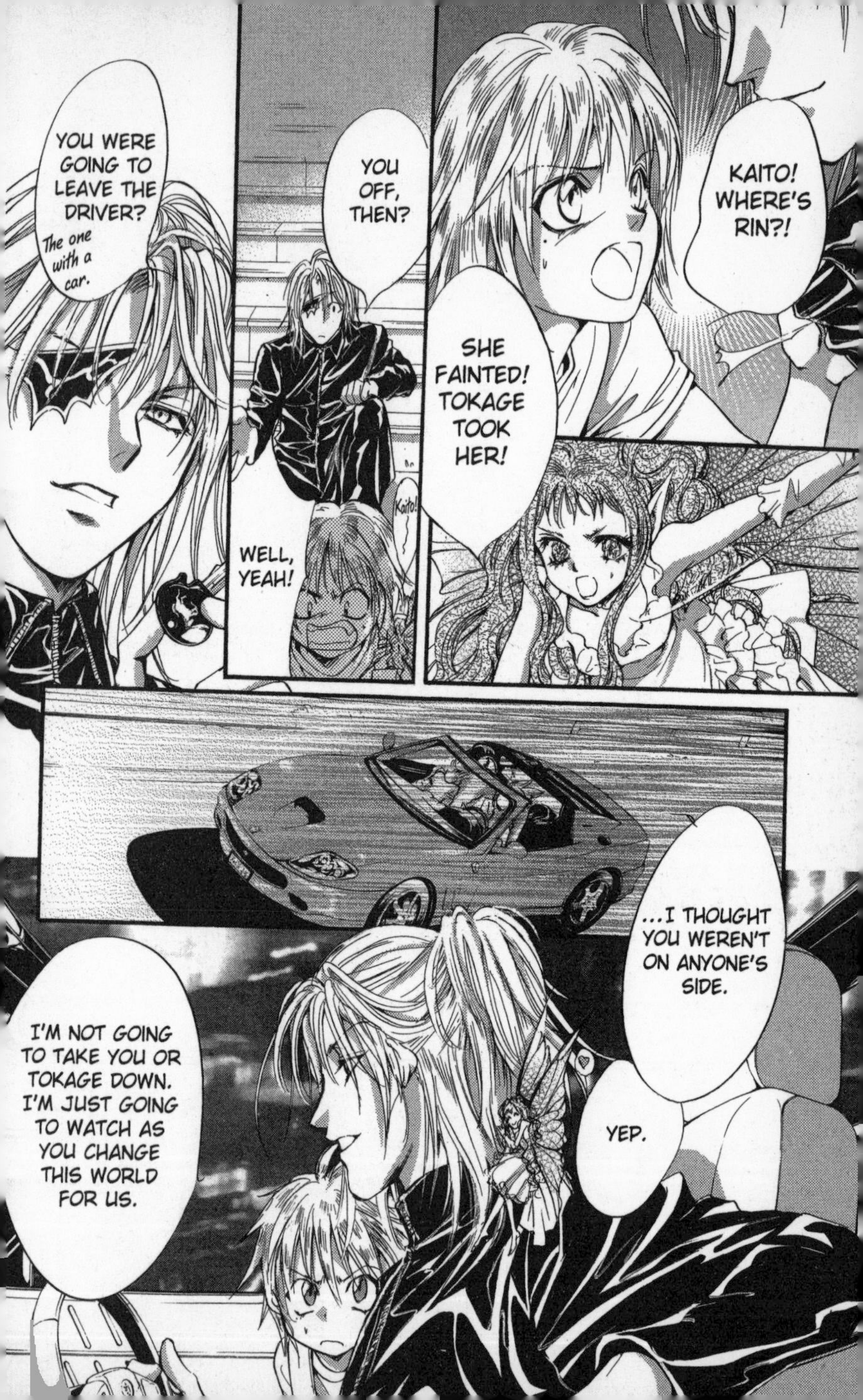
KAITO! WHERE'S RIN?!
SHE FAINTED! TOKAGE TOOK HER!
YOU OFF, THEN?
Kaito!
WELL, YEAH!
YOU WERE GOING TO LEAVE THE DRIVER?
The one with a car.
...I THOUGHT YOU WEREN'T ON ANYONE'S SIDE.
YEP.
I'M NOT GOING TO TAKE YOU OR TOKAGE DOWN. I'M JUST GOING TO WATCH AS YOU CHANGE THIS WORLD FOR US.

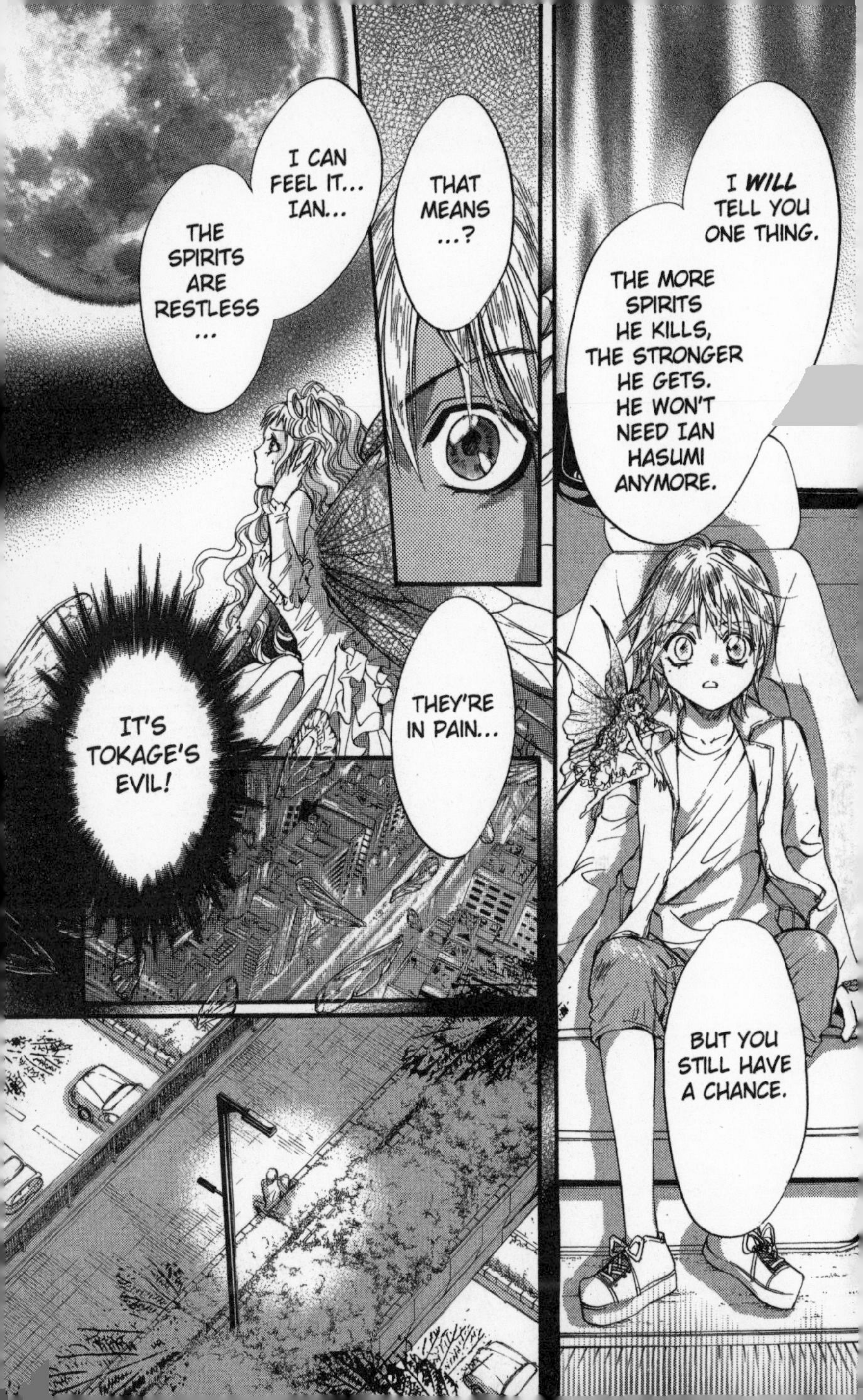
I WILL TELL YOU ONE THING.
THE MORE SPIRITS HE KILLS, THE STRONGER HE GETS. HE WON'T NEED IAN HASUMI ANYMORE.
BUT YOU STILL HAVE A CHANCE.
I CAN FEEL IT... IAN...
THE SPIRITS ARE RESTLESS...
THAT MEANS...?
THEY'RE IN PAIN...
IT'S TOKAGE'S EVIL!

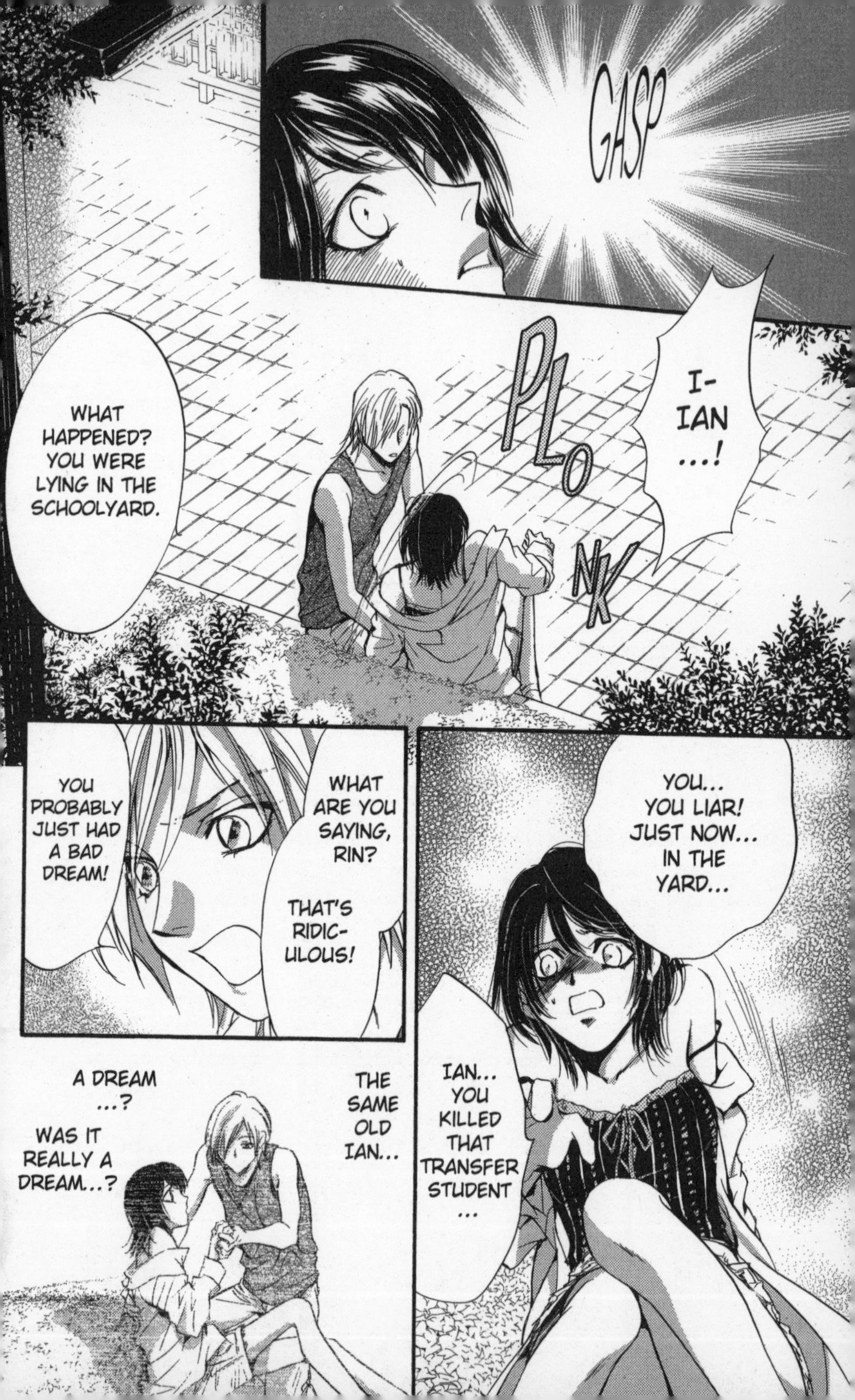
GASP
I-IAN...!
PLONK
WHAT HAPPENED? YOU WERE LYING IN THE SCHOOLYARD.
YOU... YOU LIAR! JUST NOW... IN THE YARD...
IAN... YOU KILLED THAT TRANSFER STUDENT...
WHAT ARE YOU SAYING, RIN?
THAT'S RIDIC-ULOUS!
YOU PROBABLY JUST HAD A BAD DREAM!
THE SAME OLD IAN...
A DREAM...?
WAS IT REALLY A DREAM...?

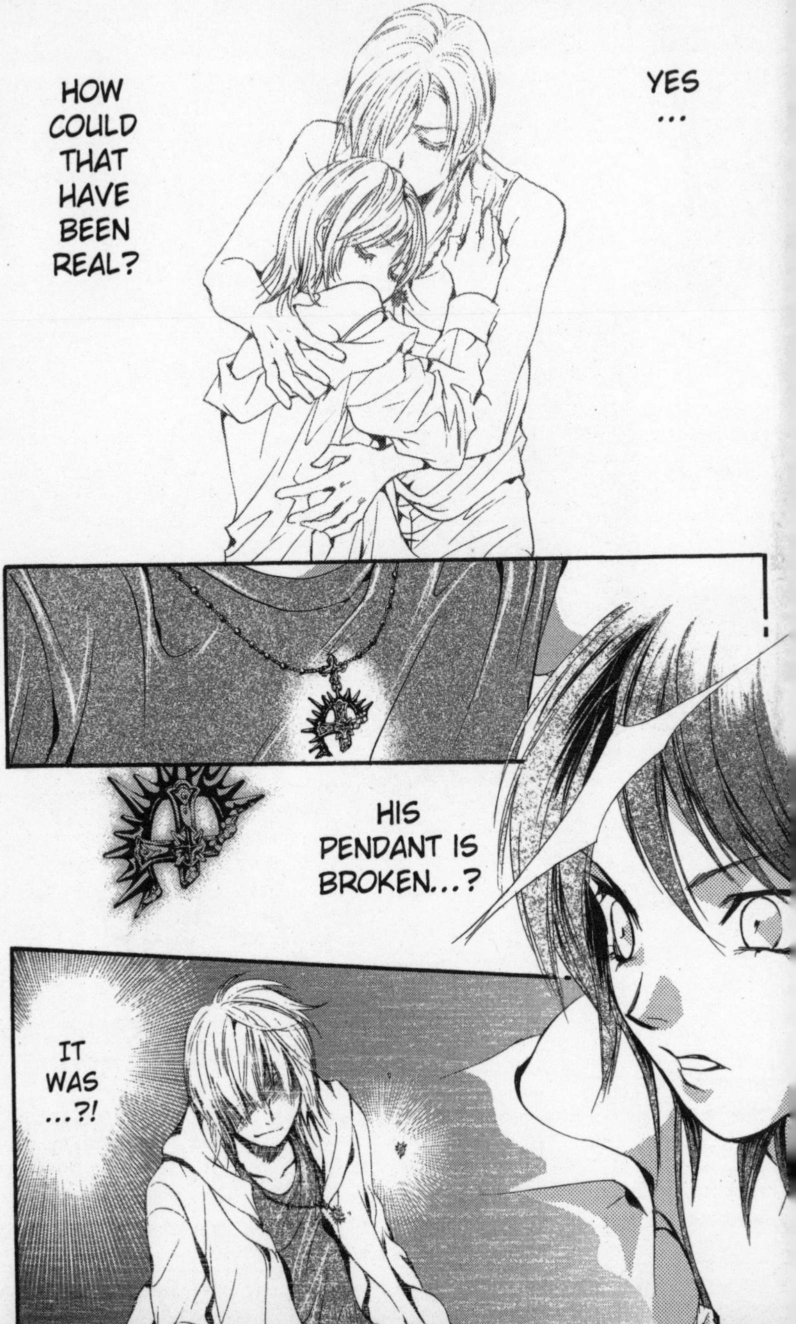
YES...
HOW COULD THAT HAVE BEEN REAL?
HIS PENDANT IS BROKEN...?
IT WAS ...?!

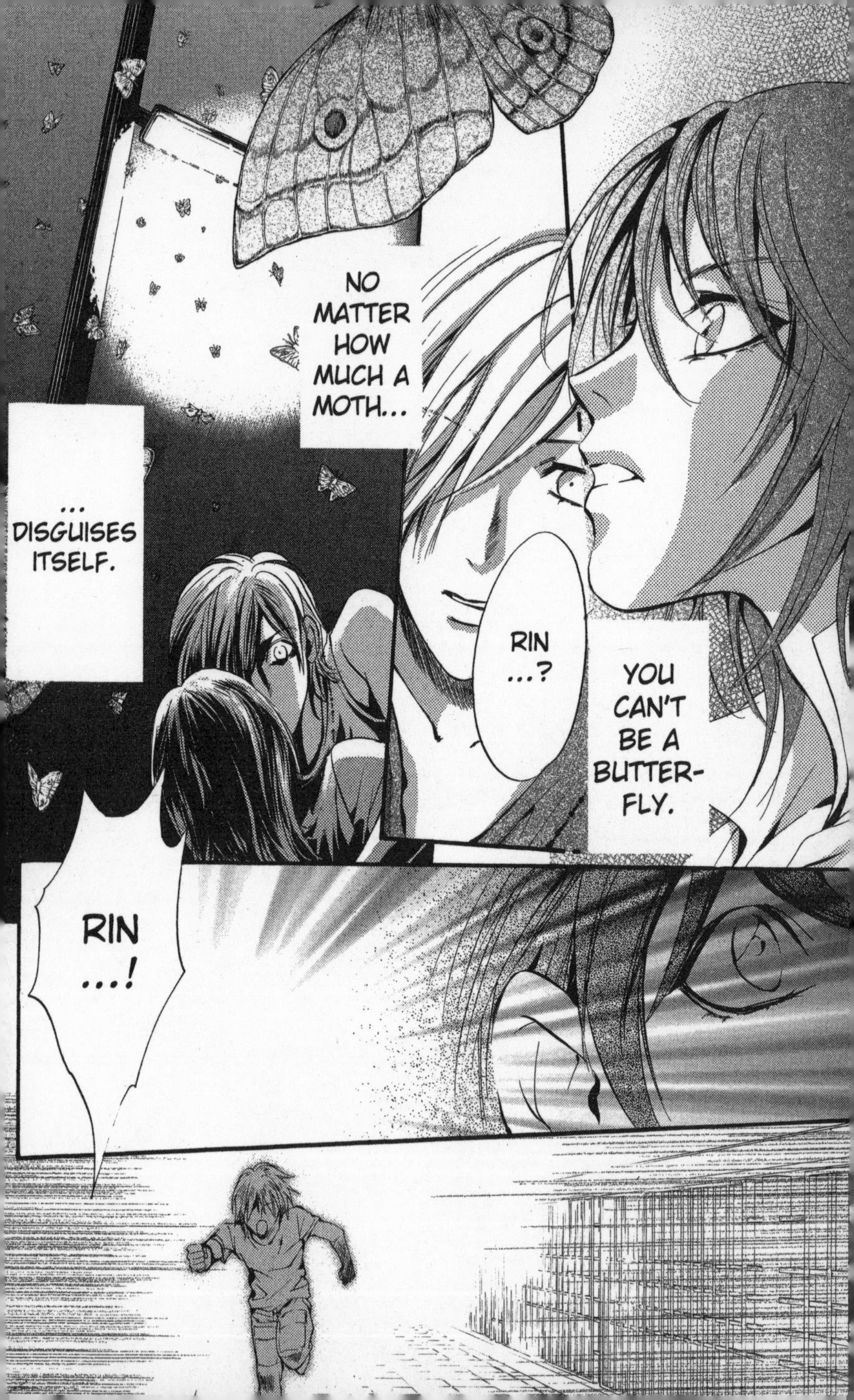
NO MATTER HOW MUCH A MOTH...
... DISGUISES ITSELF.
YOU CAN'T BE A BUTTER-FLY.
RIN ...?
RIN ...!

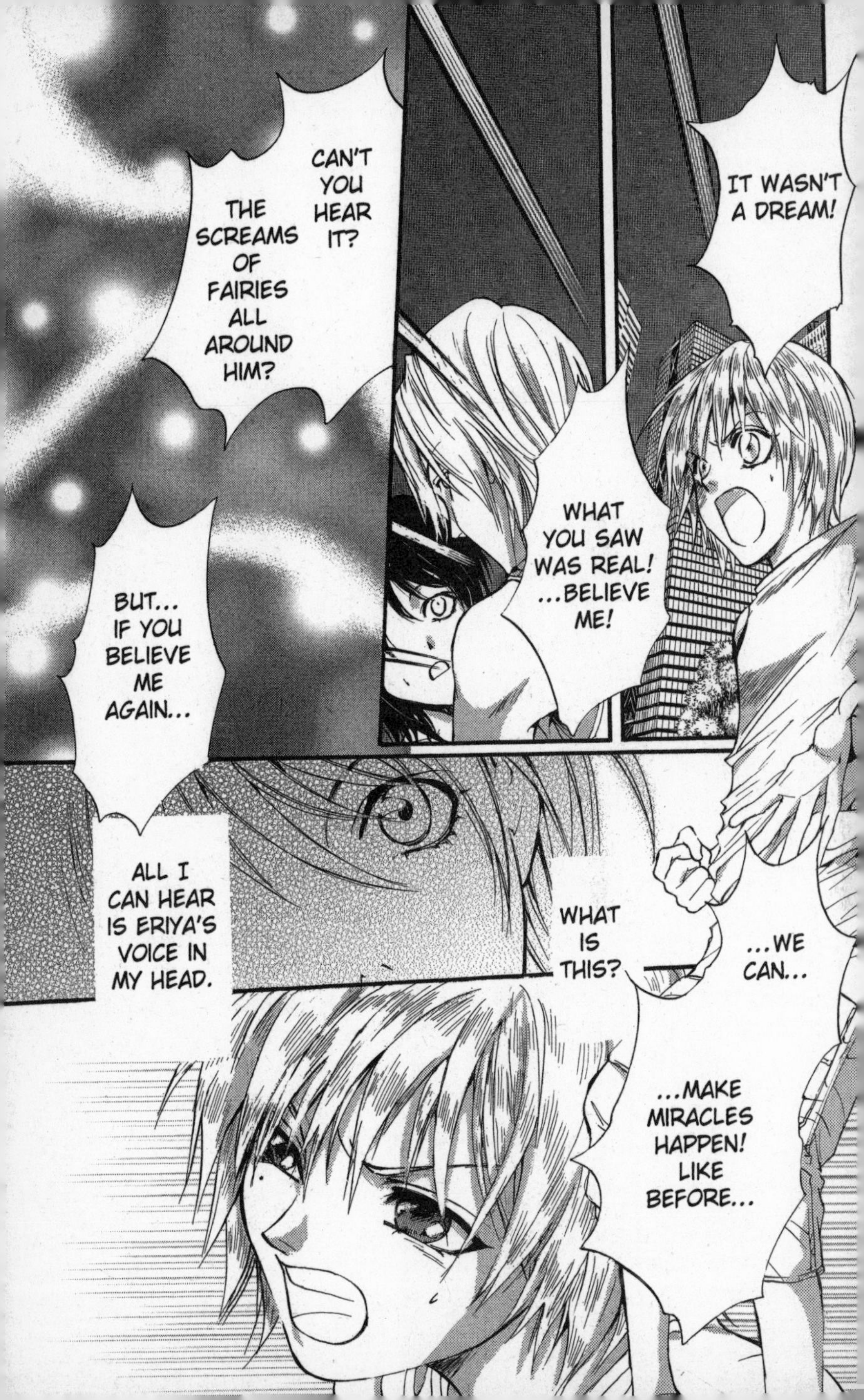
IT WASN'T A DREAM!
WHAT YOU SAW WAS REAL! ...BELIEVE ME!
CAN'T YOU HEAR IT?
THE SCREAMS OF FAIRIES ALL AROUND HIM?
BUT... IF YOU BELIEVE ME AGAIN...
WHAT IS THIS?
ALL I CAN HEAR IS ERIYA'S VOICE IN MY HEAD.
...WE CAN...
...MAKE MIRACLES HAPPEN! LIKE BEFORE...

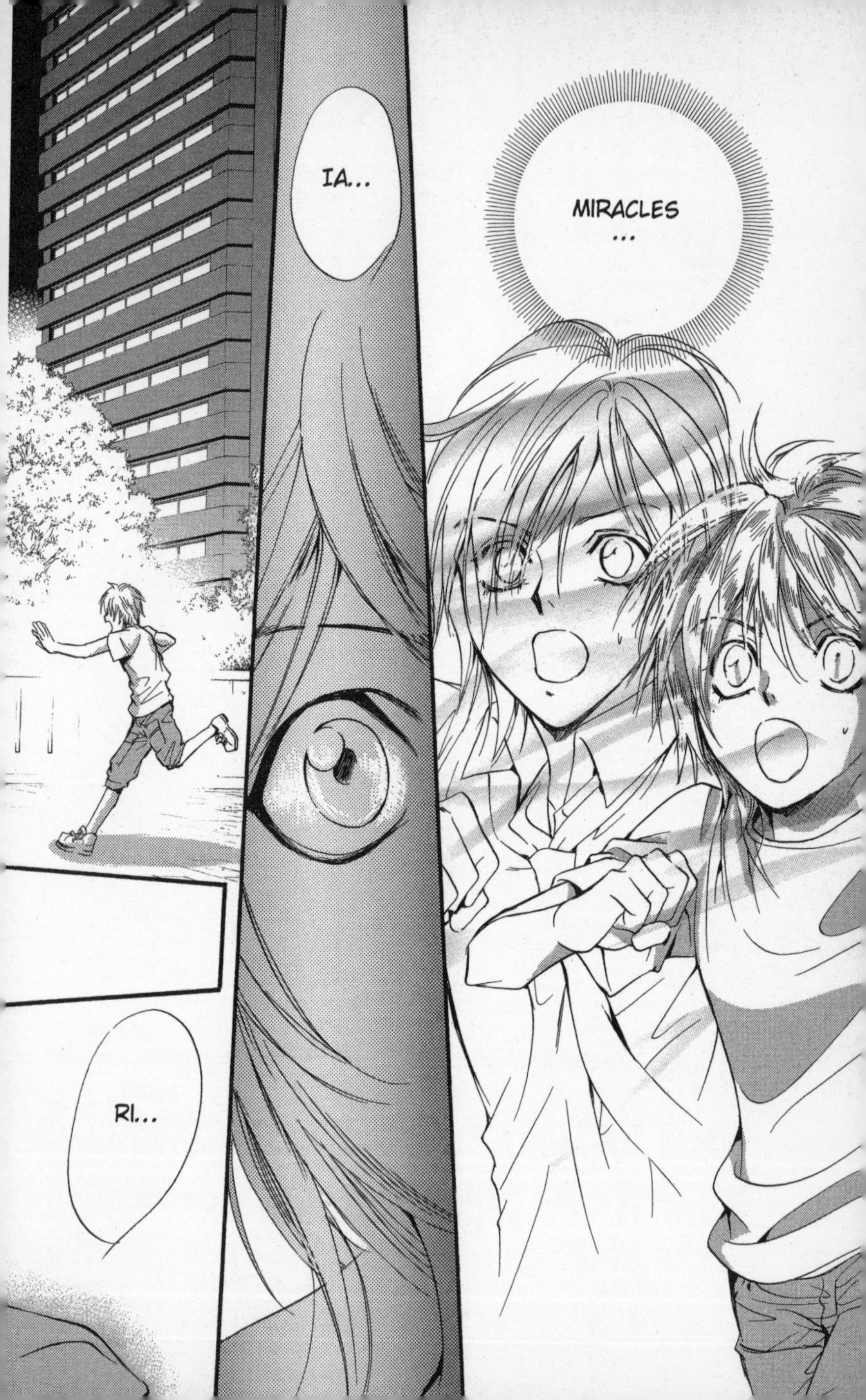
MIRACLES ...
IA...
RI...

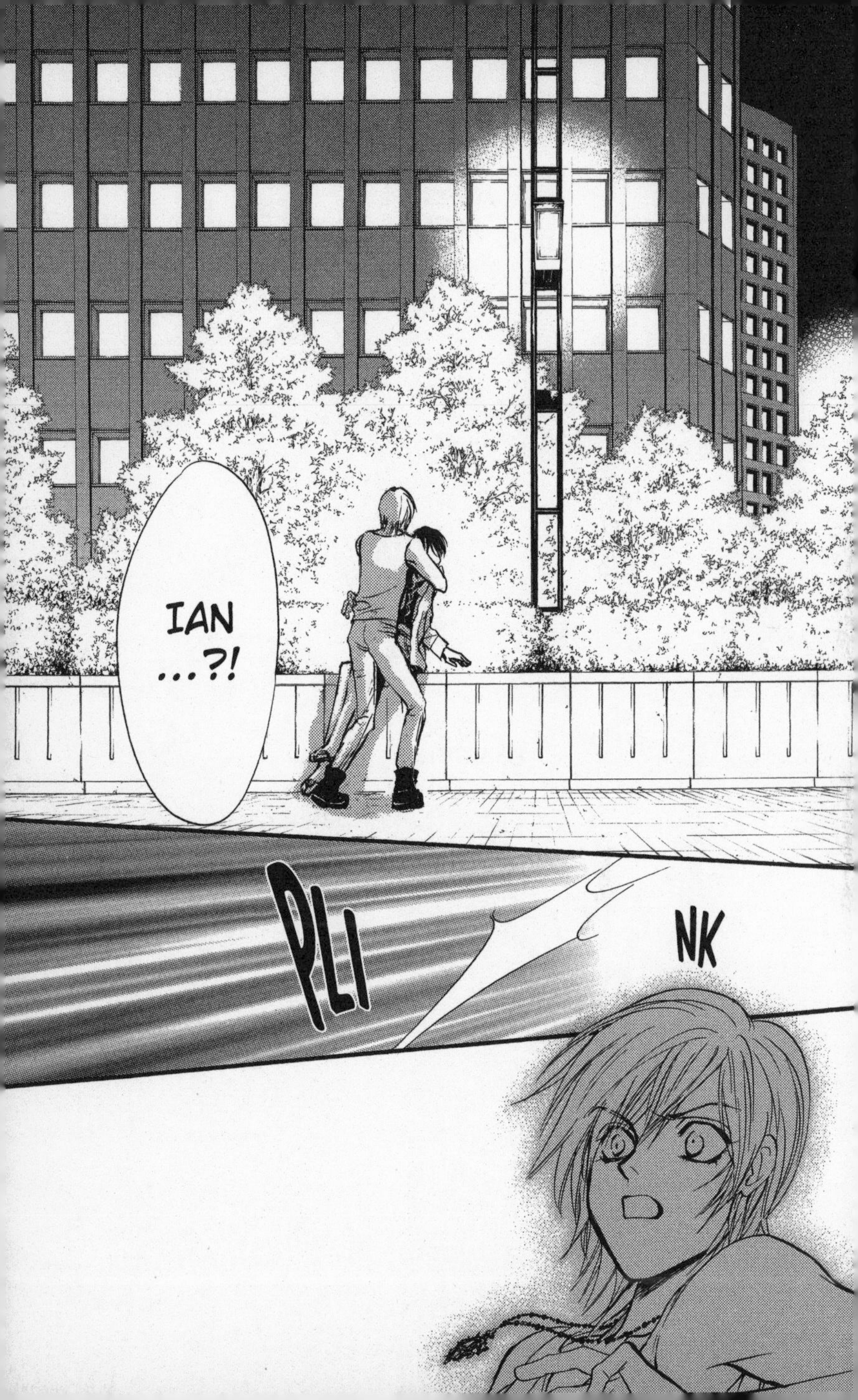
IAN ...?!
PLI NK

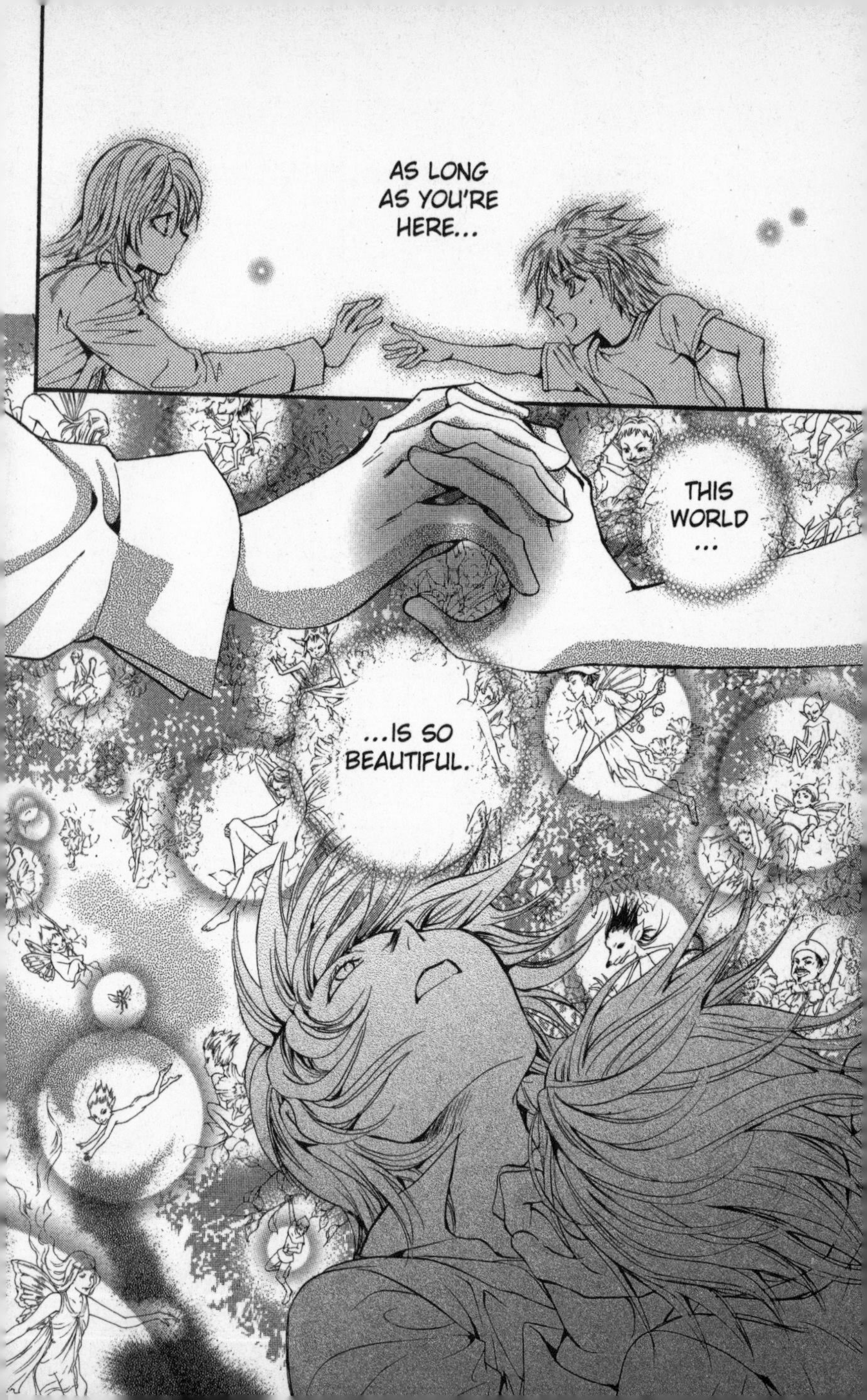
AS LONG AS YOU'RE HERE...
THIS WORLD ...
...IS SO BEAUTIFUL.

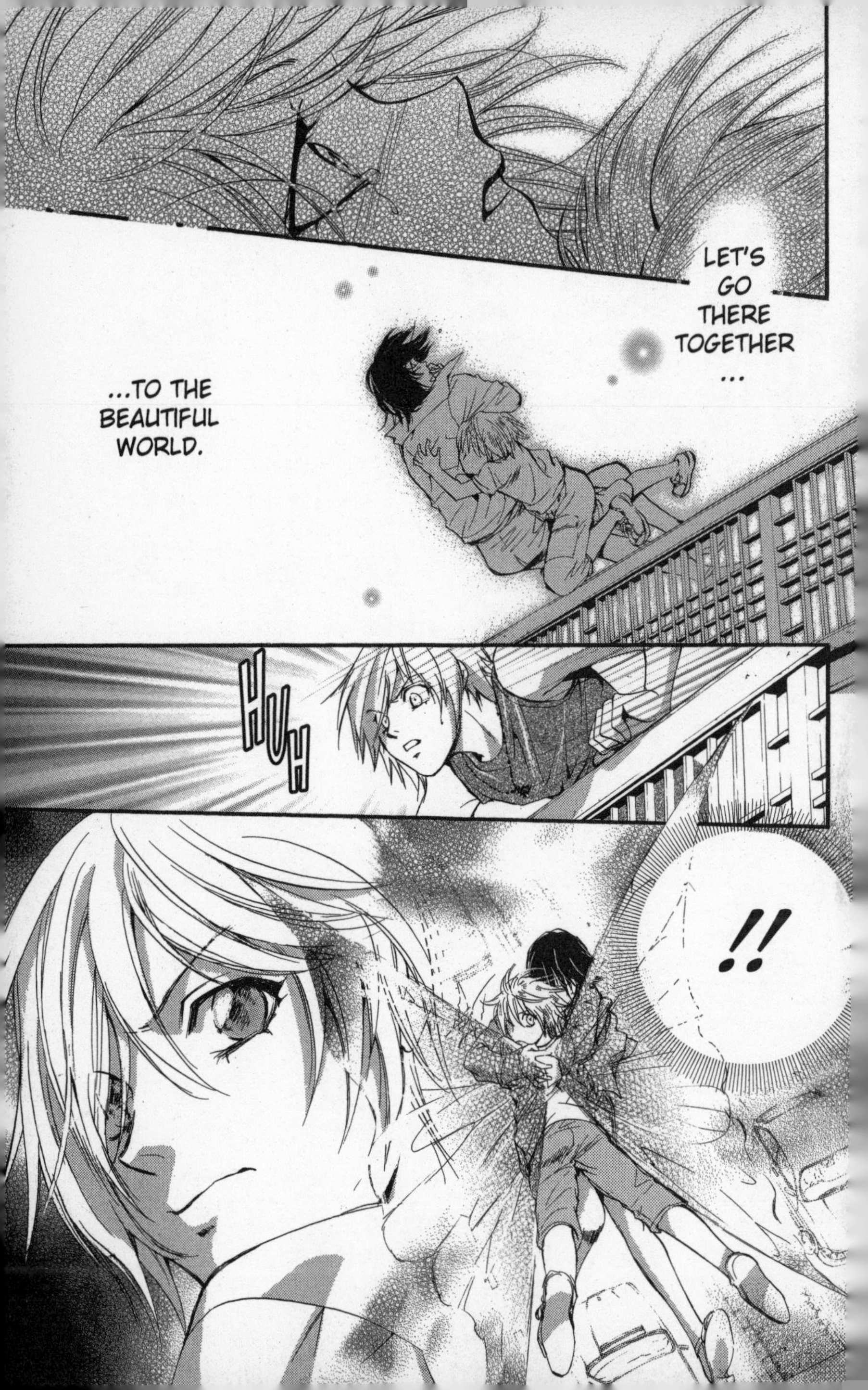
LET'S GO THERE TOGETHER ...
...TO THE BEAUTIFUL WORLD.
HUH
!!

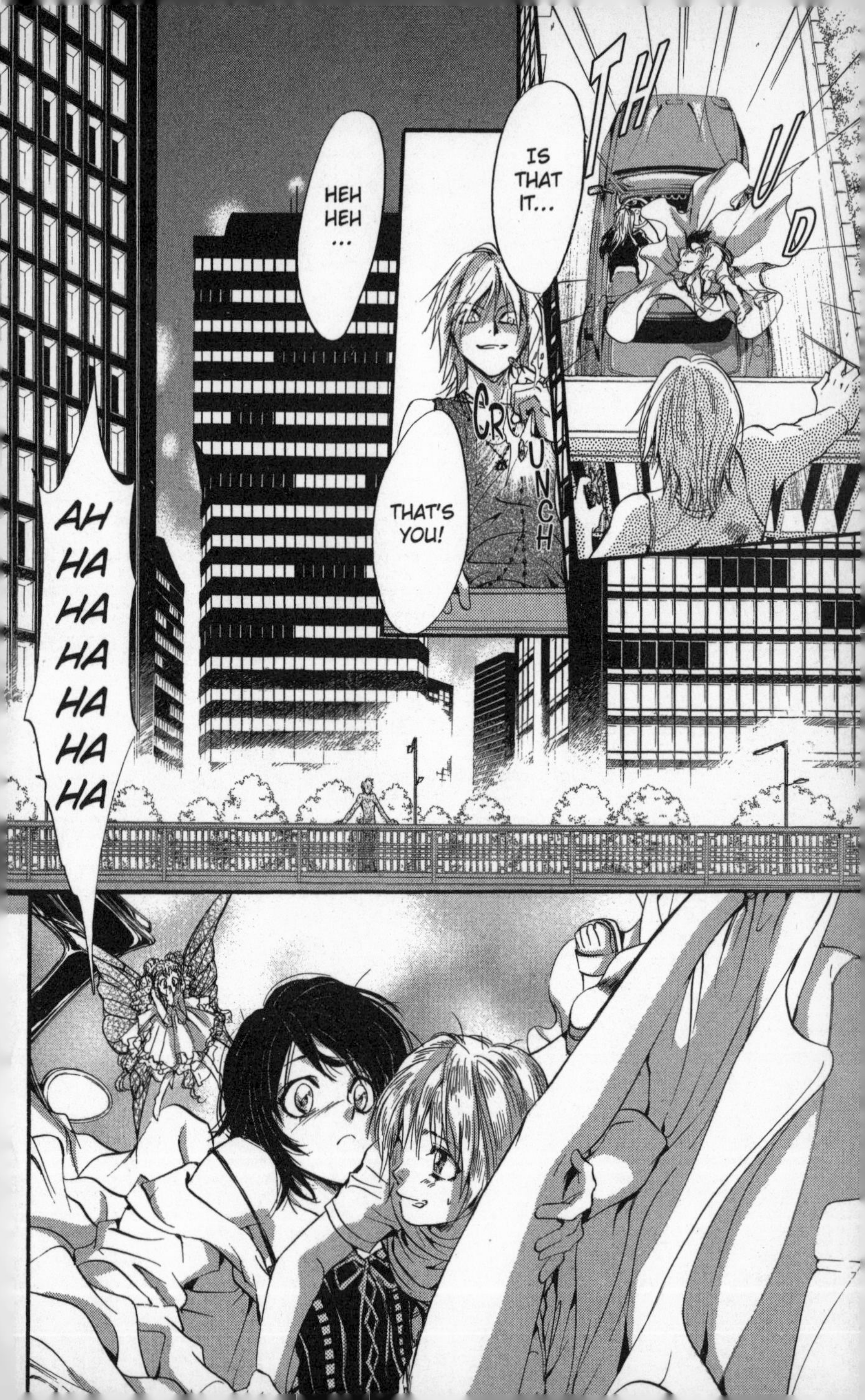
THUD
IS THAT IT...
HEH HEH...
CRUNCH
THAT'S YOU!
AH HA HA HA HA HA HA HA

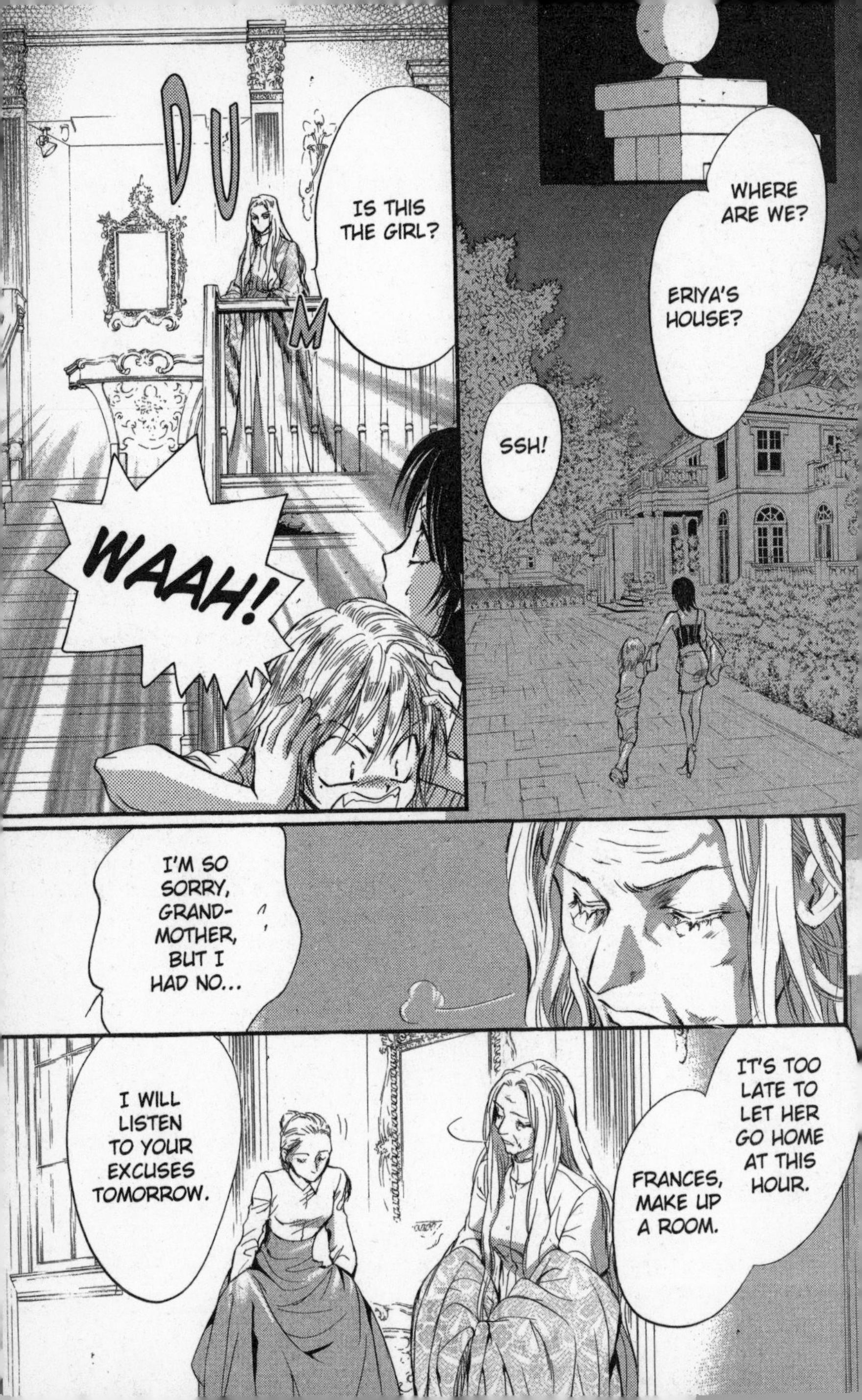
WHERE ARE WE?
ERIYA'S HOUSE?
SSH!
DUM
IS THIS THE GIRL?
WAAH!
I'M SO SORRY, GRAND-MOTHER, BUT I HAD NO...
IT'S TOO LATE TO LET HER GO HOME AT THIS HOUR.
FRANCES, MAKE UP A ROOM.
I WILL LISTEN TO YOUR EXCUSES TOMORROW.

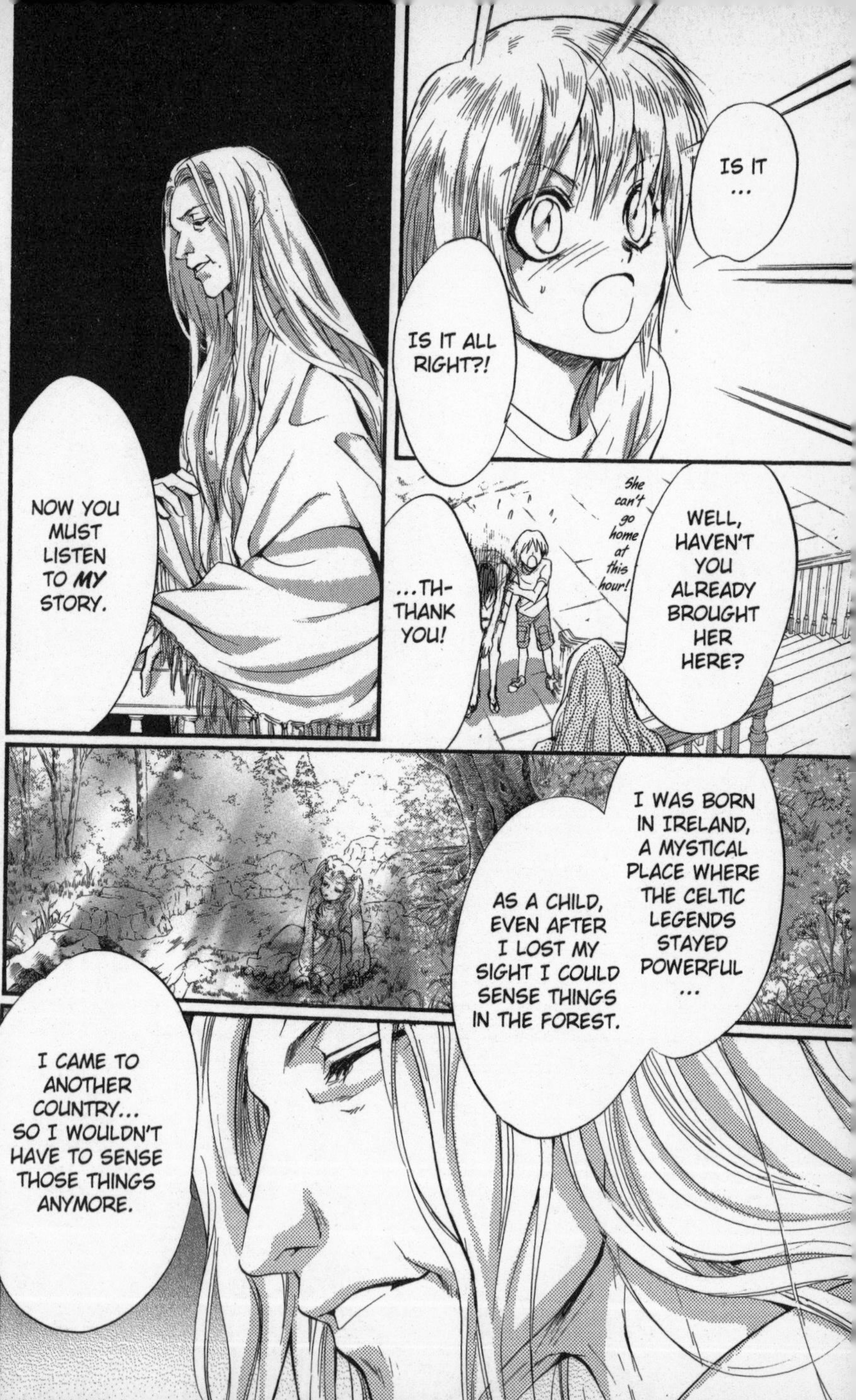
IS IT ...
IS IT ALL RIGHT?!
WELL, HAVEN'T YOU ALREADY BROUGHT HER HERE?
She can't go home at this hour!
...TH-THANK YOU!
NOW YOU MUST LISTEN TO *MY* STORY.
I WAS BORN IN IRELAND, A MYSTICAL PLACE WHERE THE CELTIC LEGENDS STAYED POWERFUL ...
AS A CHILD, EVEN AFTER I LOST MY SIGHT I COULD SENSE THINGS IN THE FOREST.
I CAME TO ANOTHER COUNTRY... SO I WOULDN'T HAVE TO SENSE THOSE THINGS ANYMORE.

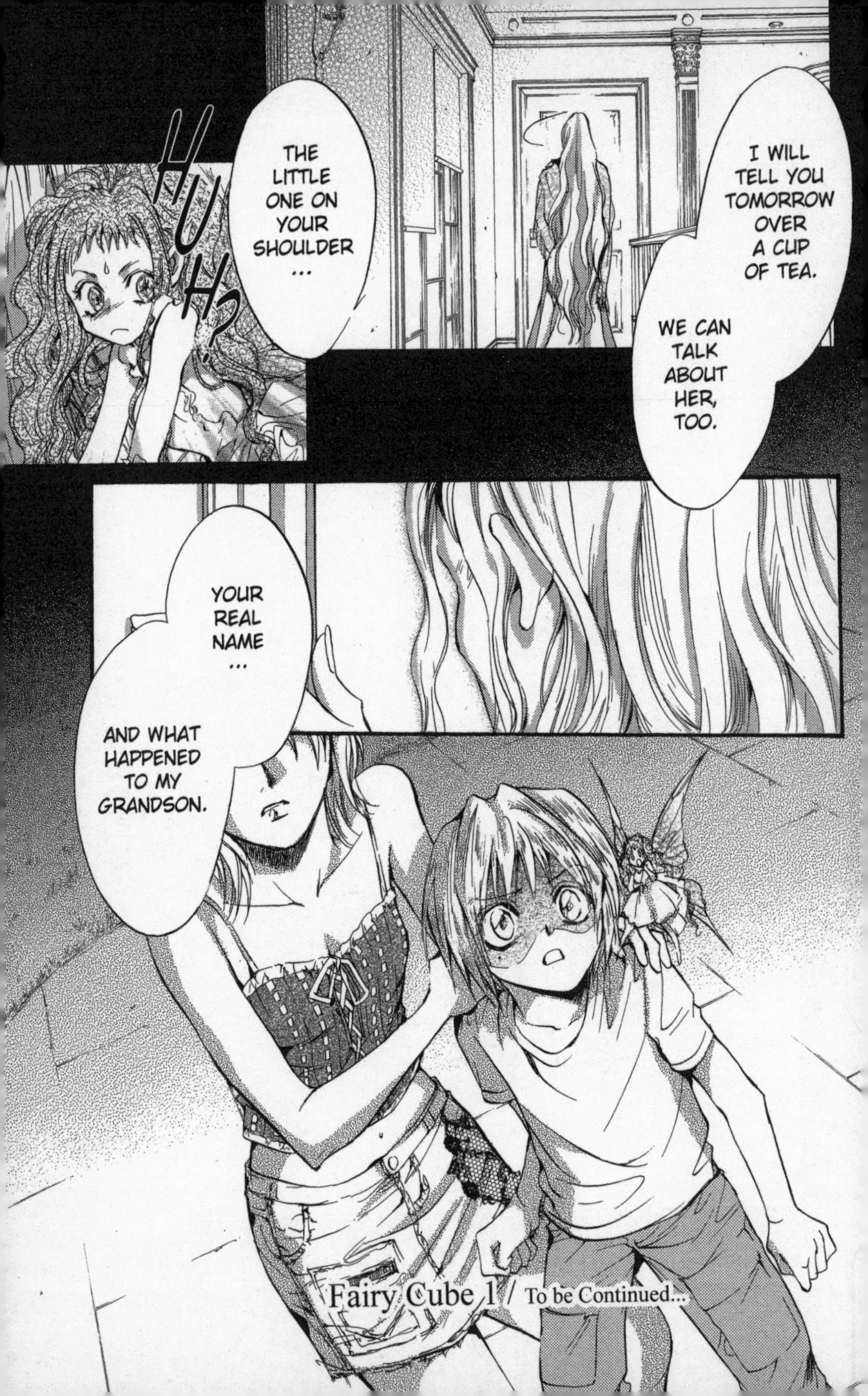
I WILL TELL YOU TOMORROW OVER A CUP OF TEA.
WE CAN TALK ABOUT HER, TOO.
THE LITTLE ONE ON YOUR SHOULDER ...
HUH?
YOUR REAL NAME ...
AND WHAT HAPPENED TO MY GRANDSON.
Fairy Cube 1 / To be Continued...

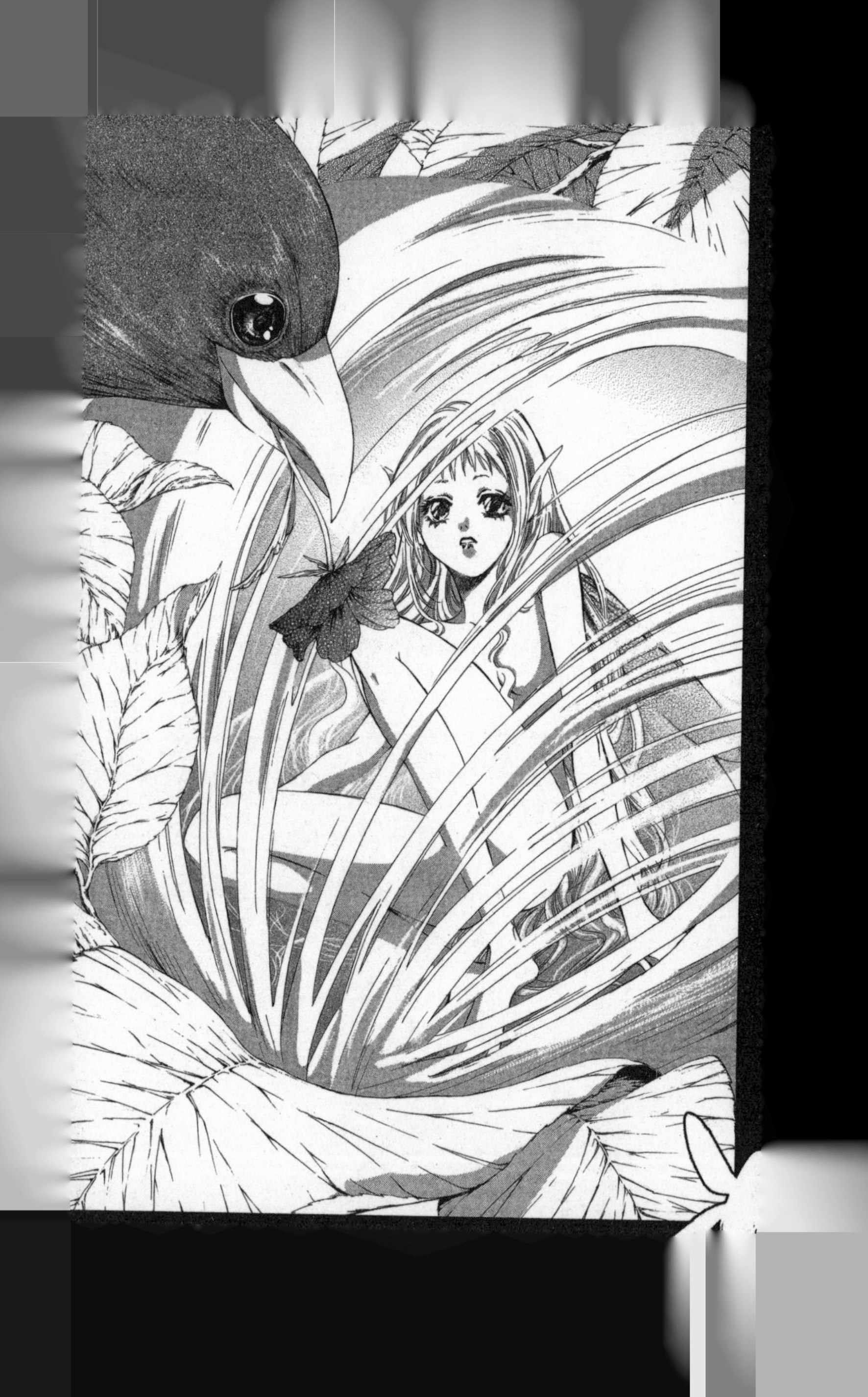

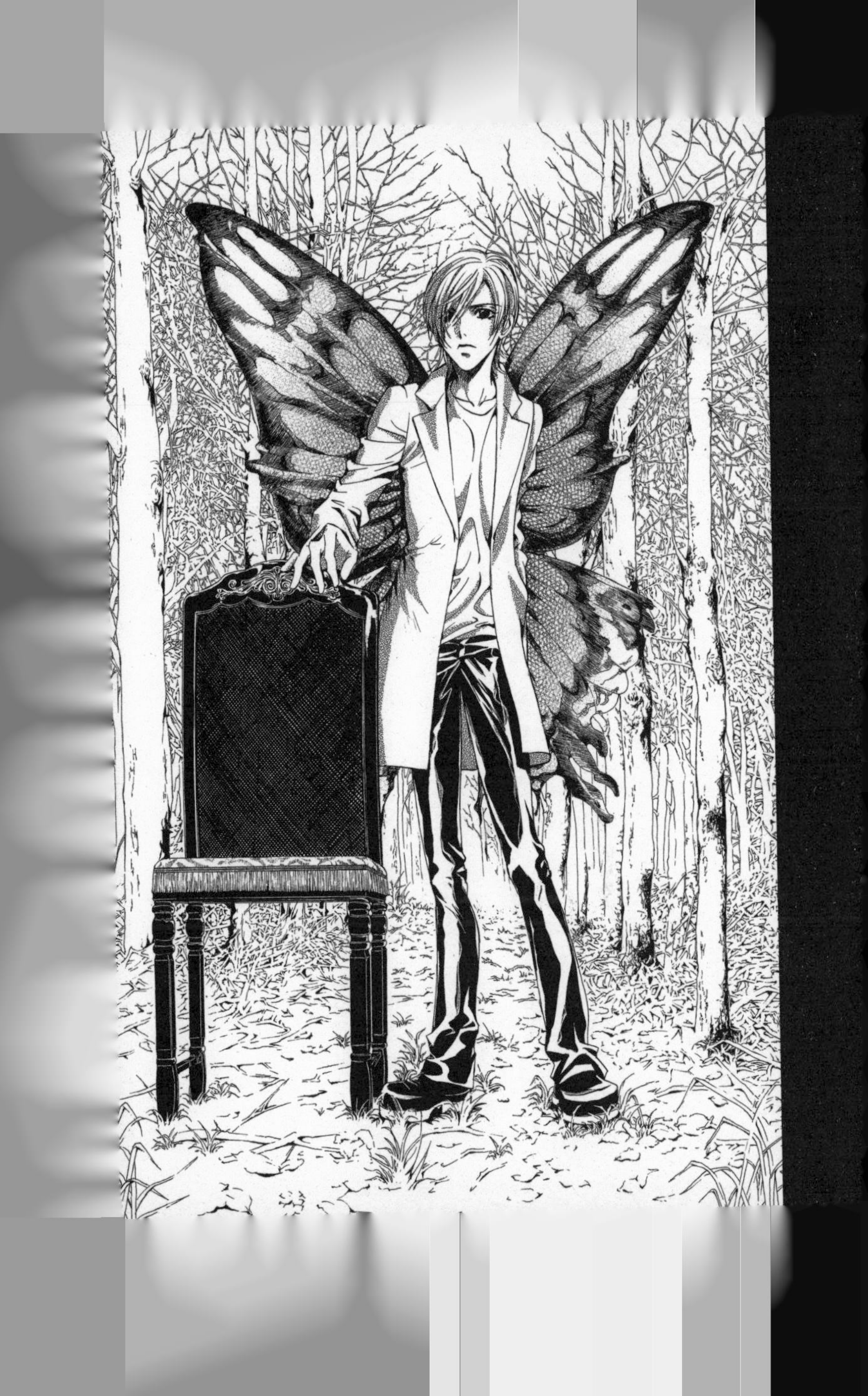

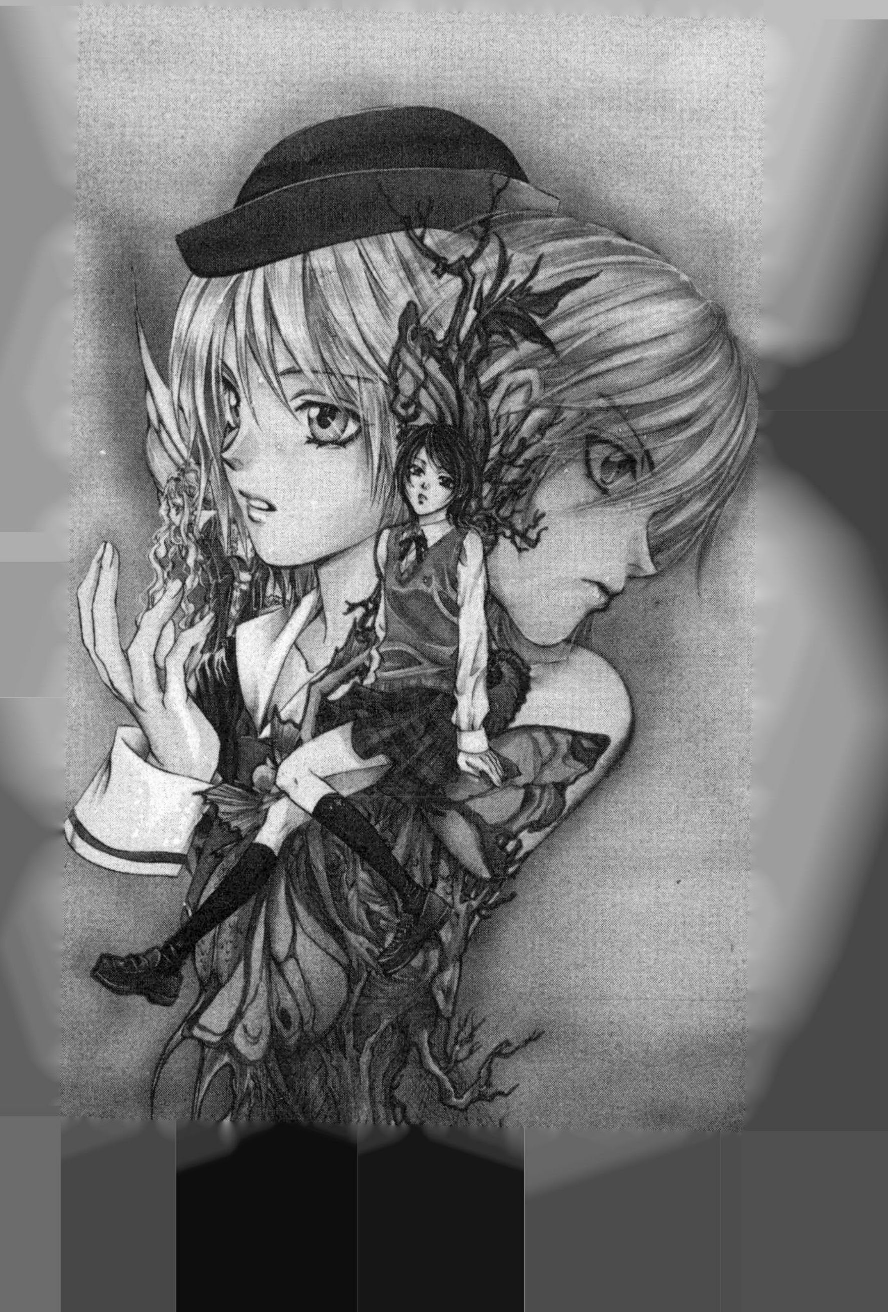

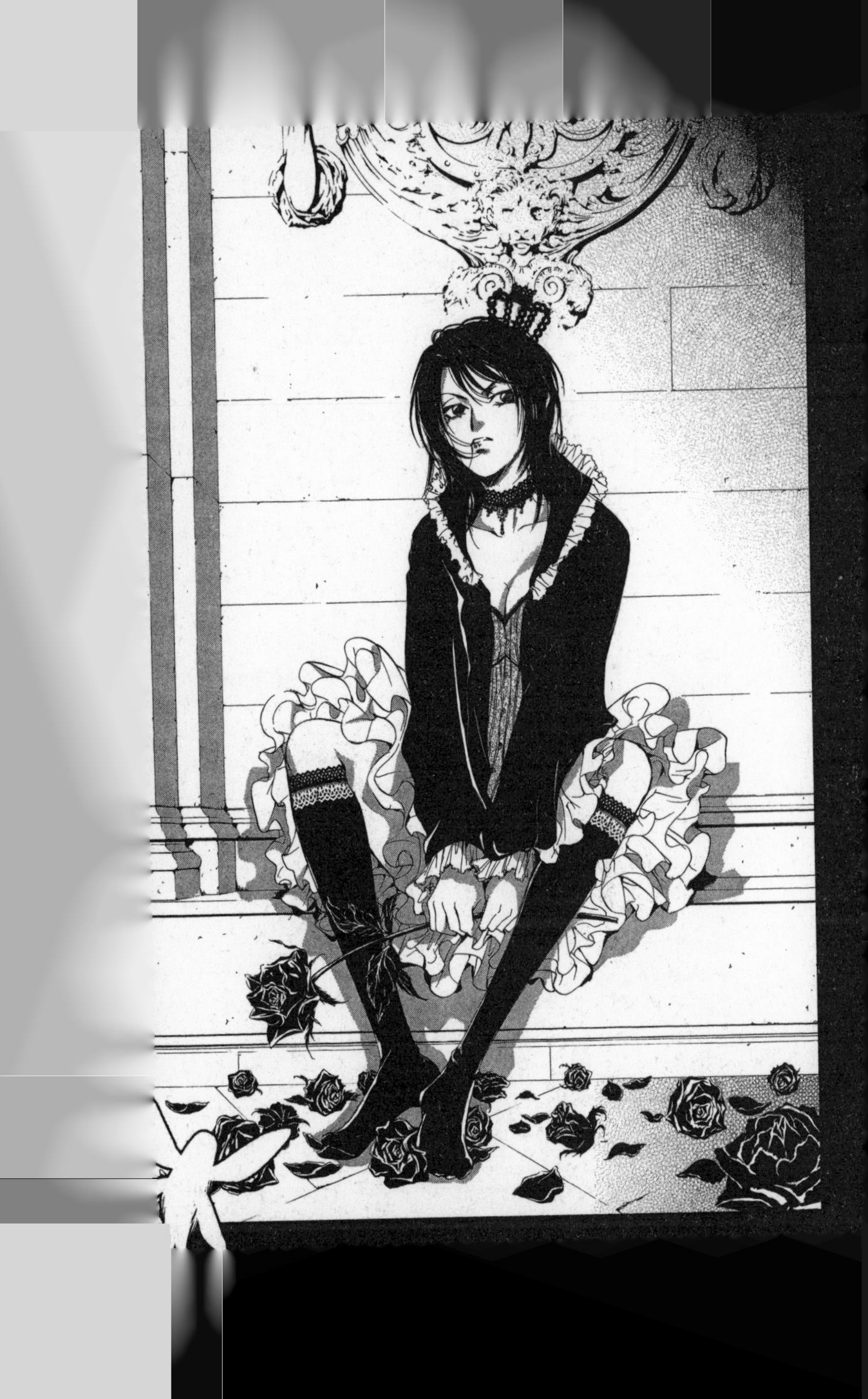

**Creator:** Kaori Yuki

**Date of Birth:** December 18

**Blood Type:** B

**Major Works:** *Angel Sanctuary* and *Godchild*

**K**aori Yuki was born in Tokyo and started drawing at a very early age. Following her debut work *Natsufuku no Erie* (Ellie in Summer Clothes) in the Japanese magazine *Bessatsu Hana to Yume* (1987), she wrote a compelling series of short stories: *Zankoku na Douwatachi* (Cruel Fairy Tales), *Neji* (Screw), and *Sareki Ōkoku* (Gravel Kingdom).

As proven by her best-selling series *Angel Sanctuary* and *Godchild*, her celebrated body of work has etched an indelible mark on the gothic comics genre. She likes mysteries and British films and is a fan of the movie *Dead Poets Society* and the television show *Twin Peaks*.

# FAIRY CUBE

VOL. 1
The Shojo Beat Manga Edition

## STORY AND ART BY KAORI YUKI

Translation/Gemma Collinge
English Adaptation/Kristina Blachere
Touch-up Art & Lettering/James Gaubatz
Design/Courtney Utt
Editor/Joel Enos

Editor in Chief, Books/Alvin Lu
Editor in Chief, Magazines/Marc Weidenbaum
VP of Publishing Licensing/Rika Inouye
VP of Sales/Gonzalo Ferreyra
Sr. VP of Marketing/Liza Coppola
Publisher/Hyoe Narita

Printed in Canada

Published by VIZ Media, LLC
P.O. Box 77010
San Francisco, CA 94107

Shojo Beat Manga Edition
10 9 8 7 6 5 4 3 2 1

First printing, May 2008

# Love Kaori Yuki?

## Read the rest of VIZ Media's Kaori Yuki Collection!

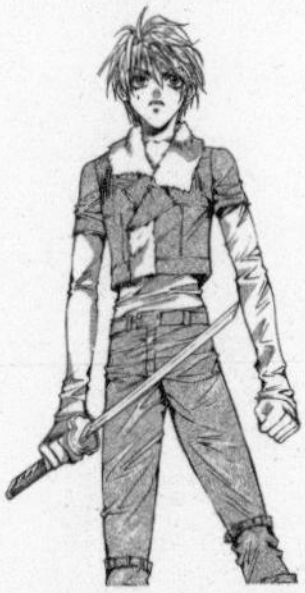

### Angel Sanctuary

Rated T+ for Older Teen
20 Volumes

The angel Alexiel loved God, but she rebelled against Heaven when she saw how disgracefully the other angels were behaving. She was finally captured and, as punishment, sent to Earth to live an endless series of tragic lives. She now inhabits the body of Setsuna Mudo, a troubled teen in love with his sister Sara.

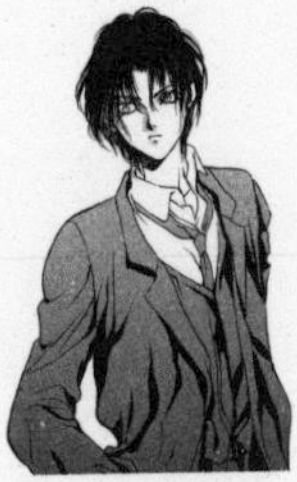

### The Cain Saga

Rated M for Mature Readers
5 Volumes

Delve into the tortured past of Earl Cain C. Hargreaves, charismatic heir to a wealthy family full of secrets, lies and unthinkable crimes. The prequel to the *Godchild* series, *The Cain Saga* follows the young Cain as he attempts to unravel the secrets of his birth, all the while solving each new mystery that comes his way.

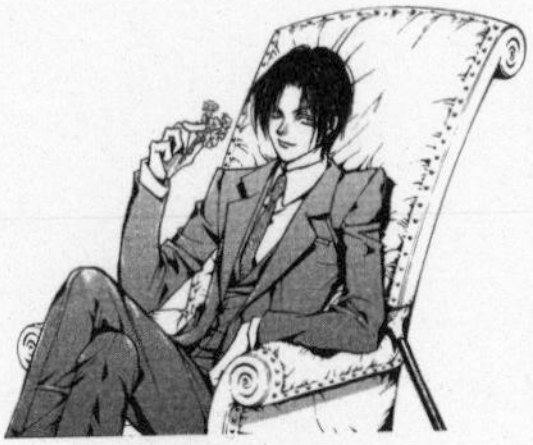

### Godchild

Rated T+ for Older Teen
8 Volumes

In 19th century London, dashing young nobleman Earl Cain Hargreaves weaves his way through the shadowy cobblestone streets that hide the dark secrets of aristocratic society. With his young sister Mary Weather and his constant companion Riff, Cain sets out to solve the dangerous mystery of his disturbing lineage.

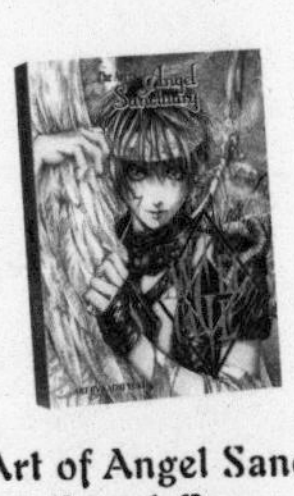

### The Art of Angel Sanctuary: Angel Cage

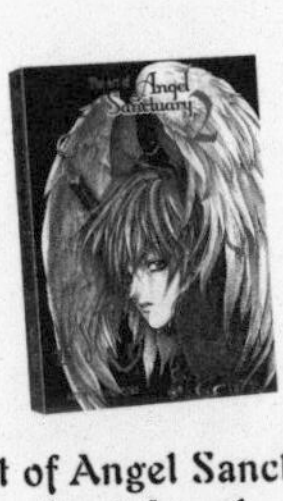

### The Art of Angel Sanctuary 2: Lost Angel

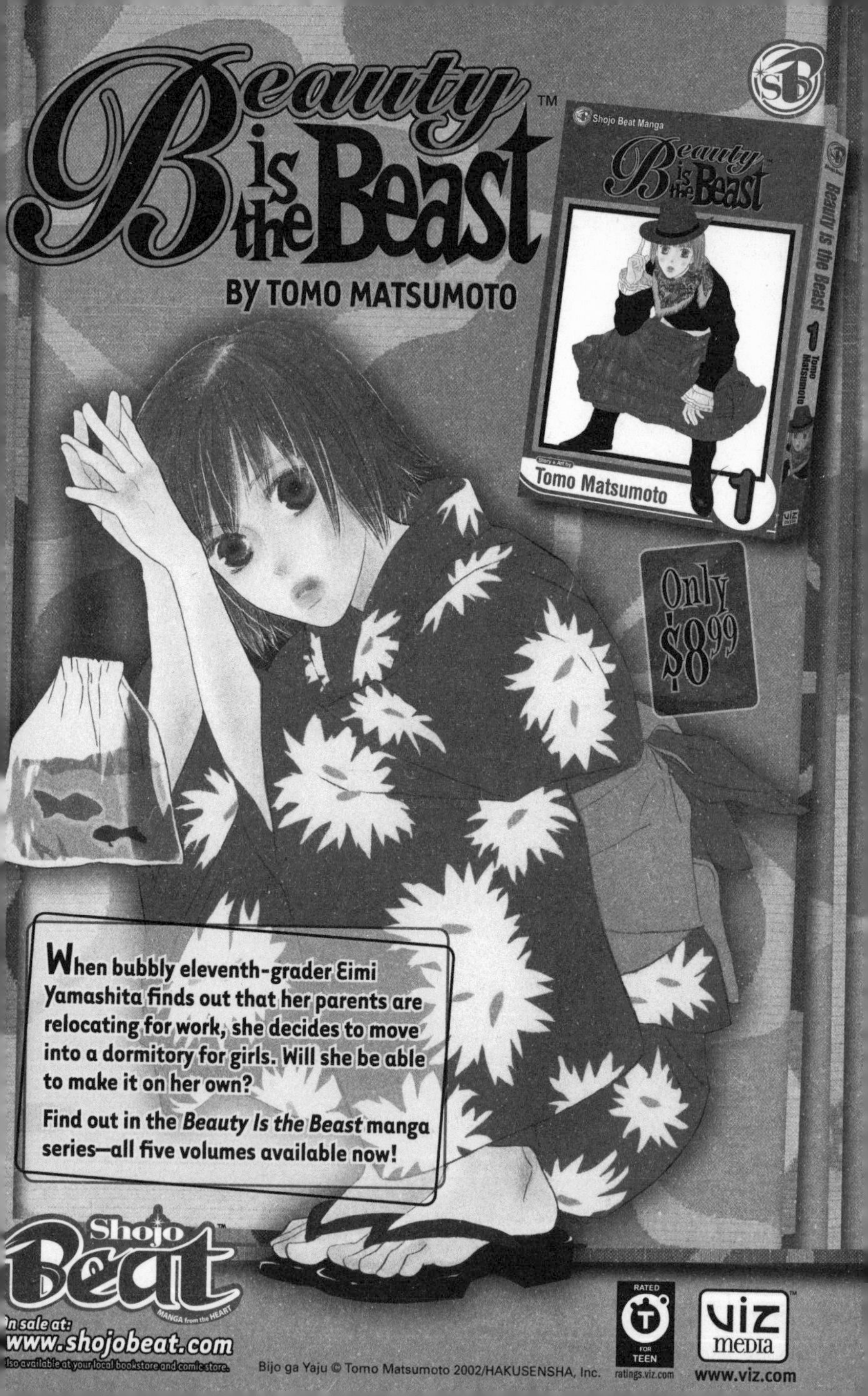
Beauty is the Beast™
BY TOMO MATSUMOTO
Shojo Beat Manga
Beauty is the Beast
Tomo Matsumoto
1
Only $8.99
When bubbly eleventh-grader Eimi Yamashita finds out that her parents are relocating for work, she decides to move into a dormitory for girls. Will she be able to make it on her own?
Find out in the *Beauty Is the Beast* manga series—all five volumes available now!
Shojo Beat
MANGA from the HEART
On sale at:
www.shojobeat.com
Also available at your local bookstore and comic store.
Bijo ga Yaju © Tomo Matsumoto 2002/HAKUSENSHA, Inc.
RATED T FOR TEEN
ratings.viz.com
viz media
www.viz.com

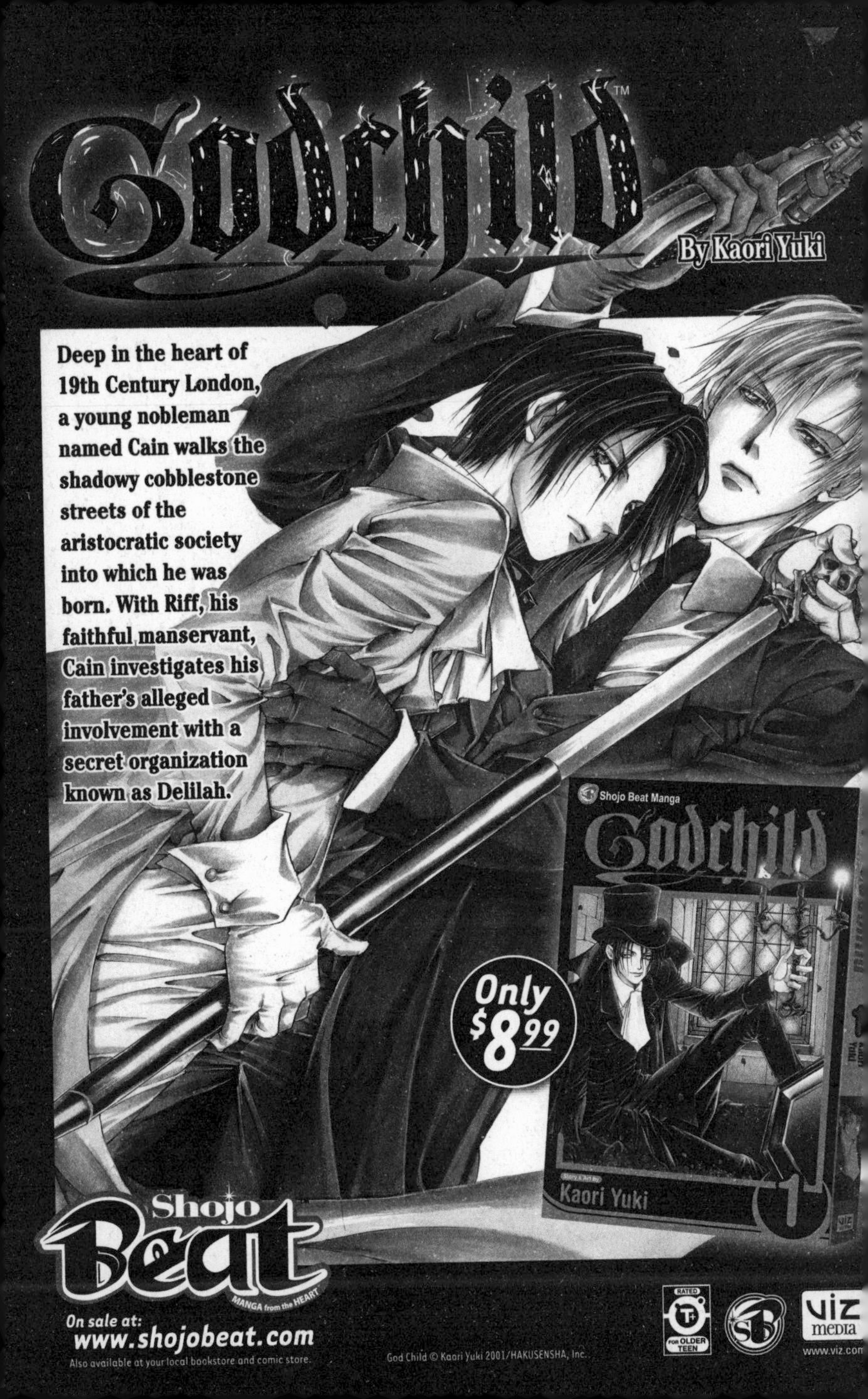
Godchild™
By Kaori Yuki
Deep in the heart of 19th Century London, a young nobleman named Cain walks the shadowy cobblestone streets of the aristocratic society into which he was born. With Riff, his faithful manservant, Cain investigates his father's alleged involvement with a secret organization known as Delilah.
Shojo Beat Manga
Godchild
Story & Art by
Kaori Yuki
Only $8.99
Shojo Beat
MANGA from the HEART
On sale at:
www.shojobeat.com
Also available at your local bookstore and comic store.
God Child © Kaori Yuki 2001/HAKUSENSHA, Inc.
RATED T+ FOR OLDER TEEN
VIZ media
www.viz.com

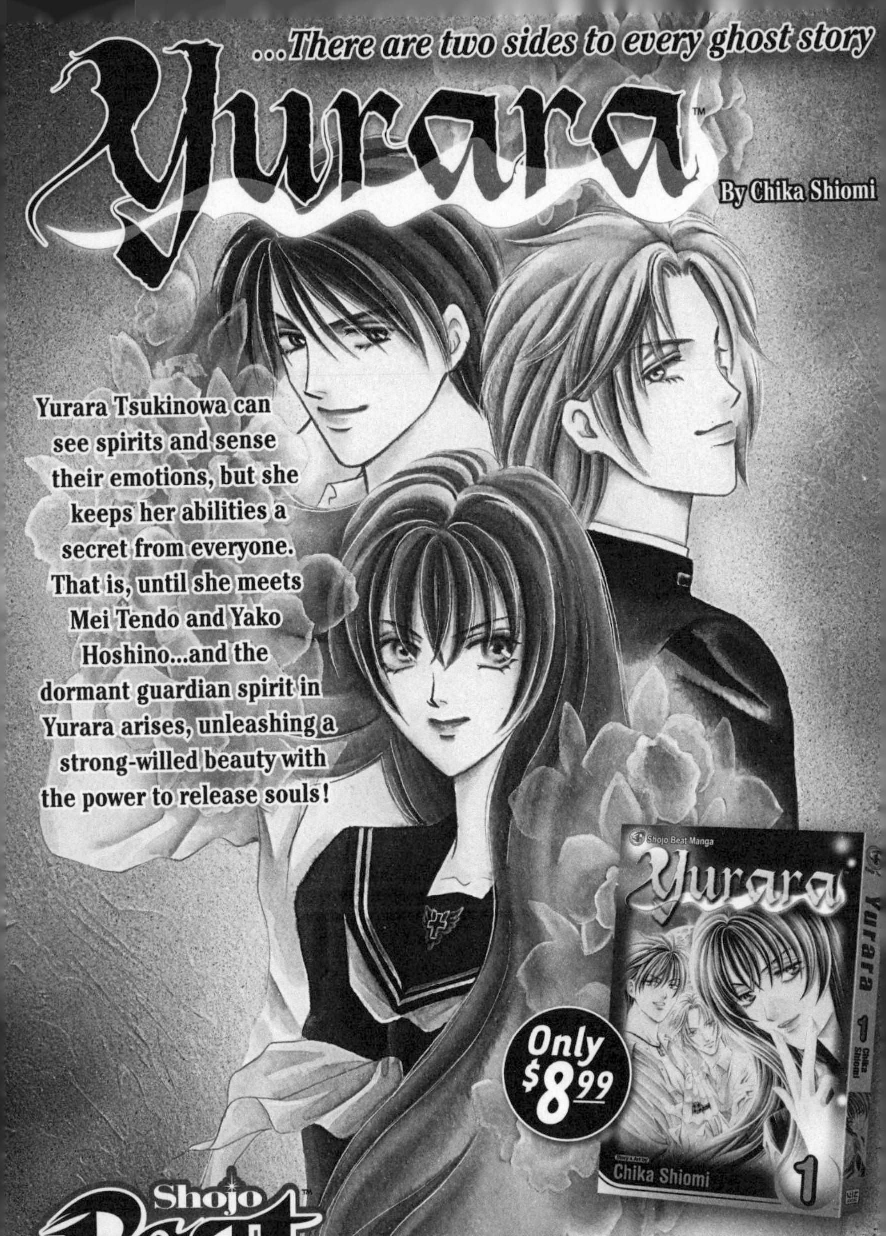

...There are two sides to every ghost story
Yurara™
By Chika Shiomi
Yurara Tsukinowa can see spirits and sense their emotions, but she keeps her abilities a secret from everyone. That is, until she meets Mei Tendo and Yako Hoshino...and the dormant guardian spirit in Yurara arises, unleashing a strong-willed beauty with the power to release souls!
Shojo Beat Manga
Yurara
Chika Shiomi
1
Yurara 1 Chika Shiomi
Only $8.99
Shojo Beat™